McGRAW-HILL
COMPUTING ESSENTIALS

Annual Edition
1993–1994

Timothy J. O'Leary

Arizona State University

Brian K. Williams

Linda I. O'Leary

 Mitchell McGRAW-HILL

New York St. Louis San Francisco Auckland Bogotá Caracas Hamburg
Lisbon London Madrid Mexico Milan Montreal New Delhi Paris
San Juan São Paulo Singapore Sidney Tokyo Toronto Watsonville

To

Pat and Tuff—T.J.O.

Stacey, Sylvia, Kirk, and Gertrude—B.K.W.

Nick, Betty, Jo, Bill, and Mill—L.I.O.

From all of us—especially to Roger

McGraw-Hill Computing Essentials Annual Edition 1993–1994

2 3 4 5 6 7 8 9 0 KGP KGP 9 0 9 8 7 6 5 4 3

ISBN 0-07-048868-1

See Illustration Credits on page 284.
Copyrights included on these pages by reference.

Sponsoring editor: Roger Howell
Editorial assistant: Laurie Boudreau
Production director: Jane Somers
Project manager: Greg Hubit, Bookworks
Text and cover designer: Christy Butterfield
Illustrator: Erik Kroha, Caliber Design
Photo researcher: Roberta Spieckerman Associates
Compositor: Caliber Division of Phoenix Color Corp.
Printer and binder: Arcata Graphics Kingsport

About the Authors

Timothy J. O'Leary *(left)* has been a professional educator since 1975. He is currently an Associate Professor in the Department of Decision and Information Systems at Arizona State University. He has written several books and articles on computers and information systems.

Linda I. O'Leary is a professional trainer in the area of computers. She has developed computer training manuals for corporations and presented seminars on the use of many computer software packages. She has also coauthored many computer lab manuals.

Brian K. Williams is a professional writer and has coauthored several books about computers. The holder of degrees from Stanford University, he was for many years an editor and manager for several book publishers before turning full time to writing. He lives in Incline Village, Nevada.

About the Board

Bob Autry *(left)*, Chuck Riden, and Jerry Booher are members of the McGraw-Hill Microcomputing Advisory Board. They are university and community college instructors who teach microcomputing courses. Their ongoing input has been invaluable to the development of this project.

Contents in Brief

Contents

3   Systems Software   36

6   **Secondary Storage   100**

7   **Communications and Connectivity   116**

9   Information Systems   152

10   Systems Analysis and Design   168

11   Programming and Languages   186

14 Your Future: Using Information Technology   242

Preface to the Instructor

This book is designed for students in an introductory computer or microcomputer course. It assumes no prerequisites.

Our Purpose: To Create Computer Competency

This book is intended to give students competency in computer-related knowledge and skills to support their academic pursuits and be of immediate value to their employers. Our goal is to prepare students to be:

- **Microcomputer-literate**—able to employ microcomputers to increase their productivity and effectiveness.

- **Familiar with commercial software**—especially word processing, spreadsheet, and database management packages.

- **Grounded in fundamental concepts**—a basic working vocabulary and knowledge of computing and information concepts.

Distinguishing Features and Benefits

Key Feature #1: Flexibility The modular design provides instructors with many opportunities to meet their particular course objectives. You are now holding one of the three standard book versions:

- **Text Only**. *McGraw-Hill Computing Essentials: Annual Edition 1993-1994* in 14 brief chapters describes basic computer and information concepts.

- **Labs Only**. *McGraw-Hill Microcomputing Labs: Annual Edition* is available in two configurations of software applications. Both are spiral-bound for convenient use in a lab setting. *Edition A* includes DOS 3.3–5.0, WordPerfect 5.1, Lotus 1-2-3 Release 2.3, and dBASE IV Version 1.1. *Edition B* includes DOS 3.3–5.0, Word-Perfect 5.1, Lotus 1-2-3 Release 2.2, and dBASE III PLUS.

- **Text Plus Labs**. *McGraw-Hill Microcomputing: Annual Edition 1993-1994* is a spiral-bound combination of the text and *Labs Edition A*.

Also available: your own "mix-and-match" combinations. If none of the above options meets your needs, *you can mix and match modules to create your own customized instructional package.* The following lab modules may be ordered—with or without *McGraw-Hill Computing Essentials*—in any combination, shrink-wrapped, with or without a three-ring binder:

DOS 5.0	Lotus 1-2-3 Release 2.01
DOS 3.3–5.0	Microsoft Excel 4.0 for Windows
Windows 3.1	Quattro Pro 4.0
Windows 3.0	Quattro*
WordPerfect for Windows	SuperCalc 4*
WordPerfect 5.1	dBASE IV Version 1.1
WordPerfect 5.0	dBASE III PLUS*
WordPerfect 4.2*	Paradox for Windows
WordStar 4.0	Paradox 4.0
Lotus 1-2-3 for Windows	Microsoft Works Release 2.0
Lotus 1-2-3 Release 2.3	on the IBM PC
Lotus 1-2-3 Release 2.2	Local Area Network (LAN)

*Educational versions of WordPerfect 4.2, Quattro Training Edition 1.01, SuperCalc 4, and dBASE III PLUS can be shrink-wrapped with these lab modules.

Your McGraw-Hill sales representative will explain this customization feature in more detail.

Key Feature #2: Revised Annually Being able to revise our materials every year allows us—and our readers—to keep pace in this dynamic field.

New to the 1993–1994 edition:

- **Revised Discussion Questions and Projects**. As before, the two student assignments at the end of each chapter are designed to be interesting, informative, and practical.

- **New Section, "The Student Buyer's Guide: How to Buy Your Own Microcomputer System."** This new section shows students in four simple steps how to buy a new or used microcomputer.

- **Update of Technology and Issues.** We have increased or added discussion of: MS DOS 5.0, DR DOS 6.0, Windows 3.1, and OS/2 2.0; viruses; multimedia; downsizing; computer ethics; hardware and software compatibility issues; conventional memory, extended memory, and expanded memory; cache memory; pen-based computing; data compression; faster modems; Open Systems Interconnection (OSI); and object-oriented programming.

- **Trends and the Future.** Charts and graphs have been added and updated to reflect the latest trends. The section at the end of each chapter, "A Look at the Future," has been updated to cover subjects such as videophones, Windows NT operating system, Taligent, holographic storage, and light-sensitive bacteria protein for storage.

- **New Lab Modules.** Our lab offerings have been expanded to include coverage of: DOS 3.3–5.0, DOS 5.0, Windows 3.1, WordPerfect for Windows, Excel 4.0 for Windows, Lotus 1-2-3 for Windows, Quattro Pro 4.0, Paradox 4.0, and Paradox for Windows. Our selection reflects the packages you've told us you use. We count on your feedback to keep pace with your needs.

- **Enhanced Interior Text Design.** The artwork and photos have been thoroughly revised to create a fresh new look and further enhance learning.

Key Feature #3: Visual Orientation We believe that our readers learn visually. Accordingly, *Computing Essentials* balances text with color graphics. Our Visual Summaries capture in a nutshell the key concepts covered in each chapter. The text also contains numerous color illustrations, photos, and charts. Adopters tell us that our visual orientation enhances their students' interest and comprehension.

Key Feature #4: "Learn-by-Doing" Approach Each chapter in *Computing Essentials* concludes with Review Questions, Discussion Questions and Projects. These pedagogical aids are designed to reinforce learning and encourage students to apply the concepts covered in each chapter to solve actual problems.

The lab modules also follow the "learn-by-doing" approach and are based on an ongoing case study that simulates real-world use of the software and leads the student step by step to the solution to the problem. Each lab module includes the following additional learning aids:

- Conceptual Overview
- Objectives
- Wealth of Screen Displays
- Summary of Key Terms
- Lab Review (Matching and Fill-in Questions)
- Practice Exercises
- Glossary of Key Terms
- Summary of Commands
- Index

The Support Package

Teaching Materials sets are available to adopters. They are available separately for *Computing Essentials* as well as for each of the lab modules. Each set includes:

- Objectives
- Schedule
- Procedural Requirements
- Teaching Tips
- Answers to Matching Problems
- Command Summary
- Answers to Practice Exercises
- Transparency Masters
- Printed Test Bank
- 3½-inch Student Data Disk and Test Questions

    Note: RHTest, a computerized testbank, is also available to adopters.

Other support materials:

- Color Transparencies
- Documentary-style Videotapes
- Hypercard Presentation Tool (Computer Resource Library)
- Computerized Glossary of Terms

    If you would like information on how to obtain the last four supplements described above, please contact your McGraw-Hill sales representative.

Acknowledgments

We were fortunate to have a great deal of fine input and ongoing advice from the McGraw-Hill Microcomputer Advisory Board: Bob Autrey, Mesa Community College; Jerry Booher, Scottsdale Community College; and Chuck Riden, Arizona State University, Mesa Community College, and Dobson High School. A special thanks goes to the industry professionals who have given invaluable insights into the use of microcomputers in today's work life. They include Bill Bauer, Ernst & Young; Brian Corke and Gene Kunkle, Sun State Seafoods; Ernie Ziak, Western Reserve Family Sports Center; and Jim Price, The Sports Authority.

We are also grateful for the helpful comments from our reviewers: David Adams, Northern Kentucky University; Henry Altieri, Norwalk State Technical College; Harvey Blessing, Essex Community College; Cathy Brotherton, Riverside Community College; Earline Cocke, Northwest Mississippi Community College; Mona Dalton, Tallahassee

Community College; Tim De Clue, Southwest Baptist University; Kevin Duggan, Midlands Technical College; Lucie Dutfield, Seneca College; Sandra Dzakovic, Niagara College; Jeannine Englehart, Coastline College; Patrick Fenton, West Valley College; Tom Gallagher, Seneca College; Nancy Gillespie, Glassboro State College; Carla Hall, St. Louis Community College–Florissant Valley; Sue Henry, Cheridian College; Jim Higgins, Mohawk College; Lister Horn, Pensacola Junior College; Ann Houck, Pima Community College; Peter Irwin, Richland College; Ruth Jaglowitz, Seneca College; Barbara Jauken, Southeast Community College; Cynthia Kachik, Santa Fe Community College; Tom Kane, Centennial College; John Keeling, Seneca College; Shelley Langman, Bellevue Community College; Philip E. Lowry, University of Nevada–Las Vegas; Deborah Ludford, Glendale Community College; Brian Monahan, Iona College; Trudy Montoya, Aims Community College; Don Myers, Vincennes University; Dean Orris, Butler University; James Payne, Kellogg Community College; Allan Peck, Springfield Technical Community College; Diane Peterson, Wisconsin Indianhead Technical College; James Phillips, Helena Vocational Technical Center; Rick Phillips, Roosevelt University; Leonard Presby, William Paterson College; Herbert Rebhun, University of Houston; Paul Ross, Millersville University; Lorilee Sadler, Indiana University; Peg Saragina, Santa Rosa Junior College; Judith Scheeren, Westmoreland County Community College; Faye Simmons, Canton College of Technology; Laurie Smith, University of South Carolina; Sandra Stalker, North Shore Community College; Hamilton Stirling, University of South Florida at St. Petersburg; Margaret Thomas, Ohio University; Nancy Tinkham, Glassboro State College; Douglas Topham; Michael Trombetta, Queensborough Community College; Jeannetta Williams, Piedmont Virginia Community College; Don Wilson, Georgian College; and Al Woodman, Seneca College.

In addition, we are again extremely appreciative of all the efforts of the Mitchell/McGraw-Hill staff and others who worked on this book: Roger Howell, Erika Berg, Laurie Boudreau, and Steve Mitchell for their enthusiastic support of the 1993–1994 edition; Jane Somers for her production supervision; John Ambrose, Kris Johnson, and Judith Hug for their marketing support; and Karen Jackson, Eric Munson, and Seibert Adams for their past and present editorial and marketing support.

We are also grateful for the contributions of those outside McGraw-Hill and Mitchell: Jim Elam for his dedication and thoughtful suggestions; Colleen Hayes for her thorough software evaluation and recommendations; Greg Hubit for his project management; Christy Butterfield for her design; Mark Poe for the new practice exercises; Peg Sallade for permission to use parts of her research paper, "Aquatic Fitness"; Roberta Spieckerman for photo research; Beverly Zegarski for copyediting; and the Caliber Division of Phoenix Color Corporation for line illustrations and composition.

Write to Us

We welcome your reactions to this book, for we would like it to be as useful to you as possible. Write to us in care of:

Microcomputer Applications Editor
Mitchell McGraw-Hill
55 Penny Lane
Watsonville, CA 95076.

Timothy J. O'Leary
Brian K. Williams
Linda I. O'Leary

1

You and Computer Competency

Competencies

After you have read this chapter, you should be able to:

1. Explain computer competency.

2. Distinguish four kinds of computers: microcomputer, minicomputer, mainframe, and supercomputer.

3. Explain the five parts of a microcomputer system: people, procedures, software, hardware, and data.

4. Distinguish applications software from systems software.

5. Describe hardware devices for input, processing, storage, output, and communications.

6. Describe the categories of data: character, field, record, and file.

7. Explain computer connectivity.

Computer competency: This notion may not be familiar to you, but it's easy to understand. The purpose of this book is to help you become *competent* in computer-related skills. Specifically, we want to help you walk into a job and immediately be of value to an employer. In this chapter, we first describe why learning about the computer is important to your future. We then present an *overview* of what makes up a computer system: people, procedures, software, hardware, and data. In subsequent chapters, we will describe these parts in detail.

Ten years ago, most people had little to do with computers, at least directly. Of course, they filled out computerized forms, took computerized tests, and paid computerized bills. But the real work with computers was handled by specialists—programmers, data-entry clerks, and computer operators.

Then microcomputers came along and changed everything. Today it is easy for nearly everybody to use a computer. People who use microcomputers today are called "end users." (*See Figure 1-1.*) Some examples:

■ Microcomputers are common tools in all areas of life. Writers write, artists draw, engineers and scientists calculate—all on microcomputers. Businesspeople do all three.

■ New forms of learning have developed. People who are homebound, who work odd hours, or who travel frequently may take courses by telephone-linked home computers. A course need not fit within the usual time of a quarter or a semester.

■ Expert knowledge is readily at hand. Whatever your field or prospective field—from animal husbandry to tax law—programs probably exist that can offer you advice. Powerful "expert systems" make the wisdom of professionals available to you.

What about you? How can microcomputers enhance *your* life?

End Users and Computer Competency

By Gaining Computer Competency, End Users Can Use Microcomputers to Improve Their Productivity and Their Value in the Workplace.

End users are people who use microcomputers or have access to larger computers. If you are not an end user already, you will probably become one in the near future. That is, you will learn to use prewritten computer programs to meet your unique needs for information. Let us point out two things here.

- By "prewritten programs," we mean programs that you can buy rather than those you have to write yourself. A video game on a diskette is an example of a prewritten program. Here we describe work-related programs, such as word processing for typing documents and electronic spreadsheets for analysis.

- By "needs," we mean various organizing, managing, or business needs. That is, they are *information-related* or *decision-making* needs. Becoming **computer competent**—learning how to use the computer to meet your information needs—will improve your productivity. It will also make you a more valuable employee.

How much do you have to know to be computer competent? Clearly, in today's fast-changing technological world, you cannot learn everything—but very few people need to. You don't have to be a computer scientist to make good use of a microcomputer. Indeed, that is precisely the point of this book. Our goal is to teach you not everything there is to know but only what you *need* to know. Thus, we present only what we think you will find most useful—both now and in the future.

Four Kinds of Computers

Computers Are of Four Types: Microcomputers, Minicomputers, Mainframes, and Supercomputers.

This book focuses principally on microcomputers. However, it is almost certain that you will come in contact at least indirectly with other kinds of computers, too. Thus, we describe many features that are common to these larger machines.

Computers are categorized into four types: *microcomputers, minicomputers, mainframe computers,* and *supercomputers*. We discuss these in detail later in the book, but here let us give a quick description for purposes of comparison.

- **Microcomputers** are small computers that can fit on a desktop. They are often called **personal computers.** Some microcomputers are small enough to be portable (*laptops* and *notebooks*). Until recently, the more powerful microcomputers, those used by engineers and scientists, were called **workstations.** However, the distinction between personal computers and workstations is now blurring. The demand for microcomputers has been growing spectacularly over the years and is projected to increase even more in the future. (*See Figure 1-2, next page.*)

Figure 1-1
End users: People are using microcomputers to meet their information needs.

3

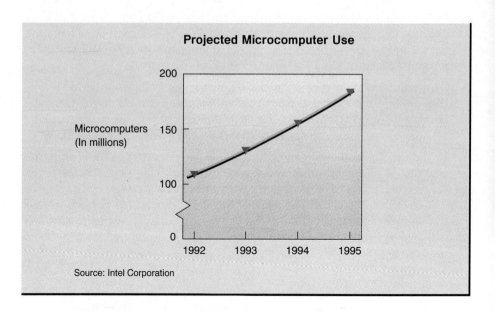

Figure 1-2
Microcomputers in use
worldwide.

■ **Minicomputers** are refrigerator-size machines that fall in between microcomputers and mainframes in their processing speeds and data-storing capacities. Medium-size companies or departments of large companies typically use them for specific purposes. For example, they might use them to do research or to monitor a particular manufacturing process. Smaller-size companies typically use minicomputers for their general data processing needs, such as accounting.

■ **Mainframe computers** are large computers occupying specially wired, air-conditioned rooms and capable of great processing speeds and data storage. They are used by large organizations—businesses, banks, universities, government agencies—to handle millions of transactions. For example, insurance companies use mainframes to process information about millions of policies.

■ **Supercomputers** are special, high-capacity computers used by very large organizations principally for research purposes. Among their uses are weapons research, oil exploration, and worldwide weather forecasting.

Let us now get started on the road to computer competency. We begin by describing the microcomputer as a system.

The Five Parts of a Microcomputer System

A Microcomputer System Has Five Parts: People, Procedures, Software, Hardware, and Data.

When you think of a microcomputer, perhaps you think of just the equipment itself. That is, you think of the video display screen or the keyboard. There is more to it than that. The way to think about a microcomputer is as a *system.* A **microcomputer system** has five parts: *people, procedures, software, hardware,* and *data. (See Figure 1-3.)*

■ *People:* It is easy to overlook people as one of the five parts of a microcomputer system. Yet that is what microcomputers are all about—making people, end users, more productive.

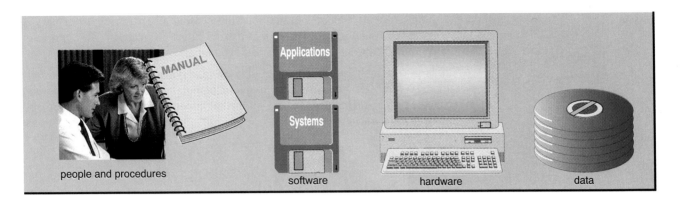

people and procedures software hardware data

- *Procedures:* **Procedures** are manuals containing rules or guidelines to follow when using software, hardware, and data. Procedures are also used for connecting to other computer systems. These manuals are usually written by computer specialists for particular organizations. Software and hardware manufacturers also provide manuals with their products. An example is the *Lotus 1-2-3 Reference Manual.*

- *Software:* **Software** is another name for a program or programs. A **program** is the step-by-step instructions that tell the computer how to do its work. The purpose of software is to convert *data* (unprocessed facts) into *information* (processed facts).

- *Hardware:* The **hardware** consists of the equipment: keyboard, monitor (video display screen), printer, the computer itself, and other devices. Examples of hardware are those for two well-known microcomputer systems—the IBM PS/2 Model 50 and the Apple Macintosh SE. (*See Figure 1-4.*)

Figure 1-3
The five parts of a microcomputer system.

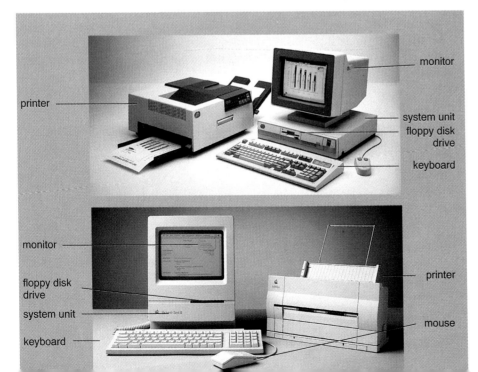

printer
monitor
system unit
floppy disk drive
keyboard

monitor
floppy disk drive
system unit
keyboard
printer
mouse

Figure 1-4
Two well-known microcomputer hardware systems: the IBM PS/2 Model 50 (*top*) and the Apple Macintosh SE.

■ *Data:* **Data** consists of the raw, unprocessed facts that are input to the system. Examples of raw facts are hours you worked and your pay rate. After data is processed through the computer, it is usually called **information.** An example of such information is the total wages owed you for a week's work.

In large computer systems, there are specialists who deal with writing procedures, developing software, and creating data. In microcomputer systems, however, end users often perform these operations. To be a competent end user, you must understand the essentials of software, hardware, and data.

Software

Software Is of Two Kinds. Applications Software, Which May Be Custom-Written or Come in Packaged Form, Does "End-User" Work. Systems Software Does "Background" Work.

Software, as we mentioned, is another name for programs. Programs are the instructions that tell the computer how to process data into the form you want. In most cases, the words *software* and *programs* are interchangeable.

There are two major kinds of software—*applications software* and *systems software.* You can think of applications software as the kind you use. Think of systems software as the kind the computer uses. (*See Figure 1-5.*)

Applications Software **Applications software** might be described as "end-user" software. Applications software performs useful work on general-purpose tasks such as word processing and cost estimating.

Applications software may be *packaged* or *custom-made.*

■ **Packaged software** consists of any program that has been prewritten by a professional programmer and is typically offered for sale on a diskette. There are over 12,000 different types of applications packages available for microcomputers alone.

■ **Custom-made software,** or **custom programs,** is what *all* software used to be. Twenty years ago organizations hired computer programmers to create all their software. The programmer custom-wrote programs to instruct the company computer to perform whatever tasks the organization wanted. A program might compute payroll checks, keep track of goods in the warehouse, calculate sales commissions, or perform similar business needs.

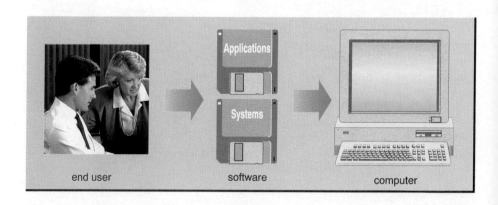

Figure 1-5
End users interact with applications software. Systems software interacts with the computer.

There are certain general-purpose programs that we call *"basic tools"* in this book. These programs are widely used in nearly all career areas. They are the kind of programs you *have* to know to be considered computer competent. We discuss these in Chapter 2.

The most popular so-called basic tools are:

- *Word processing* programs, used to prepare written documents
- *Electronic spreadsheets,* used to analyze and summarize data
- *File and database managers,* used to organize and manage data and information
- *Graphics programs,* used to present data visually, as charts and graphs
- *Communications programs,* used to transmit and receive data
- *Integrated programs,* which combine some or all of these programs in one package

Systems Software The user interacts with applications software. **Systems software** enables the applications software to interact with the computer. (*Refer to Figure 1-5.*) Systems software is "background" software. It includes programs that help the computer manage its own internal resources.

The most important systems software program is the **operating system,** which interacts between the applications software and the computer. The operating system handles such details as running ("executing") programs, storing data and programs, and processing ("manipulating") data. Systems software frees users to concentrate on solving problems rather than on the complexities of operating the computer.

Microcomputer operating systems are in the process of changing as the machines themselves become more powerful and outgrow the older operating systems. Today's computer competency, then, requires that you have some knowledge of the following most popular microcomputer operating systems:

- *DOS,* the standard operating system for International Business Machines (IBM) and IBM-compatible microcomputers.
- *DOS with Windows,* in which a program known as Microsoft Windows extends the capability of DOS on IBM and IBM-compatible microcomputers.
- *OS/2,* the operating system developed for IBM's more powerful microcomputers.
- *Macintosh operating system,* which runs only on Apple Corporation's Macintosh computers.
- *Unix,* an operating system originally developed for minicomputers. Unix is now important because it can run on many of the more powerful microcomputers.

Hardware

Microcomputer Hardware Consists of Devices for Data Input, Processing, Storage, Output, and Communications.

Microcomputer hardware—the physical equipment—falls into five categories. They are *input devices, the system unit, secondary storage, output devices,* and *communications devices.* Because we discuss hardware in detail later in the book, we will present just a quick overview here.

Input Devices **Input devices** are equipment that translates data and programs that humans can understand into a form that the computer can process. The most

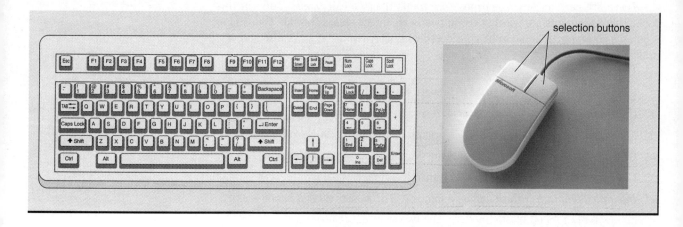

selection buttons

Figure 1-6
Microcomputer keyboard and mouse.

common input devices for the microcomputer are the keyboard and the mouse. (*See Figure 1-6.*) The **keyboard** on a computer looks like a typewriter keyboard, but it has additional specialized keys. A **mouse** is a device that can be rolled about on the desktop. It directs the **cursor,** or pointer, on the display screen. A mouse has selection buttons for entering commands. It is also used to draw figures.

The System Unit The **system unit** is housed within the computer cabinet. (*See Figure 1-7.*) The system unit consists of electronic circuitry that has two parts.

■ The **central processing unit (CPU)** controls and manipulates data to produce information. A microcomputer's CPU is contained on a single integrated circuit or microprocessor chip. These chips are called *microprocessors*. (*See Figure 1-8.*)

Figure 1-7
An open system cabinet of a Dell microcomputer.

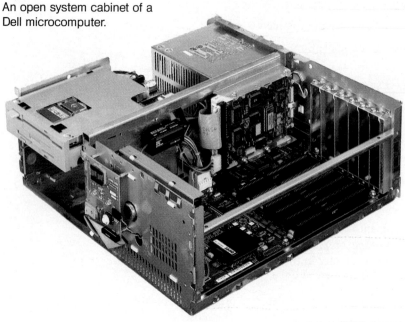

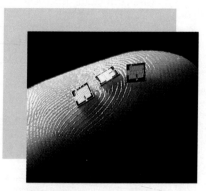

Figure 1-8
Relative size of a microprocessor chip.

■ **Primary storage,** also known as **memory,** holds data and program instructions for processing the data. It also holds the processed information before it is output. Primary storage is located in the system unit on tiny *memory chips.*

Secondary Storage   Primary storage is part of the system unit and is used to hold data and instructions only *temporarily.* That is, the data and instructions exist only as long as the electrical power to the computer is turned on. **Secondary storage** devices store data and programs *permanently.* These devices are located outside of the central processing unit, although they may still be built into the system unit cabinet.

For microcomputers, the most important kinds of secondary storage "media" are as follows:

■ **Floppy disks** (also called simply "diskettes") hold data or programs in the form of magnetized spots on plastic platters. The two sizes in most common use are 5¼-inch and 3½-inch diskettes. (*See Figure 1-9.*) The newer, smaller size, which can fit in a shirt pocket, is more durable and can hold more and therefore is gaining rapidly in popularity.

Figure 1-9
Two kinds of floppy disks: 3½-inch and 5¼-inch.

floppy-disk drive

hard-disk drive (hidden inside system cabinet)

Figure 1-10
Two kinds of disk drives: floppy and hard. Hard disks are not removable from the drives.

A floppy disk is inserted into a **disk drive.** (*See Figure 1-10.*) This mechanism **reads** data from the disk. That is, the magnetized spots on the disk are converted to electronic signals and transmitted to primary storage inside the computer. A disk drive can also **write** data. That is, it can take the electronic information processed by the computer and record it magnetically onto the disk.

Floppy-disk drives are usually built into the system cabinet, but they also may be separate units outside it.

■ A **hard disk** contains one or more metallic disks encased within a disk drive. Like floppy disks, hard disks hold data or programs in the form of magnetized spots. They also *read* and *write* data in much the same way as do floppy disks. However, the storage capacity of a hard-disk unit is many times that of a floppy disk.

Floppy disks are inserted and removed from their disk drives and are stored separately. The hard disk, by contrast, typically is not removable. Hard-disk drives are usually built into a system cabinet. (*Refer back to Figure 1-10.*) However, there are also external hard-disk drives.

Many microcomputer systems have one floppy-disk drive and one hard-disk drive. The floppy-disk unit (either 5¼-inch or 3½-inch) is referred to as drive A, and the hard-disk unit as drive C. Many other microcomputer systems have two floppy-disk drives— one that takes a 5¼-inch diskette and another that takes a 3½-inch diskette. One drive is referred to as drive A, and the other as drive B. (*See Figure 1-11.*)

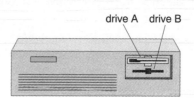

Figure 1-11
Drives A and B on a microcomputer.

Output Devices Output devices are pieces of equipment that translate the processed information from the CPU into a form that humans can understand. One of the most important output devices is the **monitor,** or **video display screen,** which may resemble a television screen. (*See Figure 1-12.*) The quality of monitors has

Figure 1-12
Newer monitors show crisp images and vivid colors.

Figure 1-13
Some printers can print color
images on paper.

improved dramatically. Many monitors now offer crisp images and vivid colors. Another important output device is the **printer,** a device that produces printed paper output. Some printers can also print in color. (*See Figure 1-13.*)

Communications Devices Communications hardware sends data and programs from one computer or secondary storage device to another. Many microcomputers use a **modem** (pronounced "*moh*-dem"). This device translates the electronic signals from the computer into electronic signals that can travel over a telephone line. A modem at the other end of the line then translates the signals for the receiving computer. A modem may be located inside a microcomputer's system cabinet. It may also be a separate unit. (*See Figure 1-14.*)

external modem | microcomputer

Figure 1-14
An external modem connects
a microcomputer and a
telephone.

Data

Data Is Organized into Characters, Fields, Records, and Files.

To be a competent end user, you must understand the essentials of hardware, software, and data. Now that we know the first two, let us describe what data is.

Data consists of the characters that are input to the computer system. Data is organized into four increasingly sophisticated levels, as follows:

- A **character** is a letter, number, or special symbol—for example, M, 3, or $.

- A **field** is an item of data consisting of one or more logically related characters. An example of a field is your last name, social security number, or driver's license number.

- A **record** is a collection of related fields. For example, all information on a driver's license would be one record. All information on a registration card for one college course would be another record.

- A **file** is a collection of related records. For example, all driver's licenses issued or renewed in your state today make one file. All information about a student's courses and grades in the registrar's office makes another file.

These categories of data can be collected together into a sophisticated structure known as a **database.** A database is a collection of integrated data.

Connectivity

Connectivity Is the Microcomputer's Ability to Communicate with Other Computers and Information Sources.

Connectivity is the capability of the microcomputer to use information from the world beyond your desk. Connectivity is a concept, not a thing. Data and information can be sent over telephone or cable lines and through the air. Thus, your microcomputer can be *connected* to other microcomputers, to many computerized data banks, and to other sources of information that lie well beyond your desk.

Connectivity is a very significant development, for it expands the uses of the microcomputer severalfold. Central to the concept of connectivity is the **computer network.** A network is a communications system connecting two or more computers and their peripheral devices. All major companies have **local area networks (LANs)**, in which computers within the same building or organization are connected by communications lines. In addition, a microcomputer may be linked to regional, national, and international networks.

With all these possible connections at your disposal, perhaps you can begin to see how important connectivity is. By using a modem and communications software, you can transmit information to other computers. You can exchange messages with other microcomputer users. (Some arrangements require a fee, but some are free, except for telephone line charges.) You can receive all kinds of information from data banks and databases—electronic libraries and catalogs—connected with large computers. Indeed, connectivity is changing the very nature of how large computers are being used.

A Look at the Future: You and Computer Competency

Computer Competency Is Understanding the Rules and the Power of Microcomputers. Competency Enables You to Take Advantage of Increasingly Productive Software and Hardware and the Connectivity Revolution That Are Expanding the Microcomputer's Capabilities.

The purpose of this book is to help you be computer competent not only in the present but also in the future. Having competency requires your having the knowledge and understanding of the rules and the power of the microcomputer. This will enable you to benefit from three important developments: more powerful software, more powerful hardware, and connectivity to outside information systems.

Powerful Software The software now available can do an extraordinary number of tasks and help you in an endless number of ways. More and more employers are expecting the people they hire to be able to use it. Thus, we spend the next two chapters describing applications software—what we call "basic tools"—and systems software.

Powerful Hardware   Microcomputers are now much more powerful than they used to be. Indeed, the newer models have the speed and power of room-size computers of only a few years ago. However, despite the rapid change of specific equipment, their essential features remain unchanged. Thus, the competent end user should focus on these features. Chapters 4 through 6 explain what you need to know about hardware: the central processing unit, input/output devices, and secondary storage.

Connectivity   The principle of *connectivity* is a revolutionary development. No longer are microcomputers and competent end users bounded by the surface of the desk. Now they can reach past the desk and link up with other computers to share data, programs, and information. Accordingly, we devote Chapters 7 through 9 to discussing connectivity: communications, files and databases, and information systems.

To competently develop access to information beyond your desktop, you must understand how information systems are created and modified. This is done with the techniques of systems analysis and design. The most successful end users not only use existing systems to generate information. They also know how to improve on these systems. They know how to evaluate and integrate new technology to improve the quality and accessibility of information. This is called *systems analysis and design.* We cover this subject in Chapter 10.

One part of systems analysis and design may include the creation of new software—specially designed programs. We describe the process of developing new software in Chapter 11.

Emerging Microcomputer Applications   In addition to certain applications programs called "basic tools," we need to explore some emerging applications programs—what we call "power tools." These are programs that, until recently, were not available on microcomputers, only on mainframe computers. However, as microcomputers have become more powerful, these programs have become more available and less expensive. Learning to use this kind of software will enable you to distinguish yourself from other computer-competent people. It will enable to work productively in innovative ways that will place you among the computer-competent of the future.

In Chapter 12, we describe the following examples of so-called power tools. *Desktop managers* are used to increase the efficiency of the end user, replacing the usual desktop "accessories" of calculators, address books, and the like. *Project management software* is used to plan, schedule, and control the people, resources, and costs of a project. *Desktop publishing* is used to create professional-quality résumés, reports, newsletters, and other publications mixing both text and graphics. What has come to be called "new media" includes hypertext and multimedia, which enable users to link related pieces of information in exciting ways. *Hypertext* is software that can connect any text or picture file with any other. *Multimedia* can link text, graphics, video, or sound. *CAD/CAM* is used to design and manufacture products.

The field of computer science known as *artificial intelligence (AI)* attempts to develop computer systems that can mimic or simulate human thought processes and actions. AI includes robotics, knowledge-based and expert systems, and virtual reality. *Robotics* is the field of study concerned with developing and using robots. *Knowledge-based systems* and *expert systems* in effect capture the knowledge of human experts and make it accessible to others through a computer program. They extend one's capacity to perform certain jobs at the level of an expert. *Virtual reality* consists of interactive sensory equipment (headgear and gloves) and software that allow one to experience alternative realities to the physical world.

Workplace Issues, Privacy, Ethics, Security, and Your Future   Very few parts of society now exist in which computers are not an important presence. Consequently, we must consider their relationship to our personal lives. Chapter 13 describes workplace issues, including how we can avoid certain physical and mental health matters associated with computers. The chapter also considers privacy and ethical issues, such as the spread of personal information without your consent. Finally, it discusses security matters, such as computer-related crimes.

The final chapter, Chapter 14, shows you how to keep up and stay ahead—to stay computer-competent in the future.

Review Questions

1. What is *computer competency?*
2. Who are *end users?*
3. What are *prewritten programs?*
4. Distinguish among the four kinds of computers: microcomputers, minicomputers, mainframes, and supercomputers.
5. Describe the five parts of a microcomputer system.
6. Distinguish between applications software and systems software.
7. How do packaged software and custom-made software differ?
8. Name some principal kinds of packaged software—what we call software "basic tools."
9. Name the five categories of microcomputer hardware.
10. What common input device will you probably use?
11. What are the two parts of the system unit, and what do they do?
12. What is the difference between primary storage and secondary storage?
13. Distinguish between floppy disks and hard disks.
14. What is a monitor?
15. What output device produces images on paper?
16. What does a modem do?
17. What are the four increasingly sophisticated levels of data?
18. What is *connectivity?*
19. Give three important reasons why gaining competency in microcomputers is important.
20. What are some software "power tools" that are emerging for microcomputer end users that formerly were found only on mainframes?

Discussion Questions and Projects

1. *Your reasons for learning computing:* How are you already using computer technology? What's happened in the computer-related world in the last six months that you might have read about or seen on television? How are companies using computers to stay on the cutting edge? These are some questions you might discuss with classmates to see why computers are an exciting part of life.

   You might also consider the reasons why *you* want to gain computer competency. Imagine your dream career. How do you think microcomputers, from what you already know, can help you do the work you want to do? What kind of after-hours interests do you have? Assuming you could afford it, how could a microcomputer bring new skills or value to those interests?

2. *Dealing with computer anxiety:* Some newcomers to computers experience *computer anxiety*, or *technophobi*a—great discomfort, even fear, about dealing with these machines. They may be afraid, for example, that they "aren't smart enough" to work with computers, that they will "mess up," that they will accidentally break something, or that they will embarrass themselves in front of others. There are a number of ways of dealing with such anxieties and fears. If you are coming to this subject with a fair amount of discomfort, discuss which of the following solutions might help.

   a. Work with a partner. Ask another newcomer if you can sit together (whether in lecture or laboratory) and try working things through together.

   b. Talk back to an imaginary critic. Write out a script in which you talk to an imaginary hostile stranger who puts you down about your computer abilities. By talking back, you demolish what are really self-criticisms.

   c. Expose yourself to computers gradually. Go into a computer lab by yourself and simply "play around" with a microcomputer. Back off whenever the discomfort becomes too great. After a while, you'll find yourself less bothered by these machines.

   d. Expose yourself to all your computer anxieties at once. In a technique psychologists call "flooding," you allow yourself to experience all your fears and anxieties at once, no matter how bad they make you feel. By hanging in there, you tolerate the discomfort until the fears run their course.

Chapter 1 You and Computer Competency

People and Procedures	Software

People

People are competent end users working to increase their productivity. **End users** use microcomputers and prewritten programs (such as word processing and spreadsheet programs) to solve information-related or decision-making problems.

Procedures

Procedures are manuals and guidelines that guide and instruct end users on how to use the software and hardware.

Software is another name for **programs**—instructions that tell the computer how process data. Two kinds of software are applications software and systems softw

Applications Software

Applications software is "end-user" software that helps perform useful work. Suc ware may be **packaged** (prewritten) or **custom-made** (written by a programmer). Examples of general-purpose packaged software ("basic tools") are:

- *Word processing* programs—to prepare written documents
- *Electronic spreadsheets*—to analyze and summarize data
- *File and database managers*—to organize and manage data and information
- *Graphics programs*—to present data visually, as charts and graphs
- *Communications programs*—to transmit and receive data
- *Integrated programs*—combine some or all of the preceding programs in one package

Systems Software

Systems software is "background" software that helps a computer manage its i resources. An example is the **operating system**, which interacts between applic software and the computer. Popular microcomputer operating systems:

- *DOS*—today's standard operating system for IBM and IBM-compatible microc ers
- *DOS with Windows*—extends capability of DOS
- *OS/2*—developed for IBM's most powerful microcomputers
- *Macintosh operating system*—runs on Apple's Macintosh computers
- *Unix*—runs on many powerful microcomputers

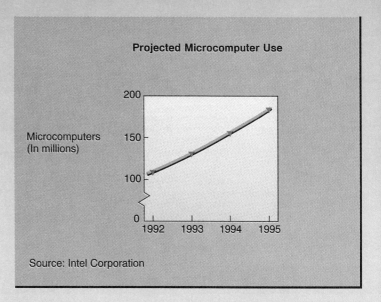

Projected Microcomputer Use

Microcomputers (In millions)

200
150
100
0

1992 1993 1994 1995

Source: Intel Corporation

Four Kinds of Computers:

- **Microcomputers**—desktop or portable size, known as **personal computers** or **workstations**
- **Minicomputers**—medium-size machines for medium-size organizations and departments within larger organizations
- **Mainframes**—large machines for large organizations
- **Supercomputers**—high-capacity machines for research

Hardware

Input Devices

Input devices take data and put it into a form the computer can process. Especially important is the **keyboard**, a typewriter-like keyboard with specialized keys.

The System Unit

The **system unit**, housed in a microcomputer's cabinet, consists of electronic circuitry with two parts:

- **The central processing unit (CPU)**—controls and manipulates data to produce information
- **Primary storage (memory)**—temporarily holds data for processing, program instructions for processing the data, and processed data before it is output

Secondary Storage

Secondary storage permanently stores data and programs. Two storage "media" are:

- **Floppy disks**—removable flexible 5¼-inch or 3½-inch plastic disks
- **Hard disk**—nonremovable, enclosed disk drive

Output Devices

Output devices output processed information from CPU. Two important output devices:

- **Monitor**—TV screen–like device to display results
- **Printer**—device that prints out images on paper

Communications Devices

These send and receive data and programs from one computer to another. A device that connects a microcomputer to a telephone is a **modem**.

Data and Connectivity

Data

Data consists of characters that are input into the computer system. Data organization:

- **Character**—letter, number, special character
- **Field**—set of related characters (e.g., person's last name)
- **Record**—set of related fields (e.g., name and address)
- **File**—set of related records (e.g., all names and addresses of companies applied to for work)
- **Database**—a collection of related files

Connectivity

Connectivity is a concept describing the ability of end users to tap into resources well beyond their desktops. With **computer networks**—communications connections—microcomputers can be linked to other microcomputers, minicomputers, or mainframes to share data and resources. Connectivity greatly expands the power of end users.

2

Applications Software: Basic Tools

Competencies

After you have read this chapter, you should be able to:

1. Explain the features common to all kinds of applications software.

2. Describe applications software for word processing, spreadsheets, database managers, graphics, and communications.

3. Describe integrated software that combines all these tasks.

Think of the microcomputer as an *enabler*. People may not consider themselves as being very good at typing. Or at doing calculations, drawing charts, or looking up information. A microcomputer, however, enables you to do all these things—and much more. All it takes is the right kind of software—the programs that go into the computer. We describe the most important ones here.

Not long ago, all the things you can now do with a microcomputer were performed mostly by trained specialists. Secretaries typed professional-looking business correspondence. Market analysts used pencils and paper and calculators to project sales. Graphic artists drew colored charts. Data processing experts stored files of records on large computers. Now you can do all these tasks—and much more—with just *one* microcomputer. And many of these tasks can be done with just *one* applications program.

Using Software Off the Shelf

Some Features Are Common to All Kinds of Applications Packages.

Word processing, electronic spreadsheets, database managers, graphics programs, communications programs, and software that combines all five tasks are *general-purpose* applications packages. That is, they may be used by many people for many different kinds of tasks. This is why we have called them "basic tools." Packaged software is also called **off-the-shelf software.** Some well-known software publishers are Lotus Corporation, famous for spreadsheets; Borland (database); and WordPerfect and Microsoft (word processors).

Some features are common to most packaged programs. The following are the most important.

Cursor The *cursor* is a blinking symbol on the screen. (*See Figure 2-1.*) It shows where you may enter data next. You can move the cursor around using cursor control keys, such as the directional arrow keys on many keyboards. You can also move the cursor using a mouse.

Scrolling is a feature that lets you move quickly through the text forward or backward. Thus, you can look at a screenful (20–22 lines) of your work. By issuing a command, you can then move ("scroll") through the screen and into the following screens.

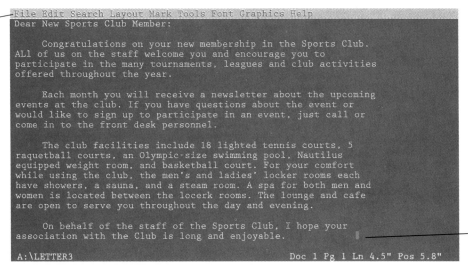

Figure 2-1
A word processing screen, with cursor and menu bar (WordPerfect, version 5.1).

Menus Most software packages have **menus,** which list commands available for manipulating data. Menus are of two kinds:

- **Menu bar:** This is a line or two across the top or bottom of the screen listing commands available. (*See Figure 2-1.*)
- **Pull-down menu:** This is a list of commands that "drops down" from a menu bar at the top of the screen. (*See Figure 2-2.*)

Most applications programs also offer a **Help menu** or **Help screen.** Help menus present a choice of step-by-step explanations on how to perform various tasks. Help menus are particularly useful when you need assistance but do not have an instruction manual handy. (*See Figure 2-3, next page.*)

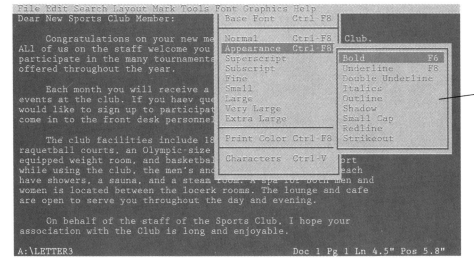

Figure 2-2
A word processing screen, with pull-down menu (WordPerfect, version 5.1).

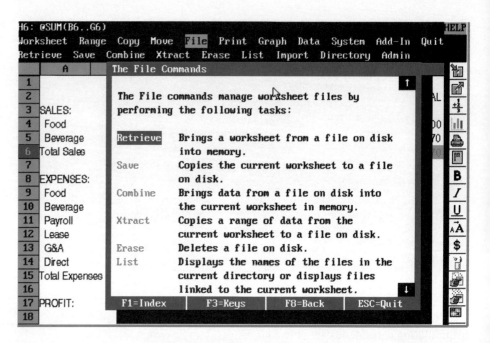

Figure 2-3
A Help screen, from a spreadsheet (Lotus 1-2-3, version 2.4).

Format   You can change the **format,** or "look," of your work. For instance, the line spacing in a letter can be altered. It can be double spaced or single spaced. Top, bottom, left, and right margins can be made narrower or wider. In a spreadsheet, the width of columns can be changed.

WYSIWYG   Pronounced "wizzy-wig," **WYSIWYG** stands for "What You See Is What You Get." This means that the image on the screen display looks the same as the final printed document. Application programs without WYSIWYG are not always able to display an exact representation of the final printed document. For instance, some word processors without WYSIWYG will not display footnotes and page numbers on the screen, although they appear on the printed copy. The WYSIWYG feature allows the user to preview the document's appearance before it is printed out.

Special-Purpose Keys   Computer keyboards have **special-purpose keys,** such as *Esc* ("Escape") and *Ctrl* ("Control"). Special-purpose keys are used to enter and edit data and execute commands. For example, in many programs, pressing *Esc* allows you to cancel a command.

Function keys are labeled *F1, F2,* and so on. These keys are positioned along the left side or along the top of the keyboard. They are used for commands or tasks that are performed frequently, such as underlining. These keys do different things in different software packages. For example, if you press *F1* in WordPerfect, it cancels the previous command you gave. If you press *F1* in the spreadsheet Lotus 1-2-3, however, it gives you access to the Help menu.

Macros   Many commonly used commands require that you press a series of keys. Many programs enable you to store these keystrokes as a macro command. For example, each time you wanted to print a spreadsheet you could press several keys. Or, by appropriately defining a macro, you could print any spreadsheet with just macro commands.

Let us now describe the categories of applications software that we are calling basic software tools.

Word Processing

Word Processing Is Used to Create, Edit, Save, and Print Documents.

Word processing software is used to create, edit, save, and print documents. (*See Figure 2-4.*) **Documents** can be any kind of *text* material. Some examples of documents are letters, memos, term papers, reports, and contracts.

If you have used a typewriter, then you know what word processing *begins* to feel like. You type in text on the keyboard. However, with word processing, you view the words you type on a monitor instead of on a piece of paper. After you are done, you "save" (store) your words on a diskette or hard disk. Then you turn on the printer and print out the results on paper.

The beauty of this method is that you can make any changes or corrections—before printing out the document. Even after your document is printed out, you can easily go back and make changes. You can then print it out again. Want to change a report from double spaced to single spaced? Alter the width of the margins on the left and right? Delete some paragraphs and add some others from yet another document? A word processor allows you to do all these with ease. Indeed, *deleting, inserting,* and *replacing*—the principal correcting activities—can be done just by pressing keys on the keyboard.

Once it was thought that only secretaries would use word processors. However, they are used extensively in managerial and professional life. Indeed, it has been found that, among the basic software tools, word processors produce the most productive gains.

Popular word processing packages include WordPerfect, Word, and MacWrite. Some interesting features shared by most word processors are described in the following sections.

Word Wrap and the Enter Key   One outstanding word processing feature is **word wrap.** On a typewriter, you must decide when to finish typing a line. You indicate the end of a line by pressing a carriage return key. A word processor decides for you and automatically moves the cursor to the next line. As you keep typing, the words "wrap around" to the next line. To begin a new paragraph or leave a blank line, you press the Enter Key.

Search and Replace   A **search** command allows you to find any word or number that you know exists in your document. When you search, the cursor will move to the first place the item appears. If you want, the program will also search for the item everywhere it appears in the document. For example, in one word processing program (WordPerfect), if you wanted to find *Chicago* in your text, you would position the cursor at the beginning of the document and then press the *F2* function key. After the word *Search* appears at the bottom of your screen, you type *Chicago.* Then press *F2* again. The cursor will then move to the word's first occurrence.

The **replace** command automatically replaces the word you search for with another word. For example, you could search for the word *Chicago* and replace it with the word *Denver.* You can do this at every place the word *Chicago* appears or only in those instances where you choose to do so. The search and replace commands are useful for finding and fixing errors—for example, if you misspell a client's name. They also may be used to revise a document intended for one person to go to another person.

Figure 2-4
The WordPerfect word processing package includes instruction manual and template—a cardboard overlay that fits on the keyboard and indicates how to key in commands. Floppy disks include program disk, self-guiding tutorial, spelling checker, and thesaurus for finding alternate words.

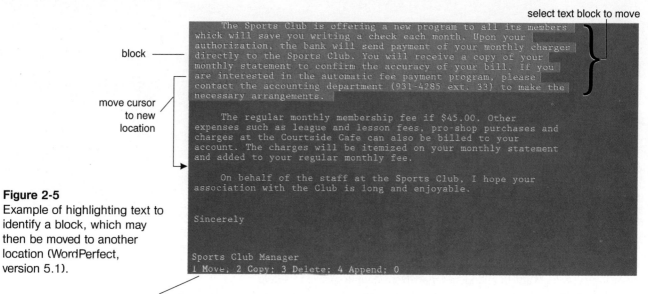

select text block to move

block

move cursor
to new
location

Figure 2-5
Example of highlighting text to identify a block, which may then be moved to another location (WordPerfect, version 5.1).

select Move command
from menu

Block and Move In writing a rough draft, typewriter users find they must use "cutting and pasting." That is, they use scissors and glue or tape when moving text from one place to another. This creates a revised draft on paper. Then this revised draft must be completely retyped. Word processors eliminate this double effort.

On a word processor, the portion of text you wish to move is a **block.** You mark the block by giving commands that produce **highlighting,** a band of light over the area. (*See Figure 2-5.*) The task of moving the block is called a **block move.**

The block command may also be used to delete text or to copy chunks of text into another document. All this occurs before the document is printed out. You can imagine the savings in time and effort.

Other Features Almost all applications software provides commands for enter, search, and move. These features are not limited to word processors. Some other features you'll usually find in word processing packages are:

- Right margins may be **justified**—that is, evened up, like the margins in this book. Or they may be **unjustified,** given a "ragged-right" appearance like correspondence typed on a standard typewriter.

- Headings may be centered. A word may be typed underlined or **boldface** (extra dark lettering) for emphasis.

- Spelling can be checked automatically, by running your text through a **spelling-checker** program.

- **Thesaurus** programs enable you to quickly find the right word or an alternative word by presenting you with an on-screen thesaurus.

- A **mail-merge** or **form-letter** feature allows you to merge different names and addresses so that you can mail out the same form letter to different people.

- **Desktop publishing** capabilities are available with some advanced word processing programs, such as WordPerfect's version 5.1. This feature enables you to mix text and graphics to produce newsletters and other publications of nearly professional quality.

- **Outlining programs** (sometimes called "idea processors") allow you to use Roman numerals, letters, and Arabic numbers to write an outline. You put in the main topic head, then the subtopics, sub-subtopics, and the like. If you decide to change the placement or importance of an idea, you simply move the block of text. The outline numbers and letters are resequenced automatically.

■ Many programs have an **importing** feature. Files may be retrieved ("imported") from nontext programs such as spreadsheets and graphics and added to the word processing program. (The process of saving a file in a form that can be retrieved by another program is called **exporting**.)

Spreadsheets

A Spreadsheet Is an Electronic Worksheet Used to Organize and Manipulate Numbers and Display Options for "What-If" Analyses.

The **electronic spreadsheet** is based on the traditional accounting worksheet. Paper worksheets have long been used by accountants and managers to work up balance sheets, sales projections, and expense budgets. The electronic spreadsheet has rows and columns that can be used to present and analyze data. (*See Figure 2-6.*) Numeric data involves numbers rather than words.

Electronic spreadsheets allow you to try out various "what-if" kinds of possibilities. That is a powerful feature. You can manipulate numbers by using stored formulas and calculate different outcomes. For example, a restaurant manager can figure out whether the business will make a profit or loss by projecting the cost of food and beverage sales over a six-month period. (*See Figure 2-6.*) The manager can then subtract expenses from sales. Expenses might include such things as payroll for employees, lease of restaurant space, and purchases of food and beverage supplies. If the expenses are too high to produce a profit, the manager can experiment on the screen with

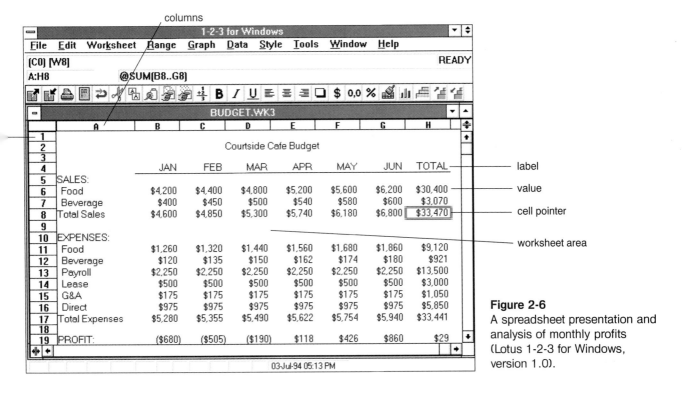

Figure 2-6
A spreadsheet presentation and analysis of monthly profits (Lotus 1-2-3 for Windows, version 1.0).

reducing some expenses. For example, the number of employees and hence payroll costs might be reduced.

Spreadsheet packages are used by financial analysts, accountants, contractors, and others concerned with manipulating numerical data. Popular spreadsheet programs are Lotus 1-2-3, Excel, and Quattro Pro.

A spreadsheet has several parts. (*See Figure 2-6.*) The **worksheet area** of the spreadsheet has **column headings** across the top and **row headings** down the left side. The intersection of a column and row is called a **cell.** The cell holds a single unit of information. The position of a cell is called the **cell address.** For example, *"A1"* is the cell address of the first position on a spreadsheet, the topmost and leftmost position. A **cell pointer**—also known as the **spreadsheet cursor**—indicates where data is to be entered or changed in the spreadsheet. The cell pointer can be moved around in much the same way that you move a cursor in a word processing program. In our illustration, the cell pointer is located in position H8.

The following are some common features of spreadsheet programs.

Format   Column and row headings are known as **labels.** Usually a label is a word or symbol, such as a pound sign (#). A number in a cell is called a **value.** Labels and values can be displayed or formatted in different ways. A label can be centered in the cell or positioned to the left or right. A value can be displayed to show decimal places, dollars, or percent (%). The number of decimal positions (if any) can be altered, and the width of columns can be changed.

Formulas   One of the benefits of spreadsheets is that you can manipulate data through the use of formulas. **Formulas** are instructions for calculations. They make connections between numbers in particular cells. For example, in our illustration, the spreadsheet is concerned with computing sales of food and beverages for a restaurant. The formula is shown near the top of the screen: *@SUM[B8..G8].* (*See Figure 2-6.*) This means sum, or add, the values in cells B8 through G8 (total sales from January to June). The total is displayed in cell H8.

Recalculation   **Recalculation** is one of the most important features of spreadsheets. If you change one or more numbers in your spreadsheet, all related formulas will recalculate automatically. Thus, you can substitute one value for another in the cells affected by your formula and recalculate the results.

By manipulating the values, you can use spreadsheet formulas to explore your options. For example, consider our illustration. If the January-to-June sales are *estimates,* you can change any or all of the values in cells B8 through G8. The total in cell H8 will change automatically. (*See Figure 2-6.*)

For more complex problems, recalculation enables you to store long, complicated formulas and many changing values and quickly produce alternatives. A contractor might need to keep the cost of building a house within a budget. The contractor can run cost calculations on various grades of materials and on the going pay rates for labor.

Windows   The screen-sized area of a spreadsheet that you are able to view is called a **window** or a **page.** Only about 20 rows and 8 columns of a spreadsheet are visible on the video display screen at one time. The total size of the spreadsheet can be much larger. Lotus 1-2-3, for instance, contains 256 rows and 8192 columns.

Other Features   Most electronic spreadsheets also include additional capabilities for visually displaying and rearranging data. Among them are the following features:

- *Data displayed in graphic form:* Most spreadsheets allow users to present their data in graphic form. That is, you can display numerical information as pie charts or bar charts (as we describe on p.28.)

- *3-D graphics:* Some spreadsheet programs even permit you to display data in graphs and charts that have a three-dimensional look.

- *Graphics on worksheet:* A new feature gives users the ability to place graphical elements such as lines, arrows, and boxes directly onto the worksheet. You can thereby create charts and graphs directly on the worksheet (rather than display them separately).

- *Consolidation feature:* Data may be consolidated from several small worksheets into one large worksheet. Thus, you can work with small worksheets, which are more manageable, and summarize the data on a large worksheet.

- *Dynamic file links:* Some software offers **dynamic file links,** which allow you to link cells in one worksheet file to cells in other worksheet files. Whenever a change occurs in one file, the linked cells in the other files are automatically updated.

Database Managers

A Database Manager Organizes a Large Collection of Data So That Related Information Can Be Retrieved Easily.

A *database* is a large collection of data that has been entered into a computer system and stored for future use. The computerized information in the database is organized so that the parts that have something in common can be retrieved easily. We describe databases in detail in Chapter 8.

A **database manager** or **database management system (DBMS)** is a software package used to set up, or *structure,* a database. It is also used to retrieve information from a database. An example of one database manager is dBASE. (*See Figure 2-7.*) This database contains information about employees. The top line is a menu. The list of

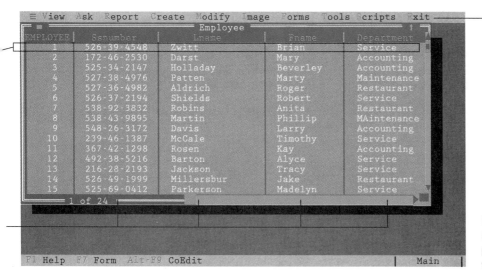

menu

Figure 2-7
A database containing employee records (dBASE IV, version 1.0).

employee names and addresses is called a *file*. Each line of information about one employee is called a *record*. Each column of information within a record is called a *field*—for example, last name.

To see the value of a computerized database, imagine that you are a filing clerk in a large corporation. The boss asks to see a list of all employees who have been with the company fewer than three years. The employee records are stored on paper, in alphabetical order by last name. It might take you days or weeks to assemble this information by hand, going through rows of four-drawer filing cabinets.

When the same information is held in an electronic database, you can get the information "on line" in a few minutes. You instruct the database software to scan just one field in every employee's record: the hire date. The computer can then print out a list of all current employees hired within the past three years.

Database management programs are used by salespeople to keep track of clients. They are also used by purchasing agents to keep track of orders and by inventory managers to monitor products in their warehouses. Database managers are used by many people inside and outside of business, from teachers to police officers. Popular database management programs include dBASE, Paradox, and FoxPro.

Database managers have different features, depending on their sophistication. A description of the principal features of database manager software for microcomputers follows.

Retrieve and Display A basic feature of all database programs is the capability to locate records in the file quickly. In our example, the program searches each record for a match in a particular field to whatever data you specify. The records can then be displayed on the screen for viewing, updating, or editing. For example, if an employee moves, the address field needs to be changed. The record is quickly retrieved by searching the database to find the employee record that matches the name field you specify. Once the record is displayed, the address field can be changed.

Sort Database managers make it easy to change the order of records in a file. Normally, records are entered into the database in the order they occur, such as the date a person is hired. This may not be the best way, however. There are a number of ways you can quickly rearrange the records in the file. For example, you might want to print out an entire alphabetical list of employees by last name. For tax purposes, you might want to list employees by social security number.

Calculate and Format Many database programs contain built-in math formulas. In the office, for example, you can use this feature to find the highest or lowest commissions earned. You can calculate the average of the commissions earned by the sales force in one part of the country. This information can be organized as a table and printed out in a report format.

Other Features Among other capabilities offered by some database management programs are the following:

■ *Customized data-entry forms:* A person new to the database program may find some of the descriptions for fields confusing. For example, a fieldname may appear as "CUSTNUM" for "customer number." However, the form on the screen may be customized so that the expression "Enter the customer number" appears in place of "CUSTNUM." Fields may also be rearranged on the screen, and boxes and lines may be added.

■ *Professional-looking reports:* A custom-report option enables you to design the elements you want in a report. Examples are the descriptions appearing above columns and the fields you wish to include. You can even add graphic elements, such as boxes or lines, so that the printed report has a professional appearance. Although the database itself may have, say, 10 fields, the report can be customized to display only the 5 or so important fields.

■ *Program control languages:* Most people using a database management program can accomplish everything they need to do by making choices from the menus. Many database management programs include a programming control language so that advanced users can create sophisticated applications. In addition, some programs, such as dBASE IV, allow direct communication to specialized mainframe databases through languages like SQL (Structured Query Language).

Graphics

A Graphics Program Can Display Numeric Data in a Visual Format for Analytical or Presentation Purposes.

Research on communications shows that people learn better when information is presented visually. A picture is indeed worth a thousand words—or numbers. The popularity of graphics programs is expected to continue. (*See Figure 2-8.*)

There are two types of graphics programs. *Analytical* graphics programs are used to analyze data. *Presentation* graphics programs are used to create attractive finished graphs for presentations or reports. As a microcomputer user, you will probably be particularly interested in analytical graphics.

Analytical Graphics   **Analytical graphics** make numerical data much easier to grasp than when it is in the form of rows and columns of numbers. Graphics may

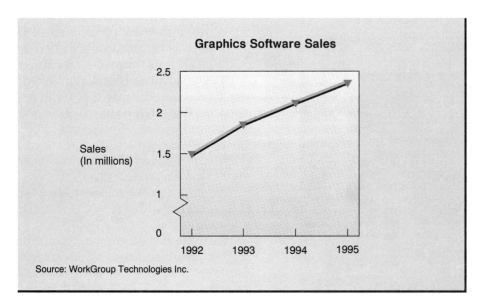

Figure 2-8
Graphics on the rise: rise in sales of graphics software packages.

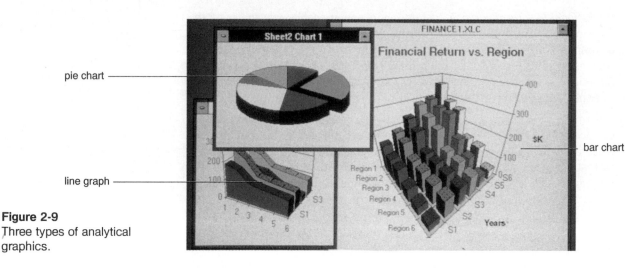

Figure 2-9
Three types of analytical graphics.

take the form of *bar charts, line graphs,* and *pie charts.* (*See Figure 2-9.*) Another kind of chart (not shown here) is the *high-low graph.* This kind of graph shows a range—for instance, of house prices. All these pictorial devices make information much easier to grasp compared to when it is presented in columns of numbers.

Most analytical graphics programs come as part of spreadsheet programs, such as Lotus 1-2-3. Thus, they are used by the same people who use spreadsheets. They are helpful in displaying economic trends, sales figures, and the like for easy analysis. Analytical graphics may be viewed on a monitor or printed out.

Presentation Graphics   You can use **presentation graphics** to communicate a message or to persuade other people, such as supervisors or clients. Thus, presentation graphics are used by marketing or sales people, for example.

Figure 2-10
Example of presentation graphics.

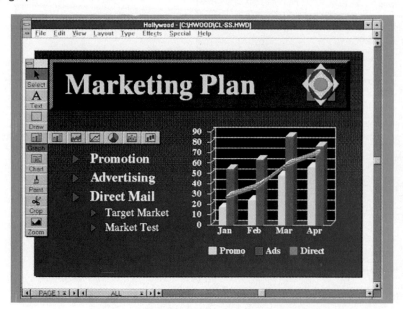

Presentation graphics look more sophisticated than analytical graphics, using color, titles, a three-dimensional look, and other features a graphic artist might use. (*See Figure 2-10.*) Using special equipment, you can convert graphics displays into slides or transparencies. High-end presentation graphics packages even include animation capabilities. These packages allow you to create and edit animated graphics on your microcomputer and then run them on your VCR.

Popular business graphics packages are Hollywood, Harvard Graphics, Persuasion and Freelance Plus.

There is yet another kind of graphics program, one that is used by professional illustrators, such as people doing commercial art or drafting. These **drawing programs** are used to help create artwork for publications work.

Communications

Communications Software Lets You Send Data to and Receive Data from Another Computer.

Communications software enables a microcomputer with a modem to send and receive data over a telephone or other communications line. Program menus show you the steps to take. An example of a communications program is Crosstalk. (*See Figure 2-11.*) A sales representative, for instance, might use this software to retrieve an electronic file from a distant, telephone-linked information source. The file might be something such as a list of clients. The representative could them copy the file to his or her own diskette or hard disk.

Communications programs are used by all kinds of people inside and outside of business. Examples are students doing research papers, travelers making plane reservations, consumers buying products, investors getting stock quotations, and economists getting government statistical data. Popular communications software includes ProComm, Smartcom, and Crosstalk.

Communications programs give microcomputers a powerful feature, as we have mentioned—namely, that of *connectivity.* Connections with microcomputers open up a world of services previously available only to users of mainframe computers. We devote all of Chapter 7 to explaining computer communications and connectivity. Here, let us briefly note some features about microcomputer communications programs.

Data Banks   With a communications program, you can access enormous computerized databases: data banks of information. Some of these, such as Dialog, resemble huge electronic encyclopedias.

Message Exchanges   Communications programs enable you to leave and receive messages on *electronic bulletin boards* or to use *electronic mail services. (See Figure 2-12, p. 30.)* Electronic bulletin boards exist for people interested in swapping all kinds of software or information. Such people might be job seekers, lawyers, femi-

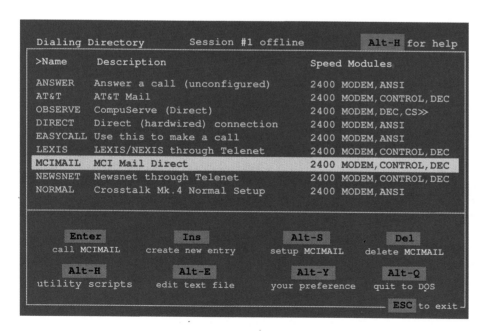

Figure 2-11
A menu from the communications program Crosstalk Mk.4, version 2.0.

nists, rock music fans, or students—the possibilities are almost endless. Many organizations have "electronic mailboxes." For instance, you can transmit a report you have created on your word processor to a faraway company executive or to a college instructor.

Financial Services With communications programs, you can look up airline reservations and stock quotations. You can order discount merchandise and even do home banking and bill paying.

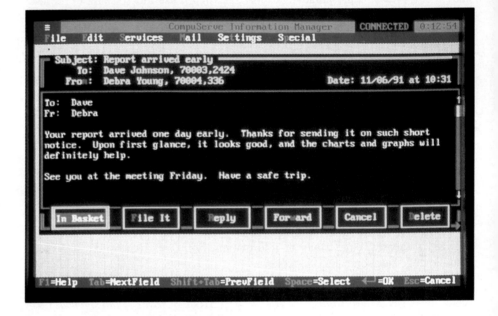

Figure 2-12
Example of an electronic mail screen.

Integrated Packages

Integrated Software Is an All-in-One Applications Package That Includes Word Processing, Spreadsheet, Database Manager, Graphics, and Communications.

We have described five important kinds of applications software. What happens if you want to take the data in one program and use it in another? Suppose you want to take information stored in the database manager and use it in a spreadsheet. This is not always possible with separate applications packages, but it is with integrated software.

An **integrated package** is a collection of applications programs that work together and share information from one program with another. With an integrated package, you can use the database manager to pull together relevant facts. An example of such facts might be the annual membership fees for a sports club for different years. You

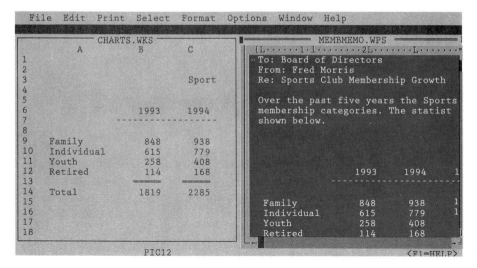

Figure 2-13
Example of an integrated package's spreadsheet and word-processor (Microsoft Works, version 2.0).

can then use the spreadsheet to compare these membership fees. (*See Figure 2-13.*) You can use the word processing program to write a memo about these membership fees for different categories of members. You can use this program to merge into the memo totals from the spreadsheet. Finally, you can use the communications program to send the memo to another computer.

Integrated packages may be categorized as two types:

- *Low end:* Low-end integrated packages provide word processing, database management, a spreadsheet, and communications all in a single program priced at less than $200. Examples are Microsoft Works and Lotus Works. Packages of this sort are easy to use. They are especially useful for microcomputers that do not have a lot of storage capacity (such as those that use floppy disks but no hard disk).

- *High end:* High-end integrated packages accomplish the same basic functions but also offer some more advanced features. However, they can cost four to five times as much as the low-end programs and require a hard disk. Examples are Symphony and Framework. These packages are not as easy to use as their low-end counterparts. However, they are less expensive than several separate "stand-alone" programs.

Whether high or low end, an integrated package has a common structure allowing data to be exchanged easily between the programs within the package. Nevertheless, each application is generally less powerful than separate "stand-alone" applications software, such as a word processing program or a spreadsheet program by itself. Moreover, stand-alone applications programs are becoming more inclusive— some word processing programs have some simple spreadsheets, for example. Finally, as we explain in the next chapter, programs such as Windows make it easy for a user to share data between *completely different* stand-alone applications programs, not just between the applications available within one integrated package.

A Look at the Future

Tutorials, Special Software, and Hardware Add-Ons Help Students Learn Complex Software Tasks.

Applications software is one of those areas in which there are always new developments. How, then, can you keep up with newer versions?

Of course you can always take a class, which is often the easiest way. Many software manufacturers also produce *tutorials*—step-by-step directions and practice sessions. These may be available in books, on floppy disks, or on videotape cassettes. In the future, as software features multiply, the pressure will increase to make the learning process more efficient.

Already some *attempts at simplification* are being marketed. An add-on console (The Simplifier) can be plugged into a microcomputer keyboard. Its special cartridges contain instructions for students to help interpret complex commands in spreadsheet programs. Assistance is also available for learning other complex tasks. For instance, one word processing program (Wordbench) forces students to learn to write by limiting the writing space, prohibiting users from going back to edit, and not allowing writers to see the words as they are written. In addition, the Help command has been made more useful in many programs. So-called *context-sensitive help systems* now provide directed assistance. They take users not just to a list of topic areas for further information but to the specific area that helps them solve their specific problems.

The very "look and feel" of most software is changing. One feature is *windowing software,* in which you can work on several applications—word processing, database searching, and the like—*simultaneously.* Another important feature that is rapidly becoming popular is *graphical user interfaces,* in which the user issues commands through pull-down menus and symbols called icons.

Review Questions

1. What, in a phrase, is off-the-shelf software?
2. Describe some common features of applications software: the cursor, scrolling, menus, format, WYSIWYG, and special keys.
3. What is a Help screen?
4. What is word processing used for?
5. Describe the following word processing operations: word wrap, search and replace, and block move.
6. Describe the principal features of the worksheet area of an electronic spreadsheet.
7. What is a window? a page?
8. How do formulas and recalculation work in a spreadsheet?
9. What is a database?
10. Describe some of the features of a database manager: retrieve and display, sort, calculate, and format.
11. Explain the purpose of analytical graphics.
12. Name three common types of graphs and charts used in analytical graphics.
13. Describe the purpose of presentation graphics.

14. What does communications software do?

15. Describe some computer connections.

16. How does integrated software work?

Discussion Questions and Projects

1. *Three ways to acquire applications software:* The following exercise can be extremely useful. Concentrate on a category of software of personal interest to you—say, word processing or spreadsheets. Go to the library and find information on the following three methods of acquiring software. Which route seems to be the best for you? Why?

   a. *Public domain software* is software you can get for free. Someone writes a program and offers to share it without charge with everyone. Generally, you find these programs by belonging to a microcomputer users group or by accessing an electronic bulletin board using your telephone-linked computer. The software may be fine, but it also may be terrible.

   b. *Shareware* is inexpensive software (perhaps $50 or less). Shareware operates on the honor system. It is distributed free, in the same way as public domain software. After you have used it for a while and decide you like it, you're supposed to pay the author for it. Again, the quality varies, but some shareware is excellent.

   c. *Commercial software* consists of brand-name packages, such as those we mentioned in this chapter. Prices vary. They are generally higher in computer stores (say, $500 for a new word processing program) and lower with mail-order software houses. Features also vary, and vary tremendously. However, there are several periodicals that provide ratings and guides. For instance, *PC World* is a magazine that specializes in IBM and IBM-compatible microcomputers. For the last several years the magazine has polled its readers to find out the best brands of software in various categories and has released the results in its October issue. Other periodicals (for example, *PC/Computing, MacWorld, Infoworld*) also have surveys, reviews, and ratings.

2. *Word processing versus desktop publishing software:* A good desktop publishing program helps you establish guidelines for consistent-looking pages, then allows you to easily break the rules and give each page a unique appearance. You should be able to extract text and graphics from any other program and alter them to your heart's content. As discussed in this chapter, the most recent versions of many word processors such as WordPerfect's version 5.1 include some desktop publishing capabilities. Ask someone familiar with the two types of programs to compare them using the following criteria:

   a. Ease of use

   b. Page design and layout

   c. Font handling

   d. Graphics handling

   e. Editing tools

   f. Price

   g. Technical support

Visual Summary

Chapter 2 — Applications Software: Basic Tools

Applications software does "useful work." The five basic tools or types of general-purpose applications programs are used by many people for different kinds of tasks.

Word Processing	Spreadsheets	Database Managers

 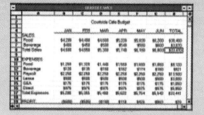 

Word Processing

Word processing software is used to create, edit, save, and print **documents**—any kind of text material. Especially useful for deleting, inserting, and replacing. Principal features:

Word Wrap and Enter Key

Word wrap automatically carries cursor to new line. **Enter key** enters new paragraph or blank line.

Search and Replace

Search command allows user to quickly find a word or number in a document. **Replace** command allows user to automatically replace word with another word.

Block and Move

A **block** is a portion of text that may be identified by **highlighting** (band of light). Moving the block to new location is done with **block move** command.

Other Features

- **Justifying**, underlining, boldfacing, and centering.
- **Spelling-checker** programs check spelling automatically.
- **Thesaurus** programs find alternative words.
- **Mail-merge** allows merging of names and addresses to personalize letters.
- Advanced features such as **desktop publishing**, **outlining**, and **importing**.

Examples of Packages

WordPerfect, Word, MacWrite

Spreadsheets

An **electronic spreadsheet**, consisting of rows and columns, is used to present and analyze data. The **worksheet area** is bounded by **column headings** across the top and **row headings** down the left side. The **cell** is the intersection of column and row; position of the cell is called **cell address**. The **cell pointer (spreadsheet cursor)** indicates where data is to be entered. Principal features:

Format

Labels (column and row headings) and **values** (numbers in cells) can be displayed in different ways (e.g., with dollar signs and decimal points).

Formulas

Formulas, instructions for calculations, may be used to manipulate data.

Recalculation

Recalculation, automatic recomputation, is an important feature.

Windows

A **window**, the screen-sized area of a spreadsheet, may be moved to show a different part of a spreadsheet.

Examples of Packages

Lotus 1-2-3, Excel, Quattro Pro

Database Managers

A **database manager** (or **database management system, DBMS**) is used to structure a database, a large collection of computerized data. Data is organized as fields and records for easy retrieval. Principal features:

Retrieve and Display

Records can be easily located and displayed on the screen for viewing or updating.

Sort

Users can sort through records and rearrange them in different ways.

Calculate and Format

Math formulas may be used to manipulate data. Data may be printed out in different report formats.

Other Features

- Customized data-entry forms
- Professional-looking reports
- Program Control languages

Examples of Packages

dBASE, Paradox, Fox Pro

Features Common to All Applications Software

- **Cursor**, blinking symbol on screen, shows where data may be entered.
- **Scrolling** allows user to move ("scroll") through text.
- **Menu** lists commands (e.g., "Delete").
- **Format**, or "look," can be altered (e.g., line spacing).
- **WYSIWYG**, "What You See Is What You Get."
- **Special-purpose keys** (e.g., *Esc, Ctrl*) and **function keys** (e.g., *F1, F2*) allow entering and editing of data and execution of commands.
- **Macro** commands combine many keystrokes in time-saving fewer strokes.

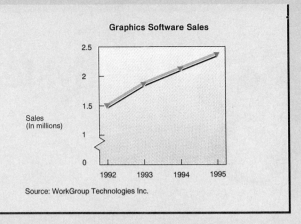

Graphics Software Sales

Sales (In millions)

Source: WorkGroup Technologies Inc.

Graphics	Communications	Integrated Packages

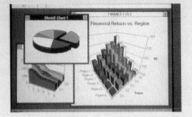

Graphics programs display results of data manipulation for easier analysis and presentation. Two types of graphics programs are analytical and presentation.

Analytical Graphics

Analytical graphics programs put data in a form easier to analyze (e.g., bar charts, line graphs).

Presentation Graphics

Presentation graphics help communicate results or persuade, using color and titles.

Examples of Packages

Most analytical graphics come as part of spreadsheet programs. Examples of presentation graphics: Hollywood, Harvard Graphics, Persuasion, Freelance Plus, Draw Applause, Graph Plus.

Communications software enables a microcomputer user with modem to send and receive data over telephone or other communications line. Communications programs permit *connectivity*—allow microcomputers to connect with other information resources.

Data Banks

Large computerized databases (e.g., electronic encyclopedias) are available.

Message Exchanges

Electronic bulletin boards and **electronic mail services** are available.

Financial Services

Users may look up stock quotations and airline reservations, order discount merchandise, and do home banking.

Examples of Packages

ProComm, Smartcom, Crosstalk

An **integrated package** is an all-in-one software package. It includes spreadsheet, database manager, graphics, and perhaps word processing and communications programs.

Some Features

- Most important, it enables programs to work together and share the same data.
- Selected data may be retrieved by the database manager, analyzed by the spreadsheet, viewed graphically, report prepared by word processor, and sent over telephone by the communication program.

Two Categories

- Low-end packages cost less than $200 and include all the basic programs. Examples include Microsoft Works and Lotus Works.
- High-end packages cost over $200 and offer more advanced features. Examples include Symphony and Framework.

3

Systems Software

Becoming a microcomputer end user is like becoming the driver of a car. You can learn just enough to start up the car, take it out on the street, and pass a driver's license test. Or you can learn more about how cars work. That way you can drive any number of vehicles, know their limitations, and compare performance. Indeed, you could go so far as to learn to be a mechanic. Similarly, by expanding your knowledge about microcomputers, you extend what you can do with them. You don't have to be the equivalent of a mechanic—a computer technician. But the more you know, the more you expand your computer competency and productivity.

Cars all do the same thing—take you somewhere. But there was a time when you could choose between different automotive power systems: steam, electricity, or gasoline. Some systems were better for some purposes than others. You could have a car that was quiet or cheap to run, for instance. However, that same car perhaps took too long to start or wouldn't take you very far.

Microcomputers are in a comparable phase of evolution. Some computers do some things better than others do—are easier to learn, for instance, or run more kinds of applications software. Why is this? One important reason is the *systems software,* the "background" software that acts as an interface between the microcomputer and the user. Systems software also acts as an interface between the applications program and the input, output, and processing devices. (*See Figure 3-1.*) The most important microcomputer systems software are *DOS, DOS with Windows, OS/2, Macintosh,* and *Unix.* Which of these you can use depends in part on what kind of computer you have.

Why Learn About Systems Software?

Because Standards Are Changing, Users Need to Know More About Systems Software Than Was Previously Required.

Are you buying a pricey racing machine that you don't really need? Or are you buying an inexpensive, practical vehicle that may nonetheless soon become obsolete? These are the kinds of things many people think about when buying cars. Similar considerations apply in buying microcomputers and software. If you are paying several thousand dollars for a computer system, it's important to know what it can and can't do. (*See Figure 3-2.*) Moreover, you hope the buying decision you make will be good for the next several years.

If the study of systems software seems to be remote from your concerns, it shouldn't be. Here's why.

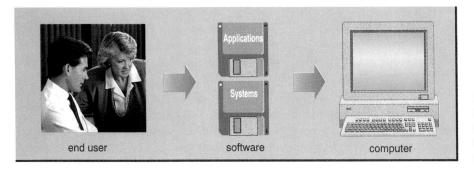

end user   software   computer

Figure 3-1
End users interact with applications software. Systems software interacts with the computer.

- *Competing systems software:* In earlier editions of this book there might not have been a need for this chapter. The kind of microcomputer systems software that predominated was the one for IBM and IBM-compatibles known as DOS. The other popular one was the one designed for the Apple Macintosh. Even then, Macintosh programs wouldn't run on IBM computers, and DOS programs wouldn't run on Macintosh computers. Today's very powerful microcomputers are demanding more and more from last year's systems software. Now there are several competing forms of systems software, leading to the lack of a standard.

- *DOS limitations:* If DOS was so popular, why didn't the microcomputer industry just stay with it? The answer is that it has some practical limitations, as we shall discuss. Because it is so widespread, DOS will probably continue to be used for the next several years. Thus, it is well worth learning. However, as more powerful microcomputers become commonplace, other systems software will replace DOS. In sum, DOS is popular today but may fade in a few years.

- *One computer, many kinds of systems software:* Even now there are microcomputers that run more than one kind of systems software. Employers may require that you know more than one kind. For instance, many office workers may need to know how to work with both DOS and the new operating system known as OS/2. These two systems may run on the same computer.

Figure 3-2
The IBM PS/2 Model 90XP 486 (left) and the Apple Macintosh IIfx (right) use different systems software. Although similar in many ways, these systems also have significant differences.

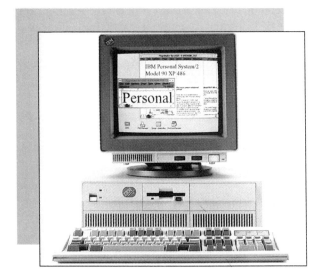

■ *More sophisticated users:* Previously, microcomputer users were satisfied with the performance offered by DOS. However, users are becoming more sophisticated, and they want to be able to fully exploit the power of these newer microcomputers. They are beginning to demand that microcomputers run programs that previously could run only on minicomputers and mainframes. To do this, more powerful systems software is required.

Even if you study only *one* kind of systems software, such as DOS, it's important to realize that such software is frequently revised. Revisions are made in order to handle new technology such as newly developed input and output devices. As systems software changes, you need to know what the effects are on your old applications software—and on your way of doing business.

Now let us see what, precisely, systems software is.

Four Kinds of Programs

Systems Software Consists of the Bootstrap Loader, Diagnostic Routines, Basic Input-Output System, and Operating System.

Systems software deals with the physical complexities of how the hardware works. Systems software consists of four kinds of programs: bootstrap loader, diagnostic routines, basic input-output system, and operating system. The last one, the operating system, is the one we are most concerned with in this chapter. However, we will briefly mention the others, which operate automatically.

■ The **bootstrap loader** is the program that is stored permanently in the computer's electronic circuitry. It starts up the computer when you turn it on. It obtains the operating system from your floppy disk (or hard disk, if you have one) and loads it into primary storage in your computer. An instruction manual will usually tell you to "boot your disk." This means you should put the operating system floppy disk in the disk drive and turn on the power. Or, if the operating system is on a hard disk, simply turn the power on.

■ The **diagnostic routines** are also programs stored in the computer's electronic circuitry. They start up when you turn the machine on. They test the primary storage, the central processing unit (CPU), and other parts of the system. Their purpose is to make sure the computer is running properly. On some computers, the screen may say "Testing RAM" (a form of computer memory) while these routines are running.

■ The **basic input-output system** consists of service programs stored in primary storage. These programs enable the computer to interpret keyboard characters or transmit characters to the monitor or to a floppy disk.

■ The **operating system,** the collection of programs of greatest interest to us, helps the computer manage its resources. The operating system takes care of a lot of internal matters so that you, the user, don't have to. For instance, it interprets the commands you give to run programs and enables you to interact with the programs while they are running.

One set of programs within the operating system is called **utility programs.** These programs perform common repetitious tasks, "housekeeping tasks." One important utility program is used for **formatting** (or **initializing**) blank floppy disks. This program is very important. Before you can use a new floppy disk out of the box you buy in a store, you must *format* (initialize) it. Formatting prepares the disk so that it will accept data or programs in your computer. After formatting a disk, you can use a utility program to **copy** or duplicate files and programs from one disk to another. You can **erase** or remove old files from a disk. You can make a **backup** or duplicate copy of a disk. You can **rename** the files on a disk—that is, give them new filenames.

Every computer has to have an operating system. A popular operating system for IBM's mainframes, for example, is MVS. Digital Equipment Corporation (DEC) uses VAX/VMS as the operating system for its minicomputers. For end users, the most important operating systems are those for microcomputers. To achieve computer competency, it is essential that you know something about the principal operating systems on the market for microcomputers today. These are *DOS, DOS with Windows, OS/2, Macintosh,* and *Unix.*

DOS: The IBM Personal Computer Standard

DOS Is the Standard for IBM Microcomputers and Compatibles. It Is Very Popular, Runs Thousands of Applications, and Is Easy to Use.

DOS stands for *Disk Operating System.* Its developer, Microsoft Corporation, sells it under the name *MS-DOS.* (The "MS," of course, stands for Microsoft.) Microsoft licenses a version called *PC-DOS* to International Business Machines for its IBM personal computers (such as models PC, XT, AT, and PS/2). A great many other microcomputer manufacturers have also been licensed to use DOS. DOS is the standard operating system for all microcomputers advertising themselves as "IBM-compatible," such as Compaq. Whatever machine it is used with, it is usually referred to simply as *DOS.*

There have been several upgrades since DOS was introduced. The 1981 original was labeled version 1.0 (*See Figure 3-3.*) Since then there have been DOS 2.0, 2.1, 3.0, 3.1, 3.2, 3.3, 4.0, 4.1, and 5.0. (The number before the period refers to a "version," the number after the period to a "release," which contains fewer refinements than a version.) An important characteristic of later DOS versions (the newer versions) is that they are "backward compatible." That is, you can still run applications programs with

Different Versions of DOS	
DOS version	**Features**
1.0	Original operating system for IBM PC and compatibles. Supported only floppy-disk drives.
2.0	Developed for IBM XT microcomputer. First version to support hard-disk drives.
3.0	Appeared about the same time as IBM AT microcomputer. Starting with 3.2 release, supported networking and 3 1/2-inch disk drives.
4.0	Included pull-down menus and other sophisticated modifications.
5.0	Allows access to more memory and task switching.

Figure 3-3
Different versions of DOS.

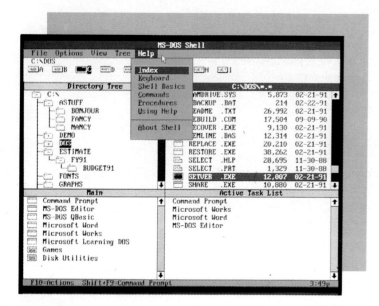

Figure 3-4
Example of pull-down menu
from DOS 5.0.

them that you could run on the earlier versions. The newest versions feature pull-down menus. (*See Figure 3-4.*) With a pull-down menu, you use your mouse-directed cursor to unfold ("pull down") a menu from the top of your display screen.

Advantages There is no question that DOS has many advantages. The reasons for learning it are very compelling.

- *Popularity:* DOS is the most popular microcomputer operating system ever sold. It is installed on 85 percent of all the microcomputers (personal computers) in the world.

- *Number of applications:* An enormous number of applications programs have been written for DOS—more than 20,000. Indeed, more specialized software is available for DOS than for any other operating system. This software includes not just the "basic tools" we mentioned in Chapter 2 but many others as well.

- *Runs on inexpensive hardware:* DOS runs on many IBM computers—the PC, XT, and AT—that are reasonably priced (in the $800 range, depending on the components of the hardware). In addition, MS-DOS is available for all kinds of domestic- and foreign-made IBM-compatible machines. The IBM Personal Computer set the standard for the business market. However, the appearance of similarly designed competitors has driven prices down, making microcomputers available to more people.

- *Ease of use:* Some operating systems are difficult to install on computers. With adequate accompanying instructions, DOS is not hard to install—and many publications and books are available. The operating system is also reasonably easy for novices to use.

Industry observers who have predicted the "death of DOS" may be acting prematurely. The system has some drawbacks, which we describe next. However, there is no doubt that we will continue to see DOS used in the 1990s. It will then slowly be replaced as the dominant operating system.

Disadvantages DOS is software, but software can only perform as well as the hardware for which it was designed. However, the hardware has evolved in significant ways. New microcomputers have more primary storage capacity and faster electronics than the old IBM PC, XT, and AT models. Let us see what these changes mean for DOS.

- *Limited primary storage:* Before an application program can be used, it must be stored in the computer's primary storage. An application program running with DOS has direct access to only 640 kilobytes (about 640,000 characters) of primary storage. With the newest version of DOS, 5.0, several additional kilobytes can be accessed. However, much of the new software available for spreadsheets, database management, and graphics requires more primary storage. New microcomputers have much more primary storage. Still, DOS by itself as the operating system cannot access all of this available primary storage. This restriction is an inherent limitation of DOS.

■ *"Single tasking" only:* **Multitasking** is the term given to operating systems that can run several applications programs at the same time. We discuss multitasking further in the next section. Unfortunately, DOS by itself can only do *single tasking:* It can support only one user and one applications program at the same time. DOS 5.0 does, however, support *task switching.* That is, it can switch or interrupt one application to do another application, but it cannot run both applications at the same time.

■ *Character-based interface:* In DOS, users issue commands by typing or by selecting items from a menu. This approach is called a **character-based interface** or **command line interface.** Many users find another arrangement for issuing commands, the graphical user interface (described below), much easier.

The widespread use and success of Microsoft's DOS has encouraged other software companies to introduce similar competing products. The best known is DR DOS version 6.0 from Digital Research, Inc. This operating system is very similar to DOS 5.0, with a few advantages in security and data storage capabilities. Despite these advantages, however, Microsoft's version of DOS is by far the most widely used.

The long-term future of DOS is not clear. By adding new windowing programs—such as Windows, discussed next—users are able to eliminate some of the previous disadvantages of DOS.

DOS with Windows

DOS with Windows Can Run Several Programs at Once (Multitasking), Can Share Data Between Programs (Dynamic Data Exchange), Offers a Graphical User Interface (GUI), and Can Access More Primary Storage.

The WINDOW command is available with several different kinds of programs. For example, using this command in a spreadsheet enables you to split the screen. That way you can look at two sections of the worksheet at the same time.

Integrated packages extend your capabilities by allowing you to work on more than one application. For instance, you can work on a word processing document or on a spreadsheet. You can even copy a section of the spreadsheet to the word processing document. However—and this is the important point—*with an integrated package, both applications cannot be running simultaneously.*

Windowing software, however, is much more. When run with DOS, these programs create an **operating environment** that actually extends the capability of DOS. For example, windowing software allows you to run a number of applications programs *simultaneously.* The most popular windowing program is Microsoft Corporation's Windows, with sales in the millions. (*See Figure 3-5.*) Others are Quarterdeck Office Systems' Desqview and Hewlett-Packard Company's NewWave.

Windows is designed to run on IBM and compatible microcomputers with particular kinds of microprocessors. They are the Intel 80286 (called "'286" chip), 80386 ("'386" chip), and 80486 ("'486" chip). Earlier versions of Windows did not use the '386 and '486 microprocessors to best advantage. Recent versions, however, have been designed specifically for the newer microprocessors.

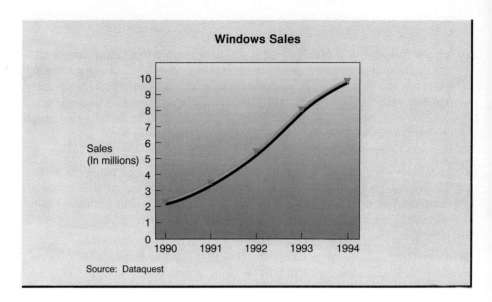

Figure 3-5
Sales of Microsoft's Windows.

Advantages Windows extends the capabilities of DOS in four ways:

- *Multitasking:* Allows you to do multitasking—to work on a number of applications ("multiple tasks") simultaneously. For instance, you could be running a word processing program and a database management program at the same time. The word processing program would appear on your screen until you opened up a window to access the database management program. While you were writing a report using the word processing program, the other program could be searching a database for more information. You could also simultaneously open up another window for a graphics program to draw a picture. Thus, you can be viewing more than one program side by side at the same time, although you can actively work on just one.

- *Dynamic data exchange:* A system called the *dynamic data exchange* will enable one program to broadcast a request for certain information to other programs currently running and to receive an automatic response. For example, a spreadsheet program could be analyzing the salaries of middle managers. At the same time, a database management program could be updating all employee data. With both programs running, you could use the spreadsheet to request and receive the most recent salary data from the database management program.

- *Graphical user interface:* Windows (and other windowing programs available for DOS) offers a **graphical user interface (GUI).** (*See Figure 3-6.*) A graphical user interface allows the user to move a mouse (or use keyboard commands) to move a pointer or cursor on the screen. The user positions the pointer on graphic symbols called **icons** or on pull-down menus and then "clicks" (presses a button on) the mouse. For example, to specify printer commands using Windows, the user could move the pointer to the icon just above Print Manager and click the mouse. Most users have found this approach to issuing commands easier to learn than the character-based approach.

- *More primary storage:* As mentioned before, DOS by itself has limited access to primary storage, thereby severely limiting software and hardware capabilities.

Windows, however, has a **memory manager** that allows access well beyond 640 kilobytes. DOS with Windows can access billions of characters of primary storage.

Disadvantages   Windows has dramatically increased the capabilities of DOS to include multitasking, sharing data, and more. Of course, DOS with Windows has some limitations.

■ *Technological limitations:* DOS and multitasking programs—particularly Windows—will continue to find more applications and more users. However, at some time in the future, the software will likely reach its inherent limitations. That is, DOS will not be able to be enhanced beyond a certain level. Then more powerful, newer operating systems will likely prevail.

■ *Minimum system configuration:* To run DOS with Windows requires a more expensive microcomputer system. To effectively use Windows, the system should have at least a '386 microprocessor. It also requires at least four times as much memory as DOS and a hard disk.

■ *Unrecoverable errors:* When running DOS with Windows, users sometimes encounter the message "Unrecoverable application error" on their screen. This means that the application program cannot proceed and the user must restart the program to begin again. These unrecoverable errors were much more common with the earlier versions of Windows. The most recent versions, however, have improved significantly and these errors occur much less frequently.

■ *Network capabilities:* In many business environments, software is shared among computers using a network. That way, several copies of the same application program are not required. Rather, a single copy is shared. This sharing is made possible and is controlled by systems software. Although network versions have been recently introduced, Windows was not originally intended for networks and is not as efficient as some other operating systems.

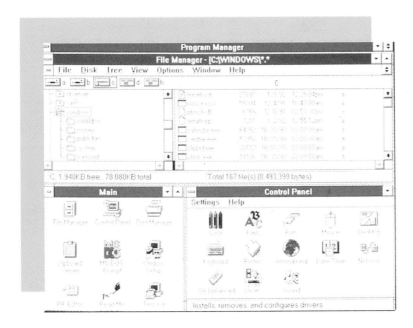

Figure 3-6
Windows 3.1 screen with graphical user interface.

OS/2

OS/2 Was Developed for Powerful Microcomputers and Networking.

OS/2, which stands for *Operating System/2,* is one of the newest operating systems for microcomputers. (*See Figure 3-7.*) Developed jointly by IBM and Microsoft Corporation (who have since gone their separate ways), the first version of OS/2 was released in December 1987. Since then there have been other versions.

OS/2 was announced almost at the same time IBM announced its new generation of powerful microcomputers—the PS/2 line. The "PS" stands for *Personal System.* However, you should not assume that every model in this line can run OS/2—some cannot.

OS/2, like Windows, is designed to run on IBM and compatible microcomputers with particular kinds of microprocessors. They are the Intel 80286 (called a "'286" chip), 80386 ("'386" chip), and 80486 ("'486" chip). The earliest version (version 1.0) of OS/2 did not use the '386 and '486 microprocessors to best advantage, but recent versions (version 2.0) do.

Let us consider both the advantages and the disadvantages of this operating system.

Advantages OS/2 offers some advantages that are simply not available with DOS without Windows. These advantages include multitasking, dynamic data exchange, graphical user interface, and more primary storage. OS/2 also has the following advantages over DOS with Windows.

- *Common user interface:* Microcomputer applications programs written specifically for OS/2 have a consistent graphics interface. Across applications, the user is provided with similar screen displays, menus, and operations. This is also true for Windows programs. Additionally, however, OS/2 offers a consistent interface with mainframes, minicomputers, and microcomputers.

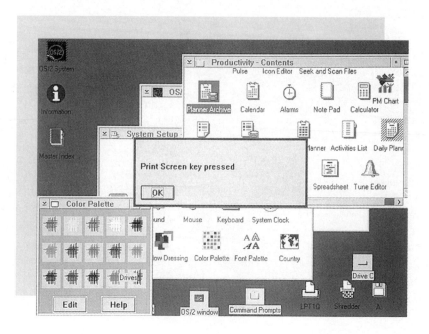

Figure 3-7
OS/2 (version 2.0) menus.

■ *Networking:* Unlike DOS with Windows, OS/2 was designed for network applications. OS/2 was initially developed and later enhanced to assist in the sharing of data and programs.

■ *Flexibility:* Unlike Windows, OS/2 is not constrained by an older operating system (DOS). Therefore, it generally processes more efficiently and is better able to be modified to meet future needs of networked users. In addition, OS/2 can run Windows applications as well as several DOS applications simultaneously.

Disadvantages   OS/2 also has some disadvantages compared to DOS with Windows.

■ *Fewer users:* Like Windows, OS/2 has far fewer users at present than DOS does. However, Windows has far more users than OS/2 does. As of mid-1992, Windows had sold over 10 million copies. OS/2 had sold only 1 million copies.

■ *Fewer applications:* OS/2 suffers because there are few applications programs developed specifically for it. Applications software developers state that it is not easy to write programs for OS/2. Although over 2,500 applications packages have been promised, few have been completed. Recently IBM estimated that over 800 completed applications were specifically designed for OS/2. In contrast, there were nearly 5,000 completed Windows applications by 1991 alone.

■ *Minimum system configuration:* OS/2 requires a more expensive microcomputer system than DOS with Windows does. Like Windows, OS/2 should be run on at least a '386 microprocessor. OS/2, however, requires twice the memory and hard disk space.

Which operating system will be more popular tomorrow? No one knows. Some observers predict that OS/2 will be widely used by large organizations, Windows by smaller organizations. Other observers say we'll have to wait until Microsoft releases its next version of Windows (Windows NT) before a fair comparison can be made.

Macintosh Operating Systems

The Macintosh Software, Which Runs Only on Macintosh Computers, Offers a High-Quality Graphical User Interface and Is Very Easy to Use.

What can you do with OS/2 or DOS with Windows that you can't already do if you have an Apple Macintosh computer? That's what many people are asking. If it's a graphical user interface you want, that's been available for some time with the Mac. In the opinion of many industry observers, OS/2 and DOS with Windows look very similar to the Macintosh operating system. To appreciate the differences, let us look at how the Macintosh works.

The Macintosh operating system is contained in two primary files—the System file and the Finder. These two files work together to perform the standard operating system procedures. These procedures include tasks such as formatting disks, copying files, erasing files, and running applications programs. These files also manage the user interface, displaying menus and activating tasks that are chosen from the menus by the user.

Apple has introduced numerous versions of its operating system. A recent version is the Apple Macintosh System 7. This version allows applications programs to exchange both data and instructions. There are also improvements in multitasking—

more than one program can be run simultaneously, each one sharing the computer's CPU. In addition, there are improvements in the user's ability to gain access over telephone lines to databases in distant locations.

We mentioned that the advantages and disadvantages of microcomputer operating systems are associated with the microprocessors for which they were originally designed. IBM microcomputers have used microprocessor chips built by Intel, most recently the '286, '386, and '486 chips. Macintoshes, on the other hand, are built around Motorola 68000, 68020, and 68030 microprocessors. These Motorola chips cannot run DOS applications programs, and the Intel chips cannot run Macintosh applications programs. In the beginning, Apple found its Macintoshes hard to sell to corporations because nearly all business applications programs—such as Lotus 1-2-3—were written to run on DOS machines. It is possible now, however, to run IBM applications on a Macintosh. Users can install a '286 electronic circuit board in their Macs or can use special applications software that permits DOS applications to run on a Macintosh.

Figure 3-8
The Macintosh graphical user interface.

Advantages The Apple Macintosh popularized the graphical user interface, including the use of windows, pull-down menus, and the mouse. (*See Figure 3-8.*) The graphical user interface has several advantages:

■ *Ease of use:* The graphical user interface has made the Macintosh popular with many newcomers to computing. This is because it is easy to learn. In fact, studies show that user training costs are *half* as much for Macintoshes as for DOS-based computers.

■ *Quality graphics:* Macintosh has established a high standard for graphics processing. This is a principal reason why the Macintosh is popular for desktop publishing. Users are easily able to merge pictorial and text materials to produce nearly professional-looking newsletters, advertisements, and the like.

■ *Consistent interfaces:* Macintosh applications have a consistent graphics interface. Across all applications, the user is provided with similar screen displays, menus, and operations.

■ *Multitasking:* Like OS/2, the Macintosh System 7 enables you to do multitasking. That is, multiple programs can run simultaneously, each one sharing the CPU.

■ *Communications between programs:* System 7 allows applications programs to share data and commands with other applications programs.

Disadvantages Many characteristics that were previously considered disadvantages may no longer prove to be so. Nevertheless, let us consider what these disadvantages are.

■ *A "business" machine?* Apple has had to struggle against the corporate perception that its products are not for "serious business users." Corporate buyers have had a history of purchasing from IBM and other vendors of large computers. Many have viewed Apple from the beginning as a producer of microcomputers for game players and hobbyists.

- *Compatibility difficulties:* The incompatibility of DOS with Macintosh microprocessors made Macintoshes less attractive to corporate users interested in compatibility and connectivity. However, as noted above, hardware and software are now available for the Mac to allow it to run DOS applications. In addition, inexpensive communications networks are available to connect Macintoshes to other computers that use DOS. Apple has cooperated with Digital Equipment Corporation (DEC) and others to produce communications links between Macintoshes, IBM PCs, and mainframe computers.

Unix: The "Portable" Operating System

Unix Can Run on Many Different Microcomputers (Is "Portable"). It Is Not Limited by Primary Storage, Can Perform Multitasking, and Can Be Shared by Several Users at Once.

Unix has been around for some time. It was originally developed by AT&T for minicomputers and is very good for multitasking. It is also good for networking between computers. It has been, and continues to be, popular on workstations.

Unix initially became popular in industry because for many years AT&T licensed the system to universities for a nominal fee. The effect of this was that Unix was carried by recent computer science and engineering graduates to their new places of employment.

One important consequence of its scientific and technical orientation is that Unix has remained popular with engineers and technical people. It is less well known with businesspeople. All that, however, is probably about to change. The reason: With the arrival of very powerful microcomputers using the '386 chip and '486 chip, Unix has become a major player in the microcomputer world.

Let us consider the advantages and disadvantages of Unix.

Advantages   Unix has the advantage of being a **portable** operating system. That means that it is able to be used with ("is portable to") many different computer systems. The other operating systems we have described are not nearly as portable. Having said this, however, we must hastily state that there are *different versions* of Unix, as we will describe. Let us first consider the advantages.

- *Multitasking:* Unix enables you to do multitasking. Assuming your microcomputer has the capability, Unix allows you to run multiple programs simultaneously, each one sharing the CPU.

- *Multiuser:* Unix not only shares the CPU among several simultaneous programs. It also shares it among multiple users, which OS/2 does not. At one point, the ability of several users to use one CPU simultaneously was considered a very significant cost advantage. Now, as hardware costs have come down, this advantage for microcomputers is not nearly as significant.

- *Not limited by primary storage:* Unix is not restricted by the hardware as the DOS and OS/2 systems are. Moreover, it can do a great many operations that were previously available only on minicomputers or mainframes. This means that, using Unix, a company can achieve the same performance and benefits using a microcomputer that previously required a large computer.

■ *Networking:* Unix is able to share files over electronic networks with several different kinds of equipment. Although the other operating systems can perform this same service, Unix systems have been successfully and reliably sharing across networks for years.

Disadvantages Unix was a minicomputer operating system used by programmers and computer science professionals some time before the rise of the microcomputer. This means it has certain qualities that make it useful to programmers—a lot of supporting utility programs and documentation, for instance. However, some of its features make it difficult for end users. Let us consider the disadvantages.

Figure 3-9
Two Unix graphical user interfaces: top, OSF/Motif; bottom, Open Look.

■ *Limited applications software:* This is a great barrier at the moment. There are many engineering applications programs. Unfortunately, there are very few business applications programs. Businesses that are dependent on off-the-shelf programs for microcomputers will find offerings very limited. Moreover, many of those business programs that do exist require customization. However, most end users knowledgeable in DOS don't have the experience to customize Unix programs. This situation may change as more DOS offerings are rewritten for Unix.

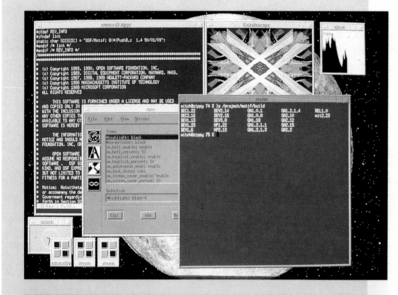

■ *No Unix standard:* This may be *the* biggest stumbling block. There is no Unix standard at any level. The principal microcomputer versions are the AT&T Unix System V, the University of California/Berkeley 4.2 Unix, and the Sun Microsystems SunOS. Microsoft has written a microcomputer version called Xenix, and Microsoft and AT&T are attempting to merge their versions to provide one standard. An organization called the Open Software Foundation is also trying to create a standard. This organization is a consortium of seven major computer suppliers led by IBM and DEC. All this means that whenever an applications program is written for one version of Unix, it may not run on other versions.

■ *No standard graphical user interface:* Just as there is no Unix standard, there is also no standard graphical user interface. For instance, an attempt has been made to combine the Sun, AT&T, and U.C. Berkeley versions of Unix to produce a graphical user interface called Open Look or Sun/Open Windows. (*See Figure 3-9.*) However, the Open Software Foundation has

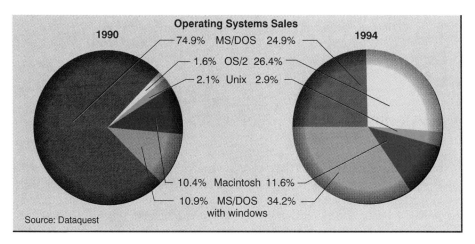

Figure 3-10
Worldwide unit sales of micro-computing operating systems—past and future.

defined its own graphical user interface called OSF/Motif. (*See Figure 3-9.*) OSF Motif offers a single, consistent graphical user interface across both OS/2 and many Unix applications.

■ *Lack of security:* Precisely because Unix is an open system, and used in a networked environment, users cannot be assured of the security of their files as much as with other operating systems.

Although Unix can do many things, it can be difficult for novice microcomputer users to understand. This is one reason why it has had a limited impact to date. Some observers think it could yet become a leader among microcomputer operating systems. However, at least one industry watcher, Dataquest, thinks its share of the market will not expand appreciably beyond what it is now. (*See Figure 3-10.*)

Comparisons of Operating Systems

Operating system	Pluses	Minuses
DOS	Many existing users, microcomputers, and applications	Limited memory; single tasking only; character-based interface
DOS with Windows	Multitasking; dynamic data exchange; graphical user interface; more primary storage	Technical limitations; unrecoverable errors; limited network capabilities
OS/2	Multitasking; dynamic data exchange; graphical user interface; common user interface; network capabilities; flexibility	Few users; few applications
Macintosh	Ease of use; quality graphics; graphical user interface; multitasking; communication among programs	Market perception; compatibility
Unix	Multitasking; multiuser; unlimited primary storage; networking capabilities	Limited business applications; no standard version; no standard graphical user interface

Figure 3-11
Pluses and minuses of present microcomputer operating systems.

On page 49 we summarize some of the principal advantages and disadvantages of the present microcomputer operating systems. (*See Figure 3-11.*)

A Look at the Future

The Popularity of Multitasking Software, Particularly Windows, May Keep DOS Strong, but Other Operating Systems May Be Adopted by Users in Large Organizations.

We continually read that this or that operating system is going to overturn DOS as the most popular microcomputer system software on the market. In fact, however, DOS remains strong and, when coupled with Windows, may very well stay strong through the next few years. The Macintosh operating system probably will not replace DOS, although its market share might grow. Unix supporters are in conflict as to which standard will prevail. Will it be Open Look from AT&T/Sun, or Motif from the Open Software Foundation? Anyone considering buying a sophisticated new microcomputer must think about these matters.

In the near future, DOS, DOS with Windows, and Macintosh will probably continue to serve people such as students, those with microcomputers at home, and owners of small businesses. DOS with Windows will probably also continue to move rapidly in the other direction—into the offices of people in small business, higher education, and local government. However, people in large organizations—corporations, universities, and major government departments—will probably find DOS with Windows insufficient after a while. As powerful desktop computers (such as those with '386 and '486 chips) begin to replace older computers and as communications links (networking) between computers become more important, these users will gradually change over to more powerful systems software. What will that be?

Microsoft Corporation, which owns DOS and Windows, is hoping that DOS and Windows users will evolve into its next generation of operating system, called *NT*, for *New Technology*. Some industry observers think OS/2 version 2.0 and future versions of OS/2 from IBM may eventually replace DOS (or DOS with Windows). There is another possible challenger, however: In 1992, the IBM and Apple Computer opened an independent joint venture known as *Taligent*. Its purpose is to develop an operating system (code-named Pink) to be used in business computers through the rest of the 1990s and into the twenty-first century. Taligent uses a technology called *object-oriented programming*, which involves creating the operating system with a series of interchangeable software objects or modules. This differs from the way DOS and other popular operating systems, which use layer after layer of lines of computer code, are constructed. With Taligent, applications software could be developed more quickly and less expensively.

Review Questions

1. What, in a phrase, is the difference between applications software and systems software?
2. What are four reasons for learning about systems software?
3. Describe what a bootstrap loader does.
4. What do diagnostic routines do?
5. What is the basic-input output system?
6. What are utility programs?
7. What is another name for initializing a blank disk?
8. What is an "IBM-compatible" microcomputer?
9. Name two principal limitations of DOS.
10. What are the principal differences between DOS and DOS with Windows?
11. What is meant by *multitasking?*
12. What is a *graphical user interface?*
13. What is a microprocessor? Will OS/2 run on Intel 80286 and 80386 microprocessors?
14. Give three advantages of OS/2 over DOS with Windows.
15. What are two advantages of the Macintosh systems software?
16. What are two disadvantages of the Macintosh when used in a business environment?
17. Unix is said to be *portable*. What does this mean?
18. What is meant by the term *multiuser?*
19. What are four advantages of Unix?
20. What are four disadvantages of Unix?

Discussion Questions and Projects

1. *Apple versus IBM—you be the judge:* Suppose you're working for a small family-run company that is in need of 10 new microcomputers. The computers must all be the same and will all be hooked together in an electronic network so that information and programs can be shared. No more computers will be purchased for another three to four years. The head of the business has put you in charge of researching this project. You need to choose between buying either all Apple Macintoshes running the Macintosh operating system or all IBM-compatibles, running either DOS with Windows or OS/2. Which operating system would you favor, and why?

2. *An operating system for everybody?* Readers always have the advantage over writers in that the words they read exist in the present rather than in the uncertain future. As we write this, we do not know how the Taligent experiment between IBM and Apple Corporation is turning out. This is the joint venture whose goal is to develop an operating system that will run on any computer, whether IBM or Apple, whether laptop or mainframe. Taligent—or another operating system that promises to be able to run on all hardware—would revolutionize systems software. To find out more about it, go to the library and do some research in various computer magazines, business magazines, and newspapers.

Chapter 3 Systems Software

Systems software does "background work" (like helping the computer do internal tasks). Five different kinds of operating systems are used on microcomputers today.

Four Kinds of Programs	DOS	DOS with Windows

Systems software is a collection of **programs** that help end users and applications programs to operate and to control a computer. There are four basic kinds of systems software programs.

- **Bootstrap loader** starts computer when turned on and loads program into primary storage.
- **Diagnostic routines** test parts of system to be sure computer is running properly.
- **Basic input output system** transmits characters from the keyboard or to a monitor or disk.
- **Operating system** helps manage computer resources. Includes **utility programs** for performing repetitive tasks such as **formatting** (or **initializing**) blank disks, **erasing**, **backing-up**, and **renaming** files.
- **DOS, DOS with Windows, OS/2, Macintosh Operating System**, and **Unix** are the most important microcomputer operating systems.

DOS, for Disk Operating System, is the most widely used operating system for IBM and IBM-compatible computers. There are five versions of DOS: 1.0, 2.0, 3.0, 4.0, 5.0. All are "backward compatible"—applications programs can run on newer versions of DOS.

Advantages

- Most popular microcomputer operating system ever sold.
- Enormous number of applications.
- Runs on inexpensive hardware.
- Is relatively easy to install and use.

Disadvantages

- An applications program running on DOS has direct access to only 640 kilobytes of primary storage.
- Can only do *single tasking* (support only one user and one applications program at the same time) although recent versions can *task switch* (interrupt one program to do another).
- Character based user interface.

Windows is a program that runs with DOS. It creates an operating environment that significantly extends the capabilities of DOS.

Advantages

- **Multitasking** is possible (several applications can be run at the same time).
- Dynamic data exchange is available. With two or more applications running at the same time, data and results can be shared back and forth.
- **Graphical user interface (GUI)** is provided. Commands can be executed by manipulating graphic symbols called icons.
- More primary storage access.

Disadvantages

- Technological limitations of DOS will likely be reached.
- Effective use requires at least an 80386 microprocessor, four times as much memory as DOS and a hard disk.
- Unrecoverable errors a problem with earlier versions although most recent versions are much better.
- Limited networking capabilities to link users.

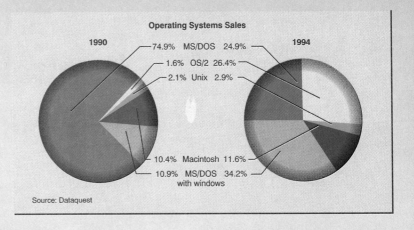

Operating Systems Sales

1990

- 74.9% MS/DOS
- 1.6% OS/2
- 2.1% Unix
- 10.4% Macintosh
- 10.9% MS/DOS with windows

1994

- 24.9% MS/DOS
- 26.4% OS/2
- 2.9% Unix
- 11.6% Macintosh
- 34.2% MS/DOS with windows

Source: Dataquest

About Systems Software?

to learn more about microcomputer systems
n was previously required because:

several competing forms of systems software.

imitations.

outers can run more than one kind of systems

t to run programs that previously ran only
mputers and mainframes.

OS/2	Macintosh Operating Systems	Unix

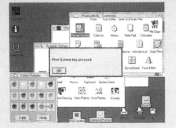

OS/2 is an operating system that has been developed to support the most advanced microcomputers.

Advantages

Like DOS with Windows, it supports multitasking, dynamic data exchange, graphical user interface, and more primary storage. Additionally:

- Common user interface across mainframes, minicomputers, and microcomputers.
- Networking capabilities to link users sharing information.
- Flexibility to adjust to changing demands and processing efficiency.

Disadvantages

- Far fewer users than either DOS or DOS with Windows.
- Fewer specialized applications programs available.
- Effective use requires at least an 80386 microprocessor, twice the memory and disk space required for DOS with Windows.

Several operating systems have been designed for Apple's **Macintosh.** New versions have been developed as new versions of the Macintosh have been developed.

Advantages

- Easy to learn and to use.
- Offers a high standard for graphics processing.
- Consistent graphics interface with all applications.
- Can do multitasking—running of multiple programs simultaneously.
- Can share data with other applications programs.

Disadvantages

- Some corporate buyers do not view Macintosh as a serious business machine.
- Programs written for DOS will not run on a Macintosh unless specialty hardware and software have been installed.

Unix, originally developed for minicomputers, is able to run on more powerful models of microcomputers. Unix is available in a number of different versions, many of which are not compatible.

Advantages

- Allows multitasking—running of multiple programs simultaneously.
- Allows multiple users to share computer simultaneously.
- Not limited by primary storage capacity.
- History of sharing files over electronic networks with different equipment.

Disadvantages

- Few business applications programs are presently available.
- No one Unix standard exists; there are several versions (principal ones: Unix System V, Berkeley 4.2 Unix, SunOS).
- No standard graphical user interface exists.
- Security can be a problem because UNIX is an open system.

4

The Central Processing Unit

Competencies

After you have read this chapter, you should be able to:

1. Describe four classes of computer systems: microcomputer, minicomputer, mainframe, and super-computer.

2. Explain the two main parts of the processor part of the central processing unit—the control unit and the arithmetic-logic unit.

3. Understand the workings and the functions of primary storage.

4. Describe how a computer uses binary codes to represent data in electrical form.

5. Describe the components of the system unit in a microcomputer.

How is the data in "data processing" actually *processed?* That is the subject of this chapter. Why do you need to know anything about it? The answer lies in three words: *speed, capacity,* and *flexibility.* After reading this chapter, you will be able to judge how fast, powerful, and versatile a particular microcomputer is. This knowledge should be valuable whenever you need to buy a computer or computer programs for yourself or for your employer.

Some time you may get the chance to watch when a technician opens up a microcomputer to fix it. You will see that it is basically a collection of electronic circuitry. (*See Figure 4-1.*) The parts will be explained in this chapter. There is no need for you to understand how all these components work. However, it is important to understand the principles because you will then be able to determine how powerful a particular microcomputer is. This will help you judge whether it can run particular kinds of programs and can meet your needs as a user.

The Four Types of Computer Systems

Computer Systems Are Classified as Microcomputers, Minicomputers, Mainframes, and Supercomputers.

You have probably already begun learning how to use a microcomputer. Do you think the day might come when you will be dealing with larger computers?

The answer is: No doubt you will—even if you never see them. The reason is that microcomputers, as we have said, are often linked by communications lines to large computers. These large computers process great quantities of information. Thus, it is worth learning about the various categories of computers and what function each category serves. We will describe them in order from smallest to largest: *microcomputers, minicomputers, mainframes,* and *supercomputers.*

Microcomputers The most familiar kind of computer is the *microcomputer.* Microcomputers cost from $800 to over $20,000 and, in the past, have been considered to be of two types—*personal computers* and *workstations.* Let's see what these are.

■ *Personal computers:* Until recently, **personal computers** were desktop or portable machines that ran comparatively easy-to-use applications software, such as the general-purpose "basic tools" we described in Chapter 2. They were usually easier to use and more affordable than workstations. However, they had less sophisticated video display screens, operating systems, and networking capabilities. Most important, they did not have the processing power that workstations did.

Figure 4-1
Inside a microcomputer: a Dell.

Examples of personal computers are Apple's Macintosh and IBM's various PS/2 models. (*See Figure 4-2.*)

■ *Workstations:* **Workstations** were—again, until recently—expensive, powerful machines used by engineers, scientists, and others who wanted to process a lot of data or run complex programs and display both work in progress and results graphically. Workstations used sophisticated display screens featuring high-resolution color graphics, operating systems such as Unix that permitted multi-tasking, and powerful networking links to other computers. The most significant distinguishing factor, however, was the powerful processor, which could churn out results much faster than personal computers.

Figure 4-2
A microcomputer: the IBM PS/2 Model 56SX desktop.

Figure 4-3
A workstation: IBM RISC
System/6000.

Examples of well-known workstations are those made by Sun, Apollo, Hewlett-Packard, NeXT, and IBM. (*See Figure 4-3.*) The number of workstations is expected to triple between 1990 and 1994. (*See Figure 4-4.*)

However, the distinction between personal computer and workstation is now blurring. The principal reason is that the microprocessors used in personal computers are now as powerful as many of those used in workstations. More powerful microprocessors and increased graphics and communications capabilities now allow end users to run applications software that previously could run only on mainframes.

More powerful has also often meant smaller. One type of personal computer that is growing in popularity is the **portable computer,** which is easily carried around. There are four categories of portable computers.

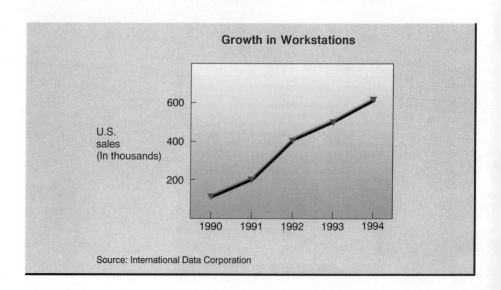

Figure 4-4
Expected surge in growth of
technical workstations.

Figure 4-5
Transportable: the IBM PS/2
Model P75.

■ *Transportables:* **Transportables,** or **luggables,** weigh between 18 and 25 pounds. They generally offer greater computing power and screens that are easier to read than those on lighter-weight portables. However, because they must be plugged into a wall socket, they are inconvenient for travelers unable to find an AC power source.

Typical users of transportables are construction engineers, who travel around with their computers and plug them in at different field offices. One transportable is the IBM PS/2 Model P75. (*See Figure 4-5.*)

■ *Laptops:* **Laptops,** which weigh between 10 and 16 pounds, may be either AC-powered, battery-powered, or both. The AC-powered laptop weighs 12 to 16 pounds. The battery-powered laptop weighs 10 to 15 pounds, batteries included, and can be carried on a shoulder strap.

The user of a laptop might be an accountant or financial person who needs to work on a computer on an airplane. An example of a laptop is the Toshiba T2200SX. (*See Figure 4-6.*)

Figure 4-6
Laptop: the Toshiba T2200SX.

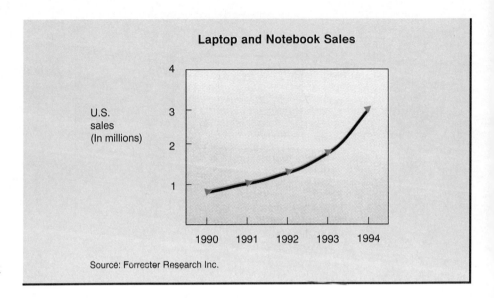

Figure 4-7
Growth of laptop and notebook
computers.

- *Notebook PCs:* **Notebook personal computers** weigh between 5 and 10 pounds and can fit comfortably into most briefcases. Laptops and notebooks are among the fastest-growing categories of computers. (*See Figure 4-7.*)

    The user of a notebook PC might be a student, salesperson, or journalist, who uses the computer for note-taking. It is especially valuable in locations where electrical connections are not available. An example of a notebook computer is the Macintosh PowerBook. (*See Figure 4-8.*)

- *Pocket PCs:* **Pocket personal computers** (sometimes called **palmtops**) are hand-held or pocket-size portables. Weighing 1 to 2 pounds, they are too small to fit on one's lap. Moreover, their keyboards are so tiny that two-handed typing is impossible. Pocket PCs are intended as complements to personal computers, not replacements. They allow you to connect with desktop computers or networks and exchange data with them. An example of a pocket PC is the 11-ounce Hewlett-Packard 95LX, nicknamed Jaguar, which comes with Lotus 1-2-3 built in. (*See Figure 4-9, next page.*)

Figure 4-8
Notebook: the Macintosh
PowerBook, with 5¼-inch
external disk drive.

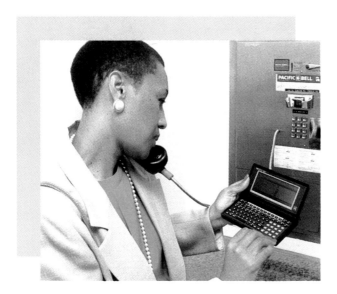

Figure 4-9
Pocket PC: the 11-ounce
Hewlett-Packard Jaguar.

The user of a pocket PC might be a beverage-delivery driver who uses one to manage orders and feed daily inventory and sales to management. Or it might be a police officer who enters license numbers in a central computer through a radio hand-held computer to detect stolen cars.

Minicomputers Costing from a few thousand dollars to over $100,000, *minicomputers* were first developed as special-purpose mainframe computers. They were used, for instance, to control a machine tool in a factory. However, now they are widely used as general-purpose computers. Thus, the line between minis and mainframes has blurred and is constantly changing. Indeed, the more powerful models are called *superminis*. One of the more popular minicomputer systems is the VAX made by Digital Equipment Corporation (DEC). (*See Figure 4-10.*)

Figure 4-10
Minicomputer: the VAX by DEC.

Figure 4-11
Mainframe: the IBM ES/9000.

Figure 4-12
Supercomputer: the Cray Y-MP/C90, and before-and-after simulations of auto crash run on this computer.

Minicomputers work well in what are known as **distributed data processing** or **decentralized** systems. That is, a company's headquarters or central office may have a mainframe computer, known as the **host** computer. It may be linked by communication lines to minicomputers in branch offices that handle work at the local sites.

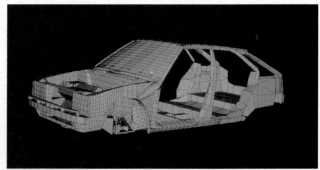

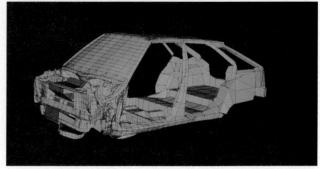

Mainframes Ranging in price from $50,000 to over $5 million, *mainframe computers* can process millions of program instructions per second. Virtually all large organizations rely on these room-size systems to handle large programs with lots of data. Mainframes are used by insurance companies, banks, airline reservation systems, and large mail-order houses, among many others.

An advanced mainframe made by International Business Machines is the IBM ES/9000. (*See Figure 4-11.*) IBM, the world's biggest computer company, is the dominant mainframe manufacturer, controlling roughly three-quarters of this market. If you peer into the computer room of any large organization, you will probably find one of the IBM 370 or 390 series of mainframe computers. Sales of these computers account for more than half of IBM's revenue.

Supercomputers Ranging in cost from $5 million to over $20 million, *supercomputers* are the fastest calculating devices ever invented. For example, the Y-MP/C90, made by Cray Research Inc., costs $20 million and can perform as many as 2.1 billion mathematical calculations per second. (*See Figure 4-12.*) Even more powerful supercomputers use a type of technology called **massively parallel processing**. These supercomputers consist of thousands of interconnected microprocessors. One massively parallel computer built by Intel Corporation is capable of performing 8.6 billion mathematical calculations per second. By 1995, several companies are expected to produce machines with speeds measured in trillions of mathematical calculations per second.

A desktop microcomputer processes data and instructions in millionths of a second, or **microseconds.** A supercomputer, by contrast, can operate at speeds measured in nanoseconds and even picoseconds—1 thousand to 1 million times as fast as microcomputers. (*See definitions, Figure 4-13.*) Most supercomputers are used by government agencies. These machines are for applications requiring very large programs and large amounts of data that must be processed quickly. Examples are such tasks as worldwide weather forecasting, oil exploration, and weapons research.

Some of the important characteristics of the four types of computers are summarized in the accompanying chart. (*See Figure 4-14.*)

Processing Speeds
Millisecond: thousandth of a second
Microsecond: millionth of a second
Nanosecond: billionth of a second
Picosecond: trillionth of a second

Figure 4-13
Processing speeds.

Types of Computers			
Type of computer	**Cost**	**Size**	**Applications**
Microcomputer	$800 to over $20,000	Palm-sized to desktop	End user
Minicomputer	$2000 to over $100,000	Closet-sized	General-purpose and special-purpose
Mainframe	$50,000 to over $5 million	Automobile-sized	General-purpose
Supercomputer	$5 million to over $20 million	Room-sized	Special-purpose

Figure 4-14
Four types of computer systems.

The CPU

The Central Processing Unit Has Two Components—the Control Unit and the Arithmetic-Logic Unit.

The part of the computer that runs the program (executes program instructions) is known as the **processor** or *central processing unit (CPU).* In a microcomputer, the CPU is on a single electronic component, a microprocessor chip, within the *system unit* or *system cabinet.* The system unit also includes circuit boards, memory chips, ports, and other components. A microcomputer's system cabinet may also house the monitor and disk drives, but these are considered separate from the CPU.

In Chapter 1 we said the system unit consists of electronic circuitry with two main parts, the processor (the CPU) and primary storage. Let us refine this further by stating that the CPU itself has two parts: the control unit and the arithmetic-logic unit. In a microcomputer, these are both on the microprocessor chip.

The Control Unit The **control unit** tells the rest of the computer system how to carry out a program's instructions. It directs the movement of electronic signals between *primary storage*—which temporarily holds data, instructions, and processed information—and the arithmetic-logic unit. It also directs these control signals between the CPU and input and output devices.

The Arithmetic-Logic Unit The **arithmetic-logic unit,** usually called the **ALU,** performs two types of operations—arithmetic and logical. *Arithmetic* operations are, as you might expect, the fundamental math operations: addition, subtraction, multiplication, and division. *Logical* operations consist of comparison. That is, two pieces of data are compared to see whether one is equal to (=), less than (<), or greater than (>) the other.

Primary Storage

Primary Storage Temporarily Holds Data, Program Instructions, and Information.

Primary storage—also known as **internal storage, main memory,** or simply *"memory"*—is the part of the microcomputer that holds

■ Data for processing

■ Instructions for processing the data—that is, the *program*

■ Information—that is, processed data—waiting to be output or sent to secondary storage such as a floppy disk in a disk drive

One of the most important facts to know about primary storage is that part of its content is held only temporarily—only as long as the microcomputer is turned on. When you turn the machine off, the contents immediately vanish. We have said this before, but it bears repeating: The stored contents in primary storage can vanish very quickly, as during a power failure, for example. It is therefore a good practice repeatedly to save your work in progress to a secondary storage medium such as a floppy disk. For instance, if you are writing a report on a word processor, every 10 to 15 minutes you should stop and save your work.

The next important fact to know about primary storage is that its capacity varies in different computers. The original IBM Personal Computer, for example, can hold up to approximately 640,000 characters of data or instructions. By contrast, the IBM Personal System/2 Model 80 can hold 16 *million* characters, or over 24 times as much. If you are using an older computer with small primary storage, it may not be able to run such powerful programs as Lotus 1-2-3. Thus, you need to look at the software package before you buy and see how much primary storage it requires.

Registers Computers also have several additional storage locations called **registers,** which appear in the control unit and ALU and make processing more efficient. Registers are sort of special high-speed staging areas that hold data and instructions temporarily during processing. They are parts of the control unit and ALU rather than primary storage. Their contents can therefore be handled much faster than can the contents of primary storage.

The Processing Cycle To locate the characters of data or instructions in main memory, the computer stores them at locations known as **addresses.** Each address is designated by a unique number. Addresses may be compared to post office mailboxes. Their numbers stay the same, but the contents continually change.

Our illustration gives an example of how primary storage and the CPU work to process information. (*See Figure 4-15, p. 64.*) Note that the various components of the CPU are linked by special electrical connections. In this example, the program will multiply two numbers—20 × 30, yielding 600. Let us assume the program to multiply these two numbers has been loaded into primary storage. The program asks the user to enter two values (20 and 30). It then multiplies the two values together (20 × 30). Finally, it prints out the result (600) on a printer. Our illustration describes the process just after the program has been loaded into primary storage. Follow the steps in the figure to walk yourself through the diagram.

Note: This figure is a simplification of the actual processing activity in order to demonstrate the essential operations of the CPU. For instance, there are actually many more primary storage addresses—thousands or millions—than are shown here. In addition, the addresses are in a form the computer can interpret—electronic signals rather than the numbers and letters shown here.

The Binary System

Data and Instructions Are Represented Electronically with a Binary, or Two-State, Numbering System. The Two Principal Binary Coding Schemes Are ASCII and EBCDIC.

We have described the storage and processing of data in terms of *characters*. How, in fact, are these characters represented inside the computer?

We said that when you open up the system cabinet of a microcomputer, you see mainly electronic circuitry. And what is the most fundamental statement you can make about electricity? It is simply this: It can be either *on* or *off*.

Indeed, there are many forms of technology that can make use of this two-state on/off, yes/no, present/absent arrangement. For instance, a light switch may be on or off, or an electric circuit open or closed. A magnetized spot on a tape or disk may have a positive charge or a negative charge. This is the reason, then, that the binary system is used to represent data and instructions.

The decimal system that we are all used to has 10 digits (0, 1, 2, 3, 4, 5, 6, 7, 8, 9). The **binary system,** however, consists of only two digits—0 and 1. In the computer, the 0 can be represented by electricity's being off, and the 1 by electricity's being on.

Figure 4-15
How the CPU and primary storage work.

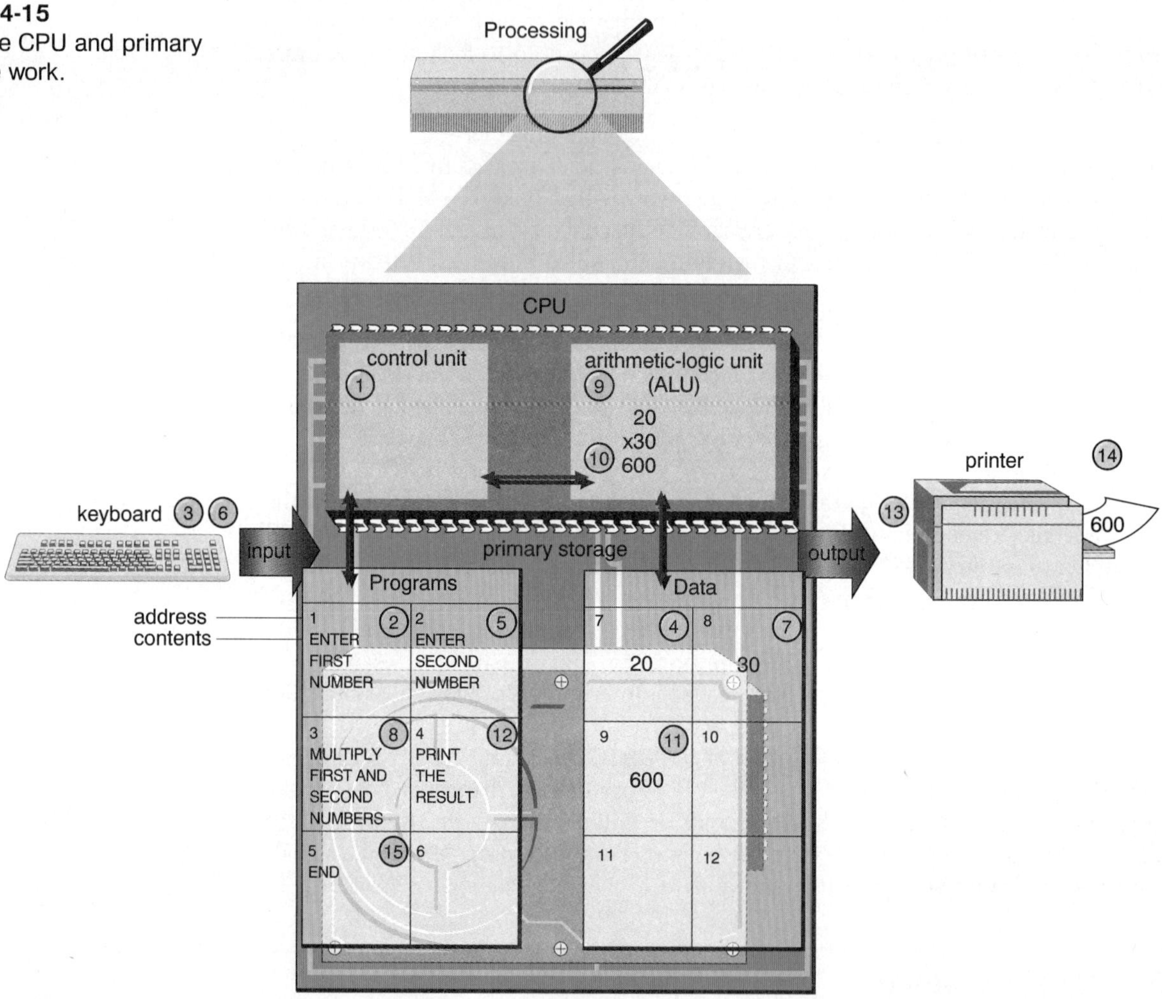

① The control unit recognizes that the entire program has been loaded into primary storage. It begins to execute the first step in the program.

② The program tells the user, ENTER FIRST NUMBER.

③ The user types the number 20 on the keyboard. An electronic signal is sent to the CPU.

④ The control unit recognizes this signal and routes the signal to an address in primary storage—address 7.

⑤ After completing the above program instruction, the control unit executes the next program instruction, which tells the user, ENTER SECOND NUMBER.

⑥ The user types the number 30 on the keyboard. An electronic signal is sent to the CPU.

⑦ The control unit recognizes this signal and routes it to primary storage address 8.

⑧ The control unit now executes the next program instruction: MULTIPLY FIRST AND SECOND NUMBERS.

⑨ To execute this instruction, the control unit informs the arithmetic-logic unit (ALU) that two numbers are coming and that the ALU is to multiply them. The control unit next sends the ALU a copy of the contents of address 7 (20) and then sends a copy of the contents of address 8 (30).

⑩ The ALU performs the multiplication: $20 \times 30 = 600$.

⑪ The control unit sends a copy of the multiplied results (600) back to primary storage, to address 9.

⑫ The control unit executes the next program instruction: PRINT THE RESULT.

⑬ To execute this instruction, the control unit sends the contents of address 9 (600) to the printer.

⑭ The printer prints the value 600.

⑮ The control unit executes the final instruction: END. The program is complete.

off   on

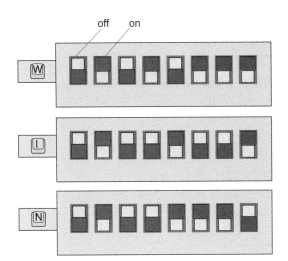

Binary Codes		
Character	**ASCII**	**EBCDIC**
A	0100 0001	1100 0001
B	0100 0010	1100 0010
C	0100 0011	1100 0011
D	0100 0100	1100 0100
E	0100 0101	1100 0101
F	0100 0110	1100 0110
G	0100 0111	1100 0111
H	0100 1000	1100 1000
I	0100 1001	1100 1001
J	0100 1010	1101 0001
K	0100 1011	1101 0010
L	0100 1100	1101 0011
M	0100 1101	1101 0100
N	0100 1110	1101 0101
O	0100 1111	1101 0110
P	0101 0000	1101 0111
Q	0101 0001	1101 1000
R	0101 0010	1101 1001
S	0101 0011	1110 0010
T	0101 0100	1110 0011
U	0101 0101	1110 0100
V	0101 0110	1110 0101
W	0101 0111	1110 0110
X	0101 1000	1110 0111
Y	0101 1001	1110 1000
Z	0101 1010	1110 1001
0	0011 0000	1111 0000
1	0011 0001	1111 0001
2	0011 0010	1111 0010
3	0011 0011	1111 0011
4	0011 0100	1111 0100
5	0011 0101	1111 0101
6	0011 0110	1111 0110
7	0011 0111	1111 0111
8	0011 1000	1111 1000
9	0011 1001	1111 1001

Everything that goes into a computer is converted into these binary numbers. (*See Figure 4-16*.) For example, the letter *W* corresponds to the electronic signal 01010111.

Units of Measure for Capacity   Each 0 or 1 in the binary system is called a **bit**—short for *bi*nary digi*t*. In order to represent numbers, letters, and special characters, bits are combined into groups of eight bits called **bytes.** Each byte typically represents one character—in many computers, one addressable storage location. The capacity of main memory, then, is expressed in numbers of bytes.

■ One **kilobyte**—abbreviated **K, KB,** or **K-byte**—is equivalent to approximately 1000 bytes. (More precisely, 1 kilobyte is equal to 1024 bytes. However, the figure is commonly rounded to 1000 bytes.) This is a common unit of measure for memory or storage capacity of microcomputers. The older IBM PCs, for example, had a top capacity of 640K, or about 640,000 characters of data.

■ One **megabyte**—**MB** or **M-byte**—represents 1 million bytes. Thus, a microcomputer system listed with a "16MB main memory" has primary storage capacity of about 16 million bytes. An example of such a microcomputer system is the IBM PS/2 Model 70.

■ One **gigabyte**—**GB** or **G-byte**—represents about 1 billion bytes—a measure used with mainframe computers and supercomputers.

■ One **terabyte**—**TB** or **T-byte**—represents about 1 trillion bytes.

Binary Coding Schemes   Now let us consider an important question. How are characters represented as 0s and 1s ("off" and "on" electrical states) in the computer? The answer is in the use of *binary coding schemes.*

Two of the most popular binary coding schemes use eight bits to form each byte. These two codes are *ASCII* and *EBCDIC*. (*See Figure 4-17*.)

■ **ASCII,** pronounced "*as*-key," stands for *A*merican *S*tandard *C*ode for *I*nformation *I*nterchange. This is the most widely used binary code for microcomputers.

■ **EBCDIC,** pronounced "*eb*-see-dick," stands for *E*xtended *B*inary *C*oded *D*ecimal *I*nterchange *C*ode. It was developed by IBM and is used on many IBM and other kinds of computers. As a result, EBCDIC is almost an industry standard for minicomputers and mainframe computers.

When you press a key on the keyboard, a character is automatically converted into a series of electronic pulses that the CPU can recognize. For example, pressing the letter W on an IBM PS/2 keyboard causes an electronic signal to be sent to the CPU, which converts it to the ASCII value of 01010111.

The Parity Bit Just as you sometimes hear static on the radio, so there can also be "static," or electronic interference, in a circuit or communications line transmitting a byte. When you are typing the letter W, for example, the W should be represented in the CPU (in ASCII) as

01010111

However, if the last 1 is garbled and becomes a 0, the byte will be read as 01010110—V instead of W. Is there a way, then, for the CPU to detect whether it is receiving erroneous data?

Indeed there is. Detection is accomplished by using a **parity bit**—an extra bit automatically added to a byte for purposes of testing accuracy. There are even-parity systems and odd-parity systems. In a computer using an even-parity system, the parity bit is set to either 0 or 1 to ensure that the number of 1s is even. (*See Figure 4-18.*) For instance, when the letter W is pressed on the keyboard, the signal 01010111 is emitted. Before the signal is sent to the CPU, the number of 1s is counted—in this case, 5. A parity bit is added to the front and set to 1, thereby making the number of 1s even. The signal 101010111 is sent. When the signal is received by the CPU, the number of 1s is checked again. If it is odd, it means an error has occurred. This is called a *parity error*. When a parity error occurs, the CPU requests that the signal be sent again. If the parity error occurs again, the message "parity error" will appear on your display. (Odd-parity systems act just the reverse of even-parity systems.)

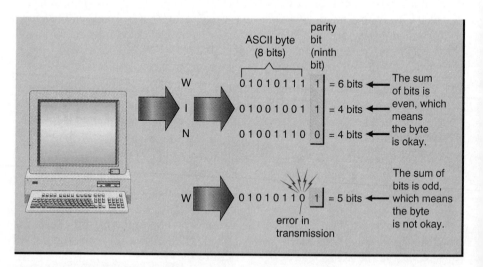

Figure 4-18
Example of parity bit.

Of course, the system does not guarantee accuracy. For example, if *two* erroneous 0s were introduced in the byte for W, the computer would accept the byte as correct, This is because the two erroneous 0s would add to an even 4 bits.

We have explained the principles by which a computer stores and processes data. We can now open up the system unit and take a look at some of the parts.

The System Unit

It's Important to Understand What's Inside the System Unit, So That You Can Talk Intelligently to Computer Specialists.

As mentioned, the part of the microcomputer that contains the CPU is called the *system unit* and is housed within the system cabinet. If you take off the cabinet, you will find that many parts can be easily removed for replacement. The IBM PS/2, for example, is modular. That is, entire sections can be replaced, as one would the parts of a car. In addition, many microcomputers are *expandable*. That is, more primary storage (main memory) may be added, as well as certain other devices.

Let us consider the following components of the system unit:

- System board
- Microprocessor chips
- Memory chips—RAM and ROM
- System clock
- Expansion slots and boards
- Bus lines
- Ports

System Board The **system board** is also called the **motherboard**. (*See Figure 4-19*.) It consists of a flat board that usually contains the CPU and some primary storage (main memory) *chips*. A chip consists of a tiny circuit board etched on a

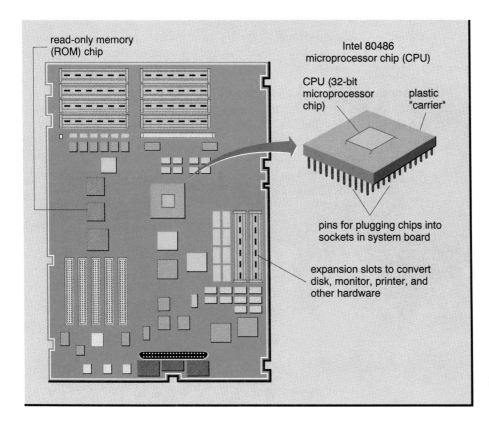

read-only memory (ROM) chip

Intel 80486 microprocessor chip (CPU)

CPU (32-bit microprocessor chip)

plastic "carrier"

pins for plugging chips into sockets in system board

expansion slots to convert disk, monitor, printer, and other hardware

Figure 4-19
A microcomputer system board. The CPU is on a tiny microprocessor chip.

Microprocessor Chips		
Microprocessor	**Application**	**Users**
Intel 80286	DOS Basic tools	Single user Office staff Home office user
80386	All of the above Windows, OS/2 Desktop publishing Project management	All of the above Professional staff
80486	All of the above Unix Artificial intelligence Multimedia	All of the above Multiusers Specialists
Motorola 68020	Macintosh operating system Basic tools	Single user Students Home office user
68030	All of the above Desktop publishing CAD/CAM	All of the above Graphic designers
68040	All of the above Multimedia	All of the above Specialists

Figure 4-20
Typical microprocessor
applications and users.

small square of sandlike material called silicon. A chip is also called a **silicon chip,**
semiconductor, or **integrated circuit.** Chips are mounted on carrier packages, which
then plug into sockets on the system board. In addition, system boards usually contain expansion slots, as we describe in another few paragraphs.

Microprocessor Chips In a microcomputer, the CPU is contained on a single
silicon chip called the *microprocessor*—"microscopic processor." Different microprocessors have different capabilities. (*See Figures 4-20 and 4-21.*)

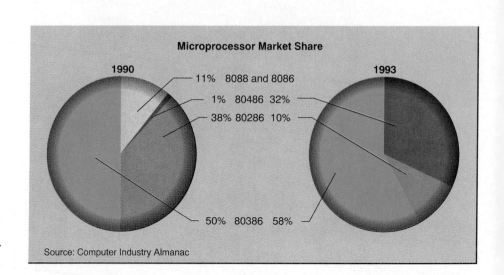

Figure 4-21
Estimated market share (percentage) of Intel microprocessors, 1990 and 1993.

Figure 4-22
The Apple Quadra 950, which uses a 68040 microprocessor.

Some chips or "families" of chips have become famous as the basis for several important lines of microcomputers. However, they are known by distinctly undramatic names: just product numbers.

Chip capacities are often expressed in word sizes. A **word** is the number of bits (such as 8, 16, or 32) that can be accessed at one time by the CPU. The more bits in a word, the more powerful—and the faster—the computer. A 32-bit-word computer can access 4 bytes at a time. An 8-bit-word computer can access only 1 byte at a time. Therefore, the 32-bit computer is faster.

As we mentioned, the growing power of microprocessor chips is what is changing everything about microcomputers. Motorola's 68040 chip, for example, is the basis for Apple's Quadra 950. (*See Figure 4-22.*) This machine can scroll through documents the length of *War and Peace* up to four times faster than the Macintosh SE. The 68040 chip is also used in the NeXTstation. (*See Figure 4-23.*) The NeXTstation runs four times faster than the first NeXT computer. NeXT, Inc. was started by former Apple

Figure 4-23
The NeXTstation, using the 68040 microprocessor.

Figure 4-24
The PS/2 486/25 "power platform" for the IBM PS/2 Model 70; it contains the Intel '486 chip.

cofounder Steve Jobs. Intel's 80486 chip is four times faster than its predecessor, the '386 chip. (*See Figure 4-24.*)

However, even more powerful microprocessors are now available. Intel's recently announced '586 chip is almost three times as large as the '486 chip. **RISC chips** (RISC stands for "reduced instruction set computer"), such as the Motorola 88000 chip, are commonly found in workstations. (*See Figure 4-25.*) RISC chips are beginning to sup-

Figure 4-25
This IBM RISC System/6000 is one of several IBM workstations using the fast RISC chip.

plant the present form of chip design (now known as *CISC,* for "complex instruction set computer"). Currently, workstations with RISC chips are being produced by Data General and IBM. These machines are being used by scientists, engineers, designers, and other professionals. You should not assume that suddenly you will find these extraordinarily powerful machines on every desktop. Because of the cost of manufacturing and availability, it will probably be some time before these microcomputers become commonplace.

Some specialized processor chips are also available. One example is a mathematics **coprocessor chip**—a chip that assists the main processor—that can help a CPU do very fast mathematical computations. Engineers generally use microcomputers with mathematics coprocessors to analyze data. The coprocessor is controlled by the main microprocessor, which sends it data and instructions.

RAM Chips   The kind of internal storage we have been calling primary storage or main memory is of a type known as **random-access memory.** This is abbreviated **RAM** (pronounced "ram"). RAM is a term frequently used in conversations about microcomputers. Random-access memory holds the program and data that the CPU is presently processing. That is, it is *temporary* storage. (Secondary storage, which we shall describe in Chapter 6, is permanent storage, such as the data stored on diskettes. Data from this kind of storage must be loaded into RAM before it can be used.)

RAM is called temporary because as soon as the microcomputer is turned off, everything in RAM is lost. It is also lost if there is a power failure that disrupts the electric current going to the microcomputer. For this reason, as we mentioned earlier, it is a good idea to save your work in progress. That is, if you are writing on your word processor, every few minutes you should save, or store, the material.

In addition, when programs or data are written, or encoded, to RAM, the previous contents of RAM are lost. This is called the *destructive write process.* However, when programs and data are read, or retrieved, from RAM, their contents are not destroyed. Rather, the read process simply makes a copy of those contents. Consequently, this activity is called the *nondestructive read process.*

RAM storage is frequently expressed in kilobytes. Thus, a microcomputer with 640K RAM has primary storage that will hold about 640,000 characters of data and programs. The IBM PS/2 Model 50 has considerably more—up to 7MB RAM, or 7 million characters.

Knowing the amount of RAM is important! Some software programs may require more primary storage capacity than a particular microcomputer offers. For instance, Lotus 1-2-3 for Windows requires 2MB of RAM to run with DOS. Additional RAM is needed to hold any data. However, many microcomputers have only 640K of RAM. This is not enough primary storage to hold the program, much less work with it.

The memory in RAM is of four types. (*See Figure 4-26, p. 72.*) You will find these types mentioned in instruction manuals when you are installing systems software such as DOS 5.0 or applications software such as Lotus 1-2-3.

- *Conventional memory:* **Conventional memory** consists of the first 640K of RAM. It is the area used by DOS and applications programs.

- *Upper memory:* **Upper memory** is located between 640K and 1MB of RAM. Although DOS uses this area to store information about the microcomputer's hardware, it is frequently underused and can be used by application programs.

- *Extended memory:* **Extended memory**, on those microprocessors that have it (e.g., Intel 80286, 80386, 80486), includes directly accessible memory above 1MB. Some programs can use extended memory (e.g., Windows), some cannot.

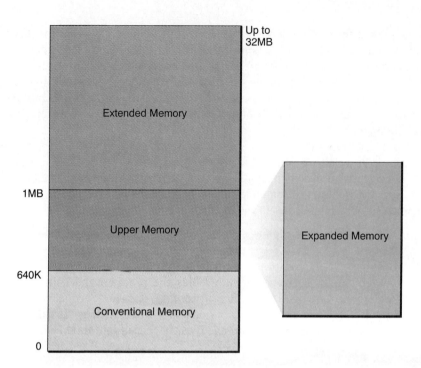

Up to
32MB

Extended Memory

1MB

Upper Memory

Expanded Memory

640K

Conventional Memory

0

Figure 4-26
Types of RAM: conventional,
upper, extended, expanded.

■ *Expanded memory:* **Expanded memory** is intended to help certain microprocessors (e.g., Intel 8088 and 8086) physically unable to directly access memory over 1MB. Expanded memory is a special "island" of memory of up to 32MB that exists outside of the DOS 640K limit. That is, it temporarily uses a portion of the reserved memory area between 640K and 1MB and switches it with information from the island.

Another term you are apt to hear about in conjunction with RAM is **cache memory.** Cache (pronounced "cash") memory is an area of RAM set aside to store the most frequently accessed information stored in RAM. The cache acts as a temporary high-speed holding zone between the primary storage and the CPU. In a computer that has a cache (not all machines do), the computer detects which information in RAM is most frequently used and copies that information into the cache, so that the CPU can access that information more quickly than usual.

ROM Chips Another type of memory, **read-only memory,** describes chips that have programs built into them at the factory. Read-only memory is abbreviated **ROM** (pronounced "rahm"). Unlike RAM chips, ROM chips cannot be changed by the user. "Read only" means that the CPU can read, or retrieve, the programs written on the ROM chip. However, the computer cannot write—encode or change—the information or instructions in ROM.

ROM chips typically contain special instructions for detailed computer operations. For example, ROM instructions may start the computer, give keyboard keys their special control capabilities, and put characters on the screen. ROMs are also called **firmware** because the programs are "firm" and cannot be easily altered.

Two important variations on the ROM chip are the following.

■ **PROM (programmable read-only memory).** This means that a software manufacturer can write instructions onto the chip using special equipment. However, once it is written, it cannot be changed.

■ **EPROM (erasable programmable read-only memory).** This is a PROM chip that can be erased with a special ultraviolet light. New instructions can then be written on it. (There are also some electrically erasable chips—EEPROM.)

System Clock The **system clock** controls how fast all the operations within a computer take place. The speed is expressed in **megahertz** (abbreviated **MHz**). One megahertz equals 1 million beats (cycles) per second. The faster the clock speed, the faster the computer can process information. In computer ads, you may see that an older IBM Personal Computer has a clock frequency of 4.77 MHz. Microcomputers built with the Intel '486 chips, by contrast, typically have a 33 MHz speed. A variant, the 486 DX chip, has 50 MHz, and Intel has even demonstrated one running at 100 MHz.

Expansion Slots and Boards Computers are known for having different kinds of "architectures." Machines that have **closed architecture** are those manufactured in such a way that users cannot easily add new devices. Most microcomputers have **open architecture.** They allow users to expand their systems by inserting optional devices known as **expansion boards.** (*See Figure 4-27.*) Expansion boards are also called **plug-in boards, controller cards, adapter cards,** or **interface cards.**

The expansion boards plug into slots inside the system unit. Ports on the boards allow cables to be connected from the expansion boards to devices outside the system unit. Among the kinds of expansion boards available are the following:

■ *Expanded primary storage:* These circuit boards consist of several additional RAM chips, which increase the capacity of the computer's primary storage. Early microcomputer users found that additional primary storage was their first requirement for handling newer, more sophisticated programs, such as integrated software. Memory can be added by using plug-in boards, which gives you expanded memory. Memory can also be added by inserting RAM chips directly onto the system board, which gives you extended memory.

■ *Display adapter cards:* These cards can be used to adapt a variety of color video display monitors to your computer.

■ *Additional secondary storage:* Expansion cards may be used to add more floppy-disk or hard-disk storage capacity.

Figure 4-27
Expansion board.

■ *Other "add-ons":* Expansion cards can be inserted to connect printers, communications devices, and other hardware.

Most computers have only a limited number of expansion slots. Thus, **multifunction boards** have been made available that combine several expansion activities on a single card. For example, a multifunction board may offer additional RAM and a display adapter of some sort.

Bus Lines   A **bus line**—or simply **bus**—connects the parts of the CPU to each other. It also links the CPU with other important hardware. Examples are RAM and ROM chips and ports connecting with outside devices. A bus is a data roadway along which bits travel. Such data pathways resemble a multilane highway. The more lanes there are, the faster traffic can go through. Similarly, the greater the capacity of a bus, the more powerful and faster the operation. A 32-bit bus has greater capacity than a 16-bit bus, for example.

Why should you even have to care about what a bus line is? The answer is that, as microprocessor chips have changed, so have bus lines. Thus, the things you used to be able to do on some computers you may no longer be able to do on new ones.

The three principal bus lines (or "architectures") are the following:

■ **Industry Standard Architecture (ISA):** This bus was developed for the IBM Personal Computer. First it was an 8-bit-wide data path, then (when the IBM AT was introduced) 16 bits wide. The '286 microprocessors and add-on expansion boards were able to satisfactorily move data along this 16-bit roadway. But then along came the '386 chip—which requires data paths that are *32* bits wide. And suddenly there was a competition between two 32-bit standards.

■ **Micro Channel Architecture (MCA):** IBM decided to support the '386 chip with a 32-bit bus line that was entirely new. You cannot simply remove your expansion boards from an IBM PC, XT, or AT and put them into an IBM PS/2 Model 80. With Micro Channel, they simply won't work. If you are not concerned about transferring boards, IBM's new standard is not a problem. You can take full advantage of the faster processor.

■ **Extended Industry Standard Architecture (EISA):** This 32-bit bus standard was proposed in September 1988 by nine manufacturers of IBM-compatibles, led by Compaq Computer Corporation. The purpose of EISA is to extend and amend the old ISA standard, so that all existing expansion boards can work with the new architecture.

As of the moment, it remains to be seen which 32-bit standard will prevail. (Apple also has a 32-bit bus standard, but it is completely incompatible with the ISA.) In making a choice, users will have to decide how their performance will be improved. They will have to decide how much it will cost and what it will do to their previous investments in hardware.

Ports   A **port** is a connecting socket on the outside of the system unit. This allows you to plug in other devices, such as video display monitors and printers. Ports may be parallel or serial. (*See Figure 4-28.*)

■ **Parallel ports** allow lines to be connected that will enable several bits to be transmitted simultaneously. An example might be an entire eight-bit ASCII character from the CPU to certain printers. Parallel lines move information faster than serial lines do. They are used for equipment, such as a printer, that is physically located close to the computer.

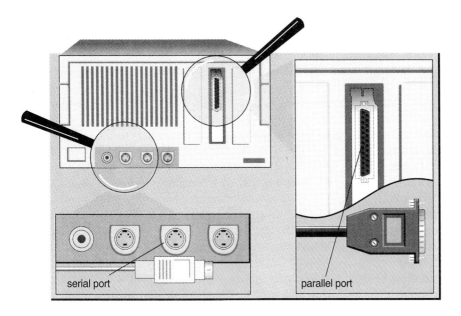

Figure 4-28
The ports in the back of
a microcomputer.

■ **Serial ports** are for connecting lines that transmit bits one after the other on a single communications line. Serial lines frequently are used to link equipment that is not located close by. Thus, they are used, for example, to send information via a modem from the computer over a telephone line.

Ports are used to connect input and output devices to the system unit. It is customary to refer to all hardware outside the system unit—but not necessarily outside the system *cabinet*—as **peripheral devices.** In many microcomputers, disk drives are built into the system cabinet. In some laptop computers, the keyboard and monitor are also an integral part of the system cabinet.

A Look at the Future

Four New Technologies Could Make Computing Faster: RISC, Superconducting, Optical Computing, and Neural Networking. The Result Will Be "Downsizing Applications."

We have already mentioned RISC (reduced instruction set computer) microprocessors. Some observers think the RISC chip will triple performance every one and a half to two years. Memory chips are also increasing in capacity. A new technology developed by Rambus Inc. promises RAM chips with ten times the speed of today's chips.

Another technological improvement may come in the form of the materials used for microprocessors. At present, microprocessor chips are made out of silicon. Such chips are called *semiconductors* because electricity flows through the material with some resistance. *Superconducting* material, in contrast, conducts electricity without resistance. Until recently, superconduction was considered impractical because the materials had to be at extremely low, subzero temperatures. However, research is now being done on "warm" superconductors, which offer the promise of faster on-and-off processing to give us lightning-quick computers.

A third area being explored is that known as *optical computing.* In this technology, a machine consisting of lasers, lenses, and mirrors uses pulses of light rather than currents of electricity to represent the on-and-off codes of data. Light is much faster than electricity. An experimental optical computer was introduced by Bell Laboratories in January 1990.

A fourth area, *neural networks,* is not a different kind of technology so much as a new arrangement using existing technology. Present computers—even supercomputers—are relatively slow because of a built-in structural limitation: the processor and the primary storage are physically separated. Although joined by a communications link, the processor must spend most of its time waiting for data to come from or go to memory. (The arrangement is known as the *von Neumann architecture,* after its originator, John von Neumann.) A neural network, however, consists of layers of processors interconnected somewhat like the neurons of biological nervous systems. One such computer developed by TRW has 250,000 processors and 5.5 million connections. As a result, data is transmitted to and from a processor at many times the speed of the old arrangements.

With these kinds of developments, it's clear that we are on the road to "downsizing applications." That is, computers will not only get smaller, as we are seeing with the newer portables, but also more powerful. Indeed, it is very easy to believe, as some industry observers suggest, that by the year 2000 desktop computers will be as powerful as the first supercomputer.

Review Questions

1. Distinguish among the four kinds of computer systems.
2. What are the two parts of the CPU, and what purpose does each serve?
3. What is the purpose of primary storage?
4. What are registers?
5. Describe how the control unit, arithmetic-logic unit, and primary storage work to process information.
6. What is the difference between the decimal system and the binary system? Why is the binary system used in the computer to represent data and instructions?
7. What is a bit? a byte?
8. What is a kilobyte? a megabyte? a gigabyte? a terabyte? What are their abbreviations?
9. What are the names (abbreviations) of the two primary coding schemes for representing letters, numbers, and special characters in binary form?
10. What does *word* mean as a measure of the power of a microprocessor?
11. Distinguish between the RAM and ROM forms of memory.
12. Why is it important to know the amount of RAM in a microcomputer?
13. Why are ROM chips also called *firmware?*
14. What are the four types of RAM memory? Define each.
15. What is the purpose of the system clock? How fast is a megahertz?
16. What is an expansion board?
17. What kinds of expansion boards are available for what purposes?
18. What do bus lines do?
19. Name the three alternative bus architectures.
20. What are two types of ports, and what are they used for?

Discussion Questions and Projects

1. *An inexpensive microcomputer system:* No doubt you've witnessed instances of price cutting in consumer electronics. There are so many very similar TVs and VCRs that you can hardly pick up a newspaper or walk into a shopping mall without seeing aggressive promotions and deep discounting.

Now the same thing is happening in personal computers, and we will probably continue to see increasing discounts over the next few years. Not until there is some major technological breakthrough such as a greatly simplified operating system or a sophisticated and inexpensive palmtop computer, experts say, will this trend toward lower prices change.

Here's your chance to do some hypothetical bargain hunting for an inexpensive microcomputer system. Look through your local newspaper for discounted systems. Bring examples to class and discuss with classmates the pros and cons of various selections, including which features are available and which are not.

2. *Buying from mail-order companies:* A lot of microcomputer users purchase hardware (and software) from mail-order companies, such as those advertising in computer magazines. The reasons are cost savings and convenience. Prices may be considerably discounted from those found at a local computer store—although you can always do some bargaining with the store by asking how close it can come to matching the mail-order company's price. Yet mail-order houses may be almost as convenient as a local store. Most offer a technical-support telephone line (often a toll-free 800 number) to help with installation problems.

An important caution, however: Nearly anyone can start a mail-order company, points out computer consumer editor Roberta Furger (*San Francisco Examiner*, February 2, 1992). The ones offering the lowest prices are precisely those that may be the most recent entrants to the field and therefore the most unstable. Thus, a company may take your order, accept your check or bill your credit card, and promise you'll receive the product within a week. And then they may go out of business without delivering, making it hard for you to get your money back. (If you do encounter questionable practices—of any sort—you can get help by mail. Submit a letter describing the transaction, along with invoices, credit card statements, or canceled checks, to The Direct Marketing Association Mail Order Action Line, 6 East 43rd St., New York, NY 10017-4646.)

Look through computer magazines or newspapers and pick out one or two mail-order companies offering hardware you might consider buying. Now check them out by contacting one of the following organizations in the city or state where the company does business: (a) the Better Business Bureau, (b) the state consumer affairs or state attorney general's office, or (c) the regional postal inspector's office. Telephone or visit a library to get help with the addresses or phone numbers. In your letter or phone call, ask if there have been many complaints against the company.

Chapter 4   The Central Processing Unit

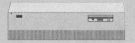

The central processing unit (CPU) and primary storage are two major parts of a microcomputer system unit.

Types of Computer Systems	The CPU and Primary Storage

From smallest to largest:

Microcomputers

Microcomputers cost from $800 to over $20,000. Two principal categories are:

- *Personal computers*—desktop or portable computers, running easy-to-use applications software. **Portable computers** may be **transportables** or **luggables** (18–30 pounds), **laptops** (10–16 pounds), **notebook PCs** (5–10 pounds), or **pocket PCs** (1–2 pounds).

- *Workstations*—machines typically used by scientists and engineers, running complex programs and with powerful processors and sophisticated display screens.

Minicomputers

Minicomputers cost from a few thousand dollars to over $100,000 and were first used as special-purpose mainframes. They work well in **distributed data processing** or **decentralized** systems, in which a **host** (central) computer is linked by communication lines to distant minicomputers.

Mainframes

Mainframes cost from $50,000 to over $5 million and process millions of instructions per second. These are room-sized systems and are used by large organizations to handle large programs with lots of data.

Supercomputers

Supercomputers cost from $5 million to over $20 million and process billions of operations per second. They are used for very large programs and very large amounts of data requiring processing in a short period of time, as in weather forecasting. Supercomputers with **massively parallel processing** use thousands of interconnected microprocessors.

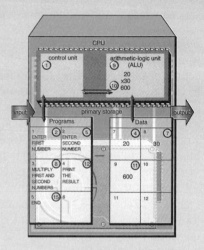

Central Processing Unit

The central processing unit (CPU) is the **processor**, the part of the computer that runs the program. The CPU has two parts:

- The **control unit** directs electronic signals between primary storage and the ALU, and between the CPU and input/output devices.

- The **arithmetic-logic unit (ALU)** performs *arithmetic* (math) operations and *logical* (comparison) operations.

Primary Storage

Primary storage **(internal storage, main memory)** holds data, instructions for processing data (the program), and information (processed data). The contents are held in primary storage only temporarily. Capacity varies with different computers.

- Additional storage units (in control unit and ALU) called **registers** help make processing more efficient.

- Characters of data or instructions are stored in primary storage locations called **addresses**.

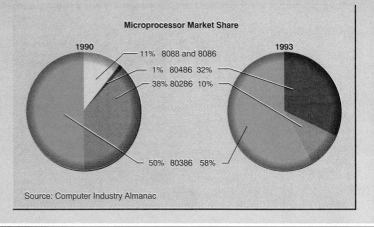

Microprocessor Market Share

1990   1993

11%   8088 and 8086

1%   80486   32%

38%   80286   10%

50%   80386   58%

Source: Computer Industry Almanac

The Binary System

off on

Data and instructions are represented electronically with a two-state **binary system** of numbers (0 and 1).

Measure of Capacity

- **Bit** (*b*inary dig*it*)—0 or 1, corresponding to electricity being *on* or *off*.
- **Byte**—eight bits. Each byte represents one character. The primary storage capacity of a computer is measured in bytes.
- **Kilobyte (K)**—about 1000 bytes.
- **Megabyte (MB)**—about 1 million bytes.
- **Gigabyte (GB)**—about 1 billion bytes.
- **Terabyte (TB)**—about 1 trillion bytes.

Binary Coding Schemes

Two popular schemes for representing bytes are:

- **ASCII**—used in microcomputers.
- **EBCDIC**—used in mini- and mainframe computers.

Parity Bit

A **parity bit** is an extra bit added to a byte for error detection purposes.

The System Unit

In a microcomputer, the system unit consists of the following:

System Board

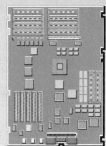

The **system board** contains the CPU and primary storage on **chips** (also called **silicon chips, semiconductors, integrated circuits**).

Microprocessor Chips

The *microprocessor chip* contains the CPU. Capacities are expressed in word sizes. A **word** is the number of bits (e.g., 16 or 32) that can be accessed at one time by the CPU.

RAM Chips

RAM (random-access memory) chips temporarily hold data and instructions in primary storage. Four types of memory are: **conventional, upper, extended,** and **expanded**.

ROM Chips

ROM (read-only memory) chips (firmware) have programs built into them for operating important system devices. Variations are:

- PROM (programmable read-only memory)
- EPROM (erasable programmable read-only memory)

System Clock

The **system clock** controls the speed of computer operations. Speed is expressed in **megahertz**—millions of beats per second.

Expansion Slots and Boards

Open architecture machines allow users to easily expand their systems (**closed architecture** machines do not). Users may add **expansion** (or **plug-in**) **boards** to:

- Expand primary storage capacity
- Adapt color display monitors
- Add floppy- or hard-disk storage capacity

Bus Lines

A **bus line** (or **bus**) is a data roadway connecting parts of the CPU. Three bus standards: **ISA, MCA,** and **EISA**.

Ports

A **port** is a connecting socket on the outside of the system unit for plugging in other devices.

- **Parallel ports** allow several bits to be transmitted simultaneously.
- **Serial ports** transmit one bit at a time.

5

Input and Output

How do you get data to the CPU? How do you get information out? Here we describe the two most important places where the computer interfaces with people. The first half of the chapter covers input devices; the second half covers output devices.

People understand language, which is constructed of letters, numbers, and punctuation marks. However, computers can understand only the binary machine language of 0s and 1s. Input and output devices are essentially *converters*. Input devices convert symbols that people understand into symbols that computers can process. Output devices do the reverse: They convert machine output to output people can comprehend. Let us, then, look at the devices that perform these conversions.

Competencies

After you have read this chapter, you should be able to:

1. Explain the difference between keyboard and direct-entry input devices and the POS terminal.

2. Describe the features of keyboards and differentiate among keyboard entry devices used with larger computer systems. These include dumb, smart, and intelligent terminals.

3. Describe direct-entry devices used with microcomputers. These include the mouse, touch screen, digitizer, light pen, image scanner, fax, bar-code reader, MICR, OCR, OMR, and voice-input devices.

4. Explain output devices, including monochrome monitors, graphics monitors, and flat-panel displays.

5. Describe printers—dot-matrix, daisy-wheel, laser, ink-jet, chain—and pen, electrostatic, and direct image plotters.

6. Describe voice-output devices.

7. Describe ergonomics.

Input

Input: Keyboard Versus Direct Entry

Input Devices Convert People-Readable Data into Machine-Readable Form. Input May Be Keyboard or Direct Entry.

Input devices take data and programs that people can read or understand and convert them to a form the computer can process. This is the machine-readable electronic signals of 0s and 1s that we described in the last chapter. Input devices are of two kinds: keyboard entry and direct entry.

■ *Keyboard entry:* Data is input to the computer through a *keyboard* that looks like a typewriter keyboard but has additional keys. In this method, the user typically reads from an original document—called the **source document**—and enters that document by typing on the keyboard.

■ *Direct entry:* Data is made into machine-readable form as it is entered into the computer; no keyboard is used.

An example of an input device that uses both is a **point-of-sale (POS) terminal.** This is the sort of "electronic cash register" you see in department stores. (*See Figure 5-1.*) When clerks sell you a sweater, for example, they can type in the information (product code, purchase amount, tax) on the keyboard. Or they can use a hand-held **wand reader** to read special characters on the price tags as direct entry. The wand reflects light on the characters. The reflection is then changed by photoelectric cells to machine-readable code. Whether keyboard entry or direct entry, the results will appear on the POS terminal's digital display. (*See Figure 5-1.*)

Keyboard Entry

In Keyboard Entry, People Type Input. The Input Usually Appears on a Monitor.

Probably the most common way in which you will input data, at least at the beginning, is through a keyboard.

Keyboards Keyboards have different kinds of keys. (*See Figure 5-2.*)

▪ *Typewriter keys:* The keys that resemble the regular letters, numbers, and punctuation marks on a typewriter keyboard are called **typewriter keys.** Note the position of the **Enter** key, which is used to enter commands into the computer. The Enter key is sometimes also called the **Return** key.

▪ *Function keys:* The keys labeled *F1, F2,* and so on, are the *function keys.* These keys are used for tasks that occur frequently (such as underlining in word processing). They save you keystrokes.

▪ *Numeric keys:* The keys 0 to 9, called the **numeric keys** or **numeric keypad,** are used for tasks principally involving numbers. These may be useful when you are working with spreadsheets.

▪ *Special-purpose and directional arrow keys:* Examples of *special-purpose keys* are *Esc* (for "Escape"), *Ctrl* (for "Control"), *Del* (for "Delete"), and *Ins* (for "Insert"). These are used to help enter and edit data and execute commands. **Directional arrow keys** are used to move the cursor.

display   keyboard

Figure 5-1
A point-of-sale terminal.

As we mentioned in Chapter 4, these keys convert letters, numbers, and other characters into electrical signals that are machine readable. These signals are sent to the computer's CPU.

Figure 5-2
Keyboard for IBM
Personal System/2.

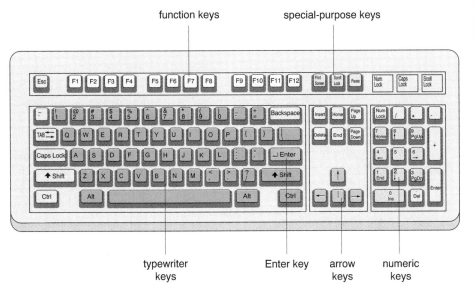

function keys   special-purpose keys

typewriter keys   Enter key   arrow keys   numeric keys

Terminals   A **terminal** is a form of input (and output) device that consists of a keyboard, a monitor, and a communications link. Terminals are of three types:

■ A **dumb terminal** can be used to input and receive data, but it cannot process data independently. It is used only to gain access to information from a computer. Such a terminal may be used by an airline reservations clerk to access a mainframe computer for flight information.

■ A **smart terminal** has some memory. It allows users to perform some editing or verification of data before it is sent to a large computer. A bank loan officer might do some calculations associated with making a loan on the smart terminal before this information is then stored in the bank's mainframe.

■ An **intelligent terminal** includes processing unit, primary storage, and secondary storage such as magnetic disk. Essentially, an intelligent terminal is a microcomputer with some communications software and a telephone hookup (modem) or other communications link. These connect the terminal to the larger computer.

Nearly all large organizations have terminals connected to their minicomputers and mainframe computers. A clear recent trend, however, has been the use of microcomputers as terminals. As prices of microcomputers have dropped and their power and flexibility have climbed, companies have tended to buy these instead of terminals. Moreover, with the appropriate software and communications links, microcomputers can communicate exactly like specialized (dedicated) terminals.

Direct Entry

Direct Entry Creates Machine-Readable Data That Can Go Directly to the CPU. Direct Entry Includes Pointing, Scanning, and Voice-Input Devices.

Direct entry is a form of input that does not require data to be keyed by someone sitting at a keyboard. Direct-entry devices create machine-readable data on paper or magnetic media or feed it directly into the computer's CPU. This reduces the possibility of human error being introduced (as often happens when data is being entered through a keyboard) and is an economical means of data entry.

Direct-entry devices may be categorized into three areas:

■ pointing devices

■ scanning devices

■ voice-input devices

Figure 5-3
A mouse.

Pointing Devices   Pointing, of course, is one of the most natural of all human gestures. There are a number of devices that use this method as a form of direct-entry input, as follows.

■ *Mouse:* A *mouse* has a ball on the bottom and is attached with a cord to the system unit. (*See Figure 5-3.*) When rolled on the table top, the mouse directs the location of the cursor or pointer on the computer screen. The pointer can then be used to draw pictures or point to a particular instruction. Selection buttons on the mouse can be used to issue commands.

At one time, the mouse was identified only with Apple microcomputers, but now it is standard for IBM's line of PS/2 models. Many people like the mouse because it reduces the need to input commands through a keyboard.

Figure 5-4
This mouselike device,
Microsoft's Ballpoint Mouse,
attaches to the side of a
portable computer.

A mouse is operated by rolling the ball beneath it along a flat surface. Sometimes no flat surface is available, as when one is on an airplane. In such cases, other pointing devices may be more convenient. An example is a mouse-like device with a ball that is attached to the side of the computer. (*See Figure 5-4.*) The device stays in one place, but the user can operate the ball with his or her thumb to guide the cursor.

- *Touch screen:* A **touch screen** is a particular kind of monitor screen covered with a plastic layer. Behind this layer are crisscrossed invisible beams of infrared light. This arrangement enables someone to select actions or commands by touching the screen with a finger. (*See Figure 5-5.*) Touch screens are easy to use, especially when people need information quickly. You are apt to see touch screen input devices used to convey visitor information in airports and hotels. However, they also have military and industrial applications. More recently, they are being used with microcomputers in applications that formerly used a mouse.

Figure 5-5
A touch screen.

Figure 5-6
A light pen.

- *Light pen:* A **light pen** is a light-sensitive penlike device. (*See Figure 5-6.*) The light pen is placed against the monitor. This closes a photoelectric circuit and identifies the spot for entering or modifying data. Light pens are used by engineers, for example, in designing anything from microprocessor chips to airplane parts.

- *Digitizer:* A **digitizer** is a device that can be used to trace or copy a drawing or photograph. The shape is converted to digital data. A computer can then represent the data on the screen or print it out on paper. A **digitizing tablet** enables you to create your own images using a special stylus. (*See Figure 5-7.*) The images are then converted to digital data that can be processed by the computer. Digitizers are often used by designers and architects.

- *Pen-based computing:* A **pen-based computer** is a small (e.g., 3.9 pounds) computer that lets you use a stylus to write directly on the display screen. (*See Figure 5-8.*) The system is less a triumph of hardware than of software. What is revolutionary is that these devices contain software that can recognize a person's handwriting. The handwriting can be stored as it was scrawled—not too difficult a task. More difficult is the task of converting a person's distinctive cursive writing (is that a "c" or an "e" or an "o"?) into typescript, which some pen-based computers attempt to do.

Scanning Devices Direct-entry scanning devices record images of text, drawings, or special symbols. The images are converted to digital data that can be processed by a computer or displayed on a monitor. Scanning devices include the following:

Figure 5-7
A digitizer.

Figure 5-8
A pen-based computer.

digitizer

Figure 5-9
An image scanner.

■ *Image scanner:* An **image scanner** identifies images on a page. (*See Figure 5-9.*) It automatically converts them to electronic signals that can be stored in a computer. The process identifies pictures or different typefaces by scanning each image with light and breaking it into light and dark dots. The dots are then converted into digital code for storage. Image scanners are becoming widely used input devices, as sales indicate. (*See Figure 5-10.*) Image scanners are commonly used in desktop publishing to scan graphic images that can then be placed in a page of text.

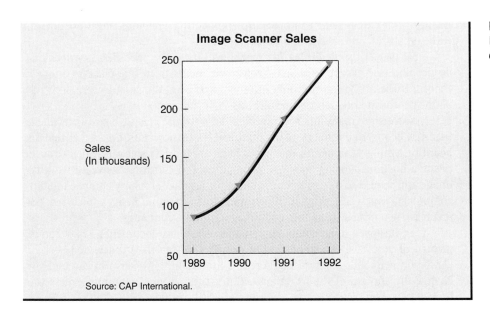

Figure 5-10
Image scanners: Sales are expected to increase.

Figure 5-11
A fax machine.

Fax machines: **Facsimile transmission machines** have become extremely popular office machines, so much so that people often ask each other, "What's your fax number?" They are commonly called **fax machines.** (*See Figure 5-11.*) Fax machines scan the image of a document and encode it as a series of instructions representing black-and-white image areas. They convert the instructions into a format (using a built-in modem) to send them electronically over telephone lines to a receiving fax machine. The receiving fax machine converts the signals back to an image and recreates it on paper. The machine uses a process much like those used by office photocopiers. Fax machines are useful to anyone who needs to send images rather than text. Examples are engineering drawings, legal documents with signatures, and sales promotional materials.

Most people use **dedicated fax machines.** These are specialized devices that do nothing else except send and receive documents from one place to another. Indeed, these are found not only in offices and print shops but even alongside phone booths in hotel lobbies and airports.

However, for many microcomputers, an optional circuit board is available that may be inserted into one of the machine's expansion slots. Called a **virtual fax board** or simply a **fax board,** this board, with appropriate software, allows you to create a document using your microcomputer. You can then convert it to a fax image and send it to a regular fax machine (or another similarly equipped microcomputer), which will print it. If you want to fax graphic images (pictures, not just text), you need a scanner to copy images into the computer.

A fax-equipped microcomputer can also receive fax documents. These can be printed, if you have the right kind of printer (dot-matrix, ink-jet, or laser), or viewed on your monitor screen. There is a limitation, however. You can't edit or change the content of the incoming fax messages on your computer unless you have a special kind of software.

- *Bar-code readers:* You are probably principally familiar with **bar-code readers** from grocery stores. (*See Figure 5-12.*) Bar-code readers are photoelectric scanners that read the **bar codes,** or vertical zebra-striped marks, printed on product containers. Supermarkets use a bar-code system called the Universal Product Code (UPC). The bar code identifies the product to the supermarket's computer, which has a description and the latest price for the product. The computer automatically tells the POS terminal what the price is and prints the price and the product name on the customer's receipt.

- *Character and mark recognition devices:* There are three kinds of scanning devices formerly used only with mainframes that are now being found in connection with the more powerful microcomputers.

  Magnetic-ink character recognition (MICR) is a direct-entry method used in banks. This technology is used to automatically read those futuristic-looking numbers on the bottom of checks. A special-purpose machine known as a **reader/sorter** reads characters made of ink containing magnetized particles.

  Optical-character recognition (OCR) uses special preprinted characters, such as those printed on utility and telephone bills. They can be read by a light source and changed into machine-readable code. A common OCR device is the hand-held *wand reader.* (*See Figure 5-13.*) These are used in department stores to read retail price tags by reflecting light on the printed characters.

  Optical-mark recognition (OMR) is also called mark sensing. An OMR device senses the presence or absence of a mark, such as a pencil mark. OMR is used in tests such as the College Board's Scholastic Aptitude Test and the Graduate Record Examination.

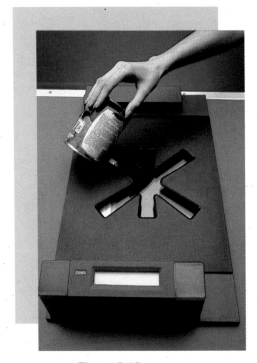

Figure 5-12
A bar-code reader.

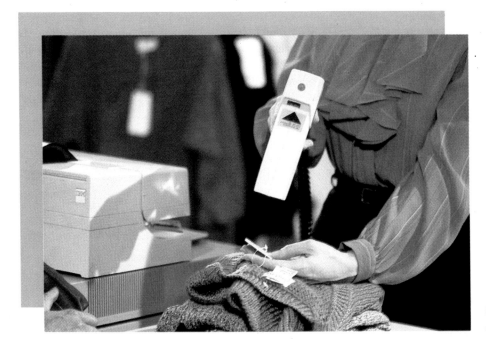

Figure 5-13
A wand reader.

Figure 5-14
A voice-input device.

Voice-Input Devices **Voice-input devices** convert a person's speech into a digital code. (*See Figure 5-14.*) Most such systems must be "trained" to the particular user's voice. This is done by matching his or her spoken words to patterns previously stored in the computer. Some systems have been devised that can recognize the same word as spoken by many different people. However, until recently the list of words has been limited. A recently developed voice-activated system, the Dragon Dictate, recognizes over 30,000 words and adapts to individual voices. There are even systems that will translate from one language to another, as from English to Japanese.

Voice-input systems enable users to keep their hands free for other tasks. Thus, they are an obvious advantage for disabled people. They are also used by people performing quality-control testing, package sorting, and baggage handling; by radiologists dictating reports; and by stockbrokers sending orders for stocks they want to buy and sell. A product called VoiceFont enables office workers to attach voice memos to their word processing, spreadsheet, and database files. All these systems are also called **speech-recognition devices** or **voice-recognition systems.**

Output

Output: Monitors, Printers, Plotters, Voice

Output Devices Convert Machine-Readable Information into People-Readable Form.

Data that is input to and then processed by the computer remains in machine-readable form until it is made people-readable by output devices.

The output devices we shall describe for microcomputers are monitors, printers, plotters, and voice-output.

Types of Monitors

Monitors May Be Single Color, or Monochrome, for Use with Text or Multicolor for Use with Graphics.

Monitors are also called **display screens** or *video display terminals (VDTs).* The kinds of monitors seem divided into two categories according to **screen resolution**—the clarity of the images on the screen. Images are represented on monitors by individual dots or "picture elements" called **pixels.** A pixel is the smallest unit on the screen that can be turned on and off or made different shades. The *density* of the dots—that is, the number of rows and columns of dots—determines the clarity of the images, the resolution.

In general, monitors with extremely high resolution are needed for such purposes as engineering workstations and computer-aided design. Monitors with lower resolution are considered suitable for general business use. However, the differences are closing fast. Thus, you should be prepared to view your work in all kinds of displays.

How many colors and how good the resolution is depend in part on the technology of the monitor. Most of those that sit on desks are built in the same way as television sets. These are called **cathode-ray tubes** and are often referred to by their abbreviation, **CRTs.** Another technology, used in portable computers, which can't fit the long tube required of the CRT, is the **flat-panel display.** Here the monitor lies flat instead of standing upright.

We will distinguish between monochrome monitors and graphics monitors.

Monochrome Monitors   In the early days of the microcomputer, you could buy a monitor that provided easily readable text or a monitor that provided color—but not both. Some people needed monitors that would mainly show words and numbers—for example, secretaries, stockbrokers, travel agents, and the like. Their preferred form of display was **monochrome monitors,** those showing one color on a dark background. The text could be viewed in white, green, or amber. (The Apple Macintosh monitor duplicated the ink-on-paper look of black on a white background.) Today monochrome monitors are used principally in portable computers, where size is a major consideration. They are able to display both text and graphics.

Because CRTs are too bulky to be transported, the flat-panel display was devised for portable computers. These monitors are more compact and consume less power than CRTs.

Portable machines use several kinds of flat-panel technology:

- **Liquid-crystal display (LCD)** was one of the first kinds of displays. (*See Figure 5-15.*) An LCD does not emit light of its own. Rather, it consists of crystal molecules. An electric field causes the molecules to line up in a way that alters their optical properties. Unfortunately, many LCDs are difficult to read in sunlight or other strong light. Many portable computers now use backlit LCDs, which are brighter and easier to read.

- The **electroluminescent (EL) display** type of flat panel is better. It actively emits light when it is electrically charged.

Figure 5-15
Liquid-crystal display (left) and gas-plasma display: Toshiba T4400SX.

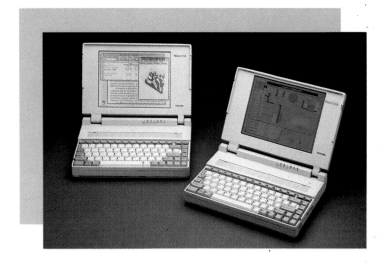

■ The **gas-plasma display** is the best type of flat screen, because it is almost as good as a CRT-type screen. (*See Figure 5-15.*) Like a neon light bulb, the plasma display uses a gas that emits light in the presence of an electric current. However, gas-plasma displays cannot be battery operated, which restricts their portability. They must be plugged into a regular wall plug offering AC current. In addition, they cannot show sharp contrast. The gas is either energized or it's not. Unlike a CRT, a gas-plasma display cannot be partially lit.

Graphics Monitors **Graphics monitors** display both alphanumeric characters and visual or graphic images. (*See Figure 5-16.*) Graphics monitors have gone through the following stages:

■ **CGA** stands for *Color Graphics Adapter.* This was a circuit board introduced by IBM that could be inserted into the computer. It was a way of giving a monitor a color display (provided the monitor was itself designed for color, not monochrome). The monochrome resolution was 640 by 350 pixels and made text easily readable. The CGA resolution for four colors was only 320 by 200 pixels. This made text display grainier and harder to read than on a monochrome monitor.

■ **EGA** stands for *Enhanced Graphics Adapter.* This board, which had a resolution of 640 by 350 pixels, was designed to support 16 colors, rather than just four. It was a significant step up in quality, offering resolution nearly like that in monochrome. Anyone upgrading to EGA from CGA, however, also had to buy a new monitor. The EGA monitor is still very popular today.

■ **VGA** stands for *Video Graphics Array.* When used just for text, the resolution of this board is 720 by 400 pixels. The VGA is far superior to the CGA and EGA boards in its handling of color. You can get 16 colors at a resolution of 640 by 480 pixels. Or you can get 16 times as many colors—256 colors—with a resolution of 320 by 200. It is useful in many applications, such as industrial design, in which precise measurements must be taken directly from the screen.

Graphics Monitors

Monitor type	Pixels	Colors
CGA	320 X 200	4
EGA	640 X 350	16
VGA	640 X 480	16
	320 X 200	256
Super VGA	800 X 600	256
	1024 X 768	256
XGA	1024 X 768	65,536

Figure 5-16
Types of graphics monitors.

- **Super VGA** is the name given to a very high resolution standard that displays up to 256 colors. Super VGA has a minimum of 800 by 600 resolution; some high-priced models have a 1024 by 768 resolution. The technology is used by highly skilled graphic designers and others who need the sharpest resolution and most color available.

- **XGA** stands for *Ex*tended *G*raphics *A*rray and has a resolution of up to 1024 by 768 pixels. Under normal circumstances, it displays up to 256 colors. However, with special equipment, it can handle up to 65,536 colors. XGA is becoming a standard for some very powerful microcomputer systems, such as the IBM 486 PS/2 models.

Printers

Five Kinds of Printers Used with Microcomputer Systems Are Dot-Matrix, Daisy-Wheel, Laser, Ink-Jet, and Chain.

The images output on a monitor screen are often referred to as **soft copy.** Information output on paper—whether by a printer or by a plotter—is called **hard copy.**

Five popular kinds of printers used with microcomputers are dot-matrix, daisy-wheel, laser, ink-jet, and chain. (*See Figure 5-17.*)

Dot-Matrix Printer **Dot-matrix printers** can produce a page of text in less than 10 seconds and are highly reliable. These inexpensive printers are the most popular machines used with microcomputers. Indeed, two-thirds of all printers

Figure 5-17
Types of printers.

Printers		
Printer	**Characteristics**	**Typical use**
Dot-matrix	Reliable, inexpensive; forms text and graphics by pixels; some color printing	In-house communications
Daisy-wheel	Letter-quality; prints text only; being replaced by other technology	External documents
Laser	Very high quality; forms text and graphics by pixels, using photocopying process	Desktop publishing
Ink-jet	High color quality; sprays drops of ink on paper	Advertising pieces
Chain	Extremely fast; can change type styles; shared by networks of microcomputers	High-quality text documents

sold are dot-matrix. In general, they are used for tasks where a high-quality image is not essential. Thus, they are often used for documents that are circulated within an organization rather than shown to clients and the public. However, some dot-matrix printers print color and *are* used for advertising and promotional purposes.

The dot-matrix printer forms characters or images using a series of small pins on a print head. (*See Figure 5-18.*) The pins strike an inked ribbon and create an image on paper. Printers are available with print heads of 9, 18, or 24 pins. The pins print a character in a manner that resembles the way individual lights spell out a number on a basketball scoreboard.

On some printers, the number of pins in the print head can be varied. This way, for example, just 9 pins can be used to rapidly print a draft-quality letter. This letter would be clear enough to read. However, it would not be as attractive as one you would want to send, say, to a customer. If the printer is set at 18 pins, it will print a near-letter-quality document, although more slowly. In 24-pin mode, the printer will print out a document that, to most people, is indistinguishable from letter-quality printing—almost as crisp as that produced by standard office typewriters.

Dot-matrix printers are especially useful because they can print any black-and-white image that the software is capable of creating. This means they will print not just letters and numbers but also shapes and graphics. As mentioned, some dot-matrix printers also print in color, using multicolored ribbons.

Daisy-Wheel Printer   The **daisy-wheel printer** is a form of letter-quality printer. In this printer, the print mechanism, the **daisy wheel,** consists of a removable wheel with a set of spokes. At the end of each spoke is a raised character. After the wheel is turned to align the correct character, it is then struck with a hammer.

Figure 5-18
A dot-matrix printer:
Epson 24-pin Action Printer.

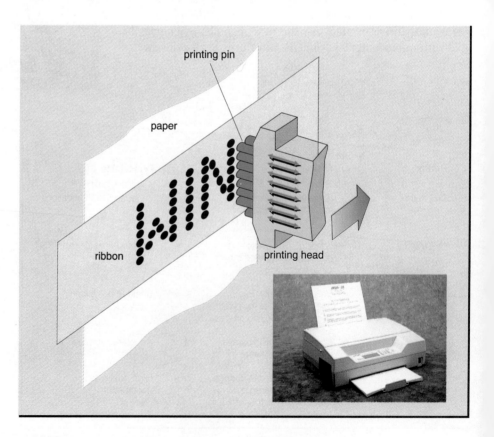

printing pin

paper

ribbon   printing head

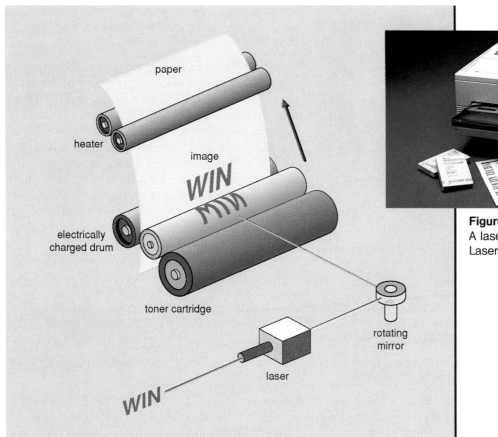

Figure 5-19
A laser printer: Hewlett-Packard LaserJet III.

These printers produce very high quality, professional-looking correspondence. However, they are slower and less reliable than dot-matrix printers. Their sales have declined dramatically as a result of the appearance of better dot-matrix printers and relatively inexpensive laser printers.

Laser Printer The **laser printer** creates dotlike images (like a dot-matrix printer) on a drum, using a laser beam light source. (*See Figure 5-19.*) The characters are treated with a magnetically charged inklike toner and then are transferred from drum to paper. A heat process is used to make the characters adhere. This technology is similar to that of a photocopying machine.

The laser printer produces images with excellent letter and graphics quality. It is widely used in applications requiring high-quality output. This has made possible the whole new industry of desktop publishing. As we've mentioned earlier, desktop publishing software enables people to merge text and graphics. The publications produced have a polish that rivals the work of some professional typesetters and graphic artists. Moreover, the laser printer can produce eight pages of text in about a minute. This printer is therefore frequently used for brochures, promotion pieces, and other tasks for which appearance is especially important.

Ink-Jet Printer An **ink-jet printer** sprays small droplets of ink at high speed onto the surface of the paper. This process not only produces a letter-quality image but also permits printing to be done in a variety of colors. (*See Figure 5-20.*) Ink-jet

Figure 5-20
An ink-jet printer: Canon.

printers are often used to duplicate color graphics from a monitor onto the printed page. Ink-jet printers are used wherever color and appearance are important, as in advertising and public relations.

Chain Printer A **chain printer** consists of several sets of characters connected together on a printing chain. (*See Figure 5-21.*) Like a bicycle chain, the chain revolves in front of the paper. Hammers are aligned with each position. When a character passes by, the hammer in that position strikes the paper and ribbon against it.

You probably won't find a chain printer on a desk next to a microcomputer standing alone by itself. This is because a chain printer is an expensive, high-speed machine designed originally to serve mainframes and minicomputers. However, you may see it in organizations that link several microcomputers together by a communications network. When several users share this resource, then the expense of serving microcomputers becomes justified.

Chain printers can reach speeds of up to 3000 lines per minute—extremely fast. They are also very reliable. A further advantage is that the chains can be changed for different type fonts or styles.

Printer Features Some general qualities to note about microcomputer printers are as follows:

- *Bidirectional:* Many of the faster printers are **bidirectional.** That is, they print in two directions. One line is printed as the print element moves to the right. The following line is printed as the print head moves to the left. This saves the time of making a carriage return, as on a typewriter.

- *Tractor feed:* Most microcomputer users buy continuous-form printer paper, the pages of which can be separated after printing. In a typewriter the paper is gripped by the roller (platen). In most microcomputer printers the paper is held in place by a **tractor feed** mechanism. This reduces the chance of the paper's getting out of alignment. The tractor feed has sprockets that advance the paper, using holes on the edges of continuous-form paper.

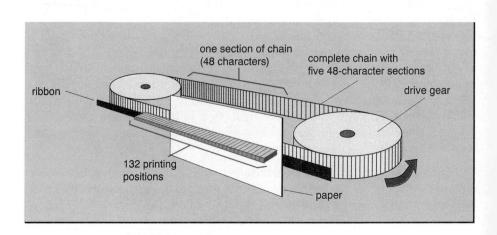

Figure 5-21
A chain printer.

- *Type styles:* Some printers allow you to change type styles by changing the printing element. Others require you to do something with the software. Still others do not allow a change in type style.

- *Shared use:* Dot-matrix and daisy-wheel printers are quite often used to serve individual microcomputers. Ink-jet and laser printers, and chain printers particularly, can be quite expensive. Thus, in organizations they are often found linked to several microcomputers through a communications network.

- *Portability:* Some people (travelers, for instance) require not only a portable computer but also a portable printer. Rugged printers are available that are battery-powered and weigh less than 7 pounds. These printers typically are either dot-matrix or ink-jet. Such printers are recharged using a special connection that can be plugged into an AC outlet. Some can even be recharged through a car's cigarette lighter.

Plotters

Plotters Are Special-Purpose Drawing Devices.

Plotters are special-purpose output devices for producing bar charts, maps, architectural drawings, and even three-dimensional illustrations. Plotters can produce high-quality multicolor documents and also documents that are larger in size than most printers can handle.

Plotters are of three types: pen, electrostatic, and direct imaging.

Pen Plotter **Pen plotters** are the most popular type of plotter, accounting for 60 percent of the market. (*See Figure 5-22.*) They are the least expensive, yet highly reliable.This type of plotter is used for a wide variety of applications including the creation of business graphs and maps.

Figure 5-22
A pen plotter.

Electrostatic Plotter While pen plotters use pens, **electrostatic plotters** use electrostatic charges to create images made up of tiny dots on specially treated paper. (*See Figure 5-23.*) The image is produced when the paper is run through a developer. Electrostatic plotters produce high-resolution images and are much faster than pen plotters. They are used for applications that require high-volume and high-quality outputs such as in advertising and graphic arts design.

Direct Imaging Plotter **Direct-image** or thermal plotters create images using heat-sensitive paper and electrically heated pins. This type of plotter is comparably priced with electrostatic plotters, is quite reliable, and good for high-volume work. However, direct-imaging plotters create only two-color output.

Voice-Output Devices

Voice-Output Devices Vocalize Prerecorded Sounds.

Voice-output devices make sounds that resemble human speech but actually are prerecorded vocalized sounds. With one Macintosh program, the computer speaks the synthesized words "We'll be right back" if you type in certain letters and numbers. (The characters are *Wiyl biy ray5t bae5k*—the numbers elongate the sounds.) Voice

Figure 5-23
An electrostatic plotter.

output is not anywhere near as difficult to create as voice input. In fact, there are many occasions when you will hear synthesized speech being used. Examples are found in soft-drink machines, on the telephone, and in cars.

Voice output can be used as a reinforcement tool for learning, such as to help students study a foreign language. Or it can help a user double-check numbers being keyed into a spreadsheet.

A Look at the Future

Developers Are Trying to Overcome Difficulties in Improving Handwritten and Voice Input. We May See Display Screens That Are Larger, Smaller, and with Lifelike Graphics. Microcomputers May Merge with Television.

We can expect some startling developments in input and output in the future. Already, some companies are giving hand-held computers *wireless communications* with more powerful, stationary computers. (We describe communications in Chapter 7.)

There are many reports that *voice-recognition technology* is rapidly progressing. However, it probably will be a few years before it is sophisticated enough to record many pages of uninterrupted speech. Still, there are many companies that say they are working on devising dictation devices that accept continuing, rather than halting, speech.

On the output side, as computers continue to shrink, we may see some hand-held, special-purpose versions sporting *1-inch display screens.* Alternatively, *screens may become larger,* with high-quality resolution. We will also probably begin to see *flat-panel,* full-color screens replace the old video-display tubes everywhere. Finally, screens may show *graphics as lifelike,* and images may be automated in ways we have not seen before. For instance, someday, technology will allow for *computerized three-dimensional video holograms,* such as might provide pictures of a patient's brain during neurosurgery.

Perhaps one of the most exciting future developments is the expected *merger of microcomputers and television.* This may come about in part through the establishment of all-digital *high-definition television (HDTV).* HDTV will deliver a much clearer and more detailed wide-screen picture. The purpose of this technology is not to allow microcomputer users to watch TV as they work, although they can indeed do that. Rather, it will enable them to freeze video sequences to create still images. These images can then be digitized and output as artwork or stored on videodisks. This technology could be useful to graphic artists, publishers, and educators.

Review Questions

1. What are the differences between keyboard entry and direct entry as forms of input?
2. What is a POS terminal? What are two input devices on it that represent the two methods of inputting data?
3. What are the four kinds of keys on a keyboard?
4. Distinguish among the three kinds of terminals: dumb, smart, and intelligent.
5. List some direct-entry input devices.
6. How does a mouse work?

7. What input device recognizes images and converts them into electronic signals?
8. How does an image scanner work?
9. Which direct-entry input device is particularly helpful to certain disabled people?
10. List four output devices.
11. What uses are monochrome monitors best suited for?
12. What are three kinds of flat-panel displays used with portable computers?
13. What are pixels? What do they have to do with screen resolution?
14. Explain how a dot-matrix printer works.
15. Explain how a daisy-wheel printer works.
16. Describe how an ink-jet printer operates.
17. State how a laser printer works.
18. What can a plotter do that a printer cannot?
19. What is the difference between a pen plotter and an electrostatic plotter?
20. Is voice output more difficult to engineer than voice input?

Discussion Questions and Projects

1. *Evaluating laser printers:* When shopping for a low-end laser printer, you can't expect to get all of the fancy fonts and speedy, sophisticated paper handling more expensive printers offer. At the very least, you'd want crisp, professional-looking output and reasonably fast performance. Evaluate your printer needs in terms of the following criteria:
   a. Output quality
   b. Print speed
   c. Price
   d. Service and support
   e. Design and construction
   f. Font/graphics options
   g. Paper handling

2. *High-definition television (HDTV):* This is a technology that you are certain to become well-acquainted with during your lifetime. HDTV—the first major technical change in TV since color came in 30 years ago—produces a sharper and more detailed picture than is available with present TV sets. However, there are presently no world technical standards, and different nations are working on different, and incompatible, systems. Some systems are based on *analog* principles, a technology that is the basis for present television. Others are based on *digital* principles. This approach eliminates image distortions and allows television to be integrated with all kinds of other digital technology, such as computerized storage communications.

   Go to the library or other sources to learn more about this evolving technology. Specifically:
   a. Define HDTV.
   b. Discuss analog versus digital technology.
   c. Discuss the potential effect of HDTV, if any, on future computer technology.

Chapter 5 Input and Output

Input devices convert symbols that people understand into symbols the computer can process. Two kinds of input are keyboard and direct entry.

Input

Keyboard Entry

Keyboard entry may be categorized as keyboards and terminals.

Keyboards

In keyboard entry, data is typed. A keyboard consists of:

- **Typewriter keys,** for regular letters, numbers, etc., and **Enter (Return)** key to enter commands.
- **Function keys** (*F1, F2,* etc.), for special tasks.
- **Numeric keys**, for typing in numbers.
- **Special-purpose keys** (e.g., *Del* for "Delete") and **directional arrow keys** (to move cursor).

Terminals

A **terminal** is an input/output device with keyboard, monitor, and communications link. Terminals are of three types:

- **Dumb**—sends and receives only; does no processing.
- **Smart**—allows some editing of data.
- **Intelligent**—has processing and primary and secondary storage and software for processing data.

Direct Entry

Direct-entry devices may be categorized as pointing, scanning, or voice-input devices.

Pointing Devices

- **Mouse**—directs cursor on screen.
- **Touch screen**—touching your finger to the screen selects actions.
- **Light pen**—recognizes a spot on the screen as input.
- **Digitizer**—converts image to digital data. A **digitizing tablet** converts images using a stylus.
- **Pen-based computing**—computer with stylus to write on display screen.

Scanning Devices

- **Image scanner (bit-mapping device)**—converts an image to digital code.
- **Facsimile transmission (fax) machine**—converts images to electronic signals for sending over telephone lines. **Dedicated fax machines** are specialized devices. **Virtual fax** boards may be inserted in microcomputers to send and receive images.

- **Bar code reader**—scans zebra-striped **bar codes** on products to reveal their prices.
- Character and mark recognition devices include: **magnetic-ink character recognition (MICR),** used by banks to read magnetized-ink numbers on checks, which are sorted by a **reader/sorter** machine; **optical-character recognition (OCR),** used to read special preprinted characters (e.g., on utility bills); **optical-mark recognition (OMR),** which senses pencil marks (e.g., on College Board tests).

Voice-Input Devices

Also called **speech-recognition devices** or **voice recognition systems, voice-input devices** convert a person's spoken words to digital code.

Output devices convert machine output to output people can understand.

Output devices include monitors, printers, plotters, and voice-output.

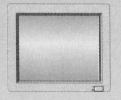

Output devices convert machine output to output that people can understand. Output devices include monitors, printers, plotters, and voice-output.

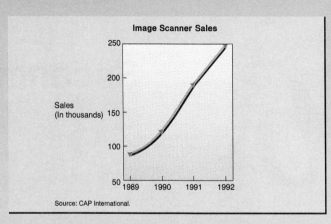

Image Scanner Sales

Sales (In thousands)

250
200
150
100
50

1989 1990 1991 1992

Source: CAP International.

Output

Monitors

Monitors **(display screens)** can be monochrome (single-color) or multicolor.

Monochrome Monitors

Monochrome monitors show one color on a dark background.

Graphics Monitors

Graphics monitors display both alphanumeric characters and graphic images. Five types are:

Graphics Monitors		
Monitor type	Pixels	Colors
CGA	320 X 200	4
EGA	640 X 350	16
VGA	640 X 480	16
	320 X 200	256
Super VGA	800 X 600	256
	1024 X 768	256
XGA	1024 X 768	65,536

Printers

Output from display screens is called **soft copy.** Output from a printer is called **hard copy.** Five types of printers are:

- **Dot-matrix**—forms text and graphic images with a matrix of pins; it is the most popular form today.
- **Daisy-wheel**—prints office-quality correspondence from a revolving wheel; it is declining in use.
- **Laser**—prints with light beam and magnetically charged toner. Lasers print high-quality text and graphics; they are becoming very popular (e.g., in desktop publishing).
- **Ink-jet**—sprays droplets of ink on paper; it is good for color and provides very good quality.
- **Chain**—characters on printing chain are hit with hammer, striking paper and ribbon; it prints at very high speeds.

Plotters

Plotters produce multicolor bar charts, maps, architectural drawings. Three types are:

- **Pen**—most popular and least expensive (shown above).
- **Electrostatic**—electrostatic charges create high-quality and high-volume work on specially treated paper (shown below).

- **Direct imaging**—electrically charged pins create two-color output on special heat-sensitive paper.

Voice-Output Devices

Voice-output devices make sounds resembling human speech.

99

6 Secondary Storage

Competencies

After you have read this chapter, you should be able to:

1. Contrast direct access and sequential access storage.

2. Describe how data is organized: characters, fields, records, files, and databases.

3. Describe how diskettes and disk drives work and how to take care of them.

4. Describe the following kinds of disks: internal hard disk, hard-disk cartridge, and hard-disk packs.

5. Discuss optical disks.

6. Describe magnetic tape streamers and magnetic tape reels.

Data may be input, processed, and output as information. But one of the best features about using a computer is the ability to save—that is, store—information permanently, after you turn off the computer. This way, you can save your work for future use, share information with others, or modify information already available. Permanent storage holds information external from the CPU. Permanent storage is also called *secondary* storage, to distinguish it from the temporary *primary* storage inside the computer. Secondary storage allows you to store programs, such as WordPerfect and Lotus 1-2-3. It also allows you to store the data processed by programs, such as text or the numbers in a spreadsheet.

What if you could buy a microcomputer and use your portable audiotape recorder to store programs and data? Actually, this was once advertised as a feature. In the early 1980s there were over 150 kinds of microcomputers being offered. Some inexpensive computers were advertised at that time that could store information on the tape in one's audiotape recorder.

To find a particular song on an audiotape, you may have to play several inches of tape. Finding a song on an LP record on a turntable, in contrast, can be much faster. You can simply lift up the record arm and quickly move it to the song of your choice. That, in brief, represents the two different approaches to external storage. These two approaches are called *sequential access* and *direct access*.

Tape storage falls in the category of **sequential access storage.** Information is stored in sequence, such as alphabetically. You may have to search a tape past all the information from A to P, say, before you get to Q. This may involve searching several inches or feet, which takes time.

Generally speaking, disk storage falls in the category of **direct access storage.** That is, it is like moving the arm on a turntable directly to the song you want. This form of storage allows you to directly access information. Therefore, retrieving data and programs is much faster with disks than with tape.

Now let us consider in detail how data is organized.

Data Organization

Data Is Organized into Characters, Fields, Records, Files, and Databases.

Computers encode data with "on" and "off" electrical states or "present" and "absent" electromagnetic charges or impulses. We saw this in Chapter 4. Individual data items are represented by 0 (off) and 1 (on) and are called *bits*. Collections of eight bits are organized into **bytes,** representing characters. Characters can be letters, numbers, or special signs such as $, ?, and !.

To be processed by the computer or stored in secondary storage, data is organized into groups or categories. Each group is more complex than the one before. (*See Figure 6-1.*)

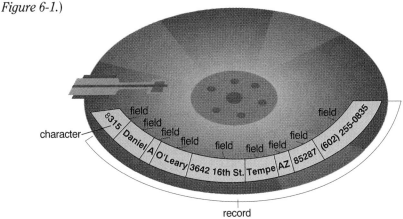

Figure 6-1
How data is organized. All records of this form would make up one file. A database is made up of several related files.

- *Character:* A *character* can be a single letter, number, or special character such as a punctuation mark or $.

- *Field:* A *field* contains a set of related characters. On a college registration form or a driver's license, a person's first name is a field. Last name is another field, street address another field, city yet another field, and so on.

- *Record:* A *record* is a collection of related fields. Everything on a person's driver's license, including number and expiration date, forms a record.

- *File:* A *file* is a collection of related records. All the driver's licenses issued in one county could be a file.

- *Database:* A *database* is a collection of related files. The department of motor vehicles in your state has a database of all vehicles registered in the state. The database consists of all files from each county and may be used in many different ways. For example, a car manufacturer might need to recall a particular car model because of a manufacturing defect. The manufacturer might ask the database for a list of all owners of that car model. The manufacturer could then notify those owners about the recall. A police department might have a partial license number (say, beginning with "ROB") of a car involved in a crime. They could ask for a list of all cars with license numbers with that beginning.

Four Kinds of Secondary Storage

Microcomputer Secondary Storage May Be on Floppy Disk, Hard Disk, Optical Disk, or Tape.

We described random-access memory (RAM) in Chapter 4. This is the *internal* and *temporary* storage of data and programs in the computer's memory. Once the power is turned off or interrupted, everything in internal storage disappears. Such storage is therefore said to be **volatile.** Thus, we need *external, more permanent,* or **nonvolatile,** ways of storing data and programs. We also need external storage because users need much more capacity than is possessed by a computer's primary memory.

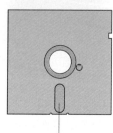

Cut-out area exposes
magnetic surface
of floppy disk.

Figure 6-2
A 5¼-inch floppy disk.

The most widely used external storage media include the following:

- Floppy disk
- Hard disk
- Optical disk
- Magnetic tape

Magnetic tape is *not* the most popular form of storage—for microcomputers or for larger computers. This is true despite all those movies you've seen that show computer rooms with reels of magnetic tape turning. For computers of all types, magnetic tape is mainly used as *backup*. That is, tape is used to make a copy in case other forms of storage are lost or damaged. The advantage of disk storage is speed.

Floppy Disks

Floppy Disks Are Removable Storage Media That Are Inserted into Disk Drives.

Floppy disks, often called diskettes or simply **disks,** are flat, circular pieces of mylar plastic that rotate within a jacket. Data and programs are stored as electromagnetic charges on a metal oxide film coating the mylar plastic. Data and programs are represented by the presence or absence of these electromagnetic charges, using the ASCII or EBCDIC data representation codes. The two most popular sizes of floppy disks are 5¼-inch diameter and 3½-inch diameter. Larger and smaller sizes are also available, although they are not standard for most microcomputers.

Floppy disks are also called **flexible disks**, and **floppies.** This is because the plastic disk inside the diskette covers is flexible, not rigid. The 5¼-inch size comes encased in a flexible plastic jacket. (*See Figure 6-2.*) The 3½-inch standard is encased in a hard plastic jacket. (*See Figure 6-3.*) Both have a flexible disk inside, and therefore both are called "floppy."

Cover slides over
to expose disk.

Figure 6-3
A 3½-inch floppy disk.

The Disk Drive The *disk drive* obtains stored data and programs from a floppy disk. It is also used to store data and programs on a floppy disk.

A disk drive consists of a box with a slot into which you insert the floppy disk. Often the slot is covered by a door, called the **drive gate.** A motor inside the drive rotates the floppy disk. As the floppy disk rotates, electronic heads can "read" data from and "write" data to it. As we stated earlier, *read* means the disk drive *copies* data (stored as magnetic impulses) from the floppy disk. *Write* means the disk drive *transfers* data, the electronic signals in the computer's memory, onto the floppy disk.

It's important to realize that reading makes a copy from the original data; it does not alter the original. Writing, on the other hand, *writes over*—and replaces—any data that is already there. This is like recording a new song over an old one on a tape recorder. The same is true of programs on a floppy disk.

Microcomputer disk drives are usually built into the computer system cabinet along with the processor unit. (*See Figure 6-4.*) Sometimes the disk drive is external, a separate component outside the system cabinet. (*See Figure 6-5.*)

Except for a few special-purpose machines, all microcomputers have at least *one* disk drive for floppy disks. This is the only way most software programs (such as word processors) initially can be entered into the computer's primary storage.

Figure 6-4
Disk drives built into system cabinet.

How a Disk Drive Works   A floppy disk is inserted into the slot in the front of the disk drive, and the drive gate is closed. (*See Figure 6-6.*) Closing the gate positions the floppy disk around a spindle and holds it so that it can revolve without slipping. When the drive is in motion, the floppy disk can turn at about 300 revolutions per minute, depending on the drive.

The magnetic data signals are transferred from floppy disk to computer (and computer to floppy disk) through **read-write heads.** (*See Figure 6-6.*) The read-write head is on an **access arm,** which moves back and forth over the floppy disk. To read or write on a particular part of the floppy disk, the access arm moves the read-write head on the floppy disk. This is called the **seek** operation. The drive then rotates the floppy disk to the proper position. This is called the **search** operation.

Drive A and Drive B   A microcomputer may operate with just one disk drive, but this involves some extra complications. (For instance, when copying from one floppy disk to another, you have to constantly switch the two floppy disks in the drive.) Most microcomputers have two disk drives. One may be a *hard-disk drive,* as we describe later, but here we are concerned with two floppy-disk drives.

Figure 6-5
External disk drive (3½-inch).

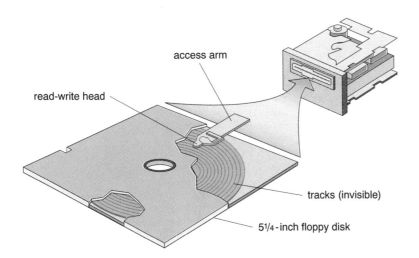

access arm

read-write head

tracks (invisible)

5¼-inch floppy disk

Figure 6-6
Reading and writing data on a floppy disk.

Figure 6-7
Two disk drives: A and B.

Normally the drive into which you put your **program disk**—the software program such as a word processor—is **drive A.** On many microcomputers, drive A is the left or upper drive, either on the front of the machine or on the side. (*See Figure 6-7.*) The drive into which you put the *data disk* is normally **drive B.** This drive is on the right or lower side on many computers. The data disk is the disk that will store the information you are creating, such as a report. (*Note:* The reference to "A" and "B" drives is used with many computer systems, notably IBM and IBM-compatibles. Even systems that do not use these terms, however, usually still have program disks and data disks.)

The Parts of a Floppy Disk Both 5¼-inch and 3½-inch floppy disks work the same way in principle, although there are some differences. (*See Figures 6-8 and 6-9.*)

Data is recorded on a floppy disk in rings called **tracks.** (*See Figure 6-8.*) These tracks are closed concentric circles, not a single spiral as on a phonograph record. Unlike a phonograph record, these tracks have no visible grooves. Looking at an exposed floppy disk, you would see just a smooth surface. Each track is divided into invisible wedge-shaped sections known as **sectors.** The fields of data within a particular record are organized according to tracks and sectors on a disk.

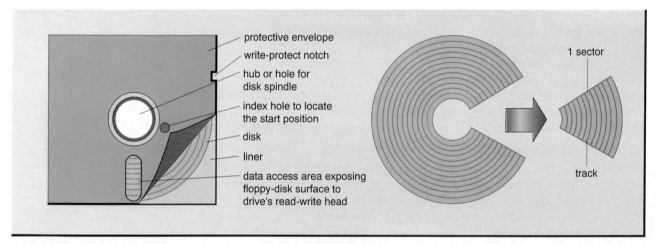

Figure 6-8
The parts of a 5¼-inch floppy disk.

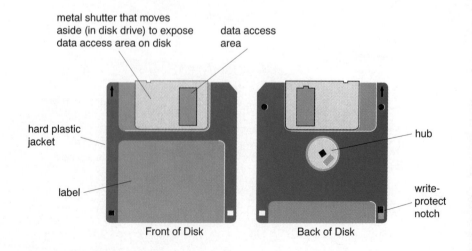

Figure 6-9
The parts of a 3½-inch floppy disk.

Almost all disks are manufactured without tracks and sectors in place. These are called **soft-sectored disks,** and they must be adapted to the particular brand of microcomputer and disk drive you are using. Thus, you must put the tracks and sectors on yourself, using a process called *formatting,* or *initializing.*

Storage capacity of floppy disks can vary considerably. (*See Figure 6-10.*) For example, you will see boxes of 5¼-inch disks labeled "DS, DD" (or "2S/2D"), which means "double-sided, double-density." A floppy disk of this sort is usually formatted to have 40 tracks on each side. Each side contains nine sectors of 512 bytes each. This adds up to 368,640 bytes, or 360K—the equivalent of 260 typewritten pages. However, as we mentioned earlier, a 3½-inch DS, DD disk typically has twice the capacity—720K. Along with their more efficient size, this high storage capacity is a major reason more microcomputers now use the 3½-inch disks.

Special note: A not uncommon problem today is that some disks can be read by one microcomputer but *not* by another. Consider two models in the IBM PS/2 line. The Model 50 might be able to read a particular 3½-inch disk. The Model 30, however, might not be able to read that same 3½-inch disk. Most likely the reason is that the data disk was originally formatted to hold 1.44 megabytes of data. The Model 50 has a high-density disk drive. It is able to read such a high-density disk as well as the standard-density data disks (720K). Model 30s and some other microcomputer systems don't have high-density drives and thus can't read such high-density disks. A similar situation may occur with IBM PCs and XTs not being able to read high-density disks formatted to run on IBM ATs. Suggestion: If you are using more than one type of disk drive—high-capacity and standard—*format all disks to be standard density.* That way your disks will run on both types of drives (even though storage capacity on the disks won't be as great).

The two most popular sizes of floppy disks have distinct differences in the ways the jacket and the write-protect notch are handled:

- *5¼-inch:* On the 5¼-inch version, the **jacket,** or liner—the protective outer covering—is made of flexible plastic or cardboard. (*Refer back to Figure 6-8.*) The disk is protected by a paper envelope, or sleeve, when it is not in the disk drive. The **write-protect notch** can be covered with a removable tab, which comes with the disk when you buy it. This prevents the computer from accidentally writing (overlaying) data over information on the disk that you want to keep.

- *3½-inch:* The 3½-inch version is the sturdier of the two. (*Refer back to Figure 6-9.*) The jacket is made of hard plastic rather than flexible plastic or cardboard. The write-protect notch is covered by a sliding shutter. When you open the shutter, the write-protect notch prevents the computer from accidentally writing over information already on the disk.

Taking Care of Floppy Disks   Taking care of floppy disks boils down to three rules:

1. *Don't bend the disks, or put heavy weights on them, or use sharp objects on them.* For 5¼-inch disks, do not write on them with ballpoint pens. Use a felt-tip pen when writing on the index label.

2. *Don't touch anything visible through the protective jacket* (such as the data access area).

3. *Keep disks away from strong magnetic fields* (like motors or telephones). Also, *keep them away from extreme heat* (like a car trunk) *and chemicals* (such as alcohol and solvents). Keep 5¼-inch disks in their paper envelopes and store them in a file box when they are not in use.

Floppy-Disk Capacity	
Description	**Bytes**
5¼-inch	
Double-sided, double-density	360 KB
Double-sided, high-density	1.2 MB
3½-inch	
Double-sided, double-density	720 KB
Double-sided, high-density	1.44 MB

Figure 6-10
Common capacities of 5¼-inch and 3½-inch floppy disks.

Of course, the best protection is to make a *backup,* or duplicate, copy of your disk.

Despite these cautions, you will find floppy disks are actually quite hardy. For instance, you can send them through the mail if you enclose them in cardboard or use special rigid mailing envelopes. They usually can also be put through the x-ray machines at airport security checkpoints without loss of data.

Hard Disks

Hard Disks Are of Three Types: Internal Hard Disk, Hard-Disk Cartridge, and Hard-Disk Pack.

Hard disks consist of metallic rather than plastic platters. They are also tightly sealed to prevent any foreign matter from getting inside. Hard disks come in three forms: *internal hard disk, hard-disk cartridge,* and *hard-disk pack.*

Internal Hard Disk An **internal hard disk** consists of one or more metallic platters sealed inside a container. The container includes the motor for rotating the disks. It also contains an access arm and read-write heads for writing data to and reading data from the disks. The operation is somewhat the same as for floppy-disk drives. That is, the disk drive has a seek operation and a search operation for reading and writing data in tracks and sectors.

From the outside of a microcomputer, an internal hard disk looks merely like part of a front panel on the system cabinet. Inside is a 5¼-inch metallic platter with an access arm that moves back and forth. (*See Figure 6-11.*) Drives with 3½-inch-diameter hard disks are also available. These provide faster access times because the access arm and read-write heads travel shorter distances across the diameter of the disk.

Internal hard disks have two advantages over floppy disks: capacity and speed. A hard disk can hold many times the information of a similar size floppy disk. One 60-megabyte internal hard disk, for instance, can hold the same amount of information as 168 double-sided, double-density floppy disks. Some *external* hard-disk drives for microcomputers (drives that are not built into the system cabinet) can store as many as 1000 megabytes. Moreover, access is faster: A hard disk spins 10 times faster than a floppy disk.

Hard-Disk Cartridges The disadvantage of hard disks or hardcards is that they have only a fixed amount of storage and cannot be easily removed. Hard-disk cartridges have the advantage of being as easy to remove as a cassette from a video-cassette recorder. (*See Figure 6-12.*) They can give microcomputer systems fast access to very large quantities of data. The amount of storage available is limited only by the number of cartridges. For instance, one self-contained removable hard-disk cartridge has a storage capacity of 40 megabytes. While a regular hard-disk system has a fixed storage capacity, a removable hard-disk cartridge system is unlimited—you can just buy more removable cartridges. One removable 20-megabyte palm-sized hard disk available weighs only 7 ounces and may be moved easily from laptop to laptop.

Hard-Disk Packs Microcomputers that are connected to other microcomputers, minicomputers, or mainframes often have access to external hard-disk packs. (*See Figure 6-13.*) Microcomputer hard-disk drives typically have only one or two disk platters and one or two access arms. In contrast, **hard-disk packs** consist of *several* platters aligned one above the other, thereby offering much greater storage capacity. These hard-disk packs resemble a stack of phonograph records. The difference is that there is space between the disks to allow the access arms to move in and out. (*See Figure 6-14.*) Each access arm has two read-write heads. One reads the disk

disk spindle
disk platter
movable access arm with read-write head

Figure 6-11
The inside of a hard-disk drive.

Figure 6-12
Removable 40-megabyte hard-disk cartridge.

Figure 6-13
Disk packs.

surface above it; the other reads the disk surface below it. A disk pack with 11 disks provides 20 recording surfaces. This is because the top and bottom outside surfaces of the pack are not used.

All the access arms move in and out together. However, only *one* of the read-write heads is activated at a given moment. **Access time** is the time between when the computer requests data from secondary storage and when the transfer of data is completed. Access time—which for most disk drives is under 25 milliseconds—depends on four things:

- How quickly the access arm can get into position over a particular track. This is known as **seek time.**

- How fast a particular read-write head can be activated. This is called **head switching time.**

- How long it takes the disk to rotate under the read-write head. This is called **rotational delay time.**

- How long it takes for data to transfer from the disk track to primary storage. This is called **data transfer time.**

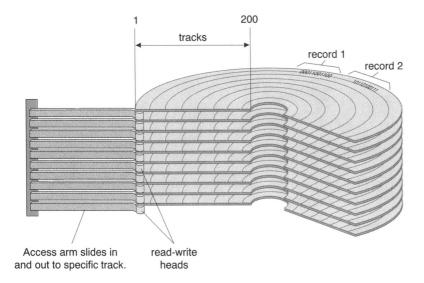

Access arm slides in and out to specific track.

read-write heads

Figure 6-14
How a disk pack operates.

You may well use your microcomputer to gain access to information over a telephone or other communications line. (We show this in the next chapter.) Such information is apt to be stored on disk packs. One large information service (named Dialog), for example, has over 300 databases. These databases cover all areas of science, technology, business, medicine, social science, current affairs, and humanities. All of these are available through a telephone link with your desktop computer. With more than 100 million items of information, including references to books, patents, directories, journals, and newspaper articles, such an information resource may be of great value to you in your work.

The reason a hard disk is enclosed in a tightly sealed container is to prevent any foreign material from getting inside. The hard disk is an extremely sensitive instrument. The read-write head rides on a cushion of air about 0.000001 inch thick. It is so thin that a smoke particle, fingerprint, or human hair could cause what is known as a head crash. A **head crash** happens when the surface of the read-write head or particles on its surface contact the magnetic disk surface. A head crash is a disaster for a hard disk. It means that some or all of the data on the disk is destroyed. Hard disks are assembled under sterile conditions and sealed from impurities within their permanent containers.

Data Compression A major complaint of many microcomputer owners is that, sooner or later, their hard disk completely fills up with data. At that point a message appears on their screen saying "Disk full." One can, of course, move files to floppy disks or tape drives or buy a bigger hard disk. A popular and less expensive alternative is to employ data compression and decompression technology.

In **data compression**, entering and existing data is automatically scanned for repeating patterns. The repeating patterns are replaced with a token, leaving enough so that the original can be rebuilt or **decompressed**. Data compression and decompression are accomplished through the use of special software and/or hardware—add-on boards inserted into the computer's expansion slots.

Data compression can regain or free as much as 70 percent of a microcomputer's hard disk. The major tradeoff is that of performance: a great deal of compression may slow down processing.

Optical Disks

Optical Disks Are Used for Storing Great Quantities of Data.

An **optical disk** may hold more than 700 megabytes of data—the equivalent of hundreds of floppy disks. Moreover, an optical disk makes an immense amount of information available even on a microcomputer. Optical disks are having a great impact on storage technology today, but we are probably only just beginning to see their effects. (*See Figure 6-15.*)

In optical-disk technology, a laser beam burns tiny pits representing data into the surface of a plastic or metallic disk. To read the data, a laser scans these areas and sends the data to a computer chip for conversion. Optical disks are made in diameters of 3½, 4¾, 5¼, 8, 12, and 14 inches.

There are three kinds of optical disks available: *CD-ROM, WORM,* and *erasable optical disks*. (*See Figure 6-16.*)

CD-ROM **CD-ROM** stands for *compact disk–read-only memory*. Like the commercial CD found in music stores, a CD-ROM is a "read-only" disk. **Read-only** means it cannot be written on or erased by the user. Thus, you as a user have access only to

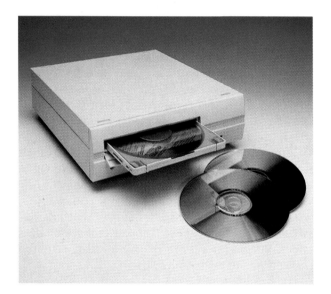

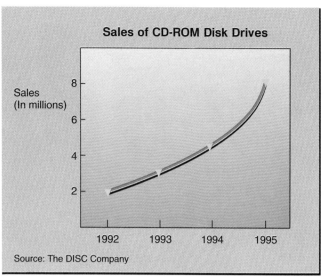

Figure 6-15
Optical disk, and past and estimated sales of CD-ROM drives.

the data imprinted by the manufacturer. CD-ROM disks are used to distribute large databases and references. An example is Computer Library, a CD-ROM containing over 50,000 computer, technical, and business articles and abstracts. A CD-ROM disk can store 540 to 748 megabytes of data.

WORM **WORM** stands for *write once, read many.* **Write-once** means that a disk can be written on just once. After that, it can be read many times without deterioration and cannot be written on or erased by the user. Because the data cannot be erased, WORM disks are ideal for use as archives. A WORM disk can store between 122 and 640 megabytes of data.

Erasable Optical Disks An **erasable optical disk** is like a CD-ROM except that it is not read-only. That is, a disk that has been written on can be erased and used over and over again. An erasable optical disk can store 281 to 320 megabytes of data. The most viable such disk runs on a *magneto-optical* (MO) disk drive, which borrows from both magnetic and optical technologies.

Optical Disks	
Technology	**Storage space**
CD-ROM	540 – 748 MB
WORM	122 – 640 MB
Erasable	281 – 320 MB

Figure 6-16
Comparison of optical disks.

Magnetic Tape

Magnetic Tape Streamers and Magnetic Tape Reels Are Used Primarily for Backup Purposes.

We mentioned the alarming consequences that can happen if a hard disk suffers a head crash. You will lose some or all of your data or programs. Of course, you can always make copies of your hard-disk files on floppy disks. However, this can be time-consuming and may require many floppy disks. Here is where magnetic tape storage becomes important. Magnetic tape falls in the category of sequential access storage and is therefore slower than direct access storage. However, it is an effective way of making a *backup,* or duplicate, copy of your programs and data.

There are two forms of tape storage. These are *magnetic tape streamers,* for use with microcomputers, and *magnetic tape reels,* for use with minicomputers and mainframes.

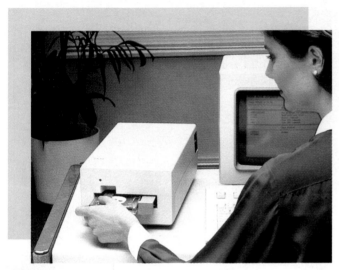

Figure 6-17
Backup tape cartridge and drive.

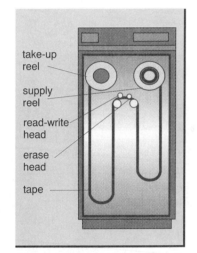

take-up
reel

supply
reel

read-write
head

erase
head

tape

Figure 6-18
Data is recorded on magnetic tape on tape reels.

Magnetic Tape Streamers   Many microcomputer users with hard disks use a device called a **magnetic tape streamer** or a **backup tape cartridge unit**. (*See Figure 6-17.*) This machine enables you to duplicate or make a backup of the data on your hard disk onto a tape cartridge. The capacities of such tape cartridges vary from 10 to 60 megabytes. Advanced forms of backup technology known as **digital audiotape (DAT) drives,** which use 2- by 3-inch cassettes, store 1.3 gigabytes or more. The copying from hard disk varies in speed from 1 to 5 megabytes per minute. On a 20-megabyte hard disk, it might take you only 5 to 20 minutes to back up the entire contents. Compare this to, say, 2 hours with 48 diskettes. If later your internal hard disk fails, you can have it repaired (or get another hard disk). You can restore all your lost data and programs in a matter of minutes.

Magnetic Tape Reels   The kind of cassette tapes you get for an audiotape recorder are only about 200 feet long. They record 200 characters to the inch. A reel of magnetic tape used with minicomputer and mainframe systems, by contrast, is ½ inch wide and ½ mile long. It stores 1600 to 6400 characters to the inch. Such tapes are run on **magnetic tape drives** or **magnetic tape units**. (*See Figure 6-18.*) You may never actually see these devices yourself. However, as a microcomputer user sharing storage devices with other users, you may have access to them through a minicomputer or mainframe.

A magnetic tape drive consists of two reels—a **supply reel** and a **take-up reel.** It also has a read-write head and an erase head. The read-write head reads (retrieves) magnetized areas on the tape, which represent data. It then converts them to electrical signals and sends them to the CPU. The read-write head also writes (records) data from the CPU onto the tape. During the writing process, any previous data on the tape is automatically erased.

Magnetic tape moves through the drive in a "start and stop" manner. The reason for this is that once a record is read, the CPU and program must process it. If the tape continues moving, the next record might pass the read-write head before the CPU and program were ready for it. Thus, the tape must pause after a record has been read and start when the computer is ready for the next record.

However, allowance must be made for the tape to "get up to speed" when it starts again. Otherwise, the data will be distorted when it is read. Consequently, some ½-inch gaps must be built into the tape between the records. These gaps give the tape enough time to gain the proper speed. These gaps are called **interrecord gaps** (**IRGs**). (*See Figure 6-19.*)

This ½ inch of space between records could add up to a lot of unused tape. It might otherwise be used for storing data. Consequently, records are often grouped together as **blocks.** These blocks are called **physical records.** The term "physical records" is used to distinguish them from the actual records, which are called **logical records.** The blocks are then separated from each other by a ½-inch gap called an **interblock gap** (**IBG**). (*See Figure 6-20.*)

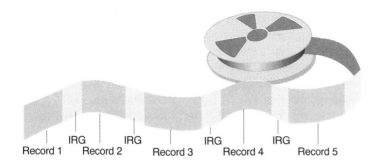

Figure 6-19
Magnetic tape with interrecord gaps.

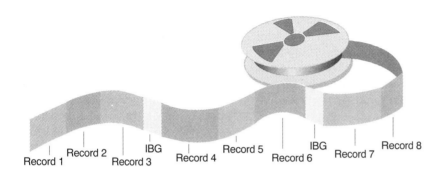

Figure 6-20
Magnetic tape with interblock gaps.

Companies often store reels of magnetic tape in **tape libraries.** This demonstrates an important advantage of tapes: a lot of data can be stored in a compact space. In addition, tapes have a feature that helps keep them reasonably secure. Before a tape can be used, a **write-enable ring** must be placed over the hub as it is mounted on the tape drive. This prevents tapes from accidentally being written over.

A Look at the Future

Floppy Disks and Hard Disks Will Continue to Increase in Capacity. Disk Arrays and Data-Compression Technology Will Also Add Storage Room. Image Processing Promises to Be a Growing Field.

The principal trend now in evidence—namely, that of packing more and more data in less and less space—will doubtless continue. For instance, 3½-inch floppy disks, which are surpassing 5¼-inch disks as the dominant storage format, can now store 2.88 megabytes of information. Other disks may become available that will store 20 megabytes or more—some say *100* megabytes or more.

Hard disks will also have greater capacity. Whereas a conventional optical disk can hold perhaps 600 megabytes (about 270,000 typewritten pages), a 12-inch optical disk being developed will hold a terabyte. That's nearly 450 million pages, about 18,000 *Encyclopedia Britannicas.*

In another move to improve storage efficiency, companies are connecting groups of small, inexpensive hard-disk drives together in a form known as *disk arrays.* These can outperform single drives of comparable capacity.

Some new storage developments are becoming particularly important for storing pictures as well as text. Presently, conventional optical disks can store large amounts of text, but pictures take up a great deal of space. One 8-by-10-inch color photo, for instance, consumes about 25 megabytes of data—about half the capacity of a typical microcomputer hard disk. But even now the makers of *Compton's Encyclopedia* are marketing all 26 volumes on a single CD-ROM disk—including 15,000 pictures. In the future, such giant storage capacity will permit the development of *multimedia*. This is a way in which computers (as we discuss in Chapter 12) can combine all sorts of media, such as video, graphics, and audio.

A particularly important development in coming years is a whole field known as *image processing*. In word processing, just the text of documents is stored. In image processing, a kind of "electronic snapshot" of a document is taken with a device resembling a copying machine. The image is then transformed into computer code and may be stored on an optical disk. Imaging technology is now used by credit card companies to make paper-based reproductions of credit card receipts. Image processing promises to be a burgeoning field in the years ahead.

On the horizon is *holographic storage*, in which information is stored on holograms, those shimmering three-dimensional images seen on credit cards. Holographic systems would store data equivalent to thousands of books in three dimensions inside a cube of special material about the size of a sugar cube, yet retrievable in 1 second. Another area being explored is *light-sensitive bacteria protein*, in which data is stored in three dimensions in a tiny block of molecules of a protein isolated from a bacteria found in salt marshes.

Review Questions

1. Explain the difference between direct access storage and sequential access storage. Which is more apt to be identified with magnetic disk and which with magnetic tape?
2. Describe the five levels of data organization, beginning with character (byte).
3. What are four kinds of secondary storage?
4. What is meant by the terms volatile and nonvolatile?
5. What are the various names given to floppy disks?
6. Describe how a floppy-disk drive works.
7. What is a seek operation? a search operation?
8. What are the three types of 3½-inch floppy disks? What are their capacities?
9. What are tracks? sectors?
10. State the three primary rules about taking care of floppy disks.
11. How does an internal hard-disk drive work?
12. What is the advantage of hard disks over floppy disks?
13. Explain what a hard-disk cartridge is.
14. How are hard-disk packs for mainframe computers different from hard disks for microcomputers?
15. Identify the following: access time; seek time; head switching time; rotational delay time; data transfer time.
16. Explain how data compression works.
17. What is so disastrous about a head crash?
18. Explain what an optical disk is.

19. What is the purpose of a tape streamer or tape backup unit for microcomputers?

20. How does a magnetic tape drive work?

21. Distinguish between an interrecord gap and an interblock gap.

22. Describe the difference between physical records and logical records.

Discussion Questions and Projects

1. *What type of storage system?* Suppose for the past few years you have owned a computer with two floppy disk drives but no hard disk drive. Your several file boxes of floppy disks include all kinds of research data comprising a college career. This is research that may be quite valuable later in college or in your career. You also have several disks containing important information about non-college matters—for example, your family history, your music collection, your personal finances.

Suppose that you're beginning to lose control and are no longer able to find things when you want them. A hard-disk drive would help. However, if a hard-disk drive suffers a head crash or other accident, you could lose all the programs and data on it. What kind of storage system should you get—hard disk, hard disk and magnetic tape backup (tape streamer), hard-disk cartridge, data-compression software and hardware, or optical disk?

2. *Looking for the right CD-ROM:* Perhaps you have had the difficulty of dealing with competing standards of media for something you want. Was a film you wanted to see available on Betamax but not on VHS videotape? Did a musical group have songs available on an LP or tape but not CD? Now you face a similar difficulty in evaluating the new storage medium of CD-ROM, for which competing versions exist. To help resolve the confusion, determine:

   a. How the CD-ROMs used for computer storage differ from those used as adjuncts to television sets, such as the CD-1 and CDTV.

   b. How "multimedia" CD-ROMs differ from computer-storage CD-ROMs.

   c. How the CD-ROMs normally associated with desktop computers differ from those used in the small electronic "book" players, such as the Data Discman put out by Sony.

   d. The difference between the CD-ROMs available for Macintosh and those available for IBM and IBM-compatible microcomputers.

Chapter 6   Secondary Storage

Primary storage in microcomputers is **volatile**; some things disappear when the power is turned off. Secondary storage is **nonvolatile**; it stores data and programs even after the power is turned off.

Data Organization	Disk

Data Organization

Access

Two different approaches to secondary storage are:

- **Sequential access storage**—information is stored in sequence (e.g., alphabetically), a characteristic of tape storage.
- **Direct access storage**—information may be stored in any order and accessed directly, a characteristic of disk storage.

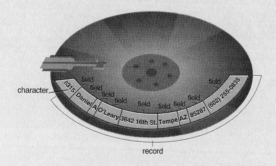

- **Character**—letter, number, special character (e.g., A, 1, %).
- **Field**—set of related characters (e.g., person's last name).
- **Record**—collection of related fields (e.g., name and address).
- **File**—collection of related records (e.g., all driver's licenses issued in one city on one day).
- **Database**—collection of related files (e.g., all driver's licenses issued in one state).

Disk

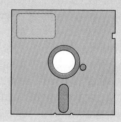

Floppy disks (disks, diskettes) are circular plastic disks. Two principal types are a 5¼-inch and 3½-inch.

Floppy-Disk Capacity	
Description	Bytes
5¼-inch	
Double-sided, double-density	360 KB
Double-sided, high-density	1.2 MB
3½-inch	
Double-sided, double-density	720 KB
Double-sided, high-density	1.44 MB

The Disk Drive

- A floppy disk is inserted through a **drive gate** into a *disk drive,* which has an **access arm** equipped with **read-write heads** that move on the disk (**seek** operation), which is rotated to the proper position (**search** operation).
- The read-write head *reads* (obtains) data or programs from the disk and sends it to the CPU or *writes* (transfers) data from the CPU to the disk.

Parts of Floppy Disk

- Data is recorded on a disk's **tracks** (rings) and **sectors** (sections). In **soft-sectored disks,** tracks and sectors must be adapted to particular microcomputers by *formatting (initializing).*

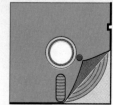

- A disk is protected by the **jacket** (liner), paper envelope, and **write-protect notch** (covered by tab or shutter).

Four Most Widely Used Secondary Storage Media

• Floppy disk
• Hard disk
• Optical disk
• Magnetic tape

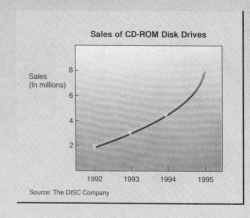

Sales of CD-ROM Disk Drives

Sales (In millions)

Source: The DISC Company

Hard Disk

A *hard disk* is an enclosed disk drive that contains one or more metallic disks. Enclosing the disk in a sealed container prevents material entering that causes a **head crash,** failure of the disk and destruction of data on it. Hard disks come in three forms:

Internal Hard Disk

An **internal hard disk** has one or more metallic platters sealed inside a container. A motor rotates the disk, and an access arm reads and writes data to and from the hard disk. Hard disks have far more capacity than a floppy disk does (e.g., a 60 MB hard disk = 168 floppy disks).

Hard-Disk Cartridges

Hard-disk cartridges can be removed when they are filled or are to be transported.

Hard-Disk Packs

Mini- and mainframe computers use **hard-disk packs,** which are hard disks consisting of several platters in a stack, accessible by multiple access arms and read-write heads.

Optical Disks

Optical Disks

An **optical disk** is a metallic disk that, using a laser beam for reading and writing, may hold more than 700 MB. Three kinds of optical disks are:

• **CD-ROM** (compact disk–read-only memory)—cannot be written on or erased by user **(read-only).**

• **WORM** (write once, read many)—can be written to one time, after which it cannot be erased by users but can be read many times without deterioration.

• **Erasable optical disks**—can be written on and erased and reused.

Optical Disks	
Technology	**Storage space**
CD-ROM	540 – 748 MB
WORM	122 – 640 MB
Erasable	281 – 320 MB

Data Compression

Entering and existing data is scanned for repeated patterns. These patterns are replaced by tokens.

Magnetic Tape

Magnetic tape storage is mainly used to back up (duplicate) programs and data on disks. Two forms are:

Magnetic Tape Streamers

Magnetic tape streamers **(backup tape cartridge units)** consist of tape cartridges used to back up microcomputer hard disks.

Magnetic Tape Reels

Magnetic tape reels, used to back up mini- and mainframe computer storage, run on **magnetic drives (magnetic tape units).**

• Drives have a **supply reel** and a **take-up reel.**

• Tape moves in "start and stop" manner. Thus, ½-inch **interrecord gaps (IRGs)** may be present to give computer take-up room.

• Records on tape may be grouped as **blocks,** with ½-inch **interblock gaps (IBGs)** between them.

• Tapes are stored in **tape libraries.** For security, before a tape can be used, a **write-enable ring** must be put over the hub.

115

7

Communications and Connectivity

A familiar instrument—the telephone—has extended our uses for the microcomputer enormously. With the telephone or other kind of communications equipment, you can connect your microcomputer to other people and other, larger computers. As we've mentioned earlier, this *connectivity* puts the power of a mainframe on your desk. The result is increased productivity—for you as an individual and for the groups and organizations of which you are a member. Connectivity has become particularly important in business, where individuals now find themselves connected in networks to other individuals and departments.

Imagine: You are a real estate salesperson, and the telephone in your car rings. It is a client, who is on the phone in his car across town. He asks you about a certain property, and you agree to meet him there. After you go back to look at the property, you connect your laptop computer to your car phone. You then dial the multiple listing service and get information on the property. This is an example of the use of communications to expand computer capabilities.

In Chapter 2, you learned about communications software. In this chapter, you will learn about communications systems. **Data communications systems** are the electronic systems that transmit data over communications lines from one location to another. You might use data communications through your microcomputer to send information to a friend using another computer. You might work for an organization whose large computer system is spread all over a building or even all over the country. That is, all the parts—input and output units, processor, and storage devices—are in different places and linked by communications. Or you might use *telecommunications* lines—telephone lines—to tap into information located in an outside data bank. You could then transmit it to your microcomputer for your own reworking and analysis.

Data communications is now considered essential in business. As we will see, an important part of communications is the *network,* a system connecting two or more computers. A popular form of network is the *local area network (LAN),* in which computers are connected together within a limited area, such as within the same building. In one survey, 82 percent of the respondents said there was a local area network within their company or organization. There are many occasions when you and coworkers need a network to gain access to one another's information. Such information may be on sales, customers, prices, schedules, or products. The list is nearly endless.

Communications and Connectivity

With Communications Capability, Microcomputer Users Can Transmit and Receive Data and Gain Access to Electronic Information Resources.

You may have a desktop microcomputer next to a telephone. You may (or may someday) have a laptop microcomputer and a cellular phone in your car. Or you may have a microcomputer that is directly connected to other computers without telephone lines at all. Whatever the case, communications systems present many opportunities for transmitting and receiving information, giving you access to many resources. This brings up the important revolution represented by this chapter, that of connectivity.

Connectivity means that you can connect your microcomputer by telephone or other telecommunications lines to other computers and sources of information anywhere. With this connection, you are linked to the world of larger computers. This includes minicomputers and mainframes and their large storage devices, such as disk packs, and their enormous volumes of information. Thus, computer competence becomes a matter of knowing not only about microcomputers. You should also know something about larger computer systems and their information resources. We describe these resources in greater detail in the next two chapters.

Let us consider the options that connectivity makes available to you. These include *fax machines, electronic bulletin boards, electronic mail, voice-messaging systems, shared resources, databases, commercial services,* and *groupware. (See Figure 7-1.)*

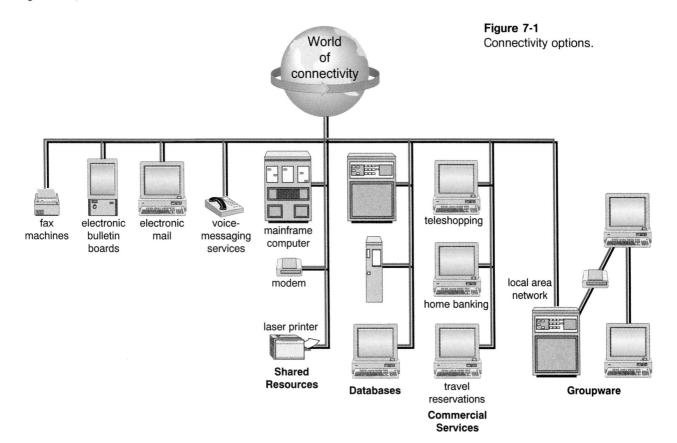

Figure 7-1
Connectivity options.

Figure 7-2
A fax machine.

Fax Machines   As we stated in Chapter 5, *fax machines*—facsimile transmission machines—are now extremely popular in offices. (*See Figure 7-2.*) Indeed, they have become essential machines in many workplaces. These devices, you'll recall, scan the image of a document. They convert the image to signals that can be sent over a telephone line to a receiving machine. This machine prints the image out on paper. Microcomputers, using virtual fax—built-in facsimile circuit boards—also can be used to send and receive fax messages. Fax circuit boards require scanners to read in hardcopy documents because the material must be put into primary storage before it can be transmitted.

Sending a document by fax is certainly faster—it arrives immediately—than any delivery service. It also is often cheaper than overnight delivery, unless you're sending more than 50 pages of a document. Almost every fax machine can exchange messages with every other fax machine, and all you need is the receiving machine's phone number. It can transmit photographs and other artwork, as well as text in various typefaces.

If you are in the business of meeting deadlines—as most people are—a fax machine can be invaluable. Construction engineers can get cost estimates to major contractors. Lawyers can get contracts to other lawyers. Advertising people can get prospective ad layouts to their clients. Just as important, because people often respond better to pictures than to text, fax can get a picture to them quickly.

Electronic Bulletin Boards   This is an activity you can begin to discover yourself if you have access to a microcomputer and the necessary telephone links. **Electronic bulletin boards** are like public bulletin boards, usually open to everybody. The difference is that you need a microcomputer, a telephone connection, and the board's telephone number. Such bulletin boards have been popular with microcomputer hobbyists and enthusiasts for many years. They are rapidly gaining favor with other people, too.

Bulletin boards exist for almost any subject. Many are concerned with new developments and problems related to particular brands of microcomputers. Others have to do with hobbies, such as rock music, science fiction, or genealogy. Still others serve special interests, such as political causes, or professional groups, such as lawyers. Finally, some companies offer bulletin boards as a means by which customers can get advice from other customers. They can also get advice from the company itself regarding a particular service or product.

Electronic Mail Also called **E-mail, electronic mail** resembles bulletin boards. (*See Figure 7-3.*) But often it uses a special communications line rather than a telephone line. In addition, electronic mail offers confidentiality. A **password**—a special sequence of numbers or letters that limits access—is required in order to get into the "mailbox." The mailbox is simply a file stored on a computer system.

To send a message, you dial the special number, specify the password and number of the mailbox, and type in the message. You can also put the same message in several mailboxes at the same time. To gain access to your own mailbox, you dial the number of the electronic mail system and type in your password. You can look through the list of file names and transmission times of the messages. You then transfer to your own computer the messages you want to keep.

Electronic mail is used within companies to help employees exchange memos, set up meetings, and the like. It may also be used between companies. Sometimes outside electronic bulletin board services are used for these business purposes.

Voice-Messaging Systems **Voice-messaging systems** are computer systems linked to telephones that convert the human voice into digital bits. They resemble conventional answering machines and also resemble electronic mail systems. However, they can receive large numbers of incoming calls and route them to the appropriate "voice mailboxes." They can deliver the same message to many people. They allow callers to leave "voice mail"—recorded voice messages. They can forward calls to your home or hotel, if you wish. When you check for your messages, you can speed through them or slow them down. You can dictate replies into the phone, and the system will send them out.

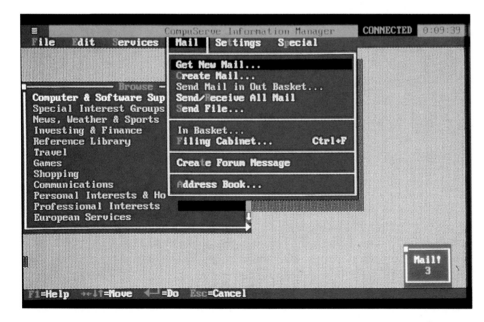

Figure 7-3
Electronic mail.

Sharing Resources An extremely important option that connectivity gives microcomputer users is that it lets them share expensive resources. We have mentioned many of these: laser printers, chain printers, disk packs, and magnetic tape storage. Only in rare instances would a single microcomputer user need the use of, say, a disk pack. However, several microcomputers linked in a network make this option not only feasible but in many cases even essential.

Communications networks also permit microcomputer users to share workstations, minicomputers, and mainframes. This is why we have stressed that it's important to know what these machines are. Finally, connectivity makes incompatible microcomputers compatible. For a long time, corporations were baffled about how to make Macintoshes and IBM PCs work with each other. Now, however, the use of local area networks to link Macintoshes and IBM microcomputers is a reality, and more and more such networks are coming into use.

Databases As we saw in Chapter 2, with a microcomputer you can have your own personal database. An example of such a database might be a collection of names and addresses. A *database,* as we mentioned, is a collection of integrated data. By "integrated," we mean the data consists of logically related files and records.

Your personal database might consist of data that only you use. However, it may also be data you share with others. The data might be stored on your microcomputer's hard disk. Or it might be located somewhere else. That is, you might use a shared database, such as one a company might provide its employees so they can share information. This could be information stored on disk packs and accessible from the company's mainframe. You could gain access by using your microcomputer linked to your telephone and **down-loading** selected data. That is, you could transfer the data from the larger computer to your microcomputer. Then you could process and manipulate the data as you chose. The reverse is **uploading**—transferring from your microcomputer to a mainframe or minicomputer.

Commercial Services Several businesses offer services specifically for microcomputer users. For example:

- *Teleshopping:* You dial into a database listing prices and descriptions of products such as appliances and clothes. You then order what you want and charge the purchase to a credit card number. The merchandise is delivered later by a package delivery service.

- *Home banking:* If you arrange it with your bank, you may be able to use your microcomputer to pay some bills (such as to big department stores and utilities). You can also make loan payments and transfer money between accounts.

- *Investing:* You can get access to current prices of stocks and bonds and enter buy and sell orders.

- *Travel reservations:* Just like a travel agent, you can get information on airline schedules and fares. You can also order tickets, charging the purchase to your credit card.

Groupware As more and more networks become established, a new kind of software may become popular. Known as **groupware** or *collaboration technology,* this software allows two or more people on a network to work on the same information at the same time. Perhaps the best-known groupware is Lotus Notes, which combines a database with electronic-mail and word processing features. (*See Figure 7-4.*)

With older technology, two people on a network working on the same document must take turns sending it back and forth. With groupware, people can work on the

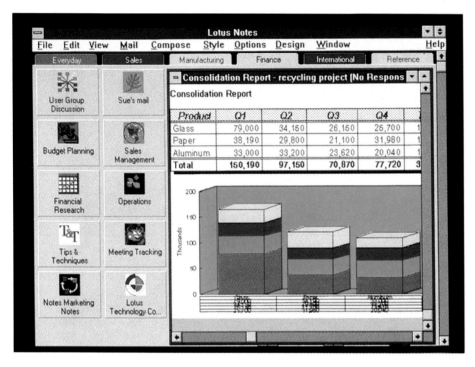

Figure 7-4
Groupware: Lotus Notes software enables network users to share information.

same document at the same time. For instance, people in a group could sit at a table in a meeting room, each person with a microcomputer. They could all watch a single large screen on the wall. They could make tentative additions and deletions on the document until everyone agrees.

Groupware can also be used to send forms throughout a corporation. The computer system can automatically remind participants of deadlines and track progress. Other groupware can be used to enable a contractor to keep track of its suppliers, who receive and acknowledge orders electronically.

User Interface

Microcomputers Require Modems to Send and Receive Messages Over Telephone Lines.

A great deal of computer communications is over telephone lines. However, because the telephone was originally designed for voice transmission, telephones typically send and receive **analog signals**. (*See Figure 7-5.*) Computers, in contrast, send and receive **digital signals.** These represent the presence or absence of an electronic pulse—the on/off binary signals we mentioned in Chapter 4. To convert the digital signals of your microcomputer to analog and vice versa, you need a modem.

Modems and Communications Speeds The word *modem* is short for "*mo*dulator-*dem*odulator." **Modulation** is the name of the process of converting from digital to analog. **Demodulation** is the process of converting from analog to digital. The modem enables digital microcomputers to communicate across analog telephone lines. Both voice communications and data communications can be carried over the same telephone line.

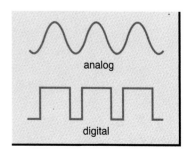

Figure 7-5
Analog versus digital signals.

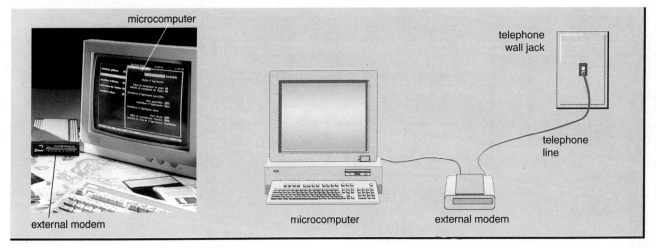

Figure 7-6
An external direct-connect modem.

The speed with which modems transmit data varies. Communications speed is often measured in **baud rate**. Baud rate represents the number of changes in the electrical state in the line per second. Unfortunately, this measure can be misleading. At low speeds, baud rate is equivalent to *bits per second* (*bps*). However, at higher speeds, baud rate is not equal to bits per second. For this reason, most communications professionals prefer to measure modem speed in bits per second.

The most popular microcomputer speeds are 1200, 2400, and 9600 bps. The higher the speed, the faster you can transmit a document—and therefore the cheaper your line costs. For example, transmitting a 10-page single-spaced report could take 20 minutes at 300 bps. It would take 5 minutes at 1200 bps and 2½ minutes at 2400 bps.

Types of Modems   The two types of modems are external and internal.

▪ The **external modem** stands apart from the computer and is connected by a cable to the computer's serial port. Another cable connects the modem to the telephone wall jack. (*See Figure 7-6.*) Some modems weigh as little as 3 ounces, making them practical for use with portable computers.

▪ The **internal modem** consists of a plug-in circuit board inside the system unit. (*See Figure 7-7.*)

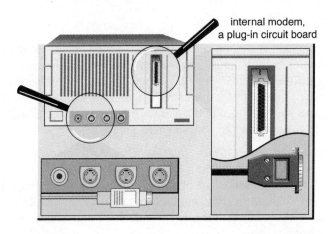

Figure 7-7
An internal modem, viewed as a plug in the back of a microcomputer.

Not all computer communications must be converted from digital to analog and back. Computer systems connected by coaxial or fiber-optic cables can transmit digital data directly through these channels.

Communications Channels

Data May Flow Through Five Kinds of Communications Channels: Telephone Lines, Coaxial Cable, Fiber-Optic Cable, Microwave, and Satellite.

The two ways of connecting microcomputers with each other and with other equipment are through the cable and through the air. Specifically, five kinds of technology are used to transmit data. These are telephone lines (twisted pair), coaxial cable, fiber-optic cable, microwave, and satellite. The diameters and transmission capacities of the three kinds of cable are compared in the illustration below. (*See Figure 7-8.*)

Telephone Lines   Most telephone lines that you see strung on poles consist of cables made up of hundreds of copper wires, called **twisted pairs.** A single twisted pair culminates in a wall jack into which you can plug your phone. Telephone lines have been the standard transmission medium for years for both voice and data. However, they are now being phased out by more technically advanced and reliable media.

Coaxial Cable   **Coaxial cable,** a high-frequency transmission cable, replaces the multiple wires of telephone lines with a single solid copper core. In terms of number of telephone connections, a coaxial cable has 80 times the transmission capacity of twisted pair. Coaxial cable is often used to link parts of a computer system in one building.

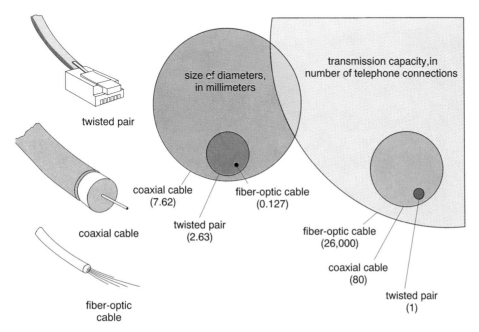

Figure 7-8
Comparing cable size and capacity: twisted pair, coaxial cable, and fiber-optic cable.

Fiber-Optic Cable In **fiber-optic cable,** data is transmitted as pulses of light through tubes of glass. In terms of number of telephone connections, fiber-optic cable has 26,000 times the transmission capacity of twisted pair. (*See Figure 7-8.*) However, it is significantly smaller. Indeed, a fiber-optic tube can be half the diameter of a human hair. Although limited in the distance they can carry information, fiber-optic cables have several advantages. Such cables are immune to electronic interference, which makes them more secure. They are also lighter and less expensive than coaxial cable and are more reliable at transmitting data. They transmit information using beams of light at light speeds instead of pulses of electricity, making them far faster than copper cable. Fiber-optic cable is rapidly replacing twisted-pair telephone lines.

Microwave In this communications channel the medium is not a solid substance but rather the air itself. **Microwaves** are high-frequency radio waves that travel in straight lines through the air. Because the waves cannot bend with the curvature of the earth, they can be transmitted only over short distances. Thus, microwave is a good medium for sending data between buildings in a city or on a large college campus. For longer distances, the waves must be relayed by means of "dishes," or antennas. These can be installed on towers, high buildings, and mountaintops, for example. (*See Figure 7-9.*)

Satellites Orbiting about 22,000 miles above the earth, **satellites** are also used as microwave relay stations. Many of these are offered by Intelsat, the *In*ternational *Tele*communications *Sat*ellite Consortium, which is owned by 114 governments and forms a worldwide communications system. Satellites rotate at a precise point and speed above the earth. This makes them appear stationary so that they can amplify and relay microwave signals from one transmitter on the ground to another. (*See Figure 7-10.*) Thus, satellites can be used to send large volumes of data. Their only drawback is that bad weather can sometimes interrupt the flow of data.

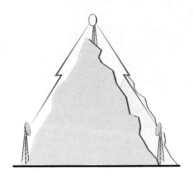

Figure 7-9
Microwave transmission.

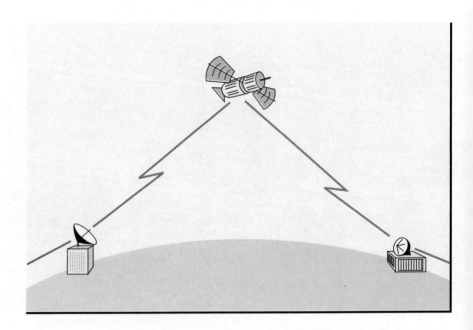

Figure 7-10
Satellite relaying microwave signals from earth.

Data Transmission

Several Technical Matters Affect Data Communications. They Are Bandwidth, Serial Versus Parallel Transmission, Direction of Flow, Modes of Transmission, and Protocols.

Several factors affect how data is transmitted. They include speed or bandwidth, serial or parallel transmission, direction of data flow, modes of transmitting data, and protocols.

Bandwidth   The different communications channels have different data transmission speeds. This bits-per-second transmission capability of a channel is called its **bandwidth.** Bandwidth may be of three types:

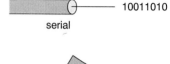

serial

- *Voiceband:* **Voiceband** is the bandwidth of a standard telephone line and used often for microcomputer transmission; the bps is 110–9600 bps.

- *Medium band:* The **medium band** is the bandwidth of special leased lines used mainly with minicomputers and mainframe computers; the bps is 9600–256,000.

- *Broadband:* The **broadband** is the bandwidth that includes microwave, satellite, coaxial cable, and fiber-optic channels. It is used for very high-speed computers whose processors communicate directly with each other. It is in the range of 256,000–1 million bps.

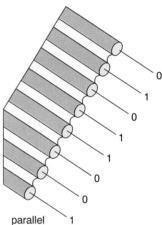

parallel

Serial and Parallel Transmission   Data travels in two ways: serially and in parallel. (*See Figure 7-11.*)

- In **serial data transmission,** bits flow in a series or continuous stream, like cars crossing a one-lane bridge. Each bit travels on its own communications line. Serial transmission is the way most data is sent over telephone lines. Thus, the plug-in board making up the serial connector in a microcomputer's modem is usually called a *serial port.* More technical names for the serial port are **RS-232C connector** and **asynchronous communications port.**

Figure 7-11
Serial versus parallel kinds of transmission.

- With **parallel data transmission,** bits flow through separate lines simultaneously. In other words, they resemble cars moving together at the same speed on a multilane freeway. Parallel transmission is not used for communications over telephone lines. It is, however, a standard method of sending data from a computer's CPU to a printer.

Direction of Data Transmission   There are three directions or modes of data flow in a data communications system. (*See Figure 7-12, next page.*)

- **Simplex communication** resembles the movement of cars on a one-way street. Data travels in one direction only. It is not frequently used in data communications systems today. One instance in which it is used may be in point-of-sale (POS) terminals in which data is being entered only.

- In **half-duplex communication,** data flows in both directions, but not simultaneously. That is, data flows in only one direction at any one time. This resembles traffic on a one-lane bridge. Half-duplex is very common and is frequently used

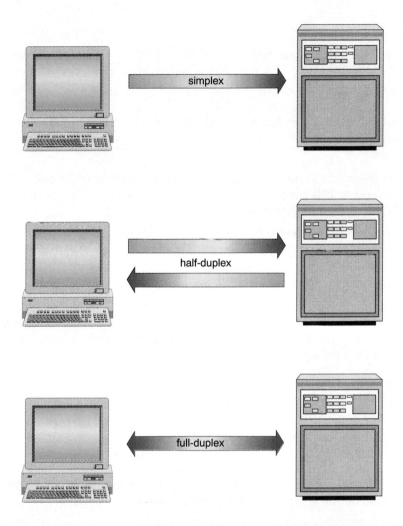

Figure 7-12
Simplex, half-duplex, and
full-duplex communication.

for linking microcomputers by telephone lines to other microcomputers, mini-computers, and mainframes. Thus, when you dial into an electronic bulletin board through your microcomputer, you may well be using half-duplex communication.

■ In **full-duplex communication,** data is transmitted back and forth at the same time, like traffic on a two-way street. It is clearly the fastest and most efficient form of two-way communication. However, it requires special equipment and is used primarily for mainframe communications. An example might be the weekly sales figures that a supermarket or regional office sends to its corporate headquarters in another state.

Modes of Transmitting Data   Data may be sent by asynchronous or synchronous transmission. (*See Figure 7-13.*)

■ In **asynchronous transmission,** the method used with most microcomputers, data is sent and received one byte at a time. Asynchronous transmission is often used for terminals with slow speeds. Its advantage is that the data can be transmitted whenever convenient for the sender.

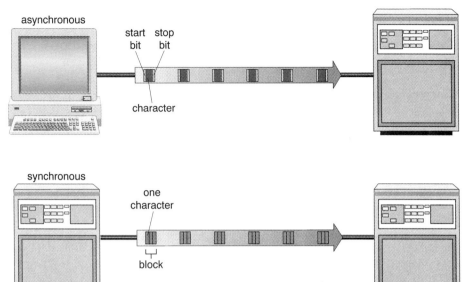

Figure 7-13
Asynchronous and synchronous communication.

■ **Synchronous transmission** is used to transfer great quantities of information by sending several bytes or a block at a time. For the data transmission to take place, the sending and receiving of the blocks of bytes must occur at carefully timed intervals. Thus, the system requires a synchronized clock. Although the equipment for this type of transmission is much more expensive, data is transmitted faster, and so transmission is often cheaper.

Protocols   For data transmission to be successful, sender and receiver must follow a set of communication rules for the exchange of information. These rules for exchanging data between computers are known as the line **protocol.** A communications software package such as Crosstalk will help define the protocol, such as speeds and modes, for connecting with another microcomputer.

When different types of microcomputers are connected in a network, the protocols can become very complex. Obviously, for the connections to work, these network protocols must adhere to certain standards. The first commercially available set of standards was IBM's Systems Network Architecture (SNA). This works for IBM's own equipment, but other machines won't necessarily communicate with them. The International Standards Organization has defined a set of communications protocols called the Open Systems Interconnection (OSI). The purpose of the OSI model is to identify functions provided by any network, whether it be NetWare for Macintosh or LAN Manager for IBM. The OSI model separates each network's functions into seven "layers" of protocols, or communication rules. (*See Figure 7-14.*) When two network systems communicate, their corresponding layers may exchange data. This assumes that the microcomputers and other equipment on each network have implemented the same functions and interfaces.

The OSI Model

Layer	Protocol	Function
7	Application:	Controls user inputs and provides network services, including file transfer.
6	Presentation:	Formats data sent from one computer so that it can be displayed and used on another.
5	Sessions:	Begin, sustain, and end connections between computers.
4	Transport:	Controls and coordinates data between sending and receiving computers.
3	Network:	Determines path of data through network and controls its transmission.
2	Data link:	Groups data into blocks, sends blocks, and checks for transmission errors.
1	Physical:	Controls voltage, electrical signals, connections, and switches.

Figure 7-14
The OSI model.

Network Configurations

A Computer Network May Have One of Four Basic Configurations: Star, Bus, Ring, or Hierarchical.

Communications channels can be connected in different arrangements, or *networks,* to suit different users' needs. A *computer network* is a communications system connecting two or more computers. This arrangement allows users to exchange information and share resources (software and hardware). A network may consist only of microcomputers, or it may integrate microcomputers (or other terminals) with larger computers. Networks may be simple or complex, self-contained or dispersed over a large geographical area.

The four principal configurations of networks are *star, bus, ring,* and *hierarchical.*

Star Network   In a **star network,** a number of small computers or peripheral devices are linked to a central unit. (*See Figure 7-15.*) This central unit may be a *host computer* or a *file server.* You may encounter these terms frequently.

- A *host computer* is a large centralized computer, usually a minicomputer or a mainframe.

- A **file server** is a large-capacity hard-disk storage device. It stores data and programs.

All communications pass through this central unit. Control is maintained by **polling.** That is, each connecting device is asked ("polled") whether it has a message to send. Each device is then in turn allowed to send its message.

One particular advantage of the star form of network is that it can be used to provide a **time-sharing system.** That is, several users can share resources ("time") on a central computer. The star is a common arrangement for linking several microcomputers to a mainframe that allows access to an organization's database.

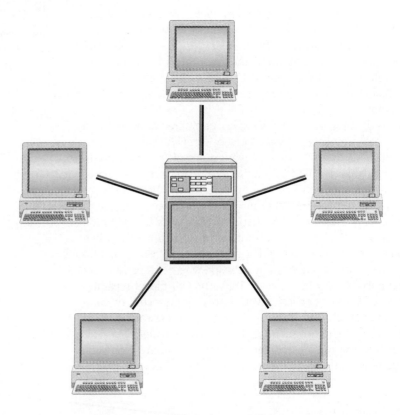

Figure 7-15
Star network.

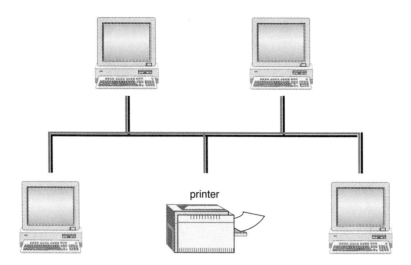

Figure 7-16
Bus network.

Bus Network In a **bus network,** each device in the network handles its own communications control. There is no host computer or file server. All communications travel along a common connecting cable called a **bus**. (*See Figure 7-16.*) As the information passes along the bus, it is examined by each device to see if the information is intended for it.

The bus network is frequently used when only a few microcomputers are to be linked together. This arrangement is common in systems for electronic mail or for sharing data stored on different microcomputers. The bus network is not as efficient as the star network for sharing common resources. (This is because the bus network is not a direct link to the resource.) However, a bus network is less expensive and is in very common use.

Ring Network In a **ring network,** each device is connected to two other devices, forming a ring. (*See Figure 7-17.*) There is no central file server or computer. Messages are passed around the ring until they reach the correct destination. With microcomputers, the ring arrangement is the least frequently used of the four

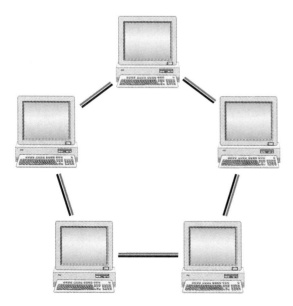

Figure 7-17
Ring network.

networks. However, it often is used to link mainframes, especially over wide geographical areas. These mainframes tend to operate fairly autonomously. They perform most or all of their own processing and only occasionally share data and programs with other mainframes.

A ring network is useful in a decentralized organization because it makes possible a *distributed data processing system.* That is, computers can perform processing tasks at their own dispersed locations. However, they can also share programs, data, and other resources with each other.

Hierarchical Network   The **hierarchical network** consists of several computers linked to a central host computer, just like a star network. However, these other computers are also hosts to other, smaller computers or to peripheral devices. (*See Figure 7-18.*)

Thus, the host at the top of the hierarchy could be a mainframe. The computers below the mainframe could be minicomputers, and those below, microcomputers. The hierarchical network—also called a **hybrid network**—thus allows various computers to share databases, processing power, and different output devices.

A hierarchical network is useful in centralized organizations. For example, different departments within an organization may have individual microcomputers connected to departmental minicomputers. The minicomputers in turn may be connected to the corporation's mainframe, which contains data and programs accessible to all.

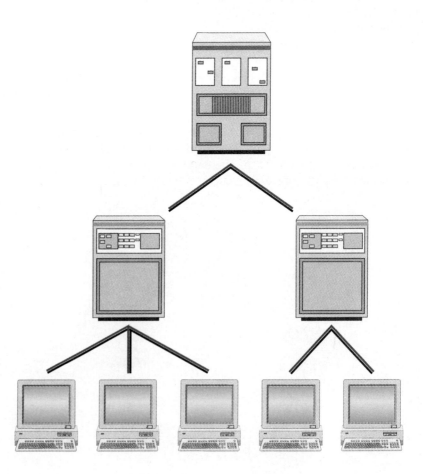

Figure 7-18
Hierarchical network.

Network Types

Communications Networks Differ in Geographical Size. Three Important Types Are LANs, MANs, and WANs.

Clearly different types of channel—cable or air—allow different kinds of networks to be formed. Telephone lines, for instance, may connect communications equipment within the same building. In fact, many new buildings—called *"smart buildings"*—have coaxial or fiber-optic cable installed inside the walls. This makes it easy to form communications networks.

Networks may also be citywide and even international, using both cable and air connections. Here let us distinguish among three types: *local area networks, metropolitan area networks,* and *wide area networks.*

Local Area Networks   Networks with computers and peripheral devices in close physical proximity—within the same building, for instance—are called **local area networks (LANs).** Linked by cable—telephone, coaxial, or fiber-optic—LANs often use a bus form of organization.

Our illustration below shows an example of a LAN. (*See Figure 7-19.*) This typical arrangement has two benefits. People can share different equipment, which lowers the cost of equipment. For instance, here the four microcomputers share the laser printer

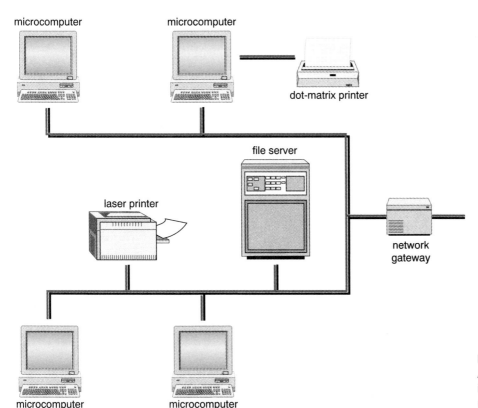

Figure 7-19
A local area network that includes a file server and network gateway.

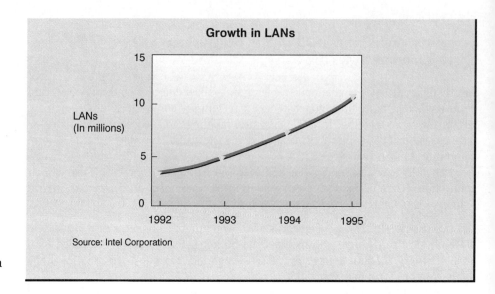

Figure 7-20
Worldwide growth in local area networks.

Figure 7-21
Example of a wide area network.

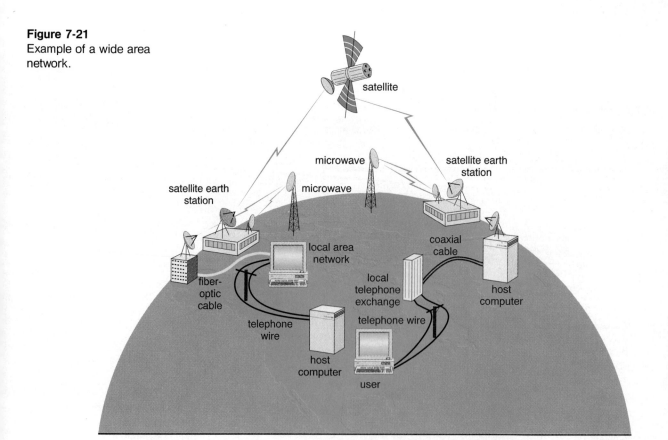

and the file server, which are expensive pieces of hardware. (Individual microcomputers many times also have their own less expensive printers, such as the dot-matrix printer shown in our illustration.) Other equipment may also be added to the LAN— for instance, mini- or mainframe computers or optical-disk storage devices.

Note that the LAN shown in our illustration also features a **network gateway.** A LAN may be linked to other LANs or to larger networks in this manner. With the gateway, one LAN may be connected to the LAN of another office group or to others in the wider world.

Experts predict great growth of microcomputer LANs. (*See Figure 7-20.*)

Metropolitan Area Networks   The next step up from the LAN might be the **MAN**—the **metropolitan area network.** Such networks have been around for some time as links between office buildings in a city. The latest innovation, however, is the *cellular phone system,* which permits the widespread use of car phones and portable phones.

Wide Area Networks   **Wide area networks (WANs)** are countrywide and worldwide networks. Among other kinds of channels, they use microwave relays and satellites to reach users over long distances—for example, from Los Angeles to Paris. (*See Figure 7-21.*) In the United States, some important WANs are Tymnet, Telenet, and Uninet.

The difference between a LAN and a WAN is the geographical range. Both may have various combinations of hardware, such as microcomputers, minicomputers, mainframes, and various peripheral devices.

A Look at the Future

New Developments in Hardware, the Telephone System, and Radio Networks Suggest New Trends: Fewer "Standalone Computers," the Era of the Portable Office, and Downsized Applications.

The next decade will see phenomenal changes in the area of communications. Consider just some improvements in hardware. *Fax machines* are no fad. It is expected that the number installed in the United States will jump to about 30 million by the end of the century. *File servers* have been introduced for microcomputers, making them more useful in networks. These file servers have a much greater storage capacity and can get access to data more quickly than ordinary desktop computers can. *Modems* will also improve, becoming easier to use and faster at sending data. *Fiber-optic cables* will become cheaper to install, opening up more and faster communication lines. *Cellular phones* are providing mobile phone service in more parts of the nation, enabling people to do computer and fax communications directly from modems in their cars. *Videophones,* or telephones with videoscreens, may soon become a practical reality.

One of the most important developments will be the expansion of the *Integrated Services Digital Network (ISDN).* In use in the United States since 1988, ISDN consists of a set of technologies and international-exchange standards that will make today's telephone system completely digital. It is estimated there are 4 million digital phone lines in the United States, likely to increase to 30 million by the year 2000. This opens up the possibility of a worldwide computer network. At that point, modems could be replaced by so-called *terminal adapters,* linking computers to the telephone network and enabling the sending of data at phenomenal speeds. ISDN also allows everything to be transmitted at once: not only data and fax but also voice and video information.

Already, however, computer networks are moving away from telephone lines. IBM and Motorola have developed a nationwide *radio network* that allows users of hand-held computers to communicate from almost anywhere. This would allow people working in the field, such as real estate brokers, package-delivery workers, and police officers, to easily tie into a central computer. Indeed, the developers think this technology might well supplant cellular phone networks.

What do all these trends suggest? First, the "standalone" computer—the type that is not connected to any network—will in the 1990s become mostly a thing of the past. Second, we have arrived at the era of the *portable office.* Hooking a portable computer or fax machine to a network while one is traveling makes one more efficient. Third, we are clearly at the point of so-called *downsized applications.* That is, more and more applications that were once available only on mainframes and minicomputers are now possible on network-linked microcomputers.

Review Questions

1. Define the term *data communications systems.*
2. What are electronic bulletin boards?
3. Describe how electronic mail differs from electronic bulletin boards.
4. What is a database?
5. Describe what is meant by *downloading* information.
6. What is a password?
7. List four kinds of commercial services available for microcomputer users with communications hookups.
8. List the five kinds of communications channels.
9. What is the difference between an analog signal and a digital signal?
10. What is the purpose of a modem?
11. Describe the two types of modems.
12. Distinguish serial from parallel transmission.
13. Describe the difference between simplex, half-duplex, and full-duplex communication.
14. Distinguish synchronous from asynchronous transmission.
15. Discuss the four basic arrangements microcomputer communications networks may take.
16. What is a file server?
17. Describe the concept of time sharing.
18. Describe what a distributed data processing system is.
19. What is a local area network? a wide area network?
20. Describe what groupware does.

Discussion Questions and Projects

1. *Electronic bulletin boards:* Unquestionably there is an area of personal interest to you that is available on an electronic bulletin board. A glance at one local microcomputer publication shows bulletin boards available on such subjects as sports, restaurants, politics, religion, business opportunities, music, mental health, drug recovery, alternative lifestyles, and many other topics.

   What kind of electronic bulletin board would be of interest to you? See if you can find a printed list of bulletin boards in a local microcomputer publication. Or try contacting a users' group for help. Users' groups are clubs or volunteer organizations. Their members meet to help each other solve problems or share interests regarding particular personal computers.

2. *The rise of telecommuting:* The number of U.S. employees working full or part time at home rose from 2.5 million in 1988 to 5.5 million in 1991. The number of telecommuters is expected to jump to 11.2 million in 1995. Discuss what you think would be some of the positive and negative consequences of this trend on:

   a. Employee accessibility
   b. Information security
   c. Productivity
   d. Communication

Chapter 7 Communications and Connectivity

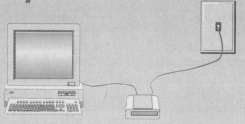

Data communications systems are the electronic systems that transmit data over communications lines from one location to another.

Communications and Connectivity	User Interface	Communications Channels

When a microcomputer is linked by a communications line, it provides the user with *connectivity*—connection to the world of larger computers and secondary storage. Options that connectivity makes available are:

Fax Machines

Fax (facsimile transmission) machines convert images to signals and send them over telephone lines to receiving fax machines.

Electronic Bulletin Boards

Electronic bulletin boards are forums on a variety of subjects available to telephone-linked microcomputer users.

Electronic Mail

Electronic mail systems resemble bulletin boards but are restricted in access. Users must use a **password** (special code) in order to read messages waiting for them.

Voice-Messaging Systems

Voice-messaging systems are telephone-linked computer systems that convert a voice message to digital bits and distribute it to many locations.

Sharing Resources

Microcomputer users may share expensive resources (e.g., laser and chain printers, disk packs, workstations, large computers).

For voice transmission, telephones use **analog signals,** which represent a range of frequencies. Computers send **digital signals,** the presence or absence of an electronic pulse (corresponding to binary 0 or 1).

Modems and Communications Speeds

- A *modem* ("*mo*dulator *demo*dulator") converts digital to analog and vice versa. **Modulation** = digital to analog. **Demodulation** = analog to digital.
- Speeds are 300, 1200, 2400 bits per second.

Types of Modems

- **External modem**—outside system cabinet and connected by cable.
- **Internal modem**—plug-in circuit board inside system unit.

Databases

Individuals may share their databases with others and vice versa. They may **download** (transfer) information from storage devices on large computers.

Commercial Services

Examples of commercial services are *teleshopping* (for ordering discount merchandise), *home banking* (for transferring between accounts and paying bills), *investment services,* and *travel reservations* services.

Groupware

Groupware, or *collaboration technology,* allows users on a network to work on same document at same time.

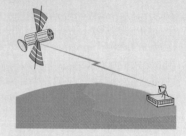

Data may be transmitted by:

Telephone Lines

Most phone lines have consisted of copper wires called **twisted pairs.**

Coaxial Cable

Coaxial cable is high-frequency, solidcore cable.

Fiber-Optic Cable

Fiber-optic cable transmits data as pulses of light through tubes of glass.

Microwave

Microwaves are high-frequency radio waves that travel in a straight line.

Satellites

Satellites act as microwave relay stations rotating above the earth.

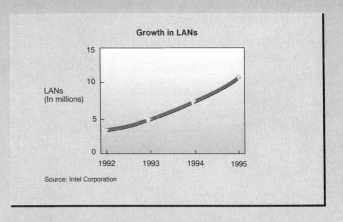

Growth in LANs

LANs
(In millions)

15
10
5
0

1992   1993   1994   1995

Source: Intel Corporation

Data Transmission	Network Configurations	Network Types

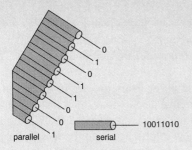

0
1
0
1
1
0
0
parallel 1   serial   10011010

Factors affecting data transmission are:

Bandwidth

Bandwidth, bits-per-second transmission capacity of a channel, may be **voiceband**—telephone line, 110–9600 bps; **medium band**—mainframe leased lines, 9600–256,000 bps; **broadband**—coaxial, fiberoptic, microwave, satellite channels, 256,000–1 million bps.

Serial and Parallel Transmission

The two ways data travels are **serial data transmission**—bits flow in a continuous stream, and **parallel data transmission**—bits flow through separate lines simultaneously.

Direction of Data Transmission

Three directions of data flow are **simplex communication**—data travels in one direction only; **half-duplex communication**—data flows in both directions, but not simultaneously; **full-duplex communication**—data is transmitted back and forth at the same time.

Modes of Transmitting Data

Two modes are **asynchronous transmission**—data is sent and received one byte at a time—and **synchronous transmission**—several bytes (a block) are sent at one time.

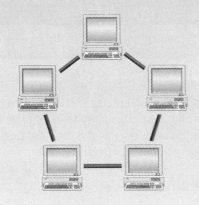

A *network* is a communications system connecting two or more computers. Four principal configurations are:

Star Network

In a **star network,** a number of small computers or peripheral devices are linked to a central unit. It is useful in a **time-sharing system,** in which several users share resources or a central computer.

Bus Network

In a **bus network,** there is no central unit. Each network device handles its own communications, which travel along the **bus,** or connecting cable.

Ring Network

In a **ring network,** there is no central unit. Each device is connected to two other devices. It is useful in decentralized organizations as a *distributed data processing system.*

Hierarchical Network

The **hierarchical network (hybrid network)** consists of several computers linked to a central host, and other computers are hosts to smaller computers or peripheral devices. It is useful in centralized organizations.

Protocols

A **protocol** defines rules by which senders and receivers may exchange information. The OSI model presents a standard set of communication protocols.

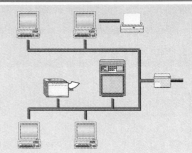

Three types of geographical networks are:

Local Area Networks

Local Area Networks (LANs) are computers and peripheral devices close together (e.g., in same building). Linked by telephone, coaxial, or fiberoptic cable, LANs often take bus form. LANs may be linked to other LANs or networks by a **network gateway.**

Metropolitan Area Networks

A **metropolitan area network (MAN)** consists of citywide networks, often using cellular phones.

Wide Area Networks

Wide area networks (WANs) are countrywide and worldwide networks, often using microwave relays and satellites.

137

8

Files and Databases

Competencies

After you have read this chapter, you should be able to:

1. Understand the difference between batch processing and real-time processing.

2. Describe the difference between master files and transaction files.

3. Define and describe the three types of file organization: sequential, direct, and index sequential.

4. Describe the advantages of a database.

5. Describe the two essential parts of a database management system (DBMS).

6. Describe three ways of organizing a DBMS: hierarchical, network, and relational.

7. Distinguish among individual, company, distributed, and proprietary databases.

8. Discuss some issues of productivity and security.

Like a library, the purpose of secondary storage is to store information. How is such information organized? What are files and databases, and why know anything about them? Perhaps the answer is: To become competent at making use of information in the Information Age, you have to know how to *find* that information.

At one time, it was not important for microcomputer users to have to know much about files and databases. However, the recent arrival of very powerful microcomputer chips and their availability to communications networks has changed that. To attain true computer competency, you need to know how to gain access to the files and databases on your own personal computer. You also need to be able to access those available from other sources. Communications lines extend the reach of your microcomputer well beyond the desktop.

Files

Understanding How Files Work Means Understanding Data Organization, Key Fields, Batch Versus Real-Time Processing, Master Versus Transaction Files, and File Organization.

You want to know if you're going to be able to graduate in June. You call your school's registrar after your last semester exams to find out your grade point average. Perhaps you are told, "Sorry, that's not in the computer yet." Why can't they tell you? How is the school's computer system any different from, say, your bank's, where deposits and withdrawals seem to be recorded right away?

Data Organization   From Chapter 6 we learned that data is organized as follows:

■ *Character:* A character is a single letter, number, or special character such as a punctuation mark or $.

■ *Field:* A field contains a set of related characters. On a college registration form or a driver's license, a person's first name is a field. Last name is another field, street address another field, city yet another field, and so on.

■ *Record:* A record is a collection of related fields. Everything on a person's driver's license, including number and expiration date, is a record.

■ *File:* A file is a collection of related records. All the driver's licenses issued in one county could be a file.

An example of how data is organized is shown in the illustration. (*See Figure 8-1.*) Note that a student's name is not one field, it is three: first name, middle initial, and last name.

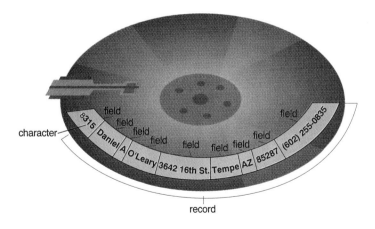

Figure 8-1
How data is organized.

The Key Field   Our illustration also shows the student's identification number. Is such a number really necessary? Certainly most people's names are different enough that at a small college, say, you might think identification numbers wouldn't be necessary. However, as anyone named Robert Smith or Susan Williams knows, there are plenty of other people around with the same name. Sometimes they even have the same middle initial. This is the reason for the student identification number: The number is unique, whereas the name may not be.

This distinctive number is called a *key field*. A **key field** is the particular field of a record that is chosen to uniquely identify each record. The key may be social security number, employee identification number, or part number.

Batch Versus Real-Time Processing   Traditionally data is processed in two ways. These are (1) *batch processing,* what we might call "later," and (2) *real-time processing,* what we might call "right away." These two methods have been used to handle common record-keeping activities such as payroll and sales orders.

- *Batch processing:* In **batch processing,** data is collected over several days or weeks. It is then processed all at once—as a "batch." If you have a gasoline credit card, your bill probably reflects batch processing. That is, during the month, you buy gas and charge it to your credit card. Each time, the gasoline dealer sends a copy of the transaction to the oil company. At some point in the month, the company's data processing department puts all those transactions (and those of many other customers) together. It then processes them at one time. The oil company then sends you a single bill totaling the amount you owe.

- *Real-time processing:* Totaling up the sales charged to your gasoline credit card is an example of batch processing. You might use another kind of card—your card for your bank's automatic teller machine (ATM)—for the second kind of processing. **Real-time processing** occurs when data is processed at the same time the transaction occurs. As you use your ATM card to withdraw cash, the system automatically computes the balance remaining in your account.

At one time, only tape storage, and therefore only sequential access storage (as we discussed in Chapter 6), was available. All processing then was batch processing and was done on mainframe computers. Even today, a great deal of mainframe time is dedicated to this kind of processing. Many smaller organizations, however, use microcomputers for this purpose.

Real-time processing is made possible by the availability of disk packs and direct access storage (as we described in Chapter 6). Direct access storage enables the user to quickly go directly to a particular record. (In sequential access storage, by contrast, the user must wait for the computer to scan several records one at a time. It continues scanning until it comes to the one that's needed.) Not long ago, specialized terminals were used to enter data and perform real-time processing. Today, however, more and more microcomputers are being used for this purpose. In addition, because microcomputers have become so powerful, smaller companies and departments of large companies use these machines by themselves for many real-time processing needs. That is, they use them without connecting to a mainframe.

Master Versus Transaction Files   Two types of files are commonly used to update data—a *master file* and a *transaction file.*

■   The **master file** is a complete file containing all records current up to the last update. An example is the data file used to prepare your last month's telephone bill or bank statement.

■   The **transaction file** contains *recent* changes to records that will be used to update the master file. An example could be a temporary "holding" file that accumulates telephone charges or bank deposits and withdrawals through the present month.

File Organization   File organization may be of three types: *sequential, direct,* and *index sequential.*

■   *Sequential file organization:* In a **sequential file,** records are physically stored one after another in some order. This order is determined by the *key field* on each record, such as the student identification number shown in our illustration. (*Refer back to Figure 8-1, p. 139.*) In this arrangement, to find the record about a particular student, the registrar's office would sequentially search through the records. It would search them one at a time until the student's number was found. If your number is 8315, the computer will start with record number 0000. It will go through 0001, 0002, and so on, until it reaches your number.

Sequential files are often stored on tape, although disk packs may also be used.

■   *Direct file organization:* For **direct file organization,** records are not stored physically one after another. Rather, they are stored on a disk in a particular location that can be determined by their key field. Knowing the key field allows the computer to access the record directly; no sequential search is necessary.

In direct file organization, data must be stored on disks. Also, a method must exist for going directly to the key fields of all records.

■   *Index sequential file organization:* **Index sequential file organization** is a compromise between sequential and direct file organizations. It stores records in a file in sequential order. However, an index sequential file also contains an index. The index lists the key to each group of records stored and the corresponding disk address for that group. When the user seeks a particular record, the computer starts searching sequentially by looking at the beginning of the group of records.

For example, the college registrar could index certain ranges of student identification numbers—0000 to 2000, 2001 to 4000, and so on. For the computer to find your number (e.g., 8315), it would first go to the index. The index would give the location of the range in which your number appears on the disk (e.g., 8001 to 10,000). The computer would then search sequentially (from 8001) to find your number.

Index sequential file organization requires disks or other direct access storage device.

All three kinds of file organization have their advantages and disadvantages.

The advantage of *sequential files* is that they are useful when all or a large part of the records need to be accessed—for example, when the next term's course offerings are being mailed out. They also have a cost advantage, since they can be stored on magnetic tape, which is less expensive than disk. The disadvantage of sequential files is that records must be ordered in a certain way and be searched one at a time.

The advantage of *direct file organization* is that it is much faster than sequential for locating a specific record. For example, if your grades were stored in a direct file, the registrar could access them very quickly. They could be accessed just by your student identification number. The disadvantage of this form of organization is cost. It needs more storage on a hard disk. It also is not as good as sequential file organization for large numbers of updates or for listing large numbers of records.

Index sequential file organization is faster than sequential but not as fast as direct access. This kind is best used when large batches of transactions must occasionally be updated, yet users also want frequent, quick access to records. For example, every month a bank will update bank statements to send to its customers. However, customers and bank tellers need to be able to have up-to-the-minute information about checking accounts.

Database

A Database Consolidates Multiple Files of Duplicate Information.

Many organizations have multiple files on the same subject or person. For example, records for the same customer may appear in different files in the sales department, billing department, and credit department. If the customer changes her or his name or moves, every file must be updated. If one file is overlooked, it can cause embarrassments. For example, a product ordered might be sent to the new address, but the bill might be sent to the old address.

Moreover, data spread around in different files is not as useful as it can be if many users have access to it. The marketing department, for instance, might want to do special promotions to customers who order large quantities of merchandise. However, they may be unable to do so because that information is in the billing department. A database can make the needed information available.

A *database* is defined as a collection of integrated data. By "integrated," we mean the data consists of logically related files and records.

The Need for Databases For both individuals and organizations, there are many advantages to having databases:

- *Sharing:* In organizations, information from one department can be readily shared with others, as we saw in the example above.

- *Security:* Users are given passwords or access only to the kind of information they need to know. Thus, the payroll department may have access to employees' pay rates, but other departments would not.

- *Fewer files:* With several departments having access to one file, there are fewer files. Excess storage, or what is called "data redundancy," is reduced. Microcomputers linked by a network to a file server, for example, could replace the hard disks located in several individual microcomputers.

- *Data integrity:* Older filing systems many times did not have "integrity." That is, a change made in the file in one department might not be made in the file in another department.

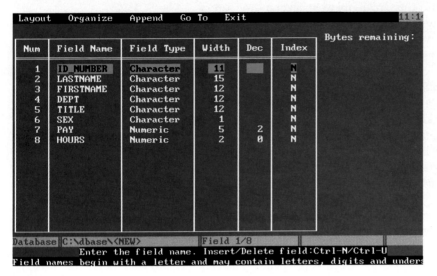

```
Layout    Organize    Append    Go To    Exit                      11:1
                                              Bytes remaining:
┌─────┬──────────────┬──────────────┬───────┬──────┬────────┐
│ Num │  Field Name  │  Field Type  │ Width │ Dec  │ Index  │
├─────┼──────────────┼──────────────┼───────┼──────┼────────┤
│  1  │ ID_NUMBER    │ Character    │  11   │      │   N    │
│  2  │ LASTNAME     │ Character    │  15   │      │   N    │
│  3  │ FIRSTNAME    │ Character    │  12   │      │   N    │
│  4  │ DEPT         │ Character    │  12   │      │   N    │
│  5  │ TITLE        │ Character    │  12   │      │   N    │
│  6  │ SEX          │ Character    │   1   │      │   N    │
│  7  │ PAY          │ Numeric      │   5   │  2   │   N    │
│  8  │ HOURS        │ Numeric      │   2   │  0   │   N    │
└─────┴──────────────┴──────────────┴───────┴──────┴────────┘

Database C:\dbase\<NEW>        Field 1/8
        Enter the field name. Insert/Delete field:Ctrl-N/Ctrl-U
Field names begin with a letter and may contain letters, digits and unders
```

Figure 8-2
The data dictionary for dBASE IV. This screen defines the structure for records in an employee payroll file.

Software for a Database Management System　In order to create, modify, and gain access to the database, special software is required. This software is called a *database management system,* which is commonly abbreviated *DBMS*.

Some DBMSs, such as dBASE, are designed specifically for microcomputers. Other DBMSs are designed for minicomputers and mainframes. Once again, increased processing power and the wide use of communications networks linked to file servers are changing everything. Now microcomputer DBMSs have become more like the ones used for mainframes—and vice versa.

DBMS software is made up of a data dictionary and a query language.

The Data Dictionary　The **data dictionary** contains a description of the structure of the data used in the database. For a particular item of data, it defines the names used for a particular field. It defines what type of data that field is (alphabetic, numeric, or alphanumeric). It also specifies the number of characters in each field and whether that field is a key field. An example of a data dictionary appears in the illustration. (*See Figure 8-2.*)

Query Language　Access to most databases is accomplished with a **query language.** This is an easy-to-use language understandable to most users. Examples of microcomputer query languages are found in dBASE and R:Base.

Query languages have commands such as DISPLAY, ADD, COMPARE, LIST, and UPDATE. For example, imagine you wanted the names of all salespeople in an organization whose sales were greater than their sales quotas. You might type the statement "DISPLAY ALL FOR SALES > QUOTA."

DBMS Organization

The Three Principal DBMS Organizations Are Hierarchical, Network, and Relational.

The purpose of a database is to integrate individual items of data—that is, to transform isolated facts into useful information. We saw that files can be organized in various ways (sequentially, for example) to best suit their use. Similarly, databases can also be organized in different ways to best fit their use. Although other arrangements have been tried, the three most common formats are *hierarchical, network,* and *relational.*

The Hierarchical Database　In a **hierarchical database,** fields or records are structured in **nodes.** Nodes are points connected like the branches of a tree (an upside-down tree). The nodes farther down the system are subordinate to the ones above, like the hierarchy of managers in a corporation. An example of a hierarchical database for part of a nationwide airline reservations system is shown in our illustration. (*See Figure 8-3.*) Each entry has one **parent node,** although a parent may have several **child nodes.** To find a particular field you have to start at the top with a parent and trace down the tree to a child.

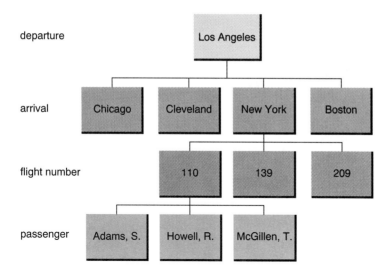

Figure 8-3
Example of a hierarchical database.

In the airline reservations system example, the parent nodes are those labeled "Departure," the airports from which planes are leaving. The first child is any of the airports labeled "Arrival," various flights' destinations. The third child is "Flight number." The fourth child is "Passenger."

The problem with a hierarchical database is that if one parent node is deleted, so are all the subordinate child nodes. Moreover, a child node cannot be added unless a parent node is added first. The most significant limitation is the rigid structure: one parent only per child, and no relationships between the child nodes themselves.

The Network Database A **network database** also has a hierarchical arrangement of nodes. However, each child node may have more than one parent node. That is, there are additional connections—called **pointers**—between parent nodes and child nodes. (*See Figure 8-4.*) Thus, a node may be reached through more than one path. It may be traced down through different branches.

An example of the use of a network organization is that shown in our illustration below for students taking courses. (*See Figure 8-4.*) If you trace through the logic of this organization, you can see that each student can have more than one teacher. Each teacher can also teach more than one course. Students may take more than a single course. This is an example of how the network arrangement is more flexible and in many cases more efficient than the hierarchical arrangement.

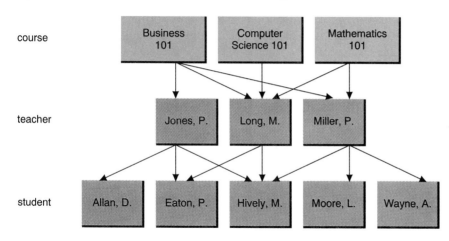

Figure 8-4
Example of a network database.

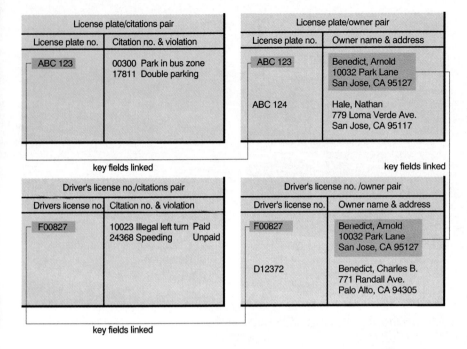

License plate/citations pair	
License plate no.	Citation no. & violation
ABC 123	00300 Park in bus zone 17811 Double parking

key fields linked

License plate/owner pair	
License plate no.	Owner name & address
ABC 123	Benedict, Arnold 10032 Park Lane San Jose, CA 95127
ABC 124	Hale, Nathan 779 Loma Verde Ave. San Jose, CA 95117

key fields linked

Driver's license no./citations pair	
Drivers license no.	Citation no. & violation
F00827	10023 Illegal left turn Paid 24368 Speeding Unpaid

key fields linked

Driver's license no. /owner pair	
Driver's license no.	Owner name & address
F00827	Benedict, Arnold 10032 Park Lane San Jose, CA 95127
D12372	Benedict, Charles B. 771 Randall Ave. Palo Alto, CA 94305

Figure 8-5
Example of a relational
database.

The Relational Database
The most flexible type of organization is the **relational database.** In this structure, there are no access paths down a hierarchy to an item of data. Rather, the data elements are stored in different tables, each of which consists of rows and columns. A table is called a **relation.**

An example of a relational database is shown in our illustration. (*See Figure 8-5.*) The second table consists of all car license plate numbers issued within a particular state. Within the table, a row resembles a record—for example, the license plate number of a car and the owner of that car. A column entry resembles a field. The car license number is one field; the owner's name and address are another field. All related tables must have a *common data item* (a key field). Thus, any piece of information stored on one table can be linked with any piece of information stored on another table. One key field might be a car license number. Another might be a person's name. Another might be a driver's license number.

Thus, police officers who stop a speeding car can radio the license plate number to the department of motor vehicles. They can use the license number as the key field. With it they can find out about any traffic violations (such as parking tickets) for which the car has been cited. Also using the license plate number as a key field, they can obtain the name and address of the car's owner. Using the car owner's name as another key field, they can obtain his or her driver's license number. With the driver's license number as another key field, they can learn if that driver has been cited for other traffic violations. They can also learn whether any fines were paid. They can do this even if the driver has been driving a dozen other cars.

The most valuable feature of relational databases is that entries can be easily added, deleted, and modified. The hierarchy and network databases are more rigid. The relational organization is common for microcomputer DBMSs, such as dBASE and R:Base. Relational databases are also becoming more popular for mainframe- and minicomputer-based systems.

Types of Databases

There Are Four Kinds of Databases: Individual, Company, Distributed, and Proprietary.

Databases may be small or large, limited in accessibility or widely accessible. Databases may be classified into four types: *individual, company* (or shared), *distributed,* and *proprietary.*

The Individual Database   The **individual database** is also called a **microcomputer database.** It is a collection of integrated files useful mainly to just one person. Typically, the data and the DBMS are under the direct control of the user. They are stored either on the user's hard-disk drive or on a LAN file server. This is the kind of database that we described in Chapter 2.

There may be many times in your life when you will find this kind of database valuable. If you are in sales, for instance, a microcomputer database can be used to keep track of customers. If you are a sales manager, you can keep track of your salespeople and their performance. If you are an advertising account executive, you can keep track of what work and how many hours to charge to which client.

The Company, or Shared, Database   Companies, of course, create databases for their own use. The **company database** may be stored on a mainframe and managed by a computer professional (known as a database administrator). Users throughout the company have access to the database through their microcomputers linked to local area networks or wide area networks.

Company databases are of two types:

- The **common operational database** contains details about the operations of the company, such as sales or production information.

- The **common user database** contains selected information both from the common operational database and from outside private (proprietary) databases. Managers can tap into this information on their microcomputers or terminals and use it for decision making.

As we will see in the next chapter, company databases are the foundation for management information systems. For instance, a department store can record all sales transactions in the database. A sales manager can use this information to see which salespeople are selling the most products and thereby determine year-end sales bonuses. Or the store's buyer can learn which products are selling well or not selling and make adjustments when reordering. A top executive might combine overall store sales trends with information from outside databases about consumer and population trends. This information could be used to change the whole merchandising strategy of the store.

The Distributed Database   Many times the data in a company is stored not in just one location but in several locations. It is made accessible through a variety of communications networks. The database, then, is a **distributed database.** That is, it is located in a place or places other than where users are located. The hard-disk drives are connected by a communications network to a mainframe.

For instance, some database information can be at regional offices. Some can be at company headquarters, some down the hall from you, and some even overseas. Sales figures for a chain of department stores, then, could be located at the various stores, but executives at district offices or at the chain's headquarters could have access to these figures.

The Proprietary Database   A **proprietary database** is generally an enormous database that an organization develops to cover certain particular subjects. It offers access to this database to the public or selected outside individuals for a fee. Sometimes proprietary databases are also called *information utilities* or *data banks*. An example is CompuServe, which sells a variety of consumer and business services to microcomputer users. (*See Figure 8-6.*)

Some important proprietary databases are the following:

- *CompuServe:* Offers consumer and business services, including electronic mail.

- *Dialog Information Services:* Offers business, technical, and scientific information.

Figure 8-6
Proprietary database:
CompuServe's opening
screens.

■ *Dow Jones News Retrieval:* Provides world news and information on business, investments, and stocks.

■ *Prodigy:* Offers news and information on business and economics, as well as leisure services.

There are also specialized proprietary databases for investors and financial analysts, such as Chase Econometric Associates.

Costs If you have a microcomputer, modem, and phone at home, many of these proprietary databases are available to you. Usually you pay a start-up fee, an hourly charge for searching the database, and the phone company or telecommunications line charges.

As you might expect, fees and charges are high during the normal nine-to-five business hours. However, proprietary databases often offer cheaper after-hours rates. Dialog Information Services, for example, offers The Knowledge Index nights and weekends for (as of this writing) a start-up fee of $35. An online search charge (which includes telecommunications line costs) is $24 an hour. This service offers comprehensive coverage of journals, abstracts, research reports, reviews, news, tax information, and bibliographies. Topics covered range from agriculture to social science.

Database Uses and Issues

Databases Help Users Keep Current and Plan for the Future, but Keeping Them Secure Is Important. Databases May Be Supervised by a Database Administrator.

Databases offer great opportunities for productivity. In fact, in corporate libraries, electronic databases are now considered more valuable than books and journals. However, maintaining databases means users must make constant efforts to keep them from being tampered with or used for the wrong purposes.

Data for Strategic Uses Databases help users keep up to date and plan for the future. Among the hundreds of databases available to help users with both general and specific business purposes are the following.

■ *Business directories* providing addresses, financial and marketing information, products, and trade and brand names.

■ *Demographic data,* such as county and city statistics, current estimates on population and income, employment statistics, census data, and so on.

■ *Business statistical information,* such as financial information on publicly traded companies, market potential of certain retail stores, and other business information.

■ *Text databases* providing articles from business publications, press releases, reviews on companies and products, and so on.

Importance of Security Precisely because databases are so valuable, their security

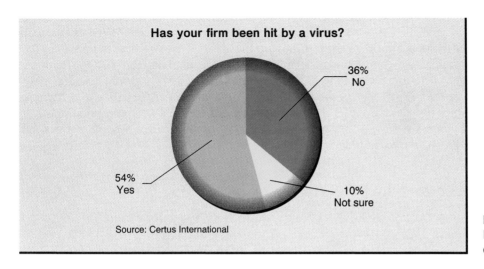

Figure 8-7
Firms reporting at least one computer virus attack.

has become a vital issue. One concern is that personal and private information about people stored in databases will be used for the wrong purposes. For instance, a person's credit or medical records might be used to make hiring or promotion decisions.

Another concern is with preventing unauthorized users from gaining access to a database. For example, there have been numerous instances in which a **computer virus** has been launched into a database or network. Computer viruses are hidden instructions that "migrate" through networks and operating systems and become embedded in different programs and databases. Some are relatively harmless, but others may destroy data. Certus International, which sells software to combat viruses, polled more than a thousand corporations. It found that a majority had suffered at least one virus attack. (*See Figure 8-7.*)

Security can require putting guards on company computer rooms and checking the identification of everyone admitted. (*See Figure 8-8.*) It can also include storing back-up tapes or disks of all valuable information in another location. We describe these and other security issues in detail in Chapter 13.

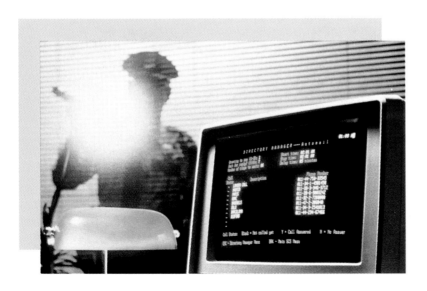

Figure 8-8
Guards are one way of ensuring computer safety.

The Database Administrator Librarians have had to be trained in the use of electronic databases so that they can help their corporate users. However, corporate databases of all sorts—not just those in the library—have become so important that many large organizations now employ a **database administrator (DBA).** He or she helps determine what kind of structure the large databases should take and evaluates the performance of the DBMS. For shared databases, the DBA also determines which people have access to what kind of data; these are called **processing rights.** In addition, the DBA is concerned with such significant issues as security, privacy, and ethics (described in Chapter 13).

A Look at the Future

Large Databases Give Us Everything from Specialty Phone Books to Census Maps. Risks Are Increased Compromises of Privacy and Security. Products Are Available to Sift Information.

Data collection and its uses are sure to get more and more sophisticated. Microcomputer users now, for instance, can get computerized *specialty phone books* loaded with corporate names, telephone numbers, and other data. A database project of awesome proportions is the huge national computer map being developed by the U.S. Census Bureau. Known as *TIGER* (for *T*opologically *I*ntegrated *G*eographic *E*ncoding and *R*eference system), it will have 23 million street intersections and can be coupled with statistics that provide a numerical or income profile of every block in the United States.

Big databases not only have great potential payoffs in productivity but also great risks for privacy and security. One worry is that corporations and governments may use them to create unnecessary or dangerous confidential files (dossiers) about private citizens. Another is that a fire, earthquake, computer virus, sabotage, or other disaster that disrupts a local communications or computer system can have nationwide or worldwide effects.

Finally, the mountains of information generated by databases have now created a new industry: products that sift the information to give us what we really want to know. These products range from personal newsletters to filtering technology that scans data for key words specified by the user.

Review Questions

1. What is the difference between batch processing and real-time processing? Give an example of each.
2. What is a master file?
3. What is a transaction file?
4. Define what is meant by *key field*.
5. Describe sequential file organization.
6. Explain direct file organization.
7. Describe index sequential file organization.
8. Why are databases needed?
9. Define what is meant by a database.
10. State four advantages of databases.
11. What is a database management system (DBMS)?

12. Describe what a data dictionary is.
13. Describe the purpose of a query language.
14. Discuss the three principal ways of organizing a database.
15. What is an individual database?
16. What is a company database?
17. What is a distributed database?
18. What is a proprietary database?
19. What is a computer virus?
20. Describe the role of the database administrator.

Discussion Questions and Projects

1. *Useful information utilities:* What is your major or prospective major? What kinds of information are you apt to be required to obtain for research papers, projects, and assignments? If you're in the health field, you may be required to learn about diet, exercise, drug recovery, and the like. If you're in marketing, you may need to know about sales forecasting and product marketing.

    Take a few minutes to list the areas of information required in your field. Then go to the library and look up which information utilities or data banks would be most valuable to you. Examples are CompuServe, Dialog or The Knowledge Index, Dow Jones New Retrieval, and Prodigy.

2. *Electronic publishing by telephone companies?* A dispute has been going on among the seven regional telephone companies (the "Baby Bells") and the newspaper industry. Following the 1984 breakup of American Telephone & Telegraph (AT&T), the regional phone companies were sharply limited from entering "electronic publishing." That is, they were prohibited from selling such database information services as news headlines, stock quotations, and computerized Yellow Pages over their own phone lines. Then some 1991 court rulings reversed this prohibition, and the phone companies are laying plans to enter the $100-billion-a-year information services market.

    Newspapers complain that the phone companies will monopolize their hold over residential phone lines and dictate what information is allowed to reach homes. In reply, critics point out that most newspapers are monopolies as well and that, unlike the phone companies, they are unregulated. In addition, they observe that newspapers have, through their editorial pages, a monopoly on the dissemination of opinion.

    Probably these struggles between the Baby Bells and the newspaper industry will continue. What do you think? Discuss the pros and cons with classmates.

Through communication lines, users can gain access to files and databases.

| Files | Database |

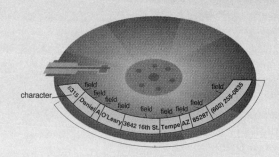

Understanding how files work means understanding the following:

Data Organization

- *Character*—letter, number, special character.
- *Field*—set of related characters.
- *Record*—collection of related fields.
- *File*—collection of related records.
- *Key field*—field of a record that uniquely identifies a record in a file.

Batch Versus Real-Time Processing

Two methods of processing:

- **Batch processing**—transactions are collected over time, then processed all at once.
- **Real-time processing**—data is processed at the same time transactions occur.

Master Versus Transaction Files

- **Master file**—a complete file containing all records current to the last update.
- **Transaction file**—a temporary "holding file" containing recent changes that will be used to update the master file.

File Organization

Three types of file organization are:

- **Sequential**—records are stored one after the other in ascending or descending order. This method is often used with magnetic tape.
- **Direct**—records are stored in order by a key field such as a special number. This method is often used with magnetic disk.
- **Index sequential**—records are stored in a file in sequential order, but the file also has an index listing the key to each group of records stored. This method is used with magnetic disk storage.

A *database* is a collection of integrated data— logically related files and records.

The Need for Databases

Advantages of databases:

- **Sharing**—users may share with others.
- **Security**—access is restricted to authorized people.
- **Fewer files**—a company avoids multiple files on the same subject.
- **Data integrity**—changes in one file are made in other files as well.

Software for a DBMS

A **database management system (DBMS)** is the software for creating, modifying, and gaining access to the database. A DBMS consists of:

- **Data dictionary**—describes the structure of the data used in the database (e.g., if data is alphabetic, numeric, alphanumeric).
- **Query language**—easy-to-use language to get access to the database.

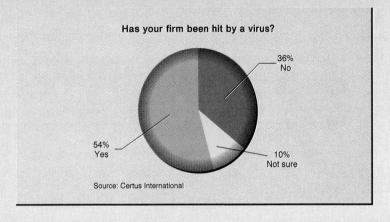

Has your firm been hit by a virus?

36% No

54% Yes

10% Not sure

Source: Certus International

| DBMS Organization | Types of Database | Database Uses and Issues |

DBMS Organization

Three principal DBMS organizations are:

Hierarchical Database

In a **hierarchical database,** fields and records are structured in **nodes,** points connected like tree branches. An entry may have a **parent** node with several **child** nodes. A node may be reached by only one path.

Network Database

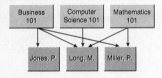

In a **network database,** nodes are arranged hierarchically, but a child node may have more than one parent. There are additional connections called **pointers.** A node may be reached by several paths.

Relational Database

Driver's name /driver's license pair	
License plate no.	Owner name & address
F00827	Benedict, Arnold 10032 Park Lane San Jose, CA 95127
D12372	Benedict, Charles B. 771 Randall Ave. Palo Alto, CA 94305

In a **relational database,** data is stored in pairs on tables (called **relations**) of rows and columns; data items are found by means of an index.

Types of Database

Four types of databases are:

Individual Database

The **individual database** (or **micro-computer database**) is a collection of integrated files useful mainly to just one person.

Company, or Shared, Database

Two types of **company (shared) data-base** are:

- **Common operational database**—contains details about company operations.
- **Common user database**—contains selected information from the common operational database and from outside private databases.

Distributed Database

The **distributed database** is spread out geographically and is accessible by communications links.

Proprietary Database

A **proprietary database** is available by subscription to customers (e.g., offering business, technical, or scientific information).

Database Uses and Issues

Databases offer increased productivity but also risks to security.

Data for Strategic Uses

Databases help users keep current and plan for the future. Among databases available are business directories, demographic data, business statistical information, and text databases.

Importance of Security

Two security concerns are that private information in databases will be used for wrong purposes and that unauthorized users will gain access. An example of a threat to databases is a **computer virus,** hidden instructions that "migrate" into programs and databases and destroy them.

The Database Administrator

The **database administrator (DBA)** is a specialist in large organizations who sets up and manages the database and determines **processing rights**—which people have access to what kind of data.

151

9 Information Systems

Communications links and databases connect you with information resources far beyond the surface of your desk. The microcomputer offers you access to a greater quantity of information than was possible a few years ago. In addition, you also have access to a better quality of information. As we show in this chapter, when you tap into a computer-based information system, you not only get information—you also get help in making decisions.

Give two reasons why computers are used in organizations. No doubt you can easily state one of them: to keep records of events. However, the second reason might be less obvious: to help make decisions. For example, as we showed earlier, point-of-sale terminals, those computerized cash registers in department stores, are used not only to record sales. They also record which salespeople made which sales. This information can be used for decision making. For instance, it can help the sales manager decide which salespeople will get year-end bonuses for doing exceptional work.

Keeping accurate records and making good decisions are extremely important in running any successful organization, small or large. Let us begin to see how information systems can help you with this.

The Information Revolution

Downsizing of Applications Allows Microcomputers to Do the Work of Mainframes and Minicomputers.

The first kind of microcomputer to which you are introduced may do just about everything you want—for the moment. Indeed, this may be so even though it is one of the less powerful models. You can use it to handle all the kinds of programs we have called "basic tools," such as word processing and spreadsheets.

However, the situation in the workplace is rapidly changing. Now technology has made microcomputers so powerful that the word *micro* is almost no longer meaningful. Indeed, people even talk about *supermicros.* If you have access to a newer microcomputer, then you practically have the power of a mainframe sitting on your desk.

As a result, a new term has come into the language: "downsizing." **Downsizing** means moving applications from larger computers to smaller ones—usually from mainframes and minicomputers to microcomputers. This trend corresponds to another significant development—the downsizing of *management staffs.* In recent years, many companies have scaled down their staffs, in the process reducing the number of middle-level managers. Since much of the company's work still remains, the microcomputer has become more important. It allows one person, typically a manager, to perform more of these tasks.

Here is what the downsizing of computers means to you. The key technology advances that support downsizing:

■ *Faster processing and more primary storage:* Many older microcomputers have only 640K or even just 256K of primary storage (main memory). Their processing capacities are limited and their speeds are relatively slow. The most recent microcomputer generation, however, has enormous power. Processing speeds and primary storage capacities approach those previously reserved for minicomputers and mainframes. As a result, a microcomputer can run not only such DBMS programs as dBASE and R:base. They can also run some even more powerful programs. These include not only more sophisticated operating systems but also high-powered applications programs, such as desktop publishing programs.

■ *More powerful secondary storage:* In large organizations, databases have always required storage devices that can hold a lot of data. This meant that company databases required disk packs in order to create and retrieve large amounts of data. The cost and the processing speeds of these disk packs could be handled only by mainframes and minis. Today two changes are taking place. (1) High-volume storage such as optical disks is available for microcomputer users. (2) In addition, when linked to communications networks, microcomputer users have access to databases stored on disk packs.

■ *Microcomputers offer easier access to large databases:* Until recently, in many large organizations, only people who could use terminals connected to a mainframe could get access to large databases. Now, however, terminals are being replaced by microcomputers connected by local area networks or other communications networks to mainframes and databases.

Today nearly everyone who needs access can readily obtain it. In fact, the role of the mainframe is changing. More and more mainframe time is being used to handle database operations. More and more processing of the data, on the other hand, is being done by microcomputers.

In short, the capabilities of the desktop computer have been dramatically expanded. (*See Figure 9-1.*) In the future, you will be able to call upon it for an enormous quantity of information for help in making decisions. Let us see how this would work. To understand this, we need to understand how an organization is structured and how information flows within it.

Figure 9-1
The capabilities of the microcomputer have been dramatically expanded, as with this high-powered Sun workstation.

How Information Flows in an Organization

Information Flows Up and Down Among Managers and Sideways Among Departments.

An **information system** (like the microcomputer system we discussed in Chapter 1) is a collection of *hardware, software, people, procedures,* and *data.* These work together to provide information essential to running an organization. This is information that will successfully produce a product or service and, for profit-oriented enterprises, derive a profit.

In large and medium-sized organizations, computerized information systems don't just keep track of transactions and day-to-day business operations. They also support the flow of information within the organization. This information flows both vertically and horizontally. In order to understand this, we need to understand how an organization is structured. One way to examine an organization's structure is to view it from a functional perspective. That is, you can study the different basic functional areas in organizations and the different types of people within these functional areas.

As we describe these, you might consider how they apply to any organization you are familiar with. Or consider how they apply to a hypothetical manufacturer of sporting goods, the HealthWise Group. Think of this as a large company that manufactures equipment for sports and physical activities, including those that interest you. These goods range from every type of ball imaginable (from golf to tennis to soccer) to hockey pads, leotards, and exercise bicycles.

Functions   Depending on the services or products they provide, most organizations have departments that perform five basic functions. These are *accounting, production, marketing, personnel,* and *research. (See Figure 9-2.)* Their purposes are as follows:

■ *Accounting:* This department keeps track of all financial activities. It pays bills, records payments, issues paychecks, and compiles periodic financial statements. At HealthWise, for example, this department performs two major activities. First, it records bills and other financial transactions with sporting goods stores and produces financial statements. Second, it produces financial budgets and forecasts of projected financial performance to help managers run the business.

■ *Production:* This department makes the product. *(See Figure 9-3.)* It takes in raw materials and puts people to work to turn out finished goods (or services). The department may be a manufacturing activity or, in the case of a retail store, for example, an operations activity. It manages purchases, inventories, and flows of

Figure 9-2
The five functions of an organization.

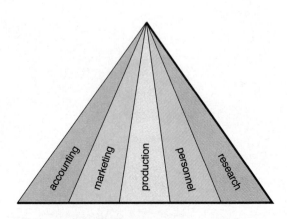

goods and services. At HealthWise, this department is a big purchaser of steel and aluminum, materials that go into weight-lifting and exercise machines.

- *Marketing:* Advertising, promotion, and sales are handled by this department. (*See Figure 9-4.*) The people in this department plan, price, promote, sell, and distribute goods and services to customers. At HealthWise they even get involved in what colors to put on the equipment that is sold.

- *Personnel:* This department finds and hires people and handles matters such as sick leave and retirement benefits. In addition, it is concerned with evaluation, compensation, and professional development. As you might imagine, HealthWise has rather good health benefits.

- *Research:* The research (or research and development) department has two tasks. First, it does product research. That is, it does basic research and relates new discoveries to the firm's current or new products. For instance, research people at HealthWise might look into new ideas from exercise physiologists about muscle development. They might use this knowledge in designing new physical fitness machines. Second, it does product development. That is, it develops and tests new products created by research people. It also monitors and troubleshoots new products as they are being produced.

Figure 9-3
Production: This department is responsible for making products—in this case, tennis balls.

Whatever your job in an organization, it is likely to be in one of these departments. Within the department, you may also be at one of the management levels.

Management Levels Most people who work in an organization are not managers, of course. At the base of the organizational pyramid are the secretaries, clerks, welders, drivers, and so on. These people produce goods and services. Above them, however, are various levels of managers—people with titles such as supervisor, director, regional manager, and vice president. These are the people who do the planning, organizing, and controlling necessary to see that the work gets done. At HealthWise, for example, the district sales manager for Oregon directs salespeople promoting exercise-related equipment to stores, gyms, and health clubs in that state. Other job titles might be vice president of marketing, director of personnel, or production manager.

Figure 9-4
Marketing: This department handles advertising, promotion, and sales.

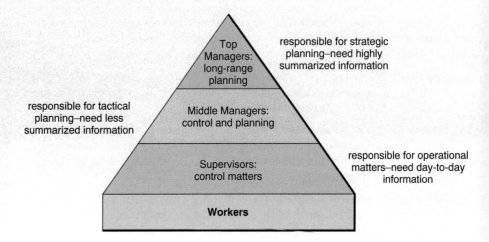

Figure 9-5
The concerns and tasks of management.

Management in many organizations is divided into three levels: supervisors, middle-level, and top-level. (*See Figure 9-5.*) They may be described as follows:

- *Supervisors:* **Supervisors** manage and monitor the employees or workers, those who actually produce the goods and services. Thus, these managers have the responsibility relating to *operational matters.* They monitor day-to-day events and immediately take corrective action, if necessary. For example, at HealthWise, a production supervisor monitors the materials needed to build exercise bicycles. If parts begin to run low, the supervisor must take action immediately.

- *Middle management:* Top managers supervise **middle-level managers,** who deal with *control and planning* (also called *tactical planning*). Middle management implements the long-term goals of the organization. For example, the HealthWise regional sales manager for the Northwest sets sales goals for district sales managers in Washington, Oregon, and Idaho. He or she also monitors their sales performance.

- *Top management:* **Top-level managers** are concerned with *long-range planning* (also called *strategic planning*). They need information that will help them to plan the future growth and direction of the organization. For example, the HealthWise vice president of marketing might need to determine the demand and the sales strategy for a new product. Such a product might be a stationary exercise bicycle with a biometric feedback mechanism.

Information Flow Each level of management has different information needs. Top-level managers need information that is summarized in capsule form to reveal the overall condition of the business. They also need information from outside the organization, because top-level managers need to try to forecast and plan for long-range events. Middle-level managers need summarized information—weekly or monthly reports. They need to develop budget projections as well as to evaluate the performance of supervisors. Supervisors need detailed, very current day-to-day information on their units so that they can keep operations running smoothly.

To support these different needs, information *flows* in different directions. (*See Figure 9-6.*) The top-level managers, such as the chief executive officer (CEO), need information not only from below and from all departments. They also need information from outside the organization. For example, at HealthWise, they are deciding whether to introduce a line of hockey equipment in the southwestern United States.

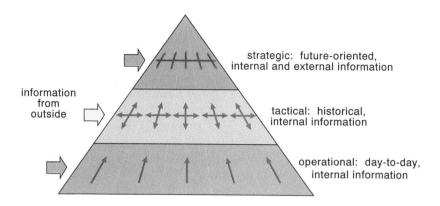

Figure 9-6
The flow of information within an organization.

The vice president of marketing must look at relevant data. Such data might include availability of ice rinks and census data about the number of young people. It might also include sales histories on related cold-weather sports equipment.

For middle-level managers, the information flow is both horizontal and vertical across functional lines within the organization. For example, the regional sales managers at HealthWise set their sales goals by coordinating with their middle-manager counterparts in the production department. They are able to tell sales managers how many products will be produced, of what kind (expensive versus inexpensive), and when. An example of a product might be exercise bicycles. The regional sales managers also must coordinate with the strategic goals set by the top managers. They must set and monitor the sales goals for the supervisors beneath them.

For supervisory managers, information flow is primarily vertical. That is, they communicate mainly with their middle managers and with the workers beneath them. For instance, at HealthWise, production supervisors rarely communicate with people in the accounting department. However, they are constantly communicating with production-line workers and with their own managers. (*See Figure 9-7.*)

Now we know how a large organization is usually structured and how information flows within the organization. But how is a computer-based information system likely to be set up to support its needs? And what do you, as a microcomputer user, need to know to use it?

Figure 9-7
For supervisory managers, information flow is vertical, from managers to workers beneath them.

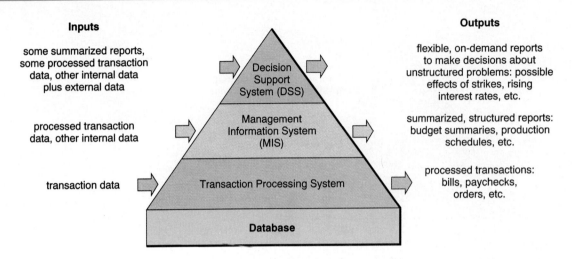

Inputs

some summarized reports, some processed transaction data, other internal data plus external data

processed transaction data, other internal data

transaction data

Outputs

flexible, on-demand reports to make decisions about unstructured problems: possible effects of strikes, rising interest rates, etc.

summarized, structured reports: budget summaries, production schedules, etc.

processed transactions: bills, paychecks, orders, etc.

Decision Support System (DSS)

Management Information System (MIS)

Transaction Processing System

Database

Figure 9-8
The three levels of information systems.

The Levels of Computer-Based Information Systems

Computer-Based Information Systems Have Three Levels: Transaction Processing System, Management Information System, and Decision Support System.

All large organizations maintain a computerized database. This database records all routine activities: employees hired, materials purchased, products produced, and the like. Such recorded events are called **transactions.** From this database of transactions, large organizations develop two kinds of computerized information systems. These systems may be thought of as forming a three-level pyramid, each primarily (but not exclusively) supporting one of the three levels of management. (*See Figure 9-8.*)

- *Transaction processing system:* The **transaction processing system** records day-to-day transactions such as customer orders, bills, inventory levels, and production output. The transaction processing system generates the database that acts as the foundation for the other two information systems.

- *Management information system:* The **management information system** (**MIS**) summarizes the detailed data of the transaction processing system in standard reports. Such reports might include production schedules and budget summaries.

- *Decision support system:* The **decision support system** (**DSS**) provides a flexible tool for analysis. The DSS helps managers make decisions about unstructured problems, such as the effect of events and trends outside the organization. Like the MIS, the DSS draws on the detailed data of the transaction processing system.

Let us describe these three kinds of information systems in more detail.

Transaction Processing Systems

A Transaction Processing System Records Routine Operations.

The purpose of a *transaction processing system* is to help an organization keep track of routine operations and to record these events in a database. The data from operations—for example, customer orders for HealthWise's products—makes up a database that records the transactions of the company. This database of transactions is used to support an MIS and a DSS.

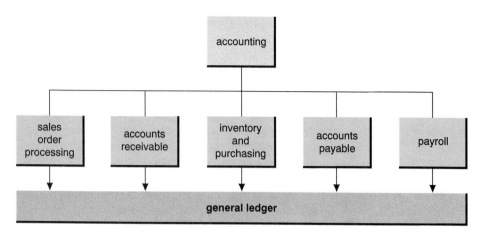

Figure 9-9
Transaction processing system for accounting.

One of the most essential transaction processing systems for any organization is in the accounting area. (*See Figure 9-9.*) Every accounting department handles six basic activities. Five of these are sales order processing, accounts receivable, inventory and purchasing, accounts payable, and payroll. All of these are recorded in the general ledger, the sixth activity. We explain these below.

Let us take a look at these six activities. They will make up the basis of the accounting system for almost any office you might work in.

- The **sales order processing** activity records the customer requests for the company's product or service. (*See Figure 9-10.*) When an order comes in—a request for a set of barbells, for example—the warehouse is alerted to ship a product.

- The **accounts receivable** activity records money received from or owed by customers. HealthWise keeps track of bills paid by sporting goods stores and also by gyms and health clubs to which it sells directly.

- The parts and finished goods that the company has in stock are called **inventory**—all exercise machines in the warehouse, for example. An *inventory control system* keeps records of the number of each kind of part or finished good in the warehouse or company storage. **Purchasing** is the buying of materials and services. Often a *purchase order* is used. This is a form that shows the name of the company supplying the material or service and what is being purchased.

Figure 9-10
Sales order processing for Canadian Airlines International.

■ **Accounts payable** refers to money the company owes its suppliers for materials and services it has received—steel and aluminum, for example.

■ The **payroll** activity is concerned with calculating employee paychecks. Amounts are generally determined by the kind of job, hours worked, and kinds of deductions (such as taxes, social security, medical insurance). Paychecks may be calculated from employee time cards or, in some cases, supervisors' time sheets.

■ The **general ledger** keeps track of all summaries of all the foregoing transactions. A typical general ledger system can produce income statements and balance sheets. *Income statements* show a company's financial performance—income, expenses, and the difference between them for a specific time period. *Balance sheets* list the overall financial condition of an organization. They include assets (for example, buildings and property owned), liabilities (debts), and how much of the organization (the equity) is owned by the owners.

Management Information Systems

A Management Information System Produces Summarized, Structured Reports.

A *management information system (MIS)* is a computer-based information system that produces standardized reports in summarized, structured form. It is used to support middle managers. An MIS differs from a transaction processing system in a significant way. Whereas a transaction processing system *creates* databases, an MIS *uses* databases. Indeed, an MIS can draw from the databases of *several* departments. (*See Figure 9-11.*) Thus, an MIS requires a *database management system* that integrates the databases of the different departments. Middle managers need summary data often drawn from across different functional areas.

An MIS produces reports that are *predetermined*. That is, they follow a predetermined format and always show the same kinds of content. Although reports may differ from one industry to another, there are three common categories of reports:

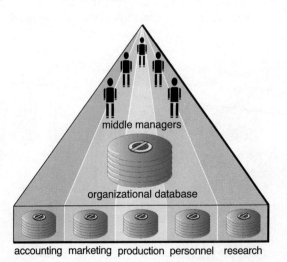

Figure 9-11
An MIS draws on the databases
of more than one department.

middle managers

organizational database

accounting marketing production personnel research

Figure 9-12
Periodic reports may be
produced weekly, monthly,
or quarterly.

- **Periodic reports** are produced at regular intervals—weekly, monthly, or quarterly, for instance. (*See Figure 9-12.*) Examples are HealthWise's monthly sales or production report. The sales reports from district sales managers are combined into a monthly report for the regional sales managers. For comparison purposes, a regional manager is also able to see the sales reports of other regional managers.

- **Exception reports** call attention to unusual events. An example is a sales report that shows that certain items are selling significantly above or below marketing department forecasts. For instance, if fewer exercise bicycles are selling than were predicted for the Northwest sales region, the regional manager will receive an exception report. That report may be used to alert the district managers and salespeople to give this product more attention.

- The opposite of a periodic report, a **demand report** is produced on request. An example is a report on the numbers of, and jobs held by, women and minorities. Such a report is not needed periodically, but it may be required when requested by the U.S. government. At HealthWise, many government contracts require this information. It's used to certify that HealthWise is achieving certain government equal-opportunity guidelines.

Decision Support Systems

A DSS Helps Decision Makers Analyze Unanticipated Situations.

Managers often must deal with unanticipated questions. For example, the HealthWise vice president in charge of manufacturing might ask, how would a strike affect production schedules? A *decision support system (DSS)* enables managers to get answers to unexpected and generally nonrecurring kinds of problems. They do this using interactive terminals (or microcomputers) and software. **Interactive** means that there is immediate communication between the user and the computer system. That is, when input data is entered into the computer, it is processed immediately. The output results are promptly displayed on the screen.

A DSS, then, is quite different from a transaction processing system, which simply records data. It is also different from a management information system, which summarizes data in predetermined reports. A DSS is used to *analyze* data. Moreover, it produces reports that do not have a fixed format. This makes the DSS a flexible tool for analysis.

Many DSSs are designed for large computer systems. However, microcomputers, with their increased power and sophisticated software, such as spreadsheet and database programs, are being used for DSS. Users of a DSS are managers, not computer programmers. Thus, a DSS must be easy to use—or most likely it will not be used at all. Commands need to be in language-like English: "SEARCH" or "FIND," for instance. A HealthWise marketing executive might want to know which territories are not meeting their sales quotas and need additional advertising support. To find out, the executive might type "FIND ALL FOR SALES < QUOTA."

How does a decision support system work? Essentially, it consists of four parts: the user, system software, data, and what are called *decision models*.

The User The user could be you. In general, the user is someone who has to make decisions—a manager, often a top-level manager.

System Software The system software is essentially the operating system—programs designed to work behind the scenes to handle detailed operating procedures. In order to give the user a good, comfortable interface, the software typically is "menu-driven." That is, the screen presents easily understood lists of commands, giving the user several options.

The Data The data in a DSS is stored in a database and consists of two kinds: *Internal* data—data from within the organization—consists principally of transactions from the transaction processing system. *External* data is data gathered from outside the organization. Examples are data provided by marketing research firms, trade associations, and the U.S. government (such as customer profiles, census data, and economic forecasts).

The Decision Models The **decision models** give the DSS its analytical capabilities. There are three basic types of models: strategic, tactical, and operational. *Strategic models* assist top-level managers in long-range planning, such as stating company objectives or planning plant locations. *Tactical models* help middle-level managers control the work of the organization, such as financial planning and sales promotion planning. Such models help middle-level managers implement top managers' long-range plans. *Operational models* help lower-level managers accomplish the day-to-day activities of the organization, such as evaluating and maintaining quality control.

Executive Information Systems

Executive Information Systems Are Specially Designed, Simplified Systems for Top Executives.

Using a DSS requires some training. Many top managers have other people in their offices running DSSs for them and reporting their findings. Top-level executives also want something more concise than an MIS—something that produces very focused, short status reports.

Executive information systems (EISs) are also known as **executive support systems (ESSs).** They consist of sophisticated software that, like an MIS or a DSS, can draw together data from an organization's databases in meaningful patterns. However, an EIS is specifically designed to be easy to use. This is so that a top executive with little spare time can obtain essential information without extensive training. Thus, information is often displayed in very condensed form and in bold graphics.

Consider an executive information system used by the president of HealthWise. It is available on his IBM PS/2 Model 70. The first thing each morning, the president calls up the EIS on his display screen, as shown in the left-hand illustration. (*See Figure 9-13.*) Note that the screen gives a condensed account of activities in the five different areas of the company. (These are Accounting, Marketing, Production, Personnel, and Research.) On one particular morning, the EIS shows business in four areas proceeding smoothly. However, in the first area, Accounting, the percentage of late-paying customers—past due accounts—has increased 3 percent. Three percent may not seem like much. But HealthWise has had a history of problems with late payers, which has left the company at times strapped for cash. The president decides to find out the details. To do so, he presses *1* (corresponding to Accounting) on his keyboard.

The right screen shows information about past due accounts expressed in graphic form. (*See Figure 9-13.*) The status of today's late payers is shown in red. The status of late payers at this time a year ago is shown in blue. The differences between today and a year ago are not appreciable for customers making their payments 11 or more days late. However, there is a significant difference between now and then for customers paying 1 to 10 days late. As a result, HealthWise has $180,653 in past due accounts today, compared to $175,391 a year ago. The president thus knows that he must take some action to speed up customer payments. (For example, he might call this to the attention of the vice president of accounting. The vice president might decide to offer discounts to early payers or charge more interest to late payers.)

EISs not only permit a firm's top executives to gain more direct access to information about the company's performance. Some of them also have electronic mail setups that allow managers to communicate directly with other executives. Some systems even have structured forms to help managers streamline their thoughts before sending electronic memos. In addition, an EIS may be organized to retrieve information from databases outside the company, such as business-news services. This enables

Figure 9-13
An executive information system. Left: information in condensed text form. Right: details in graphic form.

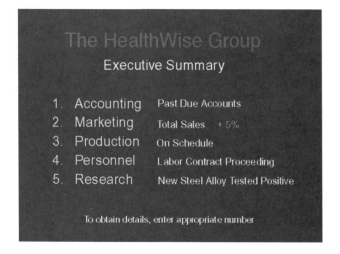

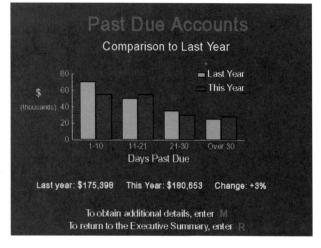

a firm to watch for stories on competitors and stay current on relevant news events that could affect its business. For example, news of increased sports injuries caused by running and aerobic dancing, and the consequent lessened interest by people in these activities, might cause HealthWise to alter its sales and production goals for its line of fitness-related shoes.

A Look at the Future

Information from Executive Information Systems Will Be Made Available in Conference-Room Microcomputers and Eventually in Laptops.

Executive information systems, still being developed in many companies, are definitely the wave of the future. Already, however, forward-looking executives are using *laptop and palmtop computers* to get EIS information while they are traveling.

Before use of laptop EISs becomes popular, experts think, large companies will equip their *conference rooms* with microcomputers that have speedy communications with corporate computers around the world. These meeting-room computers will become part of management presentations, as well as serve executives visiting from elsewhere.

As executive information systems become more a part of corporate life, something else will happen. Competent computer end users (perhaps like yourself) who have risen through the management ranks will begin to demand more from their EISs. Thus, the relatively simple kinds of EISs often seen in use today will be replaced by systems that offer much more power and many more options.

Review Questions

1. Define what an *information system* is.
2. Name five departments often found in medium-sized and large organizations.
3. What is the purpose of each department?
4. Name three levels of management common within organizations.
5. What are the responsibilities of managers on each level?
6. What are differences in the kinds of information that managers at each level need?
7. Name the three levels of computer-based information systems.
8. What does a transaction processing system do?
9. What does a management information system do?
10. What does a decision support system do?
11. Describe the six activities of an accounting department.
12. What is the general ledger, and what purpose does it serve?
13. Distinguish among the three different reports produced by a management information system.
14. What is the principal difference between a management information system and a decision support system in the kind of reports produced?
15. Distinguish between the two kinds of data used in a DSS.
16. What is a decision model?
17. Distinguish among the three types of decision models used in a DSS.
18. Explain what an executive information system is.

Discussion Questions and Projects

1. *The functions and transactions of an organization:* What is the equivalent of "production" in a hotel or "marketing" in a college? The five functions or departments of an organization—accounting, production, marketing, personnel, and research—clearly would be found in a for-profit organization such as an apparel manufacturer. However, they would not be found—at least not in the same form—in an employment agency, a department store, or a hospital. Nevertheless, these organizations do offer products or services, and they probably (if large enough) have three management levels.

   Choose an organization, such as your college, and interview someone to find out what might constitute departments and management layers. Summarize your findings in a drawing identifying the departments and the levels of management. See if you can discover the transactions that go into the database of one of the departments—for example, registrar, housing, fund raising, financial aid, or alumni affairs.

2. *Do computers really make us more productive?* The basic reason for installing and learning computers is that they help us increase our productivity. But do they really? Research has shown some of the following problems. (a) People in organizations spend more time fine-tuning their word-processing documents when such polishing is not necessary. (b) They devote time to unnecessarily putting spreadsheet information into graphic form. (c) They fill up ordinary memos with facts gleaned from expensive computer searches. (d) They create unnecessary pressure by transmitting messages via modem or fax when regular mail would do. These are serious problems that you will run across in the workplace. Discuss the following:

   a. Who or what creates this information overload?

   b. What would you do to prevent these problems if you were a supervisor in an office?

   c. What can you do from becoming a contributor to these problems yourself?

Chapter 9 Information Systems

Technology advances are making database storage and retrieval available to microcomputers everywhere. Microcomputers now have faster processing and more primary storage, more powerful secondary storage, and easier access to large databases. Computer-based information systems stored on these databases can be accessed by microcomputers. Thus, applications are being **downsized** from mainframes to microcomputers.

How Information Flows

Information flows up and down among managers and sideways among departments.

Functions

Most organizations have departments that perform five functions:

- *Accounting*—manages finances, including orders, bills, paychecks.
- *Production*—makes the product (or service).
- *Marketing*—promotes and sells the product (or service).
- *Personnel*—hires people, manages employee benefits.
- *Research*—develops new products (or services).

Management Levels

Management in many organizations has three levels:

- **Top-level managers** are concerned with long-range planning, forecasting future events.
- **Middle-level managers** are concerned with control and planning, implementing long-term goals.
- **Supervisors** are concerned with control of operational matters, monitoring day-to-day events, and supervising workers.

Information Flow

Information flows in different directions:

- For top-level managers—flow is up within the organization and into the organization from outside.
- For middle-level managers—flow is horizontally across and vertically within departments.
- For supervisors—flow is primarily vertical.

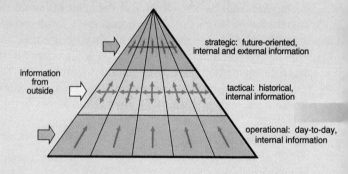

information from outside

strategic: future-oriented, internal and external information

tactical: historical, internal information

operational: day-to-day, internal information

Executive Information System

An **executive information system (EIS)** or **executive support system (ESS)** draws data together from an organization's databases but is designed to be easier to use than MISs or DSSs. Information is displayed in condensed form and in bold graphics.

Levels of Information Systems

All organizations have computerized databases holding records of routine activities called **transactions.** Three levels of computerized information systems are **transaction processing systems, management information systems,** and **decision support systems.**

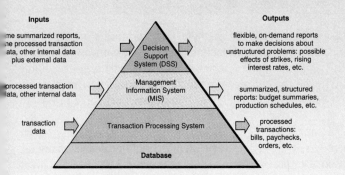

Inputs

- me summarized reports, ne processed transaction ata, other internal data plus external data → **Decision Support System (DSS)**
- processed transaction ata, other internal data → **Management Information System (MIS)**
- transaction data → **Transaction Processing System**

Database

Outputs

- flexible, on-demand reports to make decisions about unstructured problems: possible effects of strikes, rising interest rates, etc.
- summarized, structured reports: budget summaries, production schedules, etc.
- processed transactions: bills, paychecks, orders, etc.

Transaction Processing System

Records day-to-day transactions. An example is in accounting, which handles six activities:

- **Sales order processing**—records customer orders.
- **Accounts receivable**—shows money received from or owed by customers.
- **Inventory** and **purchasing**—shows availability of parts and finished goods and what supplies and services have been purchased.
- **Accounts payable**—shows money owed suppliers.
- **Payroll**—shows paychecks, deductions, benefits.
- **General ledger**—summarizes all of the above transactions.

Management Information System (MIS)

Requires database management system to integrate the databases of different departments. An MIS produces *predetermined* reports:

- **Periodic reports**—produced at regular intervals.
- **Exception reports**—show unusual events.
- **Demand reports**—produced on request.

Decision Support System (DSS)

Enables managers to get answers for unanticipated questions. A DSS consists of:

- The *user*—usually a manager.
- The *software system*—contains easily understood list of commands ("menu-driven").
- The *data*—both internal data (transactions) from the organization and external data.
- A **decision model**—gives the DSS its analytical capabilities. It may be a *strategic model* to assist top managers in long-range planning; a *tactical model* to help middle-level managers control the work of the organization; or an *operational model* to help supervisors do day-to-day activities.

10

Systems Analysis and Design

Competencies

After you have read this chapter, you should be able to:

1. Describe the six phases of the systems life cycle.

2. Discuss how problems or needs are identified during Phase 1, preliminary investigation.

3. Explain how the current system is studied and new requirements are specified in Phase 2, systems analysis.

4. Describe how a new or alternative information system is designed in Phase 3, systems design.

5. Explain how new hardware and software are acquired, developed, and tested in Phase 4, systems development.

6. Discuss how a new information system is installed and users are trained in Phase 5, systems implementation.

7. Describe Phase 6, systems maintenance, the systems audit and ongoing evaluation, to see if a new system is doing what it's supposed to.

8. Understand prototyping.

Most people in an organization are involved with an information system of some kind, as we saw in the previous chapter. Assuredly, most microcomputer users in the future will not only have access to such a system. They will also be part of one. For an organization to *establish* a system and for users to make it truly useful require considerable thought and effort. Fortunately, there is a six-step problem-solving process for accomplishing this. It is known as *systems analysis and design*.

Big organizations can make big mistakes. For example, General Motors spent $40 billion putting in factory robots and other high technology in its automaking plants. It then removed much of this equipment and reinstalled that basic part of the assembly line—the conveyor belt. Why did the high-tech production systems fail? The probable reason was that GM didn't devote enough energy to training its work force in how to use the new systems.

The government also can make big mistakes. In one year, the new Internal Revenue Service computer system was so overwhelmed it could not deliver many tax refunds on time. The reason? Despite extensive testing of much of the system, a great deal of testing was *not* done. Thus, when the new system was phased in, the IRS found it could not process tax returns as quickly as it had hoped. Many tax refunds were delayed.

Both of these examples show the necessity for thorough planning—especially when an organization is trying to implement a new kind of system. Despite the spectacular failures above, there *is* a way to avoid such mistakes. It is called *systems analysis and design*.

Why should you, as a computer end user rather than a computer professional, know anything about this procedure? There are three reasons:

■ Especially if you work for a large organization, a systems analysis and design study will sometime undoubtedly focus on your job. Knowing how the procedure works will enable you to deal with it better.

■ You can use the steps in systems analysis and design to improve your own productivity within the organization. That is, you can use the procedure to solve problems within your own corner of the organization. Or you can use it to assist professionals in solving larger problems within the organization.

■ You can use this procedure to reduce the risk of a new project's failing. Many new information systems fail or do not work well for a variety of reasons. If you use systems analysis and design, you can minimize the chances of these flaws occurring.

Systems Analysis and Design

Systems Analysis and Design Is a Six-Phase Problem-Solving Procedure for Examining an Information System and Improving It.

We described three types of information systems in the last chapter. Now let us consider: What, exactly, is a **system?** We can define it as a collection of activities and elements organized to accomplish a goal. As we saw in the last chapter, an *information system* is a collection of hardware, software, people, procedures, and data. These work together to provide information essential to running an organization. This information helps to produce a product or service and, for profit-oriented businesses, derive a profit.

Information—about orders received, products shipped, money owed, and so on—flows into an organization from the outside. Information—about what supplies have been received, which customers have paid their bills, and so on—also flows inside the organization. In order to avoid confusion, these flows of information must follow some system. However, from time to time, organizations need to change their information systems. Reasons may be organizational growth, mergers and acquisitions, new marketing opportunities, revisions in governmental regulations, availability of new technology, or other changes.

Systems analysis and design is a six-phase problem-solving procedure for examining an information system and improving it.

The six phases make up the **systems life cycle**. (*See Figure 10-1.*) The phases are as follows:

1. *Preliminary investigation:* The information problems or needs are identified.
2. *Systems analysis:* The present system is studied in depth. New requirements are specified.
3. *Systems design:* A new or alternative information system is designed.

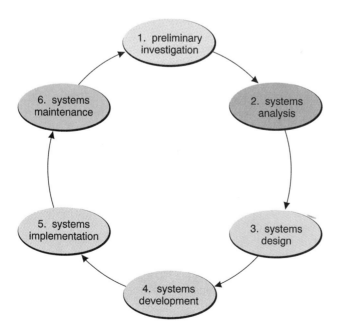

Figure 10-1
The six-phase systems life cycle.

4. *Systems development:* New hardware and software are acquired, developed, and tested.
5. *Systems implementation:* The new information system is installed and adapted to the new system, and people are trained to use it.
6. *Systems maintenance:* In this ongoing phase, the system is periodically evaluated and updated as needed.

In organizations, the six-phase systems life cycle is used by computer professionals known as **systems analysts.** These people study an organization's systems to determine what actions to take and how to use computer technology to assist them. You may well find yourself working with such professionals in evaluating and changing parts of an organization with which you are involved. It's important that you understand how the six phases work. After all, you better than anyone should understand what is needed in your part of the organization. And you should be best able to express that need. Developing a large computer-based information system requires the close collaboration of end users and systems analysts.

The procedure is also one that *you* as an end user can perform, working on your own or with a systems analyst. In fact, you may *have* to use the procedure. More and more end users are developing their own systems. This is because in many organizations there is a three-year backlog of work for systems analysts. For instance, suppose you recognize that there is a need for certain information within your organization. Obtaining this information will require the introduction of new hardware and software. You go to seek expert help from systems analysts in studying these information needs. At that point you discover they are so overworked it will take them three years to get to your request! You can see, then, why many managers are learning to do these activities themselves. In any case, learning these six steps will give you skills that raise your computer competency. They can also make you more valuable to an organization.

Let us now describe each phase in the systems life cycle.

Phase 1: Preliminary Investigation

In the Preliminary Investigation Phase, the Problems Are Briefly Identified and a Few Solutions Are Suggested.

The first phase is a **preliminary investigation** of a proposed project to determine the need for a new information system. (*See Figure 10-2.*) This usually is requested by an end user or a manager who wants something done that is not presently being done. For example, suppose you work for Advantage Advertising, a fast-growing advertising agency. Advantage Advertising produces a variety of different ads for a wide range of different clients. The agency employs both regular staff people and on-call freelancers. One of your responsibilities is to keep track of the work performed for each client and the employees who performed the work. In addition, you are responsible for tabulating the final bill for each project.

How do you figure out how to charge which clients for which work done by which employees? This kind of problem is common not only in advertising agencies. It is found in many other service organizations (such as lawyers' and contractors' offices). Indeed, it is a problem in any organization where people charge for their "time" and clients need proof of hours worked.

In Phase 1, the systems analyst—or the end user—is concerned with three tasks. These are (1) briefly defining the problem, (2) suggesting alternative solutions, and (3)

Figure 10-2
Phase 1: preliminary
investigation.

preparing a short report. This report will help management decide whether to pursue the project further. (If you are an end user employing this procedure for yourself, you may not produce a written report. Rather, you would report your findings directly to your supervisor.)

Defining the Problem Defining the problem means examining whatever current information system is in use. Determining what information is needed, by whom, when, and why, is accomplished by interviewing and making observations. If the information system is large, this survey is done by a systems analyst. If the system is small, the survey can be done by the end user.

For example, suppose at Advantage Advertising account executives, copywriters, and graphic artists at present simply keep track of the time they spend on different jobs by making notations on their desk calendars. (Examples might be "Client A, telephone conference, 15 minutes"; "Client B, design layout, 2 hours.") This approach is somewhat helter-skelter. Written calendar entries look somewhat unprofessional to be shown to clients. Moreover, often a large job has many people working on it. It is difficult to pull together all their notations to make up a bill for the client. Some freelancers work at home, and their time slips are not readily available. These matters constitute a statement of the problem: The company has a manual time-and-billing system that is slow and difficult to implement.

As an end user, you might experience difficulties with this system yourself. You're in someone else's office, and a telephone call comes in for you from a client. Your desk calendar is back in your own office. You have two choices. You can always carry your calendar with you. As an alternative, you can remember to note the time you spent on various tasks when you return to your office. The secretary to the account executive is continually after you (and everyone else at Advantage) to provide photocopies of your calendar. This is so that various clients can be billed for the work done on various jobs. Surely, you think, there must be a better way to handle time and billing.

Suggesting Alternative Systems   This step is simply to suggest some possible plans as alternatives to the present arrangement. For instance, Advantage could hire more secretaries to collect the information from everyone's calendars (including telephoning those working at home). Or it could use the existing system of network-linked microcomputers that staffers and freelancers presently use. Perhaps, you think, there is already some off-the-shelf packaged software available that could be used for a time-and-billing system. At least there might be one that would make your own job easier.

Suppose you take this notion to your boss—that you find some way to automate your time-and-billing procedures, using your own microcomputer. Your boss feels that's a fine idea but points out that whatever you do will affect other people inside and outside Advantage Advertising. The thing to do, your manager says, is to check out your suggestion with the company's systems analyst.

The systems analyst, you find, is extremely busy—so much so that this individual's current work backlog amounts to three years' worth. You might wonder how an organization could stay in business with problems piling up for this long. That is precisely the reason for learning how to do systems analysis and design yourself. This, in fact, is what the systems analyst suggests you do. You do the work yourself; the analyst will help you wherever possible.

Preparing a Short Report   For large projects, the systems analyst would write a short report summarizing the results of the preliminary investigation and suggesting alternative systems. The report may also include schedules for further development of the project. This document is presented to higher management, along with a recommendation to continue or discontinue the project. Management then decides whether to finance the second phase, the systems analysis.

For Advantage Advertising, your report might point out that billing is frequently delayed. It could say that some tasks may even "slip through the cracks" and not get charged at all. Thus, as the analyst has pointed out, you suggest the project might pay for itself merely by eliminating lost or forgotten charges.

Phase 2: Analysis

In the Systems Analysis Phase, the Present System Is Studied in Depth, and New Requirements Are Specified.

In Phase 2, **systems analysis,** data is collected about the present system. (*See Figure 10-3.*) This data is then analyzed, and new requirements are determined. We are not concerned with a new design here, only with determining the *requirements* for a new system. The design itself will be done in Phase 3. Systems analysis is concerned with gathering data and analyzing the data. It usually is completed with summarizing documentation.

Gathering Data   Here the systems analyst—or the end user doing systems analysis—expands on the data gathered during Phase 1. She or he adds details about how the current system works. Data is obtained from observation and interviews. It is also obtained from studying documents that describe the formal lines of authority and standard operating procedures. One document is the **organization chart,** which shows levels of management and formal lines of authority. (*See Figure 10-4, top.*) You might note that an organization chart resembles the hierarchy of three levels of management we described in Chapter 9. The levels are top managers, middle man-

Figure 10-3
Phase 2: analysis.

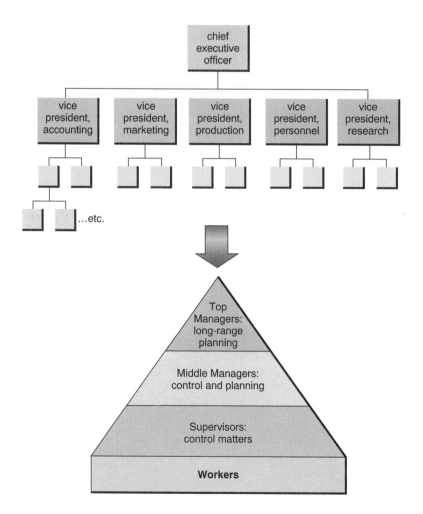

Figure 10-4
Example of an organization chart—and how it corresponds to the management pyramid.

agers, and supervisors. (*See Figure 10-4, bottom.*) In addition, data may be obtained from questionnaires given to people using the system.

Note in our illustration that we have preserved the department labeled "Production." (*See Figure 10-4, top.*) (However, the name in an advertising agency might be something like "Creative Services.") Obviously, the products an advertising agency produces are ads: radio and television commercials, magazine and newspaper ads, billboard ads, and so on. In any case, if the agency is working on a major advertising campaign, people from several departments might be involved. There might also be people from different management levels within the departments. Their time charges will vary depending on how much they are paid.

Analyzing the Data In this step, the data is analyzed to learn how information currently flows and to pinpoint why it is not flowing appropriately. The whole point of this step is to apply *logic* to the existing arrangement to see how workable it is. Many times the current system is not operating correctly because prescribed procedures are not being followed. That is, the system may not really need to be redesigned. Rather, the people in it may need to be shown how to follow correct procedures.

Many different tools are available to assist systems analysts and end users in the analysis phase. Some of the principal ones are as follows:

■ *Checklists:* Numerous checklists are available to assist in this stage. A **checklist** is a list of questions. It is helpful in guiding the systems analyst and end user through key issues for the present system.

  For example, one question might be "Can reports be easily prepared from the files and documents currently in use?" Another might be "How easily can the present time-and-billing system adapt to change and growth?"

■ *Top-down analysis methodology:* The **top-down analysis methodology** is used to identify the top-level components of a complex system. Each component is then broken down into smaller and smaller components. This kind of tool makes each component easier to analyze and deal with.

For instance, the systems analyst might look at the present kind of bill submitted to a client for a complex advertising campaign. The analyst might note the categories of costs—employee salaries, telephone and mailing charges, travel, supplies, and so on.

■ *Grid charts:* A **grid chart** shows the relationship between input and output documents. An example is shown in the illustration below, which indicates the relationship between the data input and the outputs. (*See Figure 10-5.*)

  For instance, a time card form is one of many inputs that produces a particular report, such as a client's bill. (Other inputs might be forms having to do with sup-

Forms (input)	Reports (output)		
	Report A	Report B	Report C
form 1	✓		✓
form 2	✓	✓	
form 3			✓
form 4			✓

Figure 10-5
Example of a grid chart.

Decision rules

Conditions	1	2	3	4	5	6	7
if. . .	Y	Y	Y	Y	N	N	N
And if. . .	Y	N	Y	N	Y	Y	N
And if. . .	Y	Y	N	N	Y	N	N

Actions							
Then do. . .	✓						
Then do. . .		✓	✓		✓		
Then do. . .				✓		✓	✓

Figure 10-6
Example of a decision table.

plies, travel, and other costs of an advertising campaign.) Horizontal rows represent inputs, such as time card forms. Vertical rows represent output documents, such as different clients' bills. A checkmark at the intersection of a row and column means that the input document is used to create the output document.

- *Decision tables:* A **decision table** shows the decision rules that apply when certain conditions occur. (*See Figure 10-6.*) It also shows what action should take place as a result. One rule might be "*If* creative time spent on account was by a freelance employee *and if* that employee worked overtime, *then* charge the client XXX amount." There might be different types of decision rules for different kinds of employees.

- *System flowcharts:* **System flowcharts** show the flow or input of data, processing and output, or distribution of information. An example of a system flowchart keeping track of time for advertising "creative people" is shown in the illustration at right. (*See Figure 10-7.*) The explanation of the symbols used (and others not used) appears in the illustration below. (*See Figure 10-8.*) Note this describes the present manual, or noncomputerized, system. (A *system* flowchart is not the same as a *program* flowchart, which is very detailed. Program flowcharts are discussed in the next chapter.)

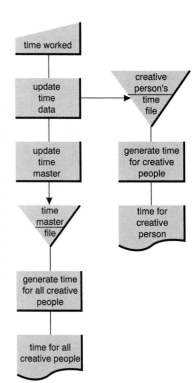

Figure 10-7
Example of a system flowchart.

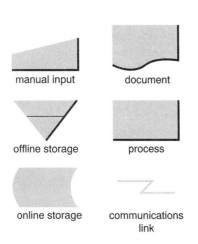

manual input   document

offline storage   process

online storage   communications link

Figure 10-8
Guide to system flowchart symbols.

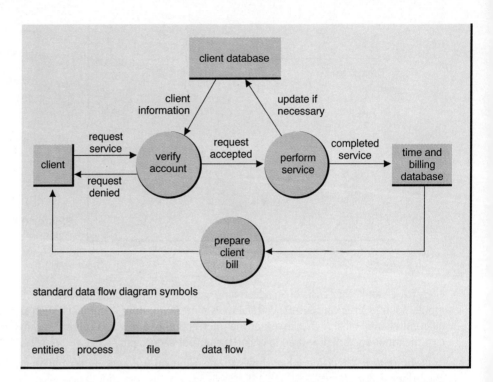

Figure 10-9
Example of a data flow diagram.

■ *Data flow diagrams:* **Data flow diagrams** show the data or information flow within an information system. The data is traced from its origination through processing, storage, and output. An example of a data flow diagram is shown in the illustration. (*See Figure 10-9.*)

■ *Automated design tools:* **Automated design tools** are software packages that evaluate hardware and software alternatives according to requirements given by the systems analyst. They are also called **computer-aided software engineering tools, or CASE tools.** They enable several systems analysts and programmers to automate and to coordinate their efforts on a project.

Documenting the Systems Analysis Stage In larger organizations, the systems analysis stage is typically documented in a report for higher management. The systems analysis report describes the current information system, the requirements for a new system, and a possible development schedule. For example, at Advantage Advertising, the system flowcharts will show the present flow of information in a manual time-and-billing system. Some of the boxes in the system flowchart might be replaced with symbols showing where a computerized information system could work better. For example, in our flowchart, the offline storage symbol ("time master file") might be replaced by an online storage symbol. (*Refer back to Figure 10-7.*) That is, the information in the file would be instantly accessible.

Management studies the report and decides whether to continue with the project. Let us assume your boss and higher management have decided to continue. You now move on to Phase 3, systems design.

Phase 3: Design

In the Systems Design Phase, a New or Alternative Information System Is Designed.

Phase 3 is **systems design**. (*See Figure 10-10.*) It consists of three tasks: (1) designing alternative systems, (2) selecting the best system, and (3) writing a systems design report.

Designing Alternative Systems   In almost all instances, more than one design can be developed to meet the information needs. Systems designers evaluate each alternative system for feasibility. By "feasibility" we mean three things:

- *Economic feasibility:* Will the costs of the new system be justified by the benefits it promises?

- *Technical feasibility:* Are reliable hardware, software, and trained people available to make the system work?

- *Operational feasibility:* Can the system actually be made to operate in the organization, or will people—employees, managers, clients—resist it?

Selecting the Best System   When choosing the best design, managers must consider these four questions. (1) Will the system fit in with the organization's overall information system? (2) Will the system be flexible enough so it can be modified in the future? (3) Can it be made secure against unauthorized use? (4) Are the benefits worth the costs?

For example, one aspect you have to consider at Advantage Advertising is security. Should freelancers and outside vendors enter data directly into a computerized time-and-billing system, or should they continue to submit time slips manually? In allowing these people outside your organization to directly input information, are you also

Figure 10-10
Phase 3: design.

allowing them access to files they should not see? Do these files contain confidential information, perhaps information of value to rival advertising agencies?

Writing the Systems Design Report The report is prepared for higher management and describes the alternative designs. It presents the costs versus the benefits and outlines the effect of alternative designs on the organization. It usually concludes by recommending one of the alternatives.

Phase 4: Development

In the Systems Development Phase, New Hardware and Software Are Developed, Acquired, and Tested.

Phase 4 is **systems development.** (*See Figure 10-11.*) It has three steps: (1) developing software, (2) acquiring hardware, and (3) testing the new system.

Developing Software Applications software for the new information system can be obtained in two ways. It can be purchased as off-the-shelf packaged software and possibly modified, or it can be custom designed. If any of the software is to be specially created, the steps we will outline on programming (in Chapter 11) should be followed.

With the systems analyst's help, you have looked at time-and-billing packaged software designed for service organizations. Such organizations might include advertising agencies, law firms, and building contractors. The systems analyst points out that it is important that the time-and-billing data be collected in an appropriate manner so that it can be used for a variety of purposes. Such a system will not only help supervisory and middle managers do their jobs but also help top managers make decisions.

Unfortunately, you find that none of the packaged software will do. Most of the packages seem to work well for one person (you). However, none seem to be designed for many people working together. It appears, then, that software will have to be custom designed. (We discuss the process of developing software in Chapter 11 on programming.)

Figure 10-11
Phase 4: development.

Acquiring Hardware Some new systems may not require new computer equipment, but others will. The kinds needed and the places they are to be installed must be determined. This is a very critical area. Switching or upgrading equipment can be a tremendously expensive proposition. Will a microcomputer system be sufficient as a company grows? Are networks expandable? Will microcomputers easily communicate with one another? Will people have to undergo costly training?

The systems analyst tells you that there are several different makes and models of microcomputers currently in use at Advantage Advertising. Fortunately, all are connected by a local area network to a file server that can hold the time-and-billing data. To maintain security, the systems analyst suggests that an electronic mailbox can be installed for freelancers and others outside the company to use to post their time charges. Thus, it appears that existing hardware will work just fine.

Testing the New System After the software and equipment have been installed, the system should be tested. Sample data is fed into the system. The processed information is then evaluated to see whether results are correct. Testing may take several months if the new system is complex.

For this step, you take some time and expense charges from an ad campaign that Advantage ran the previous year. You then ask some people in Creative Services to test it on the system. You observe that time is often charged in fractions of minutes and that the software ignores these fractions of time. You also see that some of the people in Creative Services have problems knowing where to enter their times. To solve the first problem, you must see that the software is corrected to allow for fractional minutes. To solve the second problem, you must see that the software is modified so that an improved user entry screen is displayed. After the system has been thoroughly tested and revised as necessary, you are ready to put it into use.

Phase 5: Implementation

In the Systems Implementation Phase, the New Information System Is Installed, and People Are Trained to Use It.

Another name for Phase 5, **systems implementation**, is **conversion.** (*See Figure 10-12.*) It is the process of changing—converting—from the old system to the new.

Types of Conversion There are four approaches to conversion: *direct, parallel, pilot,* and *phased.*

- In the **direct approach,** the conversion is done simply by abandoning the old and starting up the new. This can be risky. If anything is still wrong with the new system, the old system is no longer available to fall back on.

  The direct approach is not recommended precisely because it is so risky. Problems, big or small, invariably crop up in a new system. In a large system, a problem might just mean catastrophe.

- In the **parallel approach,** old and new systems are operated side by side until the new one has shown it is reliable.

  This approach is low-risk. If the new system fails, the organization can just switch to the old system to keep going. However, keeping enough equipment and people active to manage two systems at the same time can be very expensive. Thus, the parallel approach is used only in cases in which the cost of failure or of interrupted operation is great.

Figure 10-12
Phase 5: implementation.

■ In the **pilot approach,** the new system is tried out in only one part of the organization. Later it is implemented throughout the rest of the organization.

The pilot approach is certainly less expensive than the parallel approach. It also is somewhat riskier. However, the risks can be controlled because problems will be confined to only certain areas of the organization. Difficulties will not affect the entire organization.

■ In the **phased approach,** the new system is implemented gradually over a period of time.

This is an expensive proposition, because the implementation is done slowly. However, it is certainly one of the least risky approaches.

In general, the pilot and phased approaches are the most favored methods. Pilot is preferred when there are many people in an organization performing similar operations—for instance, all sales clerks in a department store. Phased is more appropriate for organizations in which people are performing different operations.

You and the systems analyst succeed in convincing the top managers of Advantage Advertising to take a pilot approach. The reason is that it is easy to select one trial group—the group of which you are a member. Moreover, this group is eager to try the new system. Thus, the new time-and-billing system is tried first with a handful of people in your particular department.

Training Training people is important, of course. Some people may begin training early, even before the equipment is delivered, so that they can adjust more easily. In some cases, a professional software trainer may be brought in to show people how to operate the system. However, at Advantage Advertising the time-and-billing software is simple enough that the systems analyst can act as the trainer.

Phase 6: Maintenance

Systems Maintenance Is First a Systems Audit and Then an Ongoing Evaluation to See Whether a System Is Performing Productively.

After implementation comes **systems maintenance,** the last step in the systems life cycle. (*See Figure 10-13.*) Maintenance has two parts—a *systems audit* and *periodic evaluation.*

In the **systems audit,** the system's performance is compared to the original design specifications. This is to determine if the new procedures are actually furthering productivity. If they are not, some further redesign may be necessary.

After the systems audit, the new information system is periodically evaluated and further modified, if necessary. All systems should be evaluated from time to time to see whether they are meeting the goals and providing the service they are supposed to.

For example, over time the transaction database at Advantage Advertising is expanded. After a year or two, the systems analyst might suggest that the time-and-billing part of it be reevaluated. For instance, the analyst might discover that telephone and mailing charges need to be separated. This might be because, with more people using the electronic mailbox and more people sharing data, telephone charges are now higher.

The six-step systems life cycle is summarized below. (*See Figure 10-14.*)

Figure 10-13
Phase 6: maintenance.

System Development Life Cycle	
Phase	**Activity**
1. Preliminary investigation	Define problem Suggest alternatives Prepare short report
2. Systems analysis	Gather data Analyze data Document
3. Systems design	Design alternatives Select best alternative Write report
4. Systems development	Develop software Aquire hardware Test system
5. Systems implementation	Convert Train
6. Systems maintenance	Perform system audit Evaluate periodically

Figure 10-14
Systems life cycle.

Prototyping

Prototyping Consists of Devising a Model of a New System for Users to Try Out.

Is it necessary to follow every phase of the six phases of systems analysis and design? It may be desirable, but often there is no time to do so. For instance, hardware may change so fast that there is no opportunity for the evaluation, design, and testing just described.

A faster alternative is prototyping. **Prototyping** means to build a model, or prototype (pronounced "*proh*-toh-type"), that can be modified before the actual system is installed. For instance, the systems analyst for Advantage Advertising might develop a menu as a possible screen display for the time-and-billing system. Users could try it before the system is put into place.

Prototyping is considered a "quickie" way of building a system. It allows users to find out right away how a change in the system can help their work. However, relying on prototyping alone can be risky. It might lead to a system's being changed or installed without all costs and other matters being considered.

A Look at the Future

The Systems Life Cycle Will Be Shortened Using a Method Called Rapid Applications Development.

The traditional systems life cycle can take a long time—sometimes years, in the case of large projects for large organizations. Because the pace of business is increasing, to stay competitive, corporations must shorten development life cycles so that products can be produced more quickly.

In the future, we will probably see increasing use of a new method called *rapid applications development (RAD),* which is intended to reduce development to months instead of years. RAD uses powerful development software (such as CASE), small teams, and highly trained people to produce applications much faster and with higher-quality results than traditional methods do.

Review Questions

1. What is a system?
2. What is the purpose of systems analysis and design?
3. What is the six-phase problem-solving procedure called?
4. List the six phases.
5. What do systems analysts do?
6. Describe the three steps required in Phase 1, preliminary investigation.
7. Describe the three steps required in Phase 2, systems analysis.
8. What is a checklist?
9. Describe top-down analysis methodology.
10. What is a grid chart?
11. Describe a decision table.
12. What is a system flowchart?

13. Explain the three steps in Phase 4, systems development.
14. Describe the four possible ways of carrying out Phase 5, systems implementation.
15. What is systems maintenance?
16. Describe prototyping.

Discussion Questions and Projects

1. *Using systems analysis in your life:* Will the systems life cycle approach work in the real world? Will it work for you? To find out, try one of the following activities:

   a. Interview a systems analyst, perhaps one working at the computer center or in the information systems department of your college. Ask the analyst's opinion of the systems approach as applied to ordinary, non–computer-related problems.

   b. Apply the systems life cycle to activities at school or work that you find inefficient or irritating: parking problems, preregistration system, financial aid deadlines, and so on. Try to apply Phase 1, preliminary investigation, briefly identifying the problem and suggesting possible solutions. Write a short report to higher management or the college administration to help them decide whether to go ahead with Phase 2. See whether you can pose a few solutions and find out who is in a position of authority to make possible changes.

2. *The requirements of a systems analyst:* Current research in systems analysis and design suggests that a systems analyst should demonstrate a wide range of characteristics. Collect several ads for systems analyst positions. What personality traits appear to be in demand? Assessing the educational requirements and work experience required may help you discuss your findings.

Chapter 10 Systems Analysis and Design

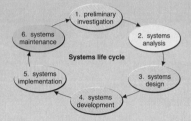

Systems analysis and design is a six-phase problem-solving procedure for examining an information system and improving it. The six phases are called the **systems life cycle.**

Phase 1: Preliminary Investigation	Phase 2: Analysis	Phase 3: Design

The **preliminary investigation** determines the need for a new information system. The tasks of this phase are:

Defining the problem—what information is needed, by whom, when, and why.

Suggesting alternative systems.

Preparing a short report—a presentation to management.

In **systems analysis** data is collected about the present system. The tasks of this phase are:

Gathering data—using observation, interviews, and questionnaires and looking at documents such as the **organization chart,** which shows a company's functions and levels of management.

Analyzing the data—using several analytical tools:

- **Checklists** show what key issues to evaluate.

- **Top-down analysis methodology** shows what are important and lesser components.

- **Grid charts** show relationship between input and output documents.

- **Decision tables** show what decision rules apply when certain conditions occur and what action should result.

- **System flowcharts** show flow or input of data, processing and output, or distribution.

- **Data flow diagrams** show data flow within an organization.

Systems design consists of the following three tasks:

Designing alternative systems—using programming tools. Systems are evaluated for feasibility—economic, technical, and operational.

Selecting the best system—considering if the system will fit, is flexible, can be made secure, and is cost-effective.

Writing the systems design report—describing this phase for higher management.

Data flow diagrams are frequently used to document and analyze the flow of data and information through a system.

- **Automated design tools** are software packages to evaluate hardware and software alternatives. They are called **computer-aided software engineering (CASE) tools.**

Documenting systems analysis stage—describing results for higher management.

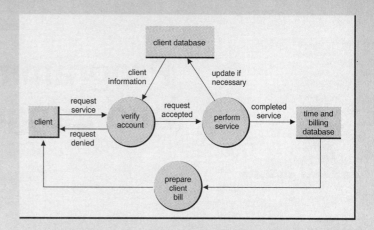

Data flow diagrams, a widely used design tool, trace information from its beginning through processing, storage, and output.

Phase 4: Development	Phase 5: Implementation	Phase 6: Maintenance

The **systems development** phase has three steps:

Developing software—determining whether packaged or custom software is needed.

Acquiring hardware—obtaining new computer equipment, if necessary.

Testing the new system—using made-up data.

Systems implementation (conversion) is the process of changing from the old system to the new.

Types of Conversion

Four ways to convert are:

- **Direct approach**—abandoning the old and starting up the new.
- **Parallel approach**—operating the old and new side by side until the new one proves its worth.
- **Pilot approach**—trying out the new system in only one part of an organization.
- **Phased approach**—implementing the new system gradually.

Training

A software trainer may be used to train end users on the new system.

Systems maintenance has two parts:

Systems audit—in which a systems analyst compares the new system to design specifications to see if it is productive.

Periodic evaluation—the new system is periodically evaluated and revised, if necessary.

11

Programming and Languages

How do you go about getting a job? You look through newspaper classified ads, check with employment services, write to prospective employers, and so on. In other words, you do some *general problem solving* to come up with a broad plan. This is similar to what you do in systems analysis and design. Once you have determined a *particular* job you would like to have, you then do some *specific problem solving.* That is what you do in programming. In this chapter, we describe programming in two parts. They are (1) the steps in the programming process and (2) some of the programming languages available.

Why should you need to know anything about programming? The answer is simple. You might need to deal with programmers in the course of your work. You may also be required to do some programming yourself in the future. A new field has emerged known as *end-user application development.* In this field, users like you create their own business application programs, without the assistance of a programmer. Thus, organizations avoid paying high software development costs. You and other end users avoid waiting months for programmers to get around to projects important to you.

In the last chapter, we described the six phases of the systems life cycle. They are (1) preliminary investigation, (2) systems analysis, (3) systems design, (4) systems development, (5) systems implementation, and (6) systems maintenance. Programming is a part of Phase 4, as illustrated on the next page. (*See Figure 11-1.*) Note that the bottom part of that illustration constitutes an outline of the steps in programming. We follow that outline in this chapter.

Programs and Programming

Programming Is a Six-Step Procedure for Producing a Program—a List of Instructions—for the Computer.

What exactly *is* programming? Many people think of it as simply typing words into a computer. That may be part of it—but certainly not all of it. Programming, as we've hinted, is actually a *problem-solving procedure.*

What Is a Program?   To see how programming works, think what a program is. A *program* is a list of instructions for the computer to follow to accomplish the task of processing data into information. The instructions are made up of statements used in a programming language, such as BASIC, Pascal, or C.

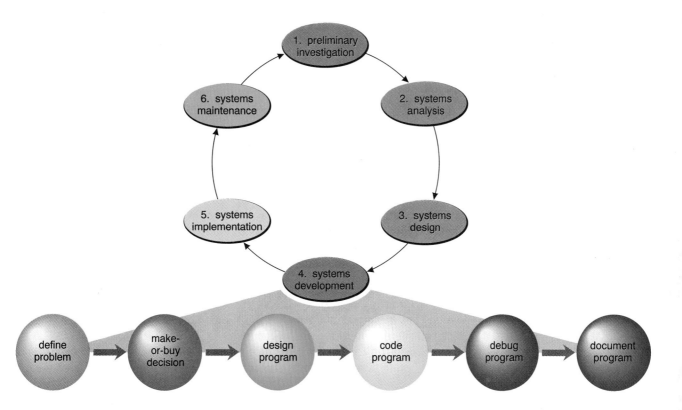

Figure 11-1
Where programming fits in the systems life cycle.

Applications software or *applications programs,* as we said in Chapter 1, are the kind of programs that do "end-user work." These are things such as word processing and accounting tasks. *Systems software,* we said, is concerned with "background" tasks such as housekeeping chores involving computer operations. In this chapter we are concerned with applications programs.

By now you are probably familiar with one kind of applications program—the *purchased, prewritten* programs. These are so-called off-the-shelf programs such as word processors, spreadsheets, and database managers, which may be purchased on floppy disks. However, applications programs may also be *created* or *custom-made*—either by a professional programmer or by you, the end user. In Chapter 10, we saw that the systems analyst looked into the availability of time-and-billing software for Advantage Advertising. Will off-the-shelf software do the job, or should it be custom written? This is one of the first things that needs to be decided in programming.

What Is Programming? A program is a list of instructions for the computer to follow to process data. **Programming** is a six-step procedure for creating that list of instructions. Only *one* of those steps consists of typing (keying) words into a computer.

The six steps are as follows. (*Refer back to Figure 11-1, bottom.*)

1. Define the problem.
2. Decide whether to make or buy software.
3. Design the program.
4. Code—that is, write—the program.
5. Test—that is, debug—the program.
6. Document the program.

Step 1: Define the Problem

In the Definition Step, the Program's Objectives, Outputs, Inputs, and Processing Requirements Are Determined.

Program definition is also called **program analysis.** It requires that the programmer—or you, the end user, if you are following this procedure—specify four tasks. They are (1) the program's objectives, (2) the desired output, (3) the input data required, and (4) the processing requirements. Let us consider these.

Determining Program Objectives   You solve all kinds of problems every day. A problem might be deciding how to commute to school or work or which homework or report to do first. Thus, every day you determine your *objectives*—the problems you are trying to solve. Programming is the same. You need to make a clear statement of the problem you are trying to solve. (*See Figure 11-2.*) An example would be "I want a time-and-billing system to keep track of the time I spend on different jobs for different clients of Advantage Advertising."

Determining the Desired Output   It is best always to specify outputs before inputs. That is, you should list what you want to *get out of* the computer system. Then you should determine what will *go into* it. The best way to do this is to draw a picture. You—the end user, not the programmer—should sketch or write what you want the output to look like in its final form. It might be printed out or displayed on the monitor.

For example, if you want a time-and-billing report, you might write out or draw something like that shown in the illustration on the next page. (*See Figure 11-3.*) Another form of output from the program might be bills to clients.

Figure 11-2
Problem definition: Make a
clear statement of the problem.

Client name: Allan Realty — Month and year: Jan '93

Date	Worker	Regular Hours & Rate	Overtime Hours & Rate	Bill
1/2	M. Jones	5 @ $10	1 @ $15	$65.00
	K. Williams	4 @ $30	2 @ $45	$210.00

Figure 11-3
End user's handwritten example of printed output desired.

Determining the Input Data Once you know the output you want, you can determine the input data and the source of this data. For example, for a time-and-billing report, you can specify that one source of data to be processed should be time cards. These are usually logs or statements of hours worked submitted on paper forms. The log shown in the illustration below is an example of the kind of input data used in Advantage Advertising's manual system. (*See Figure 11-4.*) Note that military time is used. For example, instead of writing "5:45 P.M.," people would write "1745."

Determining the Processing Requirements Here you define the processing tasks that must happen for input data to be processed into output. For Advantage, one of the tasks for the program will be to add the hours worked for different jobs for different clients.

First you must determine all the processing requirements. Then you can find out whether you need to create a special program to handle them or if you can buy an existing program. This leads to the next step, the make-or-buy decision.

Daily Log

Worker:
Date:

Client	Job	Time in	Time out
A	TV commercial	800	915
B	Billboard ad	935	1200
C	Brochure	1315	1545
A	Magazine ad	1600	1745

Figure 11-4
Example of statement of hours worked—manual system. Hours are expressed in military time.

Step 2: Make-or-Buy Decision

In the Make-or-Buy Step, You Must Determine Whether Applications Software Must Be Custom Written or May Be Prewritten.

Figure 11-5
Make-or-buy: Test software to decide if purchasing packaged software will solve the problem or if the software must be custom-made.

After the problem definition step, you have a **make-or-buy decision** to make. Will you have to *make* the software—have the program custom written by a programmer—or can you *buy* it as a prewritten program? (*See Figure 11-5.*) Obviously, just being able to use off-the-shelf purchased software can save you time. Many such programs exist. However, you may not find anything quite meets your needs. This means a programmer may have to adapt a commercially available program or create one from scratch.

Thus, you need to evaluate the feasibility of the program. You need to see whether the potential improvements of a custom-made program will outweigh the costs and time needed to write it. You should analyze the pluses and minuses.

Can you buy an existing time-and-billing program that will meet your needs? This is, in fact, a common requirement. Indeed, you find in your search with the systems analyst that several time-and-billing systems are available. Unfortunately, none of them exactly meets your needs. The systems analyst points out that if others in your organization will use the time-and-billing system, that will justify the cost of developing your own system. This system would be used for everyone working for Advantage Advertising. All workers must report their total hours. They must also state which hours (or portions) were spent working on particular projects so that clients can be billed correctly. You and the systems analyst therefore decide that you will *make* rather than *buy* the software.

Step 3: Design the Program

In the Design Step, a Solution Is Created Using Programming Techniques Such as Top-Down Program Design, Pseudocode, Flowcharts, Logic Structures, and Object-Oriented Programming (OOP).

If you decide that the software must be custom-made, you then take the **program design** step. (*See Figure 11-6.*) Here you plan a solution, preferably using **structured programming techniques.** These techniques consist of the following: (1) top-down program design, (2) pseudocode, (3) flowcharts, (4) logic structures, and (5) object-oriented programming.

Top-Down Program Design   First you determine the outputs and inputs of the computer program you will create. Then you can use **top-down program design** to identify the program's processing steps. Such steps are called **program modules** (or just **modules).** Each module is made up of logically related program statements.

An example of a top-down program design for a time-and-billing report is shown opposite. (*See Figure 11-7.*) Each of the boxes shown is a module. Under the rules of

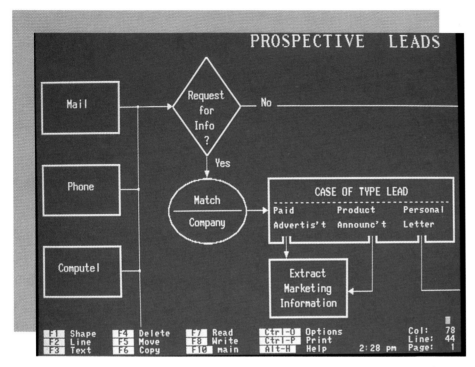

Figure 11-6
Design: In custom-made programs, diagrams are drawn to map out a solution.

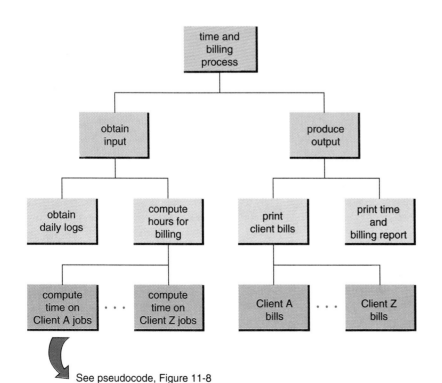

See pseudocode, Figure 11-8

Figure 11-7
Example of top-down program design.

Compute time for Client A

Set total regular hours and total overtime hours to zero.

Get time in and time out for a job.

If worked past 1700 hours, then compute overtime hours.

Compute regular hours.

Add regular hours to total regular hours.

Add overtime hours to total overtime hours.

If there are more jobs for that client, go back and compute
  for that job as well.

Figure 11-8
Example of pseudocode.

See flowchart, Figure 11-9

top-down design, each module should have a single function. The program must pass
in sequence from one module to the next until all modules have been processed by the
computer. Three of the boxes—"Obtain input," "Compute hours for billing," and
"Produce output"—correspond to the three principal computer system operations.
These operations are *input, process,* and *output.*

Pseudocode   **Pseudocode** (pronounced "*soo*-doh-code") is a narrative form of
the logic of the program you will write. It is like doing a summary or an outline
form of the program. The illustration above shows the pseudocode you might write
for one module in the time-and-billing program. (*See Figure 11-8.*) This shows the
reasoning behind determining hours—including overtime hours—worked for different jobs for one client, Client A. Again, note this expresses the *logic* of what you
want the program to do.

Flowcharts   We mentioned system flowcharts in the previous chapter. Here we
are concerned with **program flowcharts.** These graphically present the detailed
sequence of steps needed to solve a programming problem. The illustration on the
next page explains the standard flowcharting symbols and gives an example of a program flowchart. (*See Figure 11-9.*) This flowchart expresses all the logic for just *one*
module—"Compute time on Client A jobs"—in the top-down program design.

Let us proceed to explain the steps in the flowchart. (*See Figure 11-9.*)

Perhaps you can see from this why a computer is a computer, and not just a fancy
adding machine. A computer not only does arithmetic. It can also *make compari-
sons*—whether something is greater than or less than, equal to or not equal to.

But have we skipped something? How do we *know* which kind of twists and turns to
put in a flowchart so that it will logically work? The answer is the use of logic structures,
as we explain.

Logic Structures   How do you link the various parts of the flowchart? The best
way is a combination of three **logic structures** called *sequence, selection,* and *loop.*
Using these arrangements enables you to write so-called *structured programs,*
which take much of the guesswork out of programming. Let us look at the logic
structures.

■   In the **sequence structure,** one program statement follows another. (*See Figure
    11-10 on page 194.*)

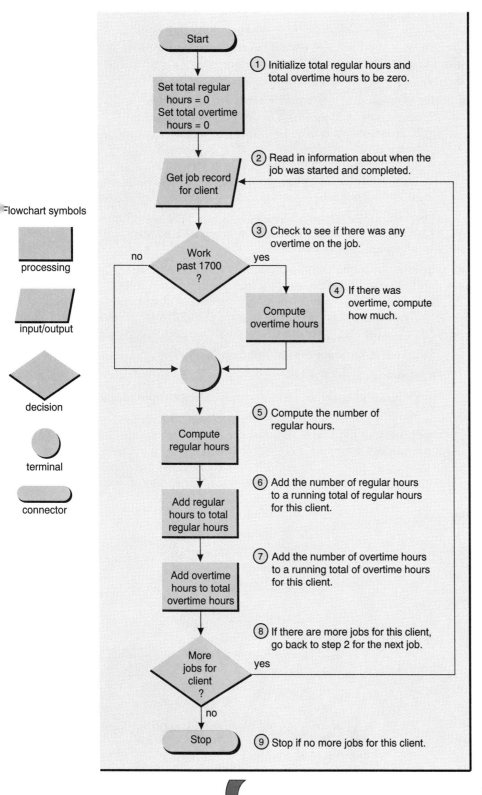

Flowchart symbols

processing

input/output

decision

terminal

connector

Start

① Initialize total regular hours and total overtime hours to be zero.

Set total regular hours = 0
Set total overtime hours = 0

② Read in information about when the job was started and completed.

Get job record for client

③ Check to see if there was any overtime on the job.

Work past 1700 ?   no   yes

④ If there was overtime, compute how much.

Compute overtime hours

⑤ Compute the number of regular hours.

Compute regular hours

⑥ Add the number of regular hours to a running total of regular hours for this client.

Add regular hours to total regular hours

⑦ Add the number of overtime hours to a running total of overtime hours for this client.

Add overtime hours to total overtime hours

⑧ If there are more jobs for this client, go back to step 2 for the next job.

More jobs for client ?   yes

no

Stop

⑨ Stop if no more jobs for this client.

See Figure 11-14

Figure 11-9
Flowchart symbols and example of a program flowchart for computing time worked.

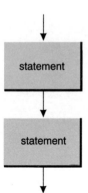

Figure 11-10
Sequence logic structure.

Consider, for example, the "compute time" flowchart. (*Refer back to Figure 11-9.*) The two "add" boxes are "Add regular hours to total regular hours" and "Add overtime hours to total overtime hours." They logically follow each other. There is no question of "yes" or "no," of a decision suggesting other consequences.

■   The **selection structure** occurs when a decision must be made. The outcome of the decision determines which of two paths to follow. (*See Figure 11-11.*) This structure is also known as an **IF-THEN-ELSE structure,** because that is how you can formulate the decision.

Consider, for example, the selection structure in the "compute time" flowchart, which is concerned about computing overtime hours. (*Refer back to Figure 11-9.*) It might be expressed in detail as follows:

**IF hour finished for this job is later than or equal to 1700 hours (5:00 P.M.),
THEN overtime hours equal the number of hours past 1700 hours.
ELSE the overtime hours equal zero.**

■   The **loop structure** describes the activity in which a process may be repeated as long as a certain condition remains true. The structure is called a "loop" or "iteration" because the program loops around (iterates or repeats) again and again.

The loop structure has two variations: *DO UNTIL* and *DO WHILE*. (*See Figure 11-12.*) The **DO UNTIL structure** is the most used form. An example is as follows.

DO read in job information UNTIL there are no more jobs.

An example of the **DO WHILE structure** is:

DO read in job information WHILE (that is, as long as) there are more jobs.

There is a difference between the two loop structures. If you have several statements that need to be repeated, the decision when to *stop* repeating them can appear at the *beginning* of the loop (DO WHILE). Or, it can appear at the *end* of the loop (DO UNTIL). The DO UNTIL loop means that the loop statements will be executed at least once. This is because the loop statements are executed *before* you are asked whether to stop.

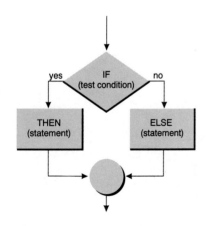

Figure 11-11
Selection (IF-THEN-ELSE) logic
structure.

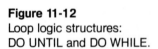

Figure 11-12
Loop logic structures:
DO UNTIL and DO WHILE.

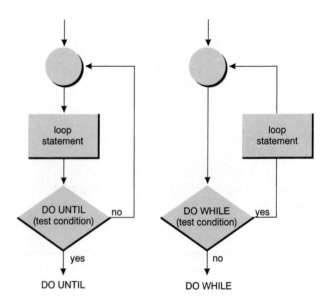

Object-Oriented Programming   Logic structures have helped to take the guess-work out of programming, but object-oriented programming has helped to improve efficiency. **Object-oriented programming (OOP)** is defined as a methodology in which a program is organized into objects, each containing both the data and processing operations necessary to perform a task. Let's explain what this means.

In the past, programs were developed as giant entities, from the first line of code to the last. This has been compared to building a car from scratch with sheet metal. Object-oriented programming is like building a car from prefabricated parts—carbu-retor, generator, fenders, and so on. Object-oriented programs use *modules* called "objects"—reusable, self-contained components. Programs built with these objects assume that certain functions are the same. For example, many programs, from word processing to spreadsheets, have an instruction that will sort lists of names in alpha-betical order. A programmer might use this module or object for alphabetizing in many other programs. There is no need to invent this activity anew every time.

Step 4: Code the Program

"Coding" Is the Actual Writing of the Program, Using a Programming Language.

Writing the program is called **coding**. Here you use the logic you developed in the pro-gram design step to actually write the program. That is, you write out—using pencil and paper or typing on a computer keyboard—the letters, numbers, and symbols that make up the program. An example of the handwritten code for the "compute time" module is shown below. (*See Figure 11-13.*) This is the "program code" that instructs the computer what to do. Coding is what many people think of when they think of

```
begin
  total_regular := 0;
  total_overtime := 0;
  while not eof(input_file) do
      begin
      readln (input_file, hour_in, minute_in, hour_out, minute_out);
      if (hour_out >= 17) then
          overtime := (hour_out - 17) + (minute_out/60)
      else
          overtime := P;
      regular := (hour_out - hour_in) + (minute_out - minute_in)/60) - overtime;

      total_regular := total_regular + regular;
      total_overtime := total_overtime = overtime;
      end;
  end.
```

See Figure 11-15

Figure 11-13
Handwritten code of "compute time" module. (The number "17" stands for "1700 hours," or 5 P.M.)

programming. As we've pointed out, however, it is only one of the six steps in the programming process.

The Good Program What are the qualities of a good program? Above all, it should be reliable; that is, it should work under most conditions. It should catch obvious and common input errors. It should also be understandable by programmers other than the person who wrote it. After all, someone may need to make changes in the program in the future. The best way to code effective programs is to write so-called *structured programs,* using the logic structures described in Step 3.

Which Language? An important decision is which language to write the program in. There are hundreds of programming languages, but for microcomputers the most popular have been BASIC and Pascal. We describe programming languages later in this chapter. First you must determine the program's logic. Then you can write (code) it in whatever language you choose that is available on your computer. A Pascal program for the "compute time" module is illustrated below. (*See Figure 11-14.*) The next step is debugging, or testing, the program.

Figure 11-14
The "compute time" program written in Pascal.

```
Program compute_time:

var
    input_file : text;
    total_regular,
    total_overtime,
    regular,
    overtime : real;
    hour_in,
    minute_in,
    hour_out,
    minute_out : integer;


begin
assign (input_file,'time.txt');
reset (input_file);

total_regular := 0;
total_overtime  := 0;
while not eof(input_file) do
  begin
  readln (input_file,hour_in,minute_in,hour_out,minute_out);
  if (hour_out >= 17) then
     overtime := (hour_out − 17) + (minute_out/60)
  else
     overtime := 0;
  regular := (hour_out-hour_in) + ((minute_out-minute_in)/60)  −overtime;
  total_regular := total_regular + regular;
  total_overtime := total_overtime + overtime;
  end;

writeln('regular = ',total_regular);
writeln('overtime = ',total_overtime);
end.
```

Step 5: Debug the Program

"Debugging" Is Testing a Program and Correcting Syntax and Logic Errors.

Debugging is a programmer's word for *testing* and then *eliminating* errors ("getting the bugs out"). It means running the program you have written on a computer and then fixing the parts that do not work. (*See Figure 11-15.*) Programming errors are of two sorts: *syntax errors* and *logic errors*.

Syntax Errors   A **syntax error** is a violation of the rules of whatever language the program is being written in. For example, in the programming language called Pascal, the instruction "write In" is wrong. It is supposed to be "writeln." That is an example of a syntax error.

Logic Errors   A **logic error** is when the programmer has used an incorrect calculation or left out a programming procedure. For instance, if you give the wrong rate for overtime hours, this is an example of a logic error.

The Debugging Process   Several methods have been devised for finding and removing both types of errors, as follows.

- *Desk checking:* In **desk checking,** a programmer sitting at a desk checks (proof-reads) a printout of the program. The programmer goes through the listing line by line looking for syntax and logic errors.

- *Manual testing with sample data:* Both correct and incorrect data is run through the program—manually, not with a computer—to test for correct processing results.

- *Attempt at translation:* The program is run through a computer, using a translator program. The translator attempts to translate the written program from the programming language (such as Pascal) into the machine language. Before the program will run, it must be free of syntax errors. Such errors will be identified by the translating program.

- *Testing sample data on the computer:* After all syntax errors have been corrected, the program is tested for logic errors. Sample data is used to test the correct execution of each program statement.

Figure 11-15
Debugging: The program is tested for errors, using sample data.

Figure 11-16
Documentation is needed so
that others may understand the
program.

Step 6: Document the Program

"Documenting" Means Writing a Description of the Purpose and Process of the Program.

Documentation consists of written descriptions and procedures about a program and how to use it. Actually, documentation is not something done just at the end of the programming process. It should be carried on throughout all the programming steps. Documentation is important for people who may be involved with the program in the future. (*See Figure 11-16.*) These people may include the following:

■ *Users:* Users need to know how to use the software. Some organizations may offer training courses to guide users through the program. However, other organizations may expect users to be able to learn a package just from the written documentation. An example of this sort of documentation is the manuals that accompany purchased software.

■ *Operators:* Documentation must be provided for computer operators. If the program sends them error messages, for instance, they need to know what to do about them.

■ *Programmers:* Even the creator of the original program may not remember much about it. Other programmers wishing to update and modify it—that is, perform **program maintenance**—may find themselves frustrated without adequate documentation. This kind of documentation should include text and program flowcharts, program listings, and sample output. It might also include system flowcharts to show how the particular program relates to other programs within an information system.

This completes the six steps of the programming process. (*See Figure 11-17.*)

Programming Steps		
Step	**Primary activity**	
1. Define problem	Determine:	program objectives desired output required input processing requirements
2. Make-or-buy decision	Consider:	purchasing prewritten software creating custom software
3. Design program	Use:	structured programming technique
4. Code program	Select: Write:	programming language the program
5. Debug program	Perform:	desk check manual check translation attempt test with sample data
6. Document program	Write procedure for:	users operators programmers

Figure 11-17
Six steps in programming.

Five Generations of Programming Languages

Languages Are Described as Occurring in "Generations," from Machine Languages to Natural Languages.

Computer professionals talk about **levels** or **generations of programming languages,** ranging from "low" to "high." Programming languages are called *lower level* when they are closer to the language the computer itself uses. The computer understands the 0s and 1s that make up bits and bytes. They are called *higher level* when they are closer to the language humans use—that is, for English speakers, more like English.

There are five generations of programming languages. These are (1) machine languages, (2) assembly languages, (3) procedural languages, (4) problem-oriented languages, and (5) natural languages. The five generations of languages are summarized on the next page. (*See Figure 11-18.*) Let us briefly consider these.

Machine Languages: The First Generation   We mentioned earlier that data starts with a *byte.* A byte is made up of *bits,* consisting of 1s and 0s. These 1s and 0s may correspond to electricity's being on or off in the computer. They may also correspond to a magnetic pulse's being present or absent on storage media such as disk or tape. From this two-state system have been built coding schemes that allow us to construct letters, numbers, punctuation marks, and other special characters. Examples of these coding schemes, as we saw, are ASCII and EBCDIC.

Data represented in 1s and 0s is said to be written in **machine language.** To see how hard this is to understand, imagine if you had to code this:

1111001001110011110100100001000001110000001010 11

Machine languages also vary according to make of computer—another characteristic that makes them hard to work with.

Assembly Languages: The Second Generation   **Assembly languages** have a clear advantage over the 1s and 0s of machine language because they use abbreviations. Abbreviations are easier for human beings to remember. The machine language code we gave above could be expressed in assembly language as

PACK 210(8,13),02B(4,7)

Programming Generations		
Generation	**Name**	**Sample statement**
First	Machine	10010001
Second	Assembly	Pack 210(8,13)
Third	Procedural	Overtime: = 0
Fourth	Problem	FIND NAME = "JONES"
Fifth	Natural	IF patient is dizzy, THEN check temperature and blood pressure

Figure 11-18
Five programming generations.

This is still pretty obscure, of course, and so assembly language is also considered low-level.

Assembly languages also vary from computer to computer. With the third generation, we advance to high-level languages, many of which are considered **portable.** That is, they can be run on more than one kind of computer—they are "portable" from one machine to another.

Procedural Languages: The Third Generation   People are able to understand languages that are more like their own language (e.g., English) than machine languages or assembly languages. However, most people require some training in order to use higher-level languages. This is particularly true of procedural languages.

Procedural languages are programming languages with names like BASIC, Pascal, C, COBOL, and FORTRAN. They are called "procedural" because they are designed to express the logic—the procedures—that can solve general problems. Procedural languages, then, are intended to solve *general* problems. COBOL, for instance, is used in all kinds of business applications, such as payroll and inventory control. It is fourth-generation languages, discussed next, that are intended to solve *specific* problems.

For a procedural language to work on a computer, it must be translated into machine language so the computer can understand it. Depending on the language, this translation is performed by either a *compiler* or an *interpreter.*

- A **compiler** converts the programmer's procedural language program, called the *source code,* into a machine language code, called the *object code.* This object code can then be saved and run later. Examples of procedural languages using compilers are Pascal, COBOL, and FORTRAN.

- An **interpreter** converts the procedural language one statement at a time into machine code just before it is to be executed. No object code is saved. An example of a procedural language using an interpreter is BASIC.

What is the difference between using a compiler and using an interpreter? When a program is run, the compiler requires two steps before the program can be executed. These two steps are source code and object code. The interpreter, in contrast, requires only one step. The advantage of a compiler language is that once the object code has been obtained, the program executes faster. The advantage of an interpreter language is that programs are easier to develop.

The principal procedural languages with which you may come in contact are as follows:

- *BASIC:* Short for *Beginner's All-purpose Symbolic Instruction Code,* **BASIC** is the most popular microcomputer language. Widely used on microcomputers and easy to learn, it is suited to both beginning and experienced programmers. It is also interactive—user and computer communicate with each other directly during the writing and running of programs.

    A new version created by the Microsoft Corporation is Visual BASIC, which has been hailed as a programming breakthrough. Visual BASIC makes it easier for novice programmers, as well as professionals, to develop customized applications for Windows. The new language is expected to become quite popular for corporate, in-house development.

- *Pascal:* Another language that is widely used on microcomputers and easy to learn is **Pascal.** It is named after Blaise Pascal, a seventeenth-century French mathematician. Pascal has become quite popular in computer science educational programs. One advantage is that it encourages programmers to follow structured coding procedures. It also works well for graphics. We showed an example of Pascal earlier. (*Refer back to Figure 11-14, p. 196.*)

- *C:* **C** is a general-purpose language that also works well with microcomputers. It is useful for writing operating systems, database programs, and some scientific applications. Programs are portable: They can be run without change on a variety of computers.

- *COBOL:* **COBOL**—which stands for *CO*mmon *B*usiness-*O*riented *L*anguage—is the most frequently used programming language in business. Until recently, COBOL was available only for use with large computers. Now, however, versions exist that run on microcomputers. Though harder to learn than BASIC, its logic is easier for a person who is not a trained programmer to understand.

    Writing a COBOL program is sort of like writing the outline for a term paper. The program is divided into four divisions. The divisions in turn are divided into sections, which are divided into paragraphs, then into statements. The *Identification Division* gives the name of the program, author, and other identifying information. The *Environment Division* describes the computer or computers to be used. The *Data Division* describes the data to be used in the program. The *Procedure Division* describes the actual processing procedures.

- *FORTRAN:* Short for *FOR*mula *TRAN*slation, **FORTRAN** is the most widely used scientific and mathematical language in the world. It is very useful for processing complex formulas. Thus, many scientific and engineering programs have been written in this language.

- *Ada:* **Ada** is named after an English countess regarded as the first programmer. It was developed under the sponsorship of the U.S. Department of Defense. Originally designed for weapons systems, it has commercial uses as well. Because of its structured design, modules (sections) of a large program can be written, compiled, and tested separately before the entire program is put together.

- *RPG:* **RPG,** short for *R*eport *P*rogram *G*enerator, enables people to prepare business reports quickly and easily. A user need not be concerned with solution procedures so much as input and output. Users can easily learn to fill out specifications in detailed coding forms for common business applications like accounts receivable and accounts payable. A report will then be produced with little effort.

Problem-Oriented Languages: The Fourth Generation   Third-generation languages are valuable, but they require training in programming. Problem-oriented languages require little special training on the part of the user.

Unlike general-purpose languages, **problem-oriented languages** are designed to solve specific problems. Some of these fourth-generation languages are used for very specific applications. For example, IFPS (interactive financial planning system) is used to develop financial models. Many consider Lotus 1-2-3 and dBASE to be flexible fourth-generation languages. This group also includes query languages and applications generators:

- *Query languages:* **Query languages** enable nonprogrammers to use certain easily understood commands to search and generate reports from a database. An example is the commands used on an airline reservations system by clerks needing flight information.

- *Applications generators:* An **applications generator** is software with numbers of modules—logically related program statements—that have been preprogrammed to accomplish various tasks. An example would be a module that calculates overtime pay. The programmer can simply state which task is needed for a particular application. The applications generator will select the appropriate modules and run a program to meet the user's needs.

Natural Languages: The Fifth Generation **Natural languages** are still being developed. They are designed to give people a more human ("natural") connection with computers. The languages are human languages: English, French, Japanese, or whatever. Researchers also hope that natural languages will enable a computer to *learn*—to "remember" information, as people do, and to improve upon it. Clearly, this area is extremely challenging.

A Look at the Future

Ways of Making Program Development More Efficient Include Computer-Aided Software Engineering (CASE) and Object-Oriented Programming (OOP).

Ten years ago, a computer program of a few thousand lines was considered long. Today a word processing program may contain 50,000 lines. Programs needed to run modern aircraft, medical equipment, or financial institutions can run to millions of lines. Thus, in the future, programming will become only more important, not less. To appreciate this, consider that in early 1990 *one* software error (bug) plunged American Telephone & Telegraph's long-distance telephone network into chaos for nine hours. During this time, AT&T was able to put through only about half of all long-distance calls attempted, severely affecting airline reservations systems, among other businesses.

Professional programmers are constantly looking for ways to make their work easier, faster, and more reliable. One tool that holds promise is one we mentioned in the last chapter: *CASE*. CASE (computer-aided software engineering) tools provide some automation and assistance in one or more phases of the programming process: designing, coding, and debugging.

Another tool is *object-oriented programming* (OOP) languages. These languages are becoming quite popular. They differ from conventional programming languages in that they use and manipulate "objects." These objects can be graphic symbols, modules or blocks of programming code, or data. These languages promise to play a significant role in program development for two primary reasons. First, they are well suited for designing and using graphical user interfaces like those used in the Macintosh, OS/2, and Unix operating systems. Second, the languages are highly modular, allowing programmers to isolate, combine, and reuse programming code very efficiently.

Review Questions

1. What is the definition of a *program?*
2. What is the difference between a prewritten program and a custom-made program?
3. What is the definition of *programming?*
4. Describe the six steps involved in programming.
5. What are the four tasks involved in Step 1, problem definition?
6. Explain Step 2, the make-or-buy decision.
7. What is the tool known as top-down program design, used in Step 3, program design?
8. What are program modules?
9. What is pseudocode?

10. What is a program flowchart?
11. What are the three logic structures used?
12. Explain the difference between the two loop (iteration) structures, DO UNTIL and DO WHILE.
13. Explain object-oriented programming.
14. Explain the differences between syntax errors and logic errors in Step 5, debugging.
15. Explain some of the debugging tools, such as desk checking.
16. Who are three kinds of people that need good documentation, Step 6?
17. What are the five generations of programming languages?
18. Explain the difference between a compiler and an interpreter.
19. Name the seven procedural languages with which you may come in contact.
20. Under problem-oriented languages, explain what query languages and applications generators are.
21. What will be the principal advantage of natural languages if researchers are successful in developing them?

Discusion Questions and Projects

1. *Pencil-and-paper programming:* Suppose you are the manager of a clothing store. Using just pencil and paper, see if you can devise the steps in a program that will do the following:
   a. Pay a sales bonus of 1 percent of total sales to salespeople who sell $50,000 worth of clothes.
   b. Pay a sales bonus of 5 percent of total sales to salespeople who sell $250,000 worth of clothes.
   c. Pay a sales bonus of 10 percent of total sales to salespeople who sell $500,000 worth of clothes.

2. *More on object-oriented programming:* Buying prewritten software allows you to do a predetermined task, such as run a spreadsheet. But unless the manufacturer already thought of a particular task, you can't do it with that software unless you know how to modify it—that is, do programming. Object-oriented programming, we said, is like building a car from prefabricated parts rather than from scratch. The attraction of object-oriented programming is that it can make programming easy for ordinary users.

   This is your chance to investigate ways to make programming fun for you. Pick one of the following subjects and use the library or other resources to look into it in detail:
   a. Hypercard, available as a standard feature on many Apple Macintoshes, uses a concept of computerized "index cards," each of which stores information. You arrange the cards into "stacks" according to whatever method of grouping you choose. Hypercard is not only modular but also highly visual.
   b. Visual BASIC, designed to work with Microsoft's Windows, has many modular elements. The user can construct the components of a Windows application by manipulating a variety of visual elements that were preassembled by Microsoft programmers.
   c. An IBM product under development called Constellation is supposed to provide blocks of software that users can mix and match as they choose.

Chapter 11 Programming and Languages

A *program* is a list of instructions for the computer to follow to do a task. The instructions are made up of statements written in a programming language (e.g., BASIC). *Programming* is a six-step procedure for producing that list.

Step 1: Define the Problem	Step 2: Make-or-Buy Decision	Step 3: Design the Program

Program definition, also called **program anaylsis,** consists of specifying four tasks:

- Determining program objectives by focusing on the specific problem to be solved.
- Determining the desired output before considering the required inputs. Typically sketches or sample reports are prepared to show final form of output.
- Determining the input data and the source of the data.
- Determining the processing requirements or steps required to use the input data to produce the output.

The **make-or-buy decision** is a choice between having the program custom written by a programmer or buying it as a prewritten software package.

- Custom-made software **(make option)** can be created to perfectly match the programming needs.
- Off-the-shelf software **(buy option)** can save time and money but generally is not a perfect fit.
- The **decision** is made by comparing the value of a perfectly fitting program to the cost and time required to create it.

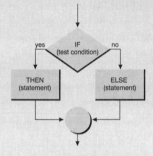

If the program is to be custom-made, in **program design** a solution is designed, using **structured programming techniques,** consisting of the following.

- **Top-down program design**— major processing steps, called **program modules,** are identified.
- **Pseudocode**—a narrative expression of the logic of the program is written.
- **Program flowcharts**—graphic representations of the steps needed to solve the programming problem are drawn.
- **Logic structures**—three arrangements are used in program flowcharts to write so-called structured programs.

Three Logic Structures

- **Sequence**—one program statement followed by another.
- **Selection** (or **IF-THEN-ELSE**)— when a decision must be made.
- **Loop**—when process is repeated as long as a condition is true. May be either **DO UNTIL** or **DO WHILE.**

Programming Generations

Generation	Name	Sample statement
First	Machine	10010001
Second	Assembly	Pack 210(8,13)
Third	Procedural	Overtime: = 0
Fourth	Problem	FIND NAME = "JONES"
Fifth	Natural	IF patient is dizzy, THEN check temperature and blood pressure

Step 4: Code the Program

Step 5: Debug the Program

Step 6: Document the Program

```
begin
total_regular :=0;
total_overtime :=0;
while not eof(input_file) do
   begin
   readln(input_file, hour_in, minute_in, hour_out, minute_out);
   if (hour_out >= 17) then
       overtime := (hour_out - 17) + (minute_out/60)
   else
       overtime := p;
   regular := (hour_out - hour_in) + (minute_out - minute_in)/60) - overtime;

   total_regular := total_regular + regular;
   total_overtime := total_overtime = overtime;
   end;
end.
```

Coding is writing a program. There are several important aspects of writing a program. Two are:

- Program quality—good programs are structured using logic structures.

- Language selection—a **programming language** should be chosen that is appropriate for the programming problem and the computer.

Debugging consists of testing the program to eliminate **syntax errors** (violation of rules of programming language) and **logic errors** (incorrect calculations or solution procedures). Debugging methods consist of:

Desk checking—careful reading of a printout of the program.

Manual testing—using sample data to test for correct processing results.

Attempt at translation—running the program through a computer, using a translator program.

Testing sample data—testing the program for logic errors on a computer, using sample data.

Documentation consists of a written description of the program and the procedures for running it for users, operators, and programmers during **program maintenance**—modifying or updating of the program.

- Users need to know how to use the program and to input the data to produce correct results

- Operators need to know how to execute the program and to recognize and correct errors.

- Programmers need to be able to explain how the program works and to maintain the program in the future.

205

12

Emerging Applications: Power Tools

Competencies

After you have read this chapter, you should be able to:

1. Describe desktop managers.

2. Discuss project management software.

3. Explain what desktop publishing is.

4. Describe new media: hypertext and multimedia.

5. Describe CAD/CAM software.

6. Explain artificial intelligence: robotics, knowledge-based and expert systems, artificial reality.

Expect surprises—exciting ones, positive ones. This is the view to take in achieving computer competency. If at first the surprises worry you, that's normal. Most people wonder how well they can handle something new. But the latest technological developments also offer you new opportunities to vastly extend your range. As we show in this chapter, for example, software that for many years was available only for mainframes has recently become available for microcomputers. Here's a chance to join the computer-competent of tomorrow.

Power tools: This is the characterization we have given to a whole new generation of software and hardware only recently available for microcomputers. Desktop managers. Project management software. Desktop publishing software. Hypertext and multimedia. CAD/CAM programs. Artificial intelligence, including robotics, knowledge-based and expert systems, and artificial reality. Is there really a need to know anything about these new developments? There is if you want to be like those professionals in every area who are at the forefront of their disciplines. They are there because they have found more efficient ways to use their talents and time. You owe it to yourself, therefore, to at least be aware of what this software and hardware can do.

Desktop Managers

A Desktop Manager Is a Program That Stays in the Computer's Primary Storage and Provides Desktop "Accessories," Such as Notepad and Calculator.

Desktop managers are programs that can be held in primary storage at the same time you are running other programs. Such other programs might include a word processor, spreadsheet, or database manager. While you are working, without having to abandon these other programs, you may call upon a desktop manager to give you the kind of "desktop accessories" that help you get your job done. Such accessories might include an appointment calendar, calculator, notepad, personal telephone directory, and automatic telephone dialer. They appear on your video display screen on top of whatever you are working on. The package known as Sidekick is one of the most popular desktop managers. Here an appointment calendar and a phone directory are displayed as windows in a word processing program. (*See Figure 12-1.*)

Desktop managers are quite handy. You may become among the thousands of managers who begin their working day by reviewing their electronic calendars to see what appointments they have. Later, while you're working on a spreadsheet, say, someone calls to schedule an important business meeting. You can simply type a com-

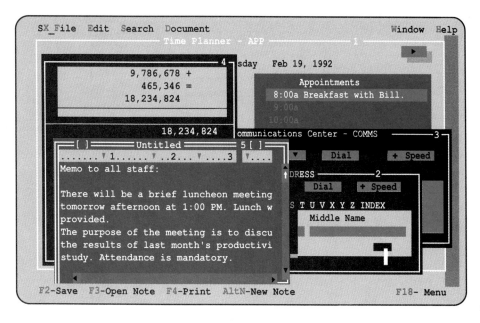

Figure 12-1
Example of desktop manager,
Sidekick 2.0.

mand that "pops up" the desktop manager on the screen, type in the meeting time on your calendar, and then save the information on your floppy disk. With another command, you make the desktop manager disappear from the screen and return to your word processing task. After you are finished for the day, you can remove your floppy disk, which stores all the information.

Desktop managers are called **memory-resident programs.** This is because they stay in the computer's memory (primary storage) all the time, until the computer is turned off. The value of a desktop manager is that it enables you to keep your desk free of notepads, phone directories, and calculators.

Project Management Software

Project Management Software Allows You to Plan, Schedule, and Control the People, Resources, and Costs of a Project.

There are many occasions in business where projects need to be watched to avoid delays and cost overruns. A **project** may be defined as a one-time operation composed of several tasks that must be completed during a stated period of time. Examples of large projects are found in construction, aerospace, or political campaigns. Examples of smaller jobs might occur in advertising agencies, corporate marketing departments, or management information systems departments.

Project management software enables users to plan, schedule, and control the people, resources, and costs needed to complete a project on time. For instance, the contractor building a housing development might use it to keep track of the materials, dollars, and people required for success. Examples of project management software are Harvard Project Manager, Microsoft Project for Windows, Project Scheduler 4, SuperProject, and Time Line.

A typical use of project management software is to show the scheduled beginning and ending dates for a particular task. It then shows the dates when the task was completed. Two important tools found in project management software are Gantt charts and PERT charts.

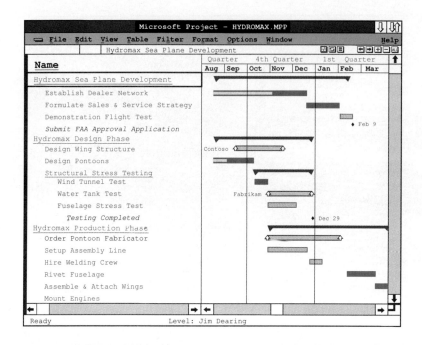

Figure 12-2
Gantt chart from Microsoft
Project for Windows project
management software.

Gantt Charts A **Gantt chart** uses bars and lines to indicate the time scale of a series of tasks. (*See Figure 12-2.*) You can see whether the tasks are being completed on schedule. The time scale may range from minutes to years.

PERT Charts A **PERT chart** shows not only the timing of a project but also the relationships among its tasks. (PERT stands for *Program Evaluation Review Technique.*) The relationships are represented by lines that connect boxes stating the tasks. (*See Figure 12-3.*) With project management software, these boxes can be easily moved around. You can see how changes in the schedule will affect various tasks.

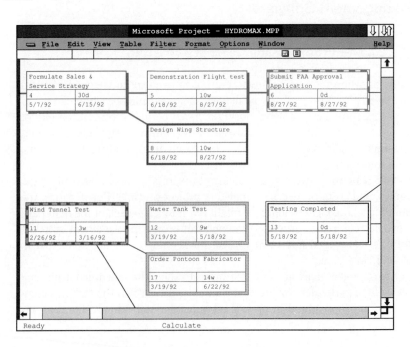

Figure 12-3
PERT chart from Microsoft
Project for Windows project
management software.

Desktop Publishing

A Desktop Publishing Program Allows You to Mix Text and Graphics to Create Publications of Nearly Professional Quality.

How would you like to generate a report that combined text and graphics and *really* impressed people with its looks? Suppose you wanted to create a report that looked like an article in a newsmagazine? When you present a report prepared on a word processing program, you are basically concerned with content; the appearance is secondary. When you do that same report with a desktop publishing program, the looks can be outstanding. An example of a page spread prepared by desktop publishing is shown below. (*See Figure 12-4.*)

Edited by Karen Bantam

Sensible Souvenirs
Egyptian design motifs and the mystical Scarab

Lorem ipsum dlor sit amet, consectetuer adipiscing elit, sed diam nonummy nibh euismod tincidunt ut laoreet dolore magna aliquam erat volutpat. Ut wisi enim ad minim veniam, quis nostrud exerci tation ullamcorper suscipit lobortis nisl ut aliup ex ea commodo consequat. Duis autem vel eum iriure dolor in hendrerit in vulputate velit esse molestie consequat, vel illum dolore eu feugiat nulla facilisis at vero eros et accumsan et iusto odio dignissim qui blandit praesent ltatum zzril delenit augue duis dolore te feugait nulla facilisi. Lorem ipsum dolor sit amet, consectetuer adipiscing elit, sed diam nonummy nibh euismod tincidunt ut laoreet dolore magna aliquam erat volutpat. Ut wisi enim ad minim veniam, quis nostrud eu feugiat nulla.

The Single Traveler
Shipboard romance... Is the Love Boat for real?

Cros et accumsan et iusto odio dignissim qui blandit praesent luptatum zzril delenit augue duis dolore te feugait nulla facilisi. Nam liber tempor cum soluta nobis eleifend option congue nihil imperdiet doming id quod mazim placerat facer possim assum. Lorem ipsum dolor sit amet, consectetuer adipiscing elit. Ut wisi enim ad minim veniam, quis nostrud exerci tation ullamcorper suscipit lobortis nisl ut aliquip ex ea commodo consequat. Duis autem vel eum iriure dolor in hendrerit in vulputate velit esse molestie consequat, vel illum dolore eu feugiat nulla facili- sis at vero eros et accumsan et iusto odio dignissim qui blandit praesent luptatum zzril delenit augue duis dolore te feugait nulla facilisi. Lorem ipsum dolor sit amet, consectetuer adipiscing elit, sed diam nonummy nibh euismod tincidunt ut laoreet dolore magna aliquam erat volutpat. Ut wisi enim ad minim veniam, quis nostrud exerci tation ullamcorper suscipit lobortis nisl ut aliquip ex ea commodo consequat. Duis autem vel eum iriure dolor in hendrerit in vulputate velit esse molestie consequat, vel illum dolore eu feugiat nulla facilisis at vero eros et accumsan et iusto odio dignissim qui blandit praesent luptatum zzril delenit augue duis dolore te.

Places with a Past
Sun worshippers abound where Greek tragedies once unfolded

Euismod tincidunt ut laoreet dolore magna aliquam erat volutpat. Ut wisi enim ad minim veniam, quis nostrud exercitation lamcorper suscipit lobortis nisl ut aliquip ex ea commodo consequat. Autem vel eum iriure dolor in

Figure 12-4
Page produced by desktop publishing software.

Many publications—most books and magazines, for instance—are created by professionals trained in graphic arts and typesetting. They use equipment that often costs several thousand dollars. However, there are many publications where such experience and expense are not necessary. Examples are newsletters, forms, catalogs, brochures, posters, menus, and advertisements. These are all candidates for desktop publishing. Real estate agents may use desktop publishing for sales sheets. Travel agents may use it for advertisements, architects for proposals, and government officials for presentations.

Desktop publishing is the process of using a microcomputer, a laser printer, and the necessary software to mix text and graphics. Some word processing programs are being developed with this capability. However, here we are concerned with specialized software that allows you to create publications that are of almost professional quality. The software enables you to select a variety of typestyles, just like those that commercial printers use. It also allows you to create and select graphic images. The laser printer produces a higher-quality printed result than is possible with other microcomputer printers. An example of a display screen of material produced using the desktop publishing program PageMaker is shown below. (*See Figure 12-5.*) Other popular programs are Ventura Publisher and First Publisher.

Desktop publishing lets you place various kinds of text and graphics together in a publication designed almost any way you want. For instance, imagine you are a marketing manager for an airplane manufacturer and you are preparing a presentation on a new aircraft. You could use a word processing program to type the text. You could then use other software to create graphics. Or you might use graphics that have already been created from a graphics program. You can even get photographs that have been copied into a computer by a special scanning device. The desktop publishing program allows you to integrate all of these and look at your work on the display screen as one page. You can also look at two facing pages in reduced size or an enlarged view of a partial page. You can rearrange text and columns. You can enlarge or reduce any element and choose from all kinds of typestyles and sizes.

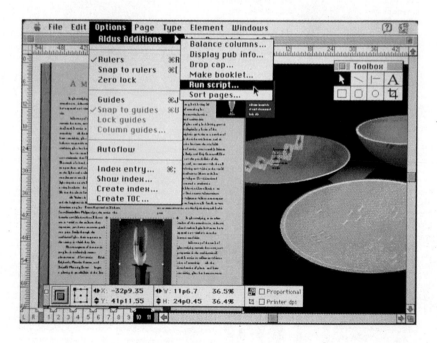

Figure 12-5
Video display screen showing a page produced by Aldus PageMaker desktop publishing software.

In Ventura Publisher, something called a **style sheet** enables you to determine the basic appearance of single or multiple pages. You can decide how many columns of type will be on a page. You can choose the size and typestyle of both text and headings. You can even select the width of lines and boxes that separate text and pictures. You can place an image anywhere on a page simply by putting a cursor at the point you wish. If a graphic image is positioned on top of text, the text will automatically realign around the image.

If you are not trained as a graphic designer, Ventura offers 25 sample style sheets. These can be used for brochures, newsletters, books, and so on. As you become more experienced, you can modify these style sheets or even create your own.

Once a document is composed on the screen, it must be transmitted to an output device that can print it out. This task is accomplished by what are known as **page description languages.** A page description language describes the shape and position of letters and graphics to the printer. An example is Adobe's PostScript, which is used in the PageMaker product. Other examples are Interpress from Xerox and Document Description Language (DDL) from Imagen.

New Media: Hypertext and Multimedia

New Media Include Hypertext and Multimedia. Hypertext Is Software That Can Connect Any Text or Picture with Any Other. Multimedia Can Link Text, Graphics, Video, and Sounds.

Where is the next area in which a revolution will happen in microcomputing? Many observers think it will be in something called "new media." *Media* refers to the formats in which information is communicated or expressed. For example, a medium may be text, graphics, animation, music, voice, or video. *New media* refers to delivery systems that combine media, using a microcomputer as the controlling framework. The two principal kinds of new media are *hypertext* and *multimedia*.

Hypertext **Hypertext** is sophisticated software that allows users to organize and access information in creative ways. It is designed to work the way people think. It enables people to link facts into sequences of information in ways that parallel the methods people use to discover knowledge. Hypertext encourages you to follow your natural train of thought as you seek information, rather than follow the restrictive search-and-retrieval methods of traditional database systems.

Much of the interest in hypertext has been generated by HyperCard, which runs on Apple's Macintosh computer. IBM's version, which runs on IBM PCs, PC-compatibles, and the IBM PS/2 line of computers, is called LinkWay. HyperCard is based on the concept of card files, just like note cards, only these are electronic. Information is recorded on basic filing units that Apple calls *cards*. A card is a computer screen filled with data comprising a single record. Cards in turn are organized into related files (bodies of information) called *stacks*. Cards and stacks are easily created and edited by the user through the use of Macintosh's typing and drawing tools.

You can create various connections between cards and stacks, and by fields of information on the cards, by means of *buttons*. A button is an area of the screen that is sensitive to the "click" of a mouse. Using your mouse to guide the cursor, you move to one of these buttons on the screen. You then press ("click") the selection button on top of the mouse, and you will be connected to another card or stack.

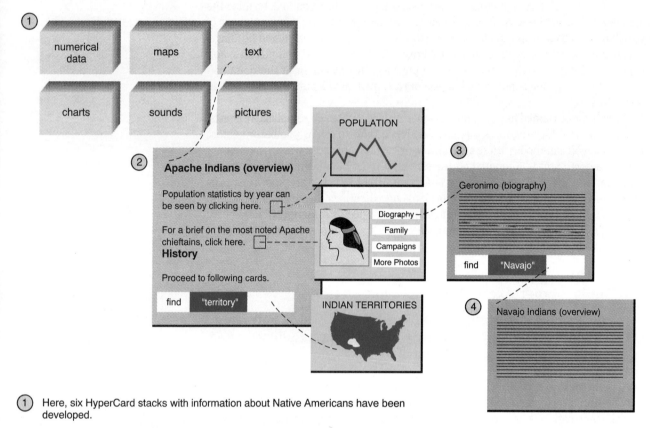

① Here, six HyperCard stacks with information about Native Americans have been developed.

② You navigate through the information by "pressing" ("clicking") on buttons that appear on the screen. Buttons call up linked data on other cards and promote self-paced, self-guided study. Information can also be accessed using the HyperCard "Find" feature.

③ Linking data is not a one-way street. From any card, you can access other cards to probe deeper into a line of thought.

④ Or you can embark on an entirely new course of investigation.

Figure 12-6
Hypertext: how HyperCard works.

By clicking buttons, you can "navigate" through the cards and stacks to locate information or to discover connections between ideas contained in the stacks. For example, suppose an electronic "encyclopedia" or "textbook" has been developed containing information about Native Americans. Our illustration above shows how you might do research in this subject. (*See Figure 12-6.*) Each stack contains pertinent data: text, statistics, maps, charts, or pictures. You can define buttons to link the information. The links may be sequential, going from one card to another in a stack. Or the links may be hierarchical, so that you can go from a summary to detailed information about a particular topic. Whatever the method, the links are varied so that you can sort through and gain access to related information in whatever ways are convenient to you.

Clearly, what is interesting about hypertext is that it enables users to search for and to link information in many different ways. Users can follow their own methods of discovery, using intuition and idea association to gain knowledge.

Multimedia   Multimedia, also called **hypermedia,** is much more than hypertext. While hypertext focuses primarily on linking textual information, **multimedia** can link all sorts of media into one form of presentation. These media may include text, graphics, animation, video, music, and voice.

An example of how these can be put together was demonstrated by a music professor as follows. Using an application written with HyperCard, the professor presented a multimedia lesson about a particular symphony. For hardware, he attached a Macintosh and a CD-ROM disk drive to a speaker system and a television monitor. The demonstration showed there were many ways to navigate through the program. For instance, the professor could call up biographical anecdotes about the composer. Or, he could present an outline of the symphony's major themes, which had music attached. When the Macintosh's mouse was clicked on the items in the outline, the audience could hear how a theme was restated as the symphony progressed. Or program notes could be made to appear that would provide a running commentary. Or, by clicking the mouse on an obscure term, the professor could call up a definition from the program's glossary.

Our illustration below shows what might be involved in developing a multimedia presentation, e.g., about events leading up to the Civil War. (*See Figure 12-7.*) In the creation stage, one could use a Macintosh and HyperCard as authoring software to integrate information. This information could come in the form of text through a

Figure 12-7
Multimedia: creation, presentation, and distribution.

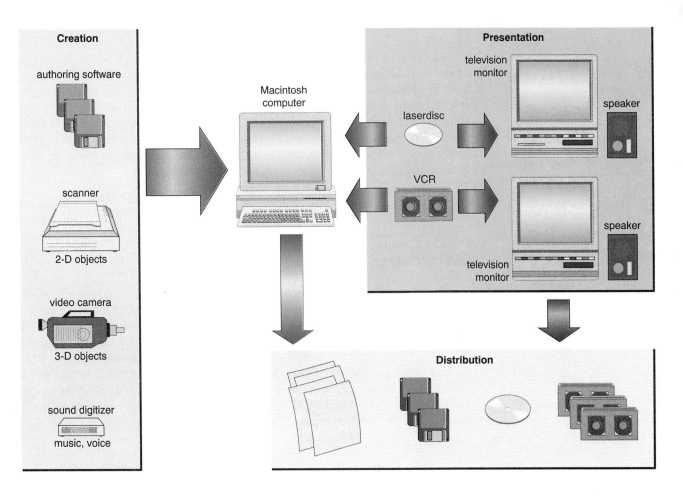

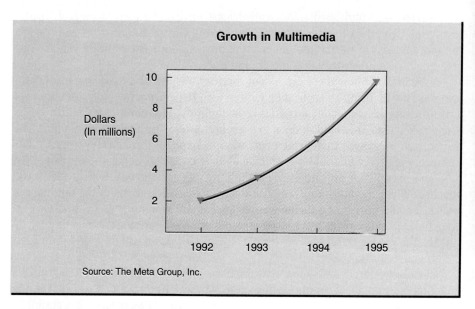

Figure 12-8
Expected sales on multimedia equipment.

scanner, graphics and animation through a video camera, and sound through a sound digitizer. The multimedia lesson could be packaged on a CD-ROM disk or videocassette tape and presented through a television monitor and speaker. The lesson could be stored and distributed on several types of media: hardcopy (text), floppy disks, CD-ROM disks, or videocassette tapes.

The sales of multimedia systems are expected to rise dramatically in the United States over the next few years. (*See Figure 12-8.*) There are four primary business areas in which multimedia is expected to be used. The first is training, in which workers are taught new skills. The second is sales and information, in which multimedia "catalogs" are used to reach customers. The third area is desktop applications. Here multimedia may be used to enhance presentations or company communications. The fourth area is industrial and scientific operations. Here voice commands may be used to direct remote computers removed from human contact.

CAD/CAM

CAD Is Computer-Aided Design. CAM Is Computer-Aided Manufacturing.

Computers have revolutionized systems for designing and manufacturing products. These are sometimes mentioned together as *CAD/CAM*—for *computer-aided design/computer-aided manufacturing.* However, they are really two separate applications.

The *really* radical change in this area is that only recently have these systems become available for microcomputer users. Just a few years ago, for example, CAD work required computer systems costing over $100,000. Today much of that same kind of work can be done on microcomputer systems costing only $6000. This means that many applications are now cost-effective—which gives you the opportunity to do creative work previously reserved for specialists.

Computer-Aided Design A product must first be designed. This is true whether it is as large as an airplane, as small as a computer chip, or as ordinary as a shoe. Until recently, industrial designers and engineers sat at drawing boards and drew rough sketches. Then they produced more refined sketches. Then they built and tested scale models. Then they made production drawings for manufacturing the product.

Some engineers and designers, however, did not design products this old-fashioned way. Rather they prepared their sketches and drawings on an expensive computer, using expensive software called **computer-aided design (CAD)** software. CAD software is a type of program that manipulates images on a screen. (*See Figure 12-9.*) One advantage of this kind of program is that the product can be drawn in three dimensions and then rotated on the screen so the viewer can see all sides.

Today, just as desktop publishing has made graphic arts and publications available to everyone, CAD is also accessible to microcomputer users. With software known as VersaCAD, for example, you can design an entire house by yourself. Or you can create clothes, furniture, industrial products, whatever your design interest—all on screen. Similar CAD software is also available for IBM microcomputers, such as AutoCAD 386 or AutoCAD for OS/2.

A variation on CAD are **computer-aided design and drafting (CADD)** systems. CADplan is one such program that is available for microcomputers. Such programs cannot really teach you to design—that is, conceptualize a drawing. However, they can help you do drafting or drawing. CADD programs come equipped with such symbols as

Figure 12-9
CAD: example of computer-aided design.

straight lines, arcs, circles, and points. These help you put together graphic elements. You can edit drawings by moving portions around, changing shapes, and rotating objects. An architect, for example, can change room dimensions and shapes, even the entire floor plan of a house. Some CADD programs also enable you to do drawings in layers, as though you were using clear plastic overlays. Another feature is that images can be stored on disk and then inserted into other drawings. Although most CADD programs perform only two-dimensional design, a few can work in three dimensions.

Computer-Aided Manufacturing Abbreviated **CAM, computer-aided manufacturing** is a term that describes programs that control automated factory equipment, including machine tools and robots. Examples are systems that regulate production in an oil refinery, that monitor nuclear power plants, and that manufacture textiles. As with CAD programs, previously CAM software was expensive and available only with mainframes. Now microcomputer CAM systems are showing up everywhere. They are used to handle communications and to route information from manufacturing equipment. They are also used to generate data and programs to run tools on the factory floor.

An instance in which both CAD and CAM have been used together on a microcomputer is found in a steel mill. A designer draws an I-beam shape with the CAD program on the computer's screen. The program then calculates the CAM instructions. It determines the exact specifications for securing clamps to a steel roll. It indicates the type of cutting needed to make the I-beam out of the steel roll. It determines where the cutting tools will start and stop and how many tool passes are required. CAD/CAM software is also used in making cars and other manufacturing applications. CAD is used to design cars; CAM is used to control factory robots and coordinate other areas of production.

As we've stated, the availability of CAD/CAM software on microcomputers is a recent and potentially far-reaching development. As others have observed, today's unfathomable is tomorrow's mundane. Whatever field you are in, as CAD/CAM applications become available, you should make it a point to become familiar with them.

Artificial Intelligence

Artificial Intelligence Attempts to Develop Computer Systems That Simulate Human Thought Processes and Actions. Three Areas Are Robotics, Knowledge-Based and Expert Systems, and Virtual Reality.

Does human intelligence really need the presence of "artificial intelligence," whatever that is? Indeed, you might worry, do we need the competition? Actually, the goal of artificial intelligence is not to replace human intelligence, which is probably not replaceable. Rather it is to help people be more productive. Let us describe how this might work.

In the past, computers used calculating power to solve *structured* problems, the kinds of tasks described throughout this book. People—using intuition, reasoning, and memory—were better at solving *unstructured* problems, whether building a product or approving a loan. Most organizations have been able to computerize the tasks once performed by clerks. However, knowledge-intensive work, such as that performed by many managers, is only beginning to be automated.

Now the field of computer science known as **artificial intelligence (AI)** is moving into the mainstream of data processing. AI attempts to develop computer systems that can mimic or simulate human thought processes and actions. These include reasoning, learning from past actions, and simulation of human senses such as vision and touch. True artificial intelligence that corresponds to human intelligence is still a long way off. However, several tools that emulate human problem solving and information processing have been developed. Many of these tools have practical applications for business, medicine, law, and many other fields.

Let us now consider three areas in which human talents and abilities have been enhanced with "computerized intelligence":

▦ Robotics

▦ Knowledge-based and expert systems

▦ Virtual reality

Robotics   **Robotics** is the field of study concerned with developing and using robots. Some toylike household robots (such as the Androbots) have been made for entertainment purposes. However, these are not the kind we are interested in here. **Robots** are machines used in factories and elsewhere. They differ from most assembly-line machines in that they can be reprogrammed to do more than one task. Among the kinds of robots are the following.

▦ *Industrial robots:* Industrial robots are used in factories to perform certain assembly-line tasks. Examples are machines used in automobile plants to do welding, painting, and loading. (*See Figure 12-10.*) In the garment industry, robot pattern cutters create pieces of fabric for clothing. Some types of robots have claws for picking up objects.

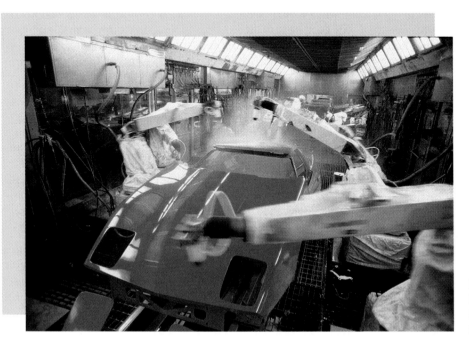

Figure 12-10
Industrial robot: spraying and polishing on car plant production line.

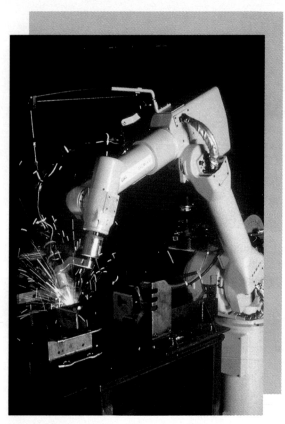

Figure 12-11
Perception system: vision-system robot, used for welding.

- *Perception systems:* Some robots imitate some of the human senses. For example, robots with television-camera vision systems are particularly useful. They can be used for guiding machine tools, for inspecting products, for identifying and sorting parts, and for welding. (*See Figure 12-11.*) Other kinds of perception systems rely on a sense of touch, such as those used on microcomputer assembly lines to put parts into place.

- *Mobile robots:* Some robots act as transporters, such as "mailmobiles." They carry mail through an office, following a preprogrammed route. Office workers can leave their desks to exchange mail when the robot comes by. Others act as computerized carts to deliver supplies and equipment at medical centers.

Knowledge-Based and Expert Systems   People who are expert in a particular area—certain kinds of law, medicine, accounting, engineering, and so on—are generally well paid for their specialized knowledge. Unfortunately for their clients and customers, they are expensive, not always available, and hard to replace when they move on.

What if you were to somehow *capture* the knowledge of a human expert? What if you then made it accessible to everyone through a computer program? This knowledge could be not only reasonably priced but also always available. Indeed, if you were an expert yourself, you could use such a program to double-check your own judgments. Moreover, as an expert yourself, you could create your own computer program containing much of what you know.

All this is exactly what is being done with so-called *knowledge-based* and *expert systems*. And again, the good news is that these programs, previously available only for mainframe computers, are now rapidly being developed for microcomputers.

Computer professionals make a distinction between two types of specialized software.

- *Knowledge-based systems:* **Knowledge-based systems** are programs that are based on "surface knowledge." This consists of facts and widely accepted rules, such as those that might be found in a firm's procedures manual. This kind of knowledge is also called "textbook knowledge"—it includes facts and rules you might find in a textbook. Such systems tell how certain decisions should be made or tasks accomplished. An example is the kind of automatic check-in machine some airlines offer. Using this machine allows passengers to avoid waiting in lines for a ticketing agent. Rather they interact with a knowledge-based system. It assigns them seats according to their preferences for window versus aisle or other seat, and so on. The system then automatically issues passengers their boarding passes.

- *Expert systems:* **Expert systems** are programs based on both "surface knowledge" and "deep knowledge." Essentially they emulate the knowledge of human experts skilled in a particular field—for instance, that of a geologist, tax lawyer, or medical doctor. These programs incorporate both textbook knowledge and "tricks of the trade" that an expert acquires after years of experience. As a result, the programs can be exceedingly complex. For example, ExperTAX, which helps accountants figure out a client's tax options, consists of over 2000 rules.

Over the past decade, expert systems have been developed in areas such as medicine, geology, chemistry, military science, and insurance. (*See Figure 12-12.*) There are expert systems with such names as Oil Spill Advisor, Bird Species Identification, and even Midwives Assistant. A system called Grain Marketing Advisor helps farmers select the best way to market their grain. Another, called Senex, shows how to treat breast cancer based on advanced treatment techniques.

Personal Machinist is an expert system designed to help the maintenance staff repair robots used in car-manufacturing operations. Personal Machinist consists of 120 rules covering the majority of the problems encountered with a particular kind of factory robot.

Expert systems are created using a programming language or a shell. **Shells** are special kinds of software that allow a person to custom-build a particular kind of expert system. For instance, the shell called VP-Expert has a database and can work with Lotus 1-2-3 and dBASE. This shell can then be used to build different kinds of expert systems. For example, VP-Expert has helped gardeners to assemble information about the most effective natural pest controls to use for specific purposes. Texas Instruments has developed an entire line of microcomputer-based shells called the Personal Consultant Series. These shells have been used to build Senex and Grain Marketing Advisor, among others we mentioned.

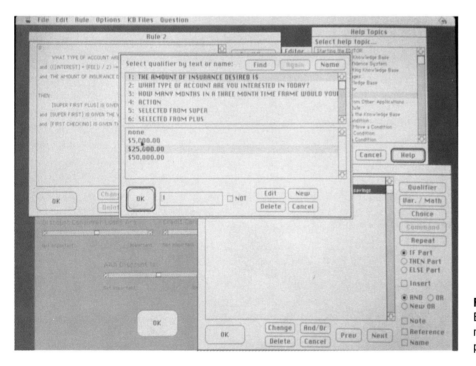

Figure 12-12
Expert system: menu for determining amount of insurance to purchase.

Virtual Reality   Suppose you could create and virtually experience any new form of reality you wish. You could see the world through the eyes of a child, a robot—or even a lobster. You could explore faraway resorts, the moon, or inside a nuclear waste dump, without leaving your chair. This simulated experience is rapidly becoming possible with a form of AI known as *virtual reality.*

Also known as **artificial reality** or **virtual environments, virtual reality** consists of headgear and gloves that you wear and software that translates data into images. The headgear (one type is called Eyephones) has earphones and three-dimensional stereoscopic screens. The glove (DataGlove) has sensors that collect data about your hand movements. When coupled with the software (such as a program called Body Electric), this interactive sensory equipment allows you to experience alternative realities to the physical world.

An example of virtual reality is shown in the three photos on these pages. (*See Figure 12-13.*) The first picture shows a man wearing interactive sensory headset and glove. When the man moves his head, the stereoscopic views change. The second picture shows what the man is looking at—a simulation of an office. The third picture shows how the view changes as the user "goes" over to a bookshelf and "reaches" up for a book.

There are several possible applications for virtual reality. The ultimate recreational use might be something resembling a "giant virtual amusement park." More seriously, we can simulate important experiences or training environments such as flying, surgical operations, spaceship repair, or nuclear disaster cleanup.

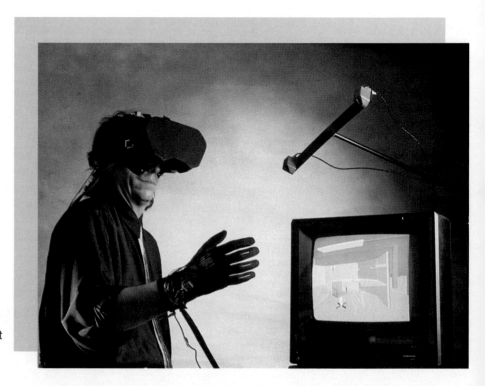

Figure 12-13
Virtual reality: sensory headset and glove, view of simulated office, reaching for a book.

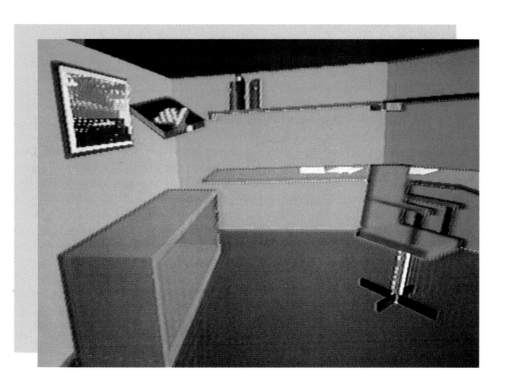

A Look at the Future

The Downsizing of Computer Applications Will Continue. So Will the Broadening of the Scope of Applications, as in Current Research into Artificial Life.

As we have pointed out elsewhere in the book, we can expect the trend of *downsizing of applications* to continue. That is, tasks that could once be performed only by mainframes will increasingly be done with microcomputers. Computer networks will link mainframes, microcomputers, workstations, and servers of all kinds—file servers, database servers, and communications servers. These developments will have an effect on the kinds of resources available to you in your career.

Just as important, we will probably also see a *broadening of the scope of applications*. Already well along in development, for instance, are *pen-based computers*. These are portable computers with handwriting-recognition capabilities that can identify printed letters, digits, and punctuation. They can even be modified to accept particular handwriting styles. Also presently being marketed are compact disk players that display audio and video programs on a TV set. These enable viewers to navigate by sight and sound through encyclopedias and atlases. These and similar devices may be forerunners to so-called *information appliances*. Such an appliance would bundle a computer, telephone, fax machine, photocopier, color printer, and laser discs or CDs into one intelligent machine.

In the 21st century, the concepts applied in artificial intelligence, such as robotics, will be applied to all sorts of things. Even now, for instance, an experimental house in Japan, the "TRON House," has microprocessors and sensors built into everything. Windows open and close to maintain optimum ventilation. Background music reduces in volume when the telephone rings. Kitchen computers take the guesswork out of cooking. Bathroom computers monitor one's health. No doubt we will see a similar extension of computer technology to the workplace.

Most spectacularly, there are already attempts to go beyond artificial intelligence to something called *artificial life*. In this field, researchers are trying to develop programs that learn and develop on their own. For instance, computers are used to simulate living systems and to make computerized environments in which simulations of organisms eat, reproduce, and die. The outcome of these investigations may produce defenses against the computer viruses that have damaged networks and databases. They may also further our understanding of how human urban communities work.

Review Questions

1. What does a desktop manager do?
2. What is meant by the term *memory-resident program?*
3. Explain what project management software does.
4. Describe what Gantt charts and PERT charts are.
5. What does a desktop publishing program let you do?
6. Describe what a page description language does.
7. What does a hypertext program do?
8. Explain how multimedia works.
9. What does CAD/CAM stand for?
10. Give an example of how CAD is used.

11. Explain what CADD does.
12. Give an example of how CAM is used.
13. What are three categories of artificial intelligence?
14. Explain the different areas of robotics.
15. Define knowledge-based systems.
16. Explain what an expert system is.
17. What is a shell?
18. Explain how virtual reality works.

Discussion Questions and Projects

1. *New areas for expert systems:* There are numerous expert systems designed to pick winning stocks in the stock market. However, not everyone using these systems has become rich. Why? List and discuss three other areas in which you think it would be difficult to devise an expert system.

2. *A picture of things to come:* Over the next 10 to 15 years, according to some experts, electronic miniaturization will give us small, portable devices that one can wear like clothing and that will do all kinds of wonderful things. For example, these wearable devices will incorporate display screens, keyboards, CD memories, faxes, telephones, scanners, cameras, and satellite transmitters and will recognize handwriting and voice. What kind of wearable, lightweight "information and entertainment machine" would you design for yourself? What would it do?

Chapter 12 Emerging Applications: Power Tools

Some recent important microcomputer applications are desktop managers, project management software, desktop publishing, hypertext and multimedia, CAD/CAM, and artificial intelligence—robotics, knowledge-based and expert systems, and artificial reality.

Desktop Managers	Project Management Software	Desktop Publishing

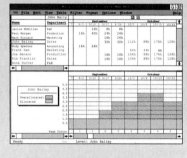

Desktop managers (also called **memory resident programs**) stay in primary storage at the same time other programs are running and provide "pop-up" assistance of such "desktop accessories" as appointment calendar, calculator, notepad, personal telephone directory, and automatic telephone dialer.

Example of Package

Sidekick

Project management software allows you to plan, schedule, and control the people, resources, and costs of a project. A **project** is a one-time operation composed of several tasks that must be completed during a stated period of time.

Two important tools found in project management software are:

Gantt Charts

A **Gantt chart** uses bars and lines to indicate the time scale of a series of tasks so you can see whether the tasks are being completed on schedule.

PERT Charts

A **PERT chart** shows not only the timing of a project but also the relationships among its tasks.

Examples of Packages

Harvard Project Manager,
Microsoft Project for Windows,
Project Scheduler 4,
SuperProject, Time Line

Desktop publishing is the process of using a microcomputer, laser printer, and necessary software to mix text and graphics and create publications of almost professional quality. Once a document is composed on the monitor screen, it is transmitted by a **page description language,** which describes the shape and position of letters and graphics, to a printer for printing out.

Examples of Packages

Ventura Publisher, PageMaker,
First Publisher

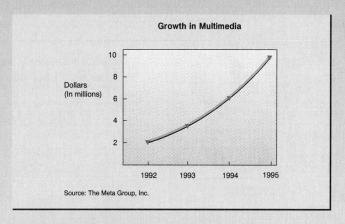

Growth in Multimedia

Dollars (In millions)

10
8
6
4
2

1992   1993   1994   1995

Source: The Meta Group, Inc.

New Media	CAD/CAM	Artificial Intelligence

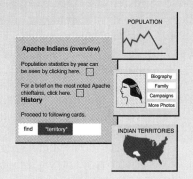

New Media

New media refers to ways of combining and controlling information in a variety of forms. These forms include text, graphics, animation, music, voice, and video. Two principal kinds of new media are **hypertext** and **multimedia.**

Hypertext

Hypertext is software that stores information in **cards** and **stacks** and allows users to navigate this information in creative and useful ways through **buttons.**

Multimedia

While hypertext relates primarily to textual information, multimedia includes much more: graphics, animation, music, voice, and video. The use of multimedia is dramatically increasing.

Example of Packages

Apple's HyperCard

CAD/CAM

CAD/CAM software is used for designing and manufacturing products.

Computer-Aided Design

Computer-aided design (CAD)—or **computer-aided design and drafting (CADD)**—software allows images to be manipulated on screen (e.g., in three dimensions).

Computer-Aided Manufacturing

Computer-aided manufacturing (CAM) software controls automated factory equipment (e.g., machine tools and robots).

Examples of Packages

VersaCAD, AutoCAD, CADplan

Artificial Intelligence

Artificial intelligence is a research field to develop computer systems simulating human thought processes and actions. Three areas include:

Robotics

Robotics is a research field to develop machines that can be reprogrammed to do more than one task. Some types are industrial robots, perception systems, and mobile robots.

Knowledge-Based and Expert Systems

These are computer programs that duplicate the knowledge humans have for performing specialized tasks.

- **Knowledge-based systems** use "surface knowledge"—facts and widely accepted rules.
- **Expert systems** use "deep knowledge," both surface knowledge and "tricks of the trade" of human experts (e.g., geologists).

Artificial Reality

Also known as **virtual reality** or **virtual environments,** this consists of interactive sensory equipment to simulate alternative realities to the physical world.

225

13 Workplace Issues, Privacy, and Security

Competencies

After you have read this chapter, you should be able to:

1. Describe health and other workplace issues.

2. Discuss privacy issues raised by the presence of large databases and electronic networks.

3. List the major laws on privacy.

4. Explain the effects of computer crimes, including the spreading of computer viruses.

5. Describe other hazards to the computer.

6. Discuss security measures that may be taken.

The tools and products of the information age do not exist in a world by themselves. As we said in Chapter 1, a computer system consists not only of software, hardware, data, and procedures but also of *people*. Because of people, computer systems may be used for both good and bad purposes. In this chapter we examine what some of the people issues are.

More than 10 million American workers now use video display terminals (VDTs) every day. About 3 million more VDTs are being added each year. Indeed, about one-third of Americans used a computer at work in 1989, according to the U.S. Census Bureau. More of these are women than men. Most of them are in clerical or administrative support jobs. What are the consequences of the widespread presence of this technology? We consider some of the effects below.

Workplace Issues

Ergonomics Helps Computer Users Take Steps to Avoid Physical and Mental Health Risks and to Increase Productivity.

Even though the cost of computers has decreased significantly, they are still expensive. Why have them, then, unless they can make workers more effective? Ironically, however, there are certain ways in which computers may actually make people *less* productive. Many of these problems are most apt to affect those working in data-entry-intensive positions, such as clerks and word processor operators. However, they may also happen to anyone whose job involves heavy use of the computer. As a result, there has been great interest in a field known as ergonomics.

Ergonomics (pronounced "er-guh-*nom*-ix") is defined as the study of human factors related to computers. It is concerned with fitting the job to the worker rather than forcing the worker to contort to fit the job. As computer use has increased, so has interest in ergonomics. People are devising ways that computers can be designed and used to increase productivity and avoid health risks.

Physical Health Matters Sitting in front of a screen in awkward positions for long periods may lead to physical problems. These can include eyestrain, headaches, back pain, and other problems. Users can alleviate these by taking frequent rest breaks and by using well-designed computer furniture. Some recommendations by ergonomic experts for the ideal setup for a microcomputer or workstation are illustrated on the next page. *(See Figure 13-1.)*

The physical health matters related to computers that have received the most attention recently are the following.

- *Avoiding eyestrain and headache:* Our eyes were made for most efficient seeing at a distance. However, VDTs require using the eyes at closer range for a long time, which can create eyestrain, headaches, and double vision.

    To make the computer easier on the eyes, take a 15-minute break every hour or two. Keep computer screens away from windows and other sources of bright light to minimize reflected glare on the screen. Special anti-glare screen coatings and "glare shields" are also available. Make sure the screen is three to four times brighter than room light. Keep everything you're focusing on at about the same distance. For example, the computer screen, keyboard, and a document holder containing your work might be positioned about 20 inches away. Clean the screen of dust from time to time.

- *Avoiding back and neck pains:* Many people work at VDT screens and keyboards that are in improper positions. The result can be pains in the back and neck.

    To avoid such problems, make sure equipment is adjustable. You should be able to adjust your chair for height and angle, and the chair should have good back support. The table on which the monitor stands should also be adjustable, and the monitor itself should be of the tilt-and-swivel kind. Keyboards should be detachable. Document holders should be adjustable.

- *Avoiding effects of electromagnetic fields:* Like many household appliances, video display terminals generate invisible electromagnetic field (EMF) emissions, which can pass through the human body. Some observers feel that there could be a connection between these EMF emissions and possible miscarriages (and even some cancers). A study by the government's National Institute of Occupational Safety and Health found no statistical relationship between VDTs and miscarriages. Even so, several companies have introduced low-emission monitors. They state that no health or safety problems exist with older monitors; rather, they are merely responding to market demands.

    One recommendation is that computer users should follow a policy of "prudent avoidance" in reducing their exposure to EMF emissions. They should try to sit about 2 feet or more from the computer screen and 3 feet from neighboring terminals. The strongest fields are emitted from the sides and backs of terminals.

- *Avoiding repetitive strain injury:* Data-entry operators in some companies may make as many as 23,000 keystrokes a day.

Figure 13-1
Recommendations for the ideal workstation.

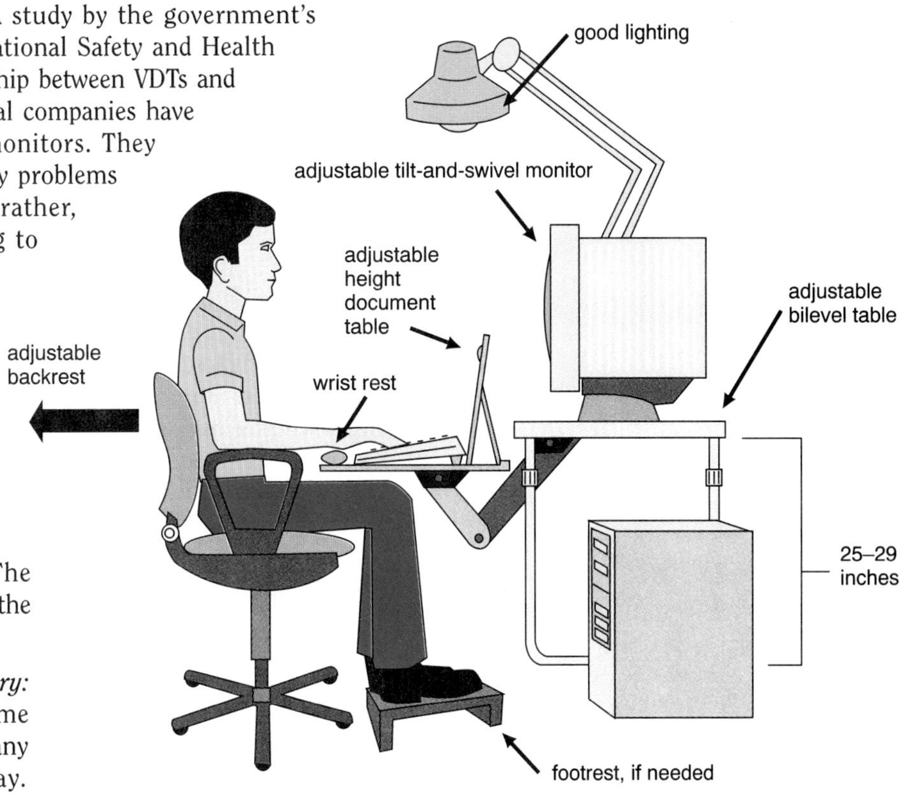

good lighting

adjustable tilt-and-swivel monitor

adjustable bilevel table

adjustable height document table

adjustable backrest

wrist rest

25–29 inches

footrest, if needed

Some of these workers and other heavy keyboard users have fallen victim to a disorder known as repetitive strain injury.

Repetitive strain injury (RSI)—also called **repetitive motion injury** and **cumulative trauma disorders**—is the name given to a number of injuries. These result from fast, repetitive work that can cause neck, wrist, hand, and arm pains. In 1988, RSI accounted for nearly half of all workplace illnesses in private industry, compared to only 18 percent in 1981. Some RSI sufferers are slaughterhouse, textile, and automobile workers, who have long been susceptible to the disorder. However, the large increase was mainly caused by the addition of so many more computer users in the intervening years. One particular RSI, **carpal tunnel syndrome,** found among heavy computer users, consists of damage to nerves and tendons in the hands. Some victims report the pain is so intense that they cannot open doors or shake hands.

Before the computer, typists would stop to change paper or make corrections, thus giving themselves tiny but frequent rest periods. Because RSI is caused by repetition and a fast work pace, avoidance consists in finding ways to take frequent short rest breaks. Experts also advise getting plenty of sleep and exercise, losing weight, sitting up straight, and learning stress-management techniques.

Mental Health Matters   Computer technology offers not only ways of improving productivity but also some irritants that may be counterproductive.

- *Avoiding noise:* Computers can be quite noisy. Working next to an impact printer for several hours, for instance, can leave one with ringing ears. Also, users may develop headaches and tension from being continually exposed to the high-frequency, barely audible squeal produced by computer monitors. This is particularly true for women, who hear high-frequency sounds better than men do. They may be affected by the noise even when they are not conscious of hearing it.

  Sound-muffling covers are available for reducing the noise from impact printers. However, there appears to be no immediate solution for abating the noise from monitors.

- *Avoiding stress from excessive monitoring:* Research shows that workers whose performance is monitored electronically suffer more health problems than do those watched by human supervisors. For instance, a computer may monitor the number of keystrokes a data-entry clerk completes in a day. It might tally the time a customer-service person takes to handle a call. The company might then decide to shorten the time allowed and to continue monitoring the employees electronically. By so doing, it may force a pace leading to physical, RSI-type problems and mental health difficulties. For example, one study found that electronically monitored employees reported more boredom, higher tension, extreme anxiety, depression, anger, and severe fatigue.

  Recently it has been shown that electronic monitoring actually is not necessary. For instance, both Federal Express and Bell Canada replaced electronic monitoring with occasional monitoring by human managers. They found that employee productivity stayed up and even increased.

A new word—*"technostress"*—has been proposed to describe the stress associated with computer use that is harmful to people. Technostress is the tension that arises when we have to unnaturally adapt to computers rather than having computers adapt to us.

Design with People in Mind   Electronic products from microwave ovens to VCRs to microcomputers offer the promise of more efficiency and speed. Often, however, the products are so overloaded with features that users cannot figure them out. Because a microprocessor chip will handle not just one operation but several, manufacturers feel obliged to pile on the "bells and whistles." Thus, many home and office products, while being fancy technology platforms, are difficult for humans to use.

A recent trend among manufacturers has been to deliberately strip down the features offered rather than to constantly do all that is possible. In appliances, this restraint is shown among certain types of "high-end" audio equipment, which come with fewer buttons and lights. In computers, there are similar trends. Surveys show that consumers want "plug and play" equipment—machines that they can simply turn on and quickly start working. Thus, computers are being made easier to use, with more menus, windows, and use of icons and pictures. For instance, the menus and pictures made popular by Macintosh are now being used with great success in Microsoft Corporation's Windows.

Similar attempts at designing computers for ease in human use are found in other areas. For example, psychologists have found that workers regard expert systems—the complex programs that emulate human experts—much as they would human expertise. To be trusted by humans, the programs must contain procedures that are very close to the logic processes used by experts. That is, they must appear to think like humans in order to be acceptable.

Computers and Privacy

Every Computer User Should Be Aware of Privacy and Ethical Matters, Including How Databases and Online Networks Are Used and the Major Privacy Laws.

We are all entitled to the right of **privacy.** This includes the right to keep personal information, such as credit ratings and medical histories, from getting into the wrong hands. Many people worry that this right is severely threatened. Let us see what some of the concerns are.

Use of Large Databases   Large organizations are constantly compiling information about us. (*See Figure 13-2.*) For instance, our social security numbers are now used routinely as key fields in databases for organizing our employment, credit, and tax records. Indeed, even children are now required to have social security numbers. Shouldn't we be concerned that cross-referenced information might be used for the wrong purposes?

Figure 13-2
Large organizations are constantly compiling information about us, such as the kinds of products we buy.

Every day, data is gathered about us and stored in large databases. For example, for billing purposes, telephone companies compile lists of the calls we make, the numbers called, and so on. A special telephone directory (called a reverse directory) lists telephone numbers followed by subscriber names. Using it, governmental authorities and others could easily get the names, addresses, and other details about the persons we call. Credit card companies keep similar records. Supermarket scanners in the grocery checkout counters record what we buy, when we buy it, how much we buy, and the price. So do publishers of magazines and newspapers and mail-order catalogs.

A vast industry of data gatherers or "information resellers" now exists that collects such personal data. They then sell it to direct marketers, fund-raisers, and others. Even government agencies contribute; some state motor vehicle departments sell the car registration data they collect. Database concerns have been able to collect names, addresses, and other information for about 80 percent of American households. The average person is on 100 mailing lists and 50 databases, according to some privacy experts.

In such ways, your personal preferences and habits become marketable commodities. This raises two questions.

■ *Spreading information without personal consent:* How would you feel if your name and your taste in movies were made available nationwide? For a while, Blockbuster, a large video rental company, considered doing just this. What if a great deal of information about your shopping habits—collected about you without your consent—was made available to any microcomputer user who wanted it? Until it dropped the project, Lotus Development Corporation and Equifax Inc. were preparing to market disks containing information on 120 million American consumers. (Lotus claimed it was only providing small businesses with the same information currently available to larger organizations.) Finally, how would you feel if your employer was using your *medical* records to make decisions about placement, promotion, and firing? A 1988 University of Illinois survey found that half of the Fortune 500 companies were using employee medical records for that purpose.

■ *Spreading inaccurate information:* How *accurate* is the information being circulated? Mistakes that creep into one computer file may find their way into other computer files. For example, credit records may be in error. Moreover, even if you correct an error in one file, the correction may not be made in other files. Indeed, erroneous information may stay in computer files for years. It's important to know, therefore, that you have some recourse. The law allows you to gain access to those records about you that are held by credit bureaus. Under the Freedom of Information Act (described below), you are also entitled to look at your records held by government agencies. (Portions may be deleted for national security reasons.)

Use of Electronic Networks   Suppose you use your company's electronic mail system to send a coworker an unflattering message about your supervisor. Later you find the boss has been spying on your exchange. Or suppose you are a subscriber to an online electronic bulletin board. You discover that the company that owns the bulletin board screens all your messages and rejects those it deems inappropriate.

Both these cases have actually happened. The first instance, of firms eavesdropping on employees, has inspired attempts at federal legislation. One proposed law would not prohibit electronic monitoring but would require employers to provide prior written notice. They would also have to alert employees during the monitoring with some sort of audible or visual signal. The second instance, in which online information services have restrictions against libelous, obscene, or otherwise offensive material, exists with most commercial services. In one case, the Prodigy Information Service terminated the accounts of eight members who were using the electronic-mail system to protest Prodigy's rate hikes.

Prodigy executives argued that the U.S. Constitution does not give members of someone else's private network the right to express their views without restrictions. Opponents say that the United States is becoming a nation linked by electronic mail. Therefore, there has to be fundamental protection for users against other people reading or censoring their messages.

The Major Laws on Privacy Some federal laws governing privacy matters are as follows:

- *Fair Credit Reporting Act:* The **Fair Credit Reporting Act of 1970** is intended to keep inaccuracies out of credit bureau files. Credit agencies are barred from sharing credit information with anyone but authorized customers. Consumers have the right to review and correct their records and to be notified of credit investigations for insurance and employment.

  Drawbacks: Credit agencies may share information with anyone they reasonably believe has a "legitimate business need." Legitimate is not defined.

- *Freedom of Information Act:* The **Freedom of Information Act of 1970** gives you the right to look at data concerning you that is stored by the federal government.

  Drawback: Sometimes a lawsuit is necessary to pry data loose.

- *Privacy Act:* The **Privacy Act of 1974** is designed to restrict federal agencies in the way they share information about American citizens. It prohibits federal information collected for one purpose from being used for a different purpose.

  Drawback: Exceptions written into the law permit federal agencies to share information anyway.

- *Right to Financial Privacy Act:* The **Right to Financial Privacy Act of 1979** sets strict procedures that federal agencies must follow when seeking to examine customer records in banks.

  Drawback: The law does not cover state and local governments.

- *Computer Fraud and Abuse Act:* The **Computer Fraud and Abuse Act of 1986** was passed to allow prosecution of unauthorized access to computers and databases.

  Drawbacks: The act is limited in scope. People with legitimate access can still get into computer systems and create mischief without penalty.

- *Video Privacy Protection Act:* The **Video Privacy Protection Act of 1988** prevents retailers from selling or disclosing video-rental records without the customer's consent or a court order.

  Drawback: The same restrictions do not apply to even more important files, such as medical and insurance records.

- *Computer Matching and Privacy Protection Act:* The **Computer Matching and Privacy Protection Act of 1988** sets procedures for computer matching of federal data. Such matching can be for verifying a person's eligibility for federal benefits or for recovering delinquent debts. Individuals are given a chance to respond before the government takes any adverse action against them.

  Drawback: Many possible computer matches are not affected, including those done for law-enforcement or tax reasons.

Currently, privacy is primarily an *ethical* issue, for many records stored by non-government organizations are not covered by existing laws. Yet individuals have shown that they are concerned about controlling who has the right to personal information and how it is used. A Code of Fair Information Practice is summarized below. (*See Figure 13-3*.). The code was recommended in 1977 by a committee established by former Secretary of Health, Education and Welfare Elliott Richardson. It has been adopted by many information-collecting businesses, but privacy advocates would like to see it written into law.

1. *No secret databases:* There must be no record-keeping systems containing personal data whose very existence is kept secret.

2. *Right of individual access:* Individuals must be able to find out what information about them is in a record and how it is used.

3. *Right of consent:* Information about individuals obtained for one purpose cannot be used for other purposes without their consent.

4. *Right to correct:* Individuals must be able to correct or amend records of identifiable information about them.

5. *Assurance of reliability and proper use:* Organizations creating, maintaining, using, or disseminating records of identifiable personal data must make sure the data is reliable for its intended use. They must take precautions to prevent such data from being misused.

Figure 13-3
Principles of the Code of Fair Information Practice.

Threats to Computers

Threats to Computer Security Are Computer Crimes, Including Viruses, Electronic Break-ins, and Natural and Other Hazards.

Keeping information private in part depends on keeping computer systems safe from criminal acts, natural hazards, and other threats.

Computer Criminals   A **computer crime** is an illegal action in which the perpetrator uses special knowledge of computer technology. Computer criminals are of four types:

- *Employees:* The largest category of computer criminals consists of those with the easiest access to computers—namely, employees. (*See Figure 13-4.*) Sometimes the employee is simply trying to steal something from the employer—equipment, software, electronic funds, proprietary information, or computer time. Sometimes the employee may be acting out of resentment and is trying to "get back" at the company.

- *Outside users:* Not only employees but also some suppliers or clients may have access to a company's computer system. Examples are bank customers who use an automatic teller machine. Like employees, these authorized users may obtain confidential passwords or find other ways of committing computer crimes.

- *"Hackers" and "crackers":* Some people think of these two groups as being the same, but they are not. **Hackers** are people who gain unauthorized access to a computer system for the fun and challenge of it. **Crackers** do the same thing but for malicious purposes. They may intend to steal technical information or to introduce what they call a "bomb"—a destructive computer program—into the system. (A similar illegal user is the "phone phreak," who explores the phone system, often with the intent of making free phone calls.)

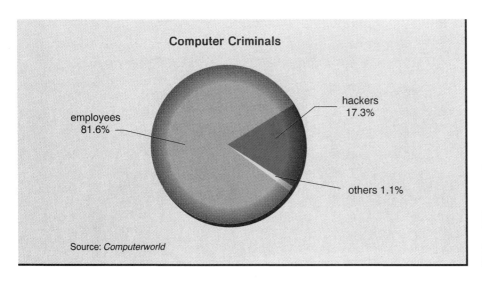

Figure 13-4
The experts reply: Whom do you consider to be a threat against your network?

■ *Organized crime:* Organized crime has discovered that computers can be used just like legitimate business people use them but for illegal purposes. For example, they are useful for keeping track of stolen goods or illegal gambling debts. In addition, counterfeiters and forgers use microcomputers and printers to produce sophisticated-looking documents, such as checks and driver's licenses.

Computer Crime Computer crime can take various forms, as follows.

■ *Damage:* Disgruntled employees sometimes attempt to destroy computers, programs, or files. For example, in a crime known as the **Trojan horse program** instructions can be written to destroy or modify software or data.

In recent years, computer viruses have gained wide notoriety. **Viruses** are programs that "migrate" through networks and operating systems and attach themselves to different programs and databases. (*See Figure 13-5.*) A variant on the virus is the **worm,** also called **bacteria.** This destructive program fills a computer system with self-replicating information, clogging the system so that its operations are slowed or stopped. Viruses typically find their way into microcomputers through copied floppy disks or programs downloaded from electronic bulletin boards. Because viruses can be so serious—certain "disk-killer" viruses can destroy all the information on one's system—computer users are advised to exercise care in accepting new programs and data from other sources. (*See Figure 13-6.*) Detection programs are available to alert users when certain kinds of viruses enter the system. Unfortunately, new viruses are being developed all the time, and not all viruses can be detected.

Figure 13-5
How a computer virus can spread.

■ *Theft:* Theft can take many forms—of hardware, of software, of data, of computer time. Thieves steal equipment, of course, but there are also "white-collar crimes." Thieves steal data in the form of confidential information such as preferred client lists or use (steal) their company's computer time to run another business.

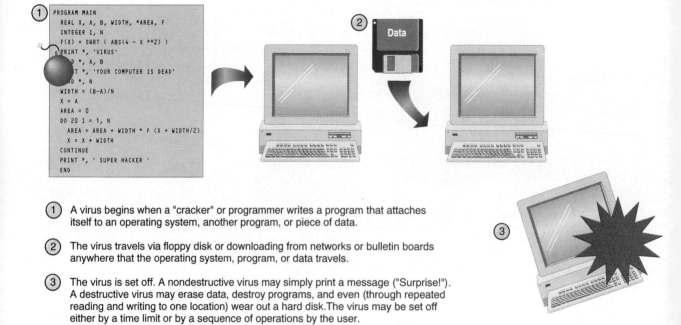

```
PROGRAM MAIN
  REAL X, A, B, WIDTH, *AREA, F
  INTEGER I, N
  F(X) = SQRT ( ABS(4 - X **2) )
  PRINT *, 'VIRUS'
     D *, A, B
     T *, 'YOUR COMPUTER IS DEAD'
     D *, N
  WIDTH = (B-A)/N
  X = A
  AREA = 0
  DO 20 I = 1, N
    AREA = AREA + WIDTH * F (X + WIDTH/2)
    X = X + WIDTH
  CONTINUE
  PRINT *, ' SUPER HACKER '
  END
```

(1) A virus begins when a "cracker" or programmer writes a program that attaches itself to an operating system, another program, or piece of data.

(2) The virus travels via floppy disk or downloading from networks or bulletin boards anywhere that the operating system, program, or data travels.

(3) The virus is set off. A nondestructive virus may simply print a message ("Surprise!"). A destructive virus may erase data, destroy programs, and even (through repeated reading and writing to one location) wear out a hard disk. The virus may be set off either by a time limit or by a sequence of operations by the user.

1. Make back-up copies of your data on a frequent basis.
2. Protect data on your floppy disks by using write/protect tabs.
3. Turn off your microcomputer when you're not using it.
4. Don't use master disks. Make a working copy and store the master.
5. Avoid downloading computer games from electronic bulletin boards.
6. Limit your use of "Shareware" programs.
7. Do not loan out your utility or other software programs.

Figure 13-6
How to prevent computer viruses and minimize damage.

Unauthorized copying—a form of theft—of programs for personal gain is called **software piracy.** According to the **Software Copyright Act of 1980,** it is legal for the owner of a program to make copies of that program for backup purposes. *It's important to note that none of these copies may be resold or given away.* This may come as a surprise to students who "borrow" copies of software from a friend, but that's the law. Such borrowing is illegal, not to mention unethical. A user may also modify a program to make it useful—again, provided it is not for purposes of resale. Penalties for violation of this law are payment of monetary damages to the developer of the program and even prison terms for offenders.

Manipulation: Finding entry into someone's computer network and leaving a prankster's message may seem like fun, which is why hackers do it. It is still against the law. Moreover, even if the manipulation seems harmless, it may cause a great deal of anxiety and wasted time among network users.

The **Computer Fraud and Abuse Act of 1986** makes it a crime for unauthorized persons even to *view* (let alone copy or damage) data using any computer across state lines. It also prohibits unauthorized use of any government computer or computer used by any federally insured financial institution. Offenders can be sentenced to up to 20 years in prison and fined up to $100,000.

Of course, using a computer in the course of performing some other crime, such as selling fraudulent products, is also illegal.

Other Hazards   There are plenty of other hazards to computer systems and data besides criminals. They include the following:

Natural hazards: Natural forces include fires, floods, wind, hurricanes, tornadoes, and earthquakes. Even home computer users should store backup disks of programs and data in safe locations in case of fire or storm damage.

Civil strife and terrorism: Wars, insurrections, and other forms of political unrest are real risks in some parts of the world. Even developed countries, however, must be mindful that acts of sabotage are possible.

■ *Technological failures:* Hardware and software don't always do what they are supposed to do. For instance, too little electricity, caused by a brownout or blackout, may cause the loss of data in primary storage. Too much electricity, as when lightning or other electrical disturbance affects a power line, may cause a **voltage surge,** or **spike.** This excess of electricity may destroy chips or other electronic components of a computer.

Many microcomputer users buy a low-cost **surge protector,** a device that separates the computer from the power source of the wall outlet. When a voltage surge occurs, it activates a circuit breaker in the surge protector, protecting the computer system.

Another technological catastrophe is when a hard disk drive suddenly "crashes," or fails, perhaps because it has been bumped inadvertently. If the user has forgotten to make backup copies of data on the hard disk, it may be lost.

■ *Human errors:* Human mistakes are inevitable. Data-entry errors are probably the most commonplace. Programmer errors also occur frequently. Some mistakes may result from faulty design, as when a software manufacturer makes a deletion command closely resemble another command. Some may be the result of sloppy procedures, as when office workers keep important correspondence under filenames that no one else in the office knows.

Security

Security Measures Consist of Restricting Access, Anticipating Disasters, and Making Backup Copies of Data.

Security is concerned with protecting information, hardware, and software. They must be protected from unauthorized use as well as from damage from intrusions, sabotage, and natural disasters. (*See Figure 13-7.*) Considering the numerous ways in which computer systems and data can be compromised, we can see why security is a growing field. Some of the principal aspects are as follows.

Restricting Access Security experts are constantly devising ways to protect computer systems from access by unauthorized persons. Sometimes security is a matter of putting guards on company computer rooms and checking the identification of everyone admitted. Oftentimes it is a matter of being careful about assigning passwords to people and of changing them when people leave a company. *Passwords,* let us recall, are the secret words or numbers that must be keyed into a computer system before it will operate. In some "dial-back" computer systems, the user telephones the computer, punches in the correct password, and hangs up. The computer then calls back at a certain preauthorized number.

Some security systems use **biometrics,** the science of measuring individual body characteristics. This may consist of using machines that can recognize one's fingerprints, signature, voice, or even photograph.

Anticipating Disasters Companies (and even individuals) that do not make preparations for disasters are not acting wisely. **Physical security** is concerned with protecting hardware from possible human and natural disasters. **Data security** is concerned with protecting software and data from unauthorized tampering or damage. Most large organizations have a **disaster recovery plan** describing ways to continue operating until normal computer operations can be restored.

Hardware can be kept behind locked doors, but often employees find this restriction a hindrance, and so security is lax. Fire and water (including the water from ceiling sprinkler systems) can do great damage to equipment. Many companies therefore will form a cooperative arrangement to share equipment with other companies in the event of catastrophe. Special emergency facilities may be created called **hot sites** if they are fully equipped computer centers. They are called **cold sites** if they are empty shells in which hardware must be installed.

Backing Up Data   Equipment can always be replaced. A company's *data,* however, may be irreplaceable. Most companies have ways of trying to keep software and data from being tampered with in the first place. They include careful screening of job applicants, guarding passwords, and auditing data and programs from time to time. The safest procedure, however, is to make frequent backups of data and to store them in remote locations.

Security for Microcomputers   If you own a microcomputer system, there are several procedures to follow to keep it safe:

- *Avoid extreme conditions:* Don't expose the computer to extreme conditions. Rain or sun from an open window, extreme temperatures, cigarette smoke, and spilled drinks or food are harmful to microcomputers. Clean your equipment regularly. Use a surge protector.

- *Guard the computer:* Put a cable lock on the computer. If you subscribe or belong to an online information service, do not leave passwords nearby. Etch your driver's license number or social security number into your equipment so that it can be identified in the event it is recovered after theft.

- *Guard programs and data:* Store disks properly, preferably in a locked container. Make backup copies of all your important files and programs. Store copies of your files in a different—and safe—location from the site of your computer.

Figure 13-7
Natural disasters such as earthquakes can play havoc with computers.

A Look at the Future

New Legislation Will Be Needed to Define Access to Government Files and to Regulate Government Interference in Free Speech in the New Electronic World.

Technology often has a way of outracing existing social and political institutions. For instance, citizens have a right to request government records under the Freedom of Information Act. But even in its most recent amendment, in 1986, the act does not mention "computer" or define the word "record." Can the government therefore legally deny, as one agency did, a legitimate request for data on corporate compliance with occupational safety and health laws? *Access laws lag* behind even as the government collects more information than ever.

In addition, there has been a rise in computer-related crimes, such as bank and credit-card fraud, viruses, and electronic break-ins of government and private computer systems. As law-enforcement agencies crack down on these computer operators, they may also be jeopardizing the rights of computer users who are not breaking the law. Such users may be suffering illegal searches and violation of constitutional guarantees of free speech. However, it is not clear how the First Amendment protects speech and the Fourth Amendment protects against searches and seizures in this electronic world. One professor of constitutional law has proposed a *new Amendment to the Constitution*. This amendment would extend the other freedoms in the Bill of Rights, such as those on free speech and restrictions on search and seizure, to cover all new technology and mediums for generating, storing, and altering information.

Review Questions

1. Define *ergonomics*.
2. What kind of activities can you take to avoid computer-related eyestrain, headaches, and back and neck pains?
3. What can you do to minimize the possible effects of electromagnetic field emissions?
4. What are *repetitive strain injuries* and how can they be avoided?
5. Describe some mental health problems associated with frequent computer use.
6. What are two major problems associated with the computer-related collection of personal data about you?
7. Discuss some of the privacy problems related to use of electronic networks.
8. Name and describe four of the seven major laws on privacy discussed in the chapter.
9. What four types of people are likely to be computer criminals?
10. How does a *computer virus* do damage?
11. What is *software piracy?*
12. What does the Computer Fraud and Abuse Act prohibit?
13. Name some of the principal hazards to computers other than computer crimes.
14. Define what is meant by *security*.
15. Name three ways of protecting the security of computers.
16. Discuss three ways of keeping microcomputers safe.

Discussion Questions and Projects

1. *Your credit record:* If you or some member of your family presently own a credit card—oil company, department store, Visa, MasterCard—you can determine your credit rating. The law allows credit-card holders access to credit records in order to determine their rating, and to correct any errors. This is an important right, because your credit rating determines your eligibility for loans in the future.

   To request a free copy of your credit record, available once per year, write to TRW Consumer Assistance, Box 2350 Chatsworth, CA 91313. Include your full name, addresses for the past five years with dates and zip codes, social security number, date of birth, and your spouse's name if you're married. Also include a photocopy of your driver's license or a utility bill showing your present name and address. Allow about four weeks for delivery. Look over the credit report, make any corrections.

2. *Your national identification number:* One characteristic of many dictatorships is that all citizens are made to carry "papers." These are a kind of internal passport, each with its own number, enabling the government to keep track of—and regulate—one's travel, employment, and so on. In the United States, the founding fathers were deeply concerned about the government's having tyranny over its citizens, and internal papers have never been required.

   Unfortunately, the social security number, or SSN, has been stretched to cover purposes for which it was never intended. It has become a national identification number that, once given out, never goes away. It can be a person's student ID, tax number, military ID, medical insurance number, criminal file number, and credit number. Every time you scrawl the number on a credit or job application or other form, it becomes available to thousands of people you don't know. It will be available to anyone with access to a legal database.

   Discuss with classmates or write an essay on your worst scenario of what could happen to you because of the easy availability of your social security number.

Chapter 13 Workplace Issues, Privacy, and Security

One-third of Americans use a computer at work. Thus, there are many "people issues" connected with computers.

| Workplace Issues | Computers and Privacy |

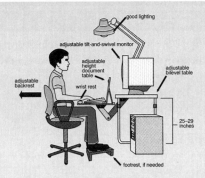

Users should take steps to increase productivity and avoid physical and mental health risks. **Ergonomics** is the study of human factors related to computers.

Physical Health Matters

Some computer-associated physical health matters that can be avoided:

- Eyestrain and headache: Take frequent breaks, avoid glare on monitor screen.
- Back and neck pains: Use adjustable chairs, tables, keyboards.
- Electromagnetic fields: May lead to miscarriages, but not proven. Sit 2 feet from screen, 3 feet from adjacent computers.
- **Repetitive strain injury (RSI):** Also known as **repetitive motion injury** and **cumulative trauma disorders,** RSIs are neck, wrist, hand, and arm injuries resulting from fast, repetitive work. **Carpal tunnel syndrome,** damage to nerves and tendons in hands, afflicts heavy keyboard users. Avoidance consists of frequent short rest breaks.

Mental Health Matters

Irritations consist of:

- Noise from clattering printers and high-frequency squeal from monitors.
- Stress from excessive monitoring.

Design with People in Mind

Computers are being designed for easier use.

Privacy is the right to keep personal information about us from getting into the wrong hands.

Use of Large Databases

Large databases are constantly compiling information about us. A vast industry of data gatherers or "information resellers" collects data about us and sells it to direct marketers and others.

Use of Electronic Networks

Some information networks have been used to eavesdrop on employees or to restrict members' messages.

Major Laws on Privacy

Some federal laws governing privacy are:

- **Fair Credit Reporting Act (1970),** restricting sharing of credit information.
- **Freedom of Information Act (1970),** giving citizens right to see federal files about them.
- **Privacy Act (1974),** restricting federal information collected for one purpose from being used for another.
- **Right to Financial Privacy Act (1979),** setting rules government must follow in seeking banks' customer records.
- **Computer Fraud and Abuse Act (1986),** prosecuting unauthorized access to computers and databases.
- **Video Privacy Protection Act (1988),** preventing retailers from disclosing customers' video-rental records.
- **Computer Matching and Privacy Protection Act (1988),** setting rules for government's matching of federal data.

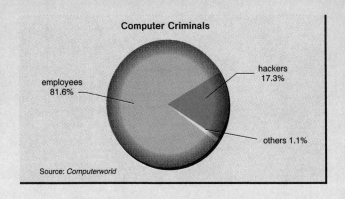

Computer Criminals

- hackers 17.3%
- employees 81.6%
- others 1.1%

Source: *Computerworld*

| Threats to Computers | Security |

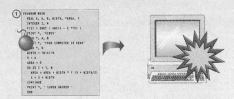

Keeping information private and secure in part depends on keeping computer systems safe.

Computer Criminals

Computer criminals are of four types:

- Employees—the largest category of computer criminals.
- Outside users—suppliers or clients.
- **Hackers,** who gain unauthorized access to computer systems for fun, and **crackers,** who do the same thing for malicious purposes.
- Organized crime figures, who use computers to assist illegal businesses or do forgeries and counterfeiting.

Computer Crime

Computer crime takes the following forms:

- Damage, as when criminals destroy files. The **Trojan horse program** is used to tamper with files or data. **Viruses** are programs that migrate through networks and operating systems and attach themselves to programs and databases, perhaps disabling them. A variant on the virus is a **worm (bacteria),** which fills the computer system until it stops.
- Theft, of hardware, software, data, or computer time. **Software piracy** is unauthorized copying of programs. The **Software Copyright Act (1980)** allows making copies for backup purposes only for personal use.
- Manipulation, as in unauthorized entry to a computer system for fun. The **Computer Fraud and Abuse Act (1986)** prohibits unauthorized persons from viewing data in computers used in crossing state lines.

Other Hazards

Other threats to computers include natural hazards, terrorism, technological failure, and human error.

Security is concerned with protecting information, hardware, and software from unauthorized use and from damage.

Restricting Access

Computer systems are protected by screening users, such as by asking them to type in correct passwords. Systems using **biometrics,** the science of measuring individual body characteristics, may recognize fingerprints or voices.

Anticipating Disasters

Physical security is concerned with protecting hardware from disasters.

Data security is concerned with protecting software and data. Many organizations have a **disaster recovery plan** prescribing ways for computer systems to operate after a disaster. **Hot sites** are alternate computer centers. **Cold sites** are sites in which hardware must be installed.

Backing Up Data

Data must be frequently backed up and stored in safe places.

Security for Microcomputers

- Avoid extreme conditions, such as heat and smoke.
- Guard the computer, using locks.
- Guard programs and data, putting backup copies in a safe place.

241

14 Your Future: Using Information Technology

Competencies

After you have read this chapter, you should be able to:

1. Explain why it's important to have an individual strategy in order to be a "winner" in the information age.

2. Describe how technology is changing the nature of competition.

3. Discuss three ways people may react to new technology.

4. Describe how you can use your computer competence to stay current and to take charge of your career.

Throughout this book, we have emphasized practical subjects that are useful to you now or will be very soon. Accordingly, this final chapter is not about the far future of, say, 10 years from now. Rather, it is about the near future—about developments whose outlines we can already see. It is about how organizations adapt to technological change. It is also about what you as an individual can do to keep your computer competency up to date.

Are the times changing any faster now than they ever have? It's hard to say. People who were alive when radios, cars, and airplanes were being introduced certainly lived through some dramatic changes. Has technology made our own times even more dynamic? Whatever the answer, it is clear we live in a fast-paced age. The challenge for you as an individual is to devise ways to stay current.

Being a Winner

To Be a Winner in the Information Revolution, You Need an *Individual* Strategy.

Most businesses have become aware that they must adapt to changing technology or be left behind. Many organizations are now making formal plans to keep track of technology and implement it in their competitive strategies. For example, banks have found that automated teller machines (ATMs) are vital to retail banking. (*See Figure 14-1.*) Not only do they require fewer human tellers, but they can also be made available 24 hours a day. More and more banks are also trying to go electronic, doing away with paper transactions wherever possible. Thus, ATM cards can now be used in certain places to buy gas or groceries. Many banks are also trying to popularize home banking, so that customers can use microcomputers for certain financial tasks. In addition, banks are exploring the use of some very sophisticated applications programs. These programs will accept and analyze cursive writing (the handwriting on checks) directly as input.

Clearly, such changes do away with some jobs—those of many bank tellers and cashiers, for example. However, they create opportunities for other people. New technology requires people who are truly capable of working with it. These are not the people who think every piece of equipment is so simple they can just turn it on and use it. Nor are they those who think each new machine is a potential disaster. In other words, new technology needs people who are not afraid to learn it and are able to manage it. The real issue, then, is not how to make technology better. Rather, it is how to integrate the technology with people.

You are in a very favorable position compared with many other people in industry today. After reading the previous 13 chapters, you have learned not only the basics of hardware, software, and connectivity. You have also learned the most *current* technology. You are therefore able to use these tools to your advantage—to be a winner.

How do you become and stay a winner? In brief, the answer is: You must form your own individual strategy for dealing with change. First let us look at how businesses are handling technological change. Then let us look at how people are reacting to these changes. Finally, we will offer a few suggestions that will enable you to keep up with—and profit by—the information revolution.

Technology and Organizations

Technology Changes the Nature of Competition by Introducing New Products, New Enterprises, and New Relationships Among Customers and Suppliers.

Technology can introduce new ways businesses compete with each other. Some of the principal changes are as follows.

New Products Technology creates products that operate faster, are priced cheaper, are often of better quality, or are wholly new. Indeed, new products can be custom tailored to a particular customer's needs. For example, financial services company Merrill Lynch took advantage of technology to launch a cash management account. This account combines information on a person's checking, savings, credit card, and securities accounts into a single monthly statement. It automatically sets aside "idle" funds into interest-bearing money market funds. The result is that customers can get a complete picture of their financial condition at one time. However, even if they don't pay much attention to their statements, their surplus funds are invested automatically.

New Enterprises Information technology can build entire new businesses. An example is the availability of facsimile (fax) machine business. Now chains of quick-print and photocopying shops offer fax services. For a few dollars you can send a fax message to, or receive one from, nearly anywhere in the United States.

Figure 14-1
Automatic teller machines are examples of technology used in business strategy.

Figure 14-2
The Sabre reservations system used by American Airlines.

A company may use its extra information systems capability to develop new services for customers outside the area it serves directly. For example, American Airlines has a reservations system called Sabre that lists the flight schedules of every major airline in the world. Travel agents with online access to Sabre pay American a fee for every reservation made on Sabre for other airlines. (*See Figure 14-2.*)

New Customer and Supplier Relationships Businesses that make their information systems easily available may make their customers less likely to take their business elsewhere. For instance, Federal Express, the overnight package delivery service, does everything possible to make its customers dependent on it. Airbills are given to the customer with the customer's name, address, and account number preprinted on them, making shipping and billing easier. Package numbers are scanned into the company's information system, so that they can be tracked from pickup point to destination. (*See Figure 14-3.*) Thus, apprehensive customers can be informed very quickly of the exact location of their packages as they travel toward their destination.

Technology and People

People May Be Cynical, Naïve, or Frustrated by Technology.

Clearly, recent technological changes, and those sure to come in the near future, will produce some upheavals in the years ahead. How should we be prepared for them?

People have different coping styles when it comes to technology. It has been suggested, for instance, that people react to the notion of microcomputers in business in three ways. These ways are *cynicism, naïveté,* and *frustration.*

Cynicism The cynic feels that, for a manager at least, the idea of using a microcomputer is overrated. (*See Figure 14-4.*) Learning and using it take too much time, time that could be delegated to someone else. Doing spreadsheets and word processing, according to the cynic, are tasks that managers should understand. However, their real job is to develop plans and set goals for the people being supervised.

Cynics may express their doubts openly, especially if they are top managers. Or they may only pretend to be interested in microcomputers, when actually they are not interested at all.

Figure 14-3
Federal Express couriers scan bar codes on every package, transferring customer and delivery data to a worldwide network that can be closely monitored by customer service agents.

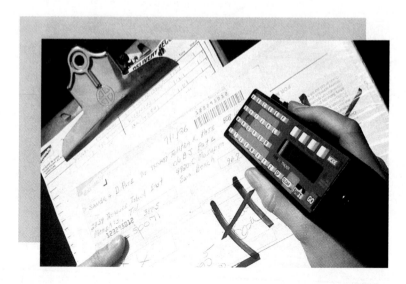

Naïveté   Naïve people may be unfamiliar with computers. Thus, they may think computers are magic boxes capable of solving all kinds of problems that they are really unable to handle. (*See Figure 14-5.*) In contrast, some naïve persons are actually quite familiar with computers. However, such people underestimate the difficulty of changing computer systems or of generating information.

Frustration   The frustrated person may already be quite busy and may hate having to take time to learn about microcomputers. Such a person feels imposed on at having to learn to keep up. Often she or he is too impatient to try to understand the manuals explaining what hardware and software are supposed to do. The result, therefore, is continual frustration. (*See Figure 14-6.*) Some people are frustrated because they try to do too much. Or they're frustrated because they find manuals difficult to understand. Oftentimes, they feel stupid, when actually the manuals are at fault.

Cynicism, naïveté, and frustration are not just confined to microcomputers, of course. They apply to all new technology. Do you see yourself reacting in any of these ways? They are actually commonplace responses—part of just being human. Knowing which, if any, of these reactions characterize you or your superiors may help you survive and react in positive ways in organizational life.

Figure 14-4
The cynic: "These gadgets are overrated."

Figure 14-5
The naïve: "Let the computer make the decision."

Figure 14-6
The frustrated: "This stuff doesn't make sense half the time."

How You Can Be a Winner

Individuals Need to Stay Current, Develop Specialties, and Be Alert to Organizational Changes and Opportunities for Innovation.

So far we have described how progressive organizations are using technology in the information age. Now let's concentrate on you as an individual. How can you stay ahead? Here are some ideas.

Stay Current   Whatever their particular line of work, successful professionals keep up both with their own fields and with the times. We don't mean you should try to become a computer expert and read a lot of technical magazines. Rather, you should concentrate on your profession and learn how computer technology is being used within it.

Every field has trade journals, whether the field is interior design, personnel management, advertising, or whatever. Most such journals regularly present articles about the uses of computers. It's important that you also belong to a trade or industry association and go to its meetings. Many associations sponsor seminars and conferences that describe the latest information and techniques.

Figure 14-7
Some books covering
computers.

Maintain Your Computer Competence   Actually, you should try to stay *ahead* of the technology. Books, journals, and trade associations are the best source of information about new technology that applies to your field. (*See Figure 14-7.*) The general business press—*Business Week, Fortune, Inc., The Wall Street Journal,* and the business section of your local newspaper—also carries computer-related articles.

However, if you wish, you can subscribe to a magazine that covers microcomputers and information more specifically. Examples are *InfoWorld, PC World,* and *MacWorld.* You may also find it useful to look at newspapers and magazines that cover the computer industry as a whole. An example of such a periodical is *ComputerWorld.*

Develop Professional Contacts   Besides being members of professional associations, successful people make it a point to maintain contact with others in their field. They stay in touch by telephone and letter and go to lunch with others in their line of work. Doing this lets them learn what other people are doing in their jobs. It tells them what other firms are doing and what tasks are being automated. Developing professional contacts can keep you abreast not only of new information but also of new job possibilities. (*See Figure 14-8.*) It also offers social benefits. An example of a professional organization that is found in many areas is the local association of realtors.

Develop Specialties   Develop specific as well as general skills. You want to be well rounded within your field, but certainly not a "jack of all trades, master of none." Master a trade or two *within* your profession. At the same time, don't become identified with a specific technological skill that might very well become obsolete.

Figure 14-8
Professional organizations and
contacts help you keep up in
your field.

The best advice is to specialize to some extent. However, don't make your specialty so tied to technology that you'll be in trouble if the technology shifts. For example, if your career is in marketing or graphics design, it makes sense to learn about desktop publishing. (*See Figure 14-9.*) That way you can learn to make high-quality, inexpensive graphics layouts. It would not make as much sense for you to become an expert on, say, the various types of monitors used to display the graphics layouts because such monitors are continually changing.

Expect to take classes during your working life to keep up with developments in your field. Some professions require more keeping up than others—that of a computer specialist, for example, compared to that of a personnel manager. Whatever the training required, always look for ways to adapt and improve your skills to become more productive and marketable. There may be times when you are tempted to start all over again and learn completely new skills. However, a better course of action is to use emerging technology to improve your present base of skills. This way you can build on your current strong points and then branch out to other fields from a position of strength.

Be Alert for Organizational Change   Every organization has formal lines of communication—for example, supervisor to middle manager to top manager. However, there is also the grapevine—informal lines of communication. (*See Figure 14-10.*) Some service departments will serve many layers of management and be abreast of the news on all levels. For instance, the art director for advertising may be aware of several aspects of a companywide marketing campaign. Secretaries and administrative assistants know what is going on in more than one area.

Being part of the office grapevine can alert you to important changes—for instance, new job openings—that can benefit you. However, you always have to assess the validity of what you hear on the grapevine. Moreover, it's not advisable to be a contributor to "office gossip." Behind-the-back criticisms of other people can have a way of getting back to the person criticized.

Be especially alert for new trends within the organization—about future hiring, layoffs, automation, mergers with other companies, and the like. Be alert for areas receiving the greatest attention from top management. One tip-off is to see what kind of outside consultants are being brought in. Independent consultants are usually invited in because a company believes it needs advice in an area with which it has insufficient experience.

Figure 14-9
Desktop publishing: a good specialty to develop for certain careers.

Figure 14-10
Informal communication can alert you to important organizational changes.

Figure 14-11
Present your ideas as saving money rather than "improving information."

Look for Innovative Opportunities You may understand your job better than anyone—even if you've only been there a few months. Look for ways to make it more efficient. How can present procedures be automated? How can new technology make your tasks easier? Discuss your ideas with your supervisor, the training director, or the head of the information systems department. Or discuss them with someone else who can see that you get the recognition you deserve. (Coworkers may or may not be receptive and may or may not try to take credit themselves.)

A good approach is to present your ideas in terms of *saving money* rather than "improving information." (*See Figure 14-11.*) Managers are generally more impressed with ideas that can save dollars than with ideas that seem like potential breakthroughs in the quality of decisions.

In general, it's best to concentrate on the business and organizational problems that need solving. Then look for a technological way of solving them. That is, avoid becoming too enthusiastic about a particular technology and then trying to make it fit the work situation.

A Look at the Future: The Rest of Your Life

Being Computer-Competent Means Always Taking Positive Control.

This is not the end; it is the beginning. Being a skilled computer end user—being computer-competent—is not a matter of thinking "Some day I'll . . ." ("Some day I'll have to learn all about that.") It is a matter of living in the present and keeping an eye on the future. It is also a matter of having the discipline to keep up with the prevailing technology. It is not a matter of focusing on vague "what-ifs." It is a matter of concentrating on your goals and learning how the computer can help you achieve them. Being an end user, in short, is not about trying to avoid failure. Rather, it is about always going toward success—about taking control over the exciting new tools available to you.

Review Questions

1. How do you become and stay a winner in the information age?
2. Give an example of how technology can change the nature of competition.
3. What are three responses or attitudes that people are apt to have when confronted by new technology?
4. Name six strategies individuals should follow in order to be successful in the information age.
5. What periodicals might you read in order to keep current on changes in microcomputer technology?

Discussion Questions and Projects

1. *Volunteering your computer skills:* What would you do if you had an old but still useful microcomputer? It might not be something you want or even something you can sell. Still, someone can benefit from it. For instance, there are several groups that collect donated hardware and software for nonprofit organizations, such as conservation, veterans, arts, and child-care groups.

   These groups also provide volunteers to assist nonprofits in learning to use their new systems. Perhaps this is a case where you can lend your own experience in a good cause. Contact one of the following or a similar organization, which you may learn about through local computer users' groups, to see how you can help:

   a. *Boston:* CONNECT, Technical Development Corporation, 30 Federal St., 5th floor, Boston, MA 02110 (telephone: 617-728-9151).

   b. *Chicago:* Information Technology Resource Center, 59 East Van Buren, Suite 2020, Chicago, IL 60605-1219 (telephone: 312-939-8050).

   c. *Dallas:* Technology Learning Center, Center for Nonprofit Management, 2900 Live Oak St., Dallas, TX 75204 (telephone: 214-823-8097).

   d. *New York:* Nonprofit Computer Exchange, Fund for the City of New York, 121 Sixth Ave., 6th floor, New York, NY 10013 (telephone: 212-925-5101).

   e. *San Francisco:* CompuMentor, 89 Stillman St., San Francisco, CA 94107 (telephone: 415-512-7784).

2. *Being careful about technology predictions:* Technology forecasts have a way of often being so wide of the mark that in looking back we may wonder how the experts could have erred so badly. For instance, nuclear-powered airplanes, household robots, and widespread use of electric cars have never realized the rosy promises of the forecasters.

   Editor Herb Brody in *Technology Review* (July 1991) suggests some guidelines for reducing erroneous predictions. Among them are the following. (a) Be wary of forecasts based on information from vested interests, such as technology developers needing financing, who may in turn exert undue influence on market-forecasting firms, the news media, and investors. (b) Expect existing technologies to keep on improving and don't expect people to abandon what they have for something only somewhat better. (c) Expect truly revolutionary technologies to take 10 to 25 years to enter widespread use.

   Given these guidelines, describe what kind of future uses and popularity you would expect for the following: neutral-network computers; pen-based computers; shirt-pocket telephones; hypermedia; computer-generated virtual realities; flat-panel display TVs to hang on living-room walls.

Chapter 14 Your Future: Using Information Technology

Being a winner in the Information Revolution means devising an individual strategy for dealing with change.

| Technology and Organizations | Technology and People |

Technology can introduce new ways businesses compete with each other.

Three common reactions to the prospect of new technology are:

New Products

Technology creates products that operate faster, are priced more cheaply, are often of better quality, or are wholly new. New products can be custom tailored to a particular customer's needs.

Cynicism

The cynics feel that new technology is overrated and too troublesome to learn.

New Enterprises

Technology can build entire new businesses (e.g., an airline charges travel agents for using its reservations system for making reservations on other airlines).

Naïveté

The naïve believe that technology can solve problems it cannot.

New Customer and Supplier Relationships

Businesses that make their information systems easily available may make their customers less likely to take their business elsewhere (e.g., overnight delivery services closely track packages and bills).

Frustration

The frustrated are impatient and irritated about taking time to learn new technology.

Being a skilled computer end user—being computer-competent—is a matter of living in the present and keeping an eye on the future. It is a matter of concentrating on your goals and learning how the computer can help you achieve them.

Six ongoing activities that can help you be successful are as follows:

Stay Current

Stay current in your field—by reading trade journals and the general business press and by joining professional associations.

Maintain Your Computer Competence

Stay current with technology—by being alert for computer-related articles in trade journals in your field, general computer magazines, and books.

Develop Professional Contacts

Develop professional contacts with others in your field.

Develop Specialties

Develop some specialties within your field, mastering a trade or two within your profession.

Be Alert for Organizational Change

Use informal lines of communication—the "grapevine"—to be alert for organizational changes.

Look for Innovative Opportunities

Improve your prospects by looking for ways to make your job more efficient—e.g., by finding ways to save money.

Glossary

Access Arm: The arm that holds the read-write head and moves back and forth over the surface of a disk.

Access Time: The period between the time that the computer requests data from a secondary storage device and the time that the transfer of data is completed.

Accounts Payable: The activity that shows the money a company owes to its suppliers for the materials and services it has received.

Accounts Receivable: The activity that shows what money has been received from or is owed by customers.

Ada: A procedural language named after Ada Augusta, daughter of the nineteenth-century English poet Lord Byron. She is considered to be the first programmer. Originally designed for weapons systems, Ada has commercial uses as well.

Adapter Card: See Expansion Board.

Address: Location in primary storage in which character of data or instruction is stored during processing.

AI: See Artificial Intelligence.

ALU (Arithmetic-Logic Unit): The part of the CPU that performs arithmetic and logical operations.

Analog Signal: A signal that represents a range of frequencies, such as the human voice.

Analytical Graphics: A form of graphics used to put numeric data into forms that are easier to analyze, such as bar charts, line graphs, and pie charts.

Applications Generator: Software with modules that have been preprogrammed to accomplish various tasks, such as calculation of overtime pay.

Applications Software: Software that can perform useful work such as word processing, cost estimating, or accounting tasks.

Artificial Intelligence (AI): A field of computer science that attempts to develop computer systems that can mimic or simulate human thought processes and actions.

Artificial Reality: Interactive sensory equipment (headgear and gloves) that allows user to experience alternative realities to the physical world.

ASCII (American Standard Code for Information Interchange): A binary coding scheme widely used on all computers, including microcomputers.

Assembly Languages: The second generation of programming languages. These languages use abbreviations for program instructions.

Asynchronous Communications Port: See Serial Port.

Asynchronous Transmission: The method whereby data is sent and received one byte at a time.

Automated Design Tool: Software package that evaluates hardware and software alternatives according to requirements given by the systems analyst.

Backup Disk: Duplicate copy of program or data disk.

Backup Tape Cartridge Unit: See Magnetic Tape Streamer.

Bacteria: See Worm.

Bandwidth: The bit-per-second transmission capability of a channel.

Bar Code: A code consisting of vertical zebra-striped marks printed on cans, boxes, and other containers, read with a bar-code reader.

Bar-Code Reader: Input device consisting of photoelectric scanner that reads bar codes for processing.

BASIC (Beginner's All-purpose Symbolic Instruction Code): An easy-to-learn procedural programming language widely used on microcomputers.

Basic Input Output System: See BIOS.

Batch Processing: Processing performed all at once on data that has been collected over several days.

Baud Rate: Communications speed; the number of changes in the electrical state in the line per second. At low speeds, baud rate is equal to *bits per second* (*bps*), but at higher speeds it is not.

Bidirectional: Characteristic of printer, in which print element moves first to the right on one line, then to the left on the following line.

Binary System: A numbering system in which all numbers consist of only two digits—0 and 1.

Biometrics: Science of measuring individual body characteristics. Some security systems use biometric machines that can recognize a person's fingerprints, signature, or voice.

BIOS (Basic Input-Output System): Type of systems software. Consists of programs that interpret keyboard characters or transmit characters to monitor or disk.

Bit (Binary Digit): A 0 or 1 in the binary system.

Block: A portion of text that is marked before being processed further.

Block (of records): Group of records on magnetic tape.

Block Move: The process of moving a unit of text that has been marked (blocked).

Boldface: Printing consisting of extra dark lettering.

Bootstrap Loader: Systems software that starts up the computer when the machine is turned on and loads the operating system into primary storage.

bps: Acronym for bits per second.

Broadband: The bandwidth that includes microwave, satellite, coaxial cable, and fiber-optic channels. It is used for very high speed computers.

Bus Line (Bus): An electronic data roadway that connects parts of the CPU with each other and the CPU with other important devices. Also a connecting cable in a bus network.

Bus Network: A network where all communications travel along a common path. Each device in the network handles its own communications control. There is no host computer or file server.

Byte: A unit consisting of eight bits. There are 256 possible bit combinations in a byte.

C: A general-purpose procedural language originally designed for writing operating systems. Widely used and portable.

Cache Memory: Area of random access memory (RAM) set aside to store the most frequently accessed information stored in RAM. Acts as temporary high-speed holding zone between primary storage and CPU.

CAD (Computer-Aided Design): A type of computer program that manipulates images such as three-dimensional objects on the screen.

CAD/CAM: Acronym for Computer-Aided Design/Computer-Aided Manufacturing.

CADD (Computer-Aided Design and Drafting): Programs that come equipped with straight lines, arcs, circles, and other elements for making graphic designs.

CAM (Computer-Aided Manufacturing): A type of program that controls automated factory equipment, including machine tools and robots.

Carpal Tunnel Syndrome: A disorder found among heavy computer users, consisting of damage to nerves and tendons in the hands. *See also* Repetitive Strain Injury.

CASE (Computer-Aided Software Engineering) Tool: *See* Automated Design Tool.

CD-ROM (Compact Disk–Read-Only Memory): A form of optical disk that allows data to be read but not recorded.

Cell: The intersection of a row and a column in a spreadsheet.

Cell Address: The position of a cell in a spreadsheet.

Cell Pointer: An indicator for the place where data is to be entered or changed in a spreadsheet.

CGA (Color Graphics Adapter): Circuit board that may be inserted into a microcomputer that changes some monitors from monochrome to color display. It offers four colors.

Chain Printer: Printer used mainly with mainframes and microcomputers. It consists of a printing chain with several sets of characters that moves at high speed in front of the paper. A hammer strikes paper and ribbon against the character.

Character: A letter, number, or other symbol.

Character-Based Interface: Arrangement for issuing commands, in which users type commands or select items from a menu. *Compare* Graphical User Interface.

Checklist: List of questions that helps show whether key elements are being evaluated in the present system.

Child Node: A node one level below the node being considered in a hierarchical database or network.

Chip: Integrated electronic circuit consisting of a tiny (⅛-inch square) circuit board etched on silicon. Examples are CPU and memory chips.

Closed Architecture: Computer designed so that users cannot get inside to add any new devices.

Coaxial Cable: A high-frequency transmission cable that replaces the multiple wires of telephone lines with a single solid copper core.

COBOL (COmmon Business-Oriented Language): A procedural language most frequently used in business, originally developed by Admiral Grace Hopper.

Coding: The fourth step of the programming procedure, during which the actual program is written in a programming language.

Cold Site: Special emergency facility in which hardware must be installed but which is available to a company in the event of disaster to its computer system. *Compare* Hot Site.

Column Headings: The labels across the top of the worksheet area of a spreadsheet.

Command Line Interface: *See* Character-Based Interface.

Common Operational Database: An integrated collection of records that contains details about the operations of a company.

Common User Database: A type of company database that contains selected information both from the common operational database and from outside proprietary databases.

Common User Interface: Similar software screen that can be used to access different hardware.

Communications System: *See* Data Communications System.

Company Database: A collection of integrated records shared throughout a company or other organization.

Compatible: Low-cost microcomputer made by a competitor that is compatible with microcomputers made by a major manufacturer, such as International Business Machines. "Compatible" means it will run most of the same software as will run on IBM machines.

Competency: *See* Computer Competency.

Compiler: Software that converts the programmer's procedural-language program (source code) into machine language (object code).

Computer Competency: Achievement of sufficient knowledge about and skill with computers so that end users can meet their information needs and improve their productivity.

Computer Crime: Illegal action in which the perpetrator uses special knowledge of computer technology. Criminals may be employees, outside users, hackers and crackers, and organized crime members.

Computer Fraud and Abuse Act (1986): Law allowing prosecution of unauthorized access to computers and databases.

Computer Matching and Privacy Protection Act (1988): Law setting procedures for computer matching of federal data for verifying eligibility for federal benefits or for recovering delinquent debts.

Computer Network: A communications system connecting two or more computers and their peripheral devices.

Computer Program: *See* Program.

Computer System: A system consisting of people, procedures, software, hardware, and data.

Computer Virus: Hidden instructions that migrate through networks and operating systems and become embedded in different programs. They may be designed to destroy data or simply to display messages.

Connectivity: The electronic connections between computers and information resources and the resulting connections between people that such technology allows.

Controller Card: *See* Expansion Board.

Control Unit: The section of the CPU that tells the rest of the computer how to carry out program instructions.

Conventional Memory: The first 640K of RAM in primary storage.

Conversion: *See* Systems Implementation.

Coprocessor Chip: A chip that is subordinate to the main processor (CPU). It assists the main processor in performing very fast mathematical computations.

Copy: Duplicate.

CPU (Central Processing Unit): Part of the computer that consists of the control unit, arithmetic-logic unit, and primary storage. It executes program instructions.

Cracker: Person who gains unauthorized access to a computer system for malicious purposes. *Compare* Hacker.

CRT (Cathode-Ray Tube): An output display device that resembles a television screen.

Cumulative Trauma Disorders: *See* Repetitive Strain Injury.

Cursor: A blinking symbol on the screen that shows where data may be entered next.

Custom-Made Software (Custom Program): Software designed by a professional programmer for a particular purpose.

Daisy Wheel: A wheel consisting of spokes, with each spoke ending in a raised character.

Daisy-Wheel Printer: Letter-quality printer that uses a daisy wheel. When a spoke on the wheel is struck with a hammer against an inked ribbon, the character image is transferred to paper.

Data: The raw, unprocessed facts that are input to a computer system.

Data Bank: *See* Proprietary Database.

Database: A collection of integrated data that gives different people access to the same data to use for different purposes.

Database Manager: *See* DBMS.

Data Communications System: An electronic system that transmits data over communications lines from one location to another.

Data Compression: A method of extending space-saving capabilities of a hard disk. Data in a file is scanned to repeating patterns, which are replaced with a token, leaving enough in the file so that the original can be rebuilt (decompressed).

Data Dictionary: A dictionary that contains a description of the structure of data used in a database.

Data Flow Diagram: Diagram used by systems analyst to show data or information flow within an information system.

Data Processing System: *See* Transaction Processing Information System.

Data Security: Activity concerned with protecting software and data from unauthorized tampering or damage.

Data Transfer Time: The time taken for data to be transferred from the disk track to primary storage.

DBA (Database Administrator): The person who helps determine the structure of, performance of, and access to databases in a company.

DBMS (Database Management System): A program for setting up a database and retrieving information from it later. Consists of a data dictionary and a query language.

Debugging: The fifth step of the programming procedure. A programmer's word for testing the program and then eliminating errors.

Decentralized System: *See* Distributed Data Processing System.

Decision Model: A model that is based on statistical packages, simulations, long-range plans, and other concepts. It gives the decision support system its analytical capabilities.

Decision Table: Shows the decision rules that apply when certain conditions occur and what action should take place as a result.

Dedicated Fax Machine: Specialized machine for sending and receiving images of documents over telephone lines.

Demand Report: The opposite of a scheduled report. A demand report—for example, a revised sales forecast—is produced on request.

Demodulation: The process performed by modems in converting analog signals to digital signals.

Desk Checking: The process of checking out a computer program by studying the program listing while sitting at a desk.

Desktop Manager: Program that stays in microcomputer's memory (primary storage) at the same time other programs are being run. The desktop manager allows the user to interrupt the other program and gain access to "desktop accessories" such as appointment calendar, notepad, and calculator.

Desktop Publishing: The process of using a microcomputer, laser printer, and the necessary software to mix text and graphics to produce final, composed pages.

Diagnostic Routine: Program in systems software that starts up when a microcomputer is turned on. Diagnostic routines test the primary storage, CPU, and other parts of the system to make sure the computer is running properly.

Digital Signal: A signal that represents the presence or absence of an electronic pulse.

Digitizer: Input device that can be used to trace a copy of a drawing or photograph. The shape is converted to digital data, which can then be represented on a monitor screen or printed out on paper.

Digitizing Tablet: A tablet that can be used to create images by moving a special stylus over its surface. The image is then converted to electronic signals that can be processed by a computer.

Direct Access Storage: A form of storage that allows any particular piece of information to be retrieved directly.

Direct Approach: The approach for systems implementation whereby the old system is simply abandoned for the new.

Direct Entry: Form of input that does not require data to be keyed by someone sitting at a keyboard. Direct-entry devices create machine-readable data on paper or magnetic media or feed it directly into the computer's CPU.

Direct File Organization: A file organization that makes use of key fields to go directly to the record being sought rather than reading records one after another.

Directional Arrow Keys: The keys labeled with arrows, used to move the cursor.

Disaster Recovery Plan: Plan used by large organizations describing ways to continue operating following disaster until normal computer operations can be restored.

Disk Address: The identifiable location on a disk where data is stored.

Disk Drive: Input mechanism that obtains stored data and programs from a disk. It also stores data and programs on a disk.

Disk Pack (Hard-Disk Pack): A disk pack that uses the same basic technology as hard disks but resembles a stack of phonograph records with multiple recording surfaces and read-write heads.

Display Screen: *See* Monitor.

Distributed Database: A database that can be made accessible through a variety of communications networks. That allows portions of the database to be located in different places.

Distributed Data Processing System: A data processing system that consists of a mainframe and minicomputers that are geographically separated but linked together by communications.

Document: Any kind of text material, such as a letter or a report.

Documentation: The sixth (and final) step of the programming procedure. Consists of written descriptions and procedures about a program and how to use it. Should be carried on throughout all steps of the programming procedure.

DOS (Disk Operating System): The standard operating system for all computers advertised as "IBM-compatible."

Dot-Matrix Printer: A printer that forms characters or images using a matrix of pins that strike an inked ribbon.

DO UNTIL and DO WHILE Structures: Two particular forms of loop structures.

Downloading: The process of transferring information from a remote computer to the computer that you are operating.

Downsizing: Describes applications being moved from larger computers to smaller ones, as from mainframes and minicomputers to microcomputers.

Drawing Programs: Software used by professional illustrators to create artwork for publications work.

Drive A: Normally the disk drive into which a microcomputer user inserts the program disk. On many microcomputers, drive A is the left or upper drive.

Drive B: Normally the disk drive into which a microcomputer user inserts the data disk. It is often the right or lower drive.

Drive Gate: The door covering the slot in a disk drive into which a disk is inserted.

Drum Plotter: A plotter that produces images by moving a pen linearly as the paper is rolled on a drum.

DSS (Decision Support System): A system that draws on an organization's MIS and outside databases to produce flexible, on-demand reports for managers.

Dumb Terminal: A terminal that can be used to input and receive data, but cannot process the data independently.

EBCDIC (Extended Binary Coded Decimal Interchange Code): A binary coding scheme that is a standard for minicomputers and mainframe computers.

EGA (Enhanced Graphics Adapter): Circuit board that may be inserted into a microcomputer producing 16 colors on a monitor. It offers higher-quality resolution than CGA.

EIS (Executive Information System): Software that draws data from an organization's databases together in patterns meaningful to top executives.

EISA: See Extended Industry Standard Architecture.

EL (Electroluminescent) Display: A display that actively emits light when electrically charged.

Electronic Bulletin Board: Electronically posted information on a computer that can be accessed by other computers using telephone lines.

Electronic Spreadsheet: A form based on the traditional accounting worksheet that can be used to present and analyze numeric data.

E-Mail (Electronic Mail): Similar to an electronic bulletin board, but provides confidentiality and may use special communications rather than telephone lines.

End User: A person who uses microcomputers or has access to large computers.

Enter Key: The key used to enter a command into the computer after it has been typed.

EPROM (Erasable Programmable Read-Only Memory): A chip that contains instructions that can be written and then erased with ultraviolet light so that the instructions can be changed.

Erasable Optical Disk: An optical disk on which the disk drive can write information and also erase and rewrite information.

Erase: Remove, as in removing obsolete electronic files from a disk.

Ergonomics: The study of human factors related to computers.

ESS (Executive Support System): See EIS.

Exception Report: Report that calls attention to unusual events, such as problems with a production schedule.

Expanded Memory: A technique that allows certain microprocessors to expand primary storage. A portion of the reserved memory area between conventional memory and memory is switched back and forth with an outside component of memory of up to 32MB.

Expansion Board: Optional device board that is usually added inside the system cabinet.

Expert System: Sophisticated knowledge-based system that essentially emulates the knowledge of human experts skilled in a particular field.

Exporting: Feature that allows file to be saved in a form so that it can be inserted into another program, as from a word processing program into a spreadsheet. *Compare* Importing.

Extended Industry Standard Architecture (EISA): Standard for bus line developed by nine manufacturers of IBM-compatible microcomputers. This bus line has a 32-bit-wide data path, but it is designed to extend the old ISA (Industry Standard Architecture) bus standard.

Extended Memory: On those microprocessors that have it, all available memory above 1MB, up to 16MB.

External Modem: A modem that stands apart from the computer and is connected by a cable to the computer's serial port.

Facsimile Transmission (Fax) Machine: Device that scans an image and sends it electronically over telephone lines to receiving fax machine, which converts electronic signals back to an image and recreates it on paper.

Fair Credit Reporting Act (1970): Law prohibiting credit agencies from sharing credit information with anyone but authorized customers and giving consumers right to review and correct their credit records.

Fax Board: *See* Virtual Fax Board.

Fiber-Optic Cable: A special transmission cable made of glass tubes that are immune to electronic interference. Data is transmitted through fiber-optic cables in the form of pulses of light.

Field: An item consisting of one or more logically related characters.

File: A collection of logically related records.

File Server: A hard-disk storage device with large capacity.

Firmware: *See* ROM.

Flatbed Plotter: Plotter that holds the paper stable while a pen moves around the paper.

Flat-Panel Display: Display that uses technologies that allow the screen to be a flat panel instead of a bulky tube such as that used in television receivers.

Flat Tension Mask: A new technology that produces a much more brilliant video image than other conventional graphics monitors.

Flexible-Disk Drive: The device used to retrieve information from and store information on a disk.

Floppy Disk (Floppy): A flat, circular piece of magnetically treated mylar plastic that rotates within a jacket.

Flowchart: *See* Program Flowchart; System Flowchart.

Format: Appearance of a text document, such as spacing or margins.

Formatting: The process of placing tracks and sectors on a disk before using it to record data and programs.

Form-Letter Feature: *See* Mail-Merge Feature.

Formula: The instructions for a calculation in a spreadsheet.

FORTRAN (FORmula TRANslation): The most widely used scientific and mathematical procedural language.

Freedom of Information Act (1970): Law giving citizens right to examine data about them in federal government files, except for that restricted for national security reasons.

Front-End Processor: A specialized computer that helps handle the input data from other devices. This leaves the mainframe computer free for other tasks.

Full-Duplex Communications: A mode of communications in which data is transmitted back and forth at the same time.

Function Keys: Keys labeled *F1, F2,* and so on, used for tasks that occur frequently, such as underlining in word processing.

Gantt Chart: Chart using bars and lines to indicate the time scale of a series of tasks.

Gas-Plasma Display: Form of technology used in some flat screens for portable computers. Like a neon light bulb, the monitor uses a gas that emits light in the presence of an electric current.

Gate: *See* Drive Gate.

Gateway: *See* Network Gateway.

GB or G-byte (Gigabyte): A unit of capacity equal to 1,073,741,824 bytes (about one billion bytes).

General Ledger: The activity that produces income statements and balance sheets based on all transactions in a company.

Generations of Programming Languages: The five generations are machine languages, assembly languages, procedural languages, problem-oriented languages, and natural languages.

Graphical User Interface (GUI): Special screen that allows software commands to be issued through the use of graphic symbols (icons) or pull-down menus.

Graphics Monitor: Monitor that displays both alphanumeric characters and visual or graphic images.

Grid Chart: Chart that shows the relationship between input and output documents.

Groupware: Software that allows two or more people on a communications network to work on the same document at the same time.

Hacker: Person who gains unauthorized access to a computer system for the fun and challenge of it. *Compare* Cracker.

Half-Duplex Communications: A mode of communications in which data flows in both directions, but not simultaneously.

Hard Copy: Images output on paper by a printer or plotter.

Hard Disk: Enclosed disk drive that contains one or more metallic disks. A hard disk has many times the capacity of a floppy disk.

Hard-Disk Cartridge: A device containing a hard disk, which can be removed from and inserted into a drive as easily as a cassette in a videotape recorder.

Hard-Disk Drive: A nonremovable, enclosed disk drive that reads data from and writes data to a hard disk.

Hardware: Equipment that includes a keyboard, monitor, printer, the computer itself, and other devices.

Head Crash: A hard-disk disaster that happens when the surface of the read-write head itself or particles on the surface of the head come into contact with the magnetic disk surface. A head crash causes the loss of some or all of the data on the disk.

Head Switching Time: The time required for a particular read-write head to be activated.

Help Menu (Help Screen):   Explanations of how to perform various tasks presented on the screen.

Hierarchical Database: A database in which the fields or records are structured in nodes, like the hierarchy of managers in a corporation.

Hierarchical Network: A network consisting of several computers linked to a host computer, just like a star network. However, the computers linked to the host are themselves hosts to other computers.

Highlighting: Special lighting of a block of text or data displayed on the screen.

Host Computer: A central computer, such as a mainframe computer at a company's headquarters or central office. The central computer in a star network.

Hot Site: Special emergency facility consisting of fully equipped computer center, available to a company in the event of disaster to its computer system. *Compare* Cold Site.

Hybrid Network: *See* Hierarchical Network.

Hypermedia: *See* Multimedia.

Hypertext: Software that enables users to organize and access information so that any file can be connected with any other file.

IBG (Interblock Gap):   The separation between blocks of records on magnetic tape.

IBM-Compatible: *See* Compatible.

Icon: Graphic symbol on a screen representing a command (e.g., a trash can for a deletion command).

IF-THEN-ELSE Structure: A logical selection structure whereby one of two paths is followed according to IF, THEN, and ELSE statements in a program.

Image Scanner: A direct-entry device that identifies images on paper and automatically converts them to electronic signals that can be stored in a computer.

Importing: Feature that allows file to be retrieved from one program and inserted into the program the user is working on, as from a spreadsheet to a word processing program. *Compare* Exporting.

Index Sequential File Organization: A compromise between sequential and direct file organizations. Records are stored sequentially, but an index is used to access a group of records directly.

Individual Database: A collection of integrated records useful mainly to just one person.

Industry Standard Architecture (ISA):   Standard for bus line developed for IBM Personal Computer. It first consisted of an 8-bit-wide data path, then a 16-bit-wide data path.

Information: Data that has been processed by a computer system.

Information System: A collection of hardware, software, people, data, and procedures that work together to provide information essential to running an organization.

Initializing: *See* Formatting.

Ink-Jet Printer: Printer that forms characters by spraying small droplets of ink at high speed onto the surface of the paper.

Input Device: Piece of equipment that takes data and puts it into a form that a computer can process.

Integrated Circuit: *See* Chip.

Integrated Package: A collection of computer programs that work together and share information.

Intelligent Terminal: A terminal that includes a processing unit, primary storage, secondary storage, and software for processing data.

Interactive: Describes activity in which there is immediate communication between the user and the computer system.

Interface Card: *See* Expansion Board.

Internal Hard Disk: Storage device consisting of one or more metallic platters stored inside a container. Internal hard disks are installed inside the system cabinet of a microcomputer.

Internal Modem: A modem that is a plug-in circuit board located inside the computer.

Internal Storage: *See* Primary Storage.

Interpreter: Software that converts a procedural language one statement at a time into machine language just before the statement is executed.

Inventory: The material or products that a company has in stock.

IRG (Interrecord Gap):   Gap between records on magnetic tape required to give the tape enough time to gain the proper speed.

ISA: *See* Industry Standard Architecture.

Jacket: The protective outer covering for a floppy disk.

Justification (Justified Margins): The process of evening up margins, such as the right margin in a printed book.

K, KB, or K-byte (Kilobyte): A unit of capacity equal to 1024 bytes (about one thousand bytes).

Keyboard: Input device that looks like a typewriter keyboard but has additional keys.

Key Field: A group of logically related characters in a file record used for sorting purposes.

Knowledge-Based System: Program that is based on facts and widely accepted rules about how certain decisions should be made or tasks accomplished.

Labels: The column and row headings in spreadsheets.

LAN (Local Area Network): Network that consists of computers and other devices that are physically near each other, such as within the same building.

Laptop: Portable computer weighing 10–16 pounds.

Laser Printer: Printer that creates dotlike images on a drum using a laser beam. The characters are then treated with magnetically charged inklike toner and transferred from the drum to the paper.

LCD (Liquid-Crystal Display): Display that consists of liquid crystal molecules whose optical properties can be altered by an applied electric field. Does not emit light of its own.

Letter-Quality Printer: Printer that produces output with the quality of that produced by an office typewriter. Used for formal correspondence and reports.

Light Pen: A light-sensitive penlike device used with a special monitor to enter commands by touching the monitor with the pen.

Logical Record: The actual record on magnetic tape.

Logic Error: Error that occurs when a programmer has used an incorrect calculation or left out a programming procedure.

Logic Structure: Structure that controls the logical sequence in which computer program instructions are executed. The three structures are sequence, selection, and loop.

Loop Structure: A logic structure in which a process may be repeated as long as a certain condition remains true.

Luggable: *See* Transportable.

Machine Languages: The first generation of programming languages. In them only the binary digits (0 and 1) are used to express program statements and data.

Macro: A keyboard command that enables users to consolidate several keystrokes for a command into only one or two keystrokes.

Magnetic Tape: Tape used to store data or programs.

Magnetic Tape Drive (Magnetic Tape Unit): Device used to read data from and store data on magnetic tape.

Magnetic Tape Streamer: Device that allows duplication (backup) of the data stored on a hard disk.

Mail-Merge Feature: A word processing feature that allows names, addresses, and other material to be inserted into documents from other files.

Mainframe Computer: Computer that can process millions of program instructions per second. Mainframes usually occupy a special room to accommodate special wiring and air conditioning. They are used by large companies.

Main Memory: *See* Primary Storage.

Make-or-Buy Decision: The second step in the programming procedure when a decision is made to buy a prewritten program or have it custom-written by a programmer.

MAN (Metropolitan Area Network): This type of network serves customers in the same city or region and can be accessed by mobile (cellular) telephone. Often created by a local telephone company.

Mark Sensing: *See* OMR.

Massively Parallel Processing: Technology used in form of supercomputers that consists of thousands of interconnected microprocessors. *See also* Supercomputer.

Master File: A complete file containing all records current up to the last update.

MB or M-byte (Megabyte): A unit of capacity equal to 1,048,576 bytes (about one million bytes).

MCA: *See* Micro Channel Architecture.

Medium Band: The bandwidth of special leased lines, used mainly with minicomputers and mainframe computers.

Memory: *See* Primary Storage.

Memory-Resident Program: *See* Desktop Manager.

Menu: A list of available commands presented on the screen.

Menu Bar: Line or two across the top or bottom of screen listing available software commands.

MHz (Megahertz): A unit of frequency equal to one million cycles (beats) per second.

MICR (Magnetic-Ink Character Recognition): A direct-entry method used in banks to read the stylized numbers on the bottoms of checks.

Micro Channel Architecture (MCA): Standard for a bus line developed to support IBM's line of PS/2 microcomputers based on the 80386 microprocessor. The MCA bus has a data path that is 32 bits wide.

Microcomputer: A small, low-cost computer designed for individual users.

Microcomputer Database: *See* Individual Database.

Microcomputer System: System involving a microcomputer that has five parts: people, procedures, software, hardware, and data.

Microprocessor: A CPU for a microcomputer contained on a single sliver of silicon. *See also* Chip.

Microsecond: One-millionth of a second.

Microwave: Radio wave that travels in straight line through the air. Microwaves are relayed by means of antennas installed on high buildings, mountaintops, or satellites.

Middle-Level Manager: Person who oversees the supervisory (lower-level) managers and deals with control and planning. Middle-level managers implement the goals of the organization.

Millisecond: One-thousandth of a second.

Minicomputer: Computer that is larger than desktop in size. First developed as special-purpose mainframe computers, minicomputers have capabilities between those of microcomputers and those of mainframe computers.

MIS (Management Information System): System that expresses the transactions of a data processing system in a summarized, structured form.

Modem (MOdulator-DEModulator): A device that changes the digital electronic signals of the computer into the analog electronic signals that can travel over a telephone line and vice versa.

Modulation: The process performed by modems in converting digital signals to analog signals.

Module: *See* Program Module.

Monitor: An output device like a television screen that displays data processed by the computer.

Monochrome Monitor: Monitor that displays characters in only one color, such as amber or green.

Motherboard: *See* System Board.

Mouse: An input device that can be rolled on a tabletop to direct the position of the cursor on the screen. Has selection buttons for entering commands.

MS-DOS (Microsoft Disk Operating System): *See* DOS.

Multifunction Board: Expansion board that combines several functions on a single card.

Multimedia: Technology that presents information on more than one delivery medium, including text, graphics, animation, video, music, and voice.

Multitasking Software: Term given to operating systems that can run several applications programs at the same time. *See also* Windowing Software.

Nanosecond: One-billionth of a second.

Natural Languages: The fifth generation of programming languages. These languages use human languages such as English to give people a more natural connection with computers.

Network: *See* Computer Network.

Network Database: Database that is similar to a hierarchical database, except that each child node may have more than one parent node.

Network Gateway: Connection by which a local area network may be linked to other LANs or to larger networks.

New Media: Information delivery systems that combine media, such as text, graphics, voice, and video, using a microcomputer as the controlling framework.

Nodes: Points connected in a database or network like the branches of a tree.

Nonvolatile Storage: Permanent storage used to preserve data and programs.

Notebook PC: Portable computer weighing 5–10 pounds.

Numeric Keypad: The keys 0 to 9, located on separate keys adjacent to the typewriter keyboard.

Object-Oriented Programming: A methodology in which a program is organized into modules or objects, each containing both the data and the processing operations necessary to perform a task.

OCR (Optical-Character Recognition): A direct-entry method that uses special preprinted characters that can be read by a light source.

Offline Storage: Data that is not directly accessible to the CPU until the tape or disk has been loaded onto an input device.

Off-the-Shelf Software: *See* Packaged Software.

OMR (Optical-Mark Recognition): A direct-entry method that senses the presence or absence of a mark, such as a pencil mark.

Online Storage: Data that is directly accessible to the CPU.

Open Architecture: Computer that contains expansion slots inside that anyone can use for adding extra memory chips or other accessories.

Operating Environment: *See* Windowing Software.

Operating System: System that consists of several programs that help the computer manage its own resources, such as manipulating files, running programs, and controlling the keyboard and screen.

Optical Disk: A device that can hold as much as 500 megabytes of data. Lasers are used to record and read data on the disk.

Organization Chart: Chart that shows an organization's functions and levels of management.

OS/2 (Operating System/2):   A multitasking operating system for microcomputers developed jointly by IBM and Microsoft Corporation.

Outlining Program: Program that allows users to use Roman numerals, then capital letters, then Arabic numbers, etc., to write an outline. To organize ideas, the user puts in the main topic head, then the subtopics, sub-subtopics, etc. When the placement of an idea is changed, the outline is resequenced automatically.

Output Device: Device that displays the information processed by the computer.

Packaged Software: Any program for sale that has been prewritten by professional programmers.

Page: *See* Window.

Page Description Language: Language that describes the format of a page to a printer in a standard way.

Palmtop: *See* Pocket PC.

Parallel Approach: The approach for systems implementation whereby the old and new systems are operated side by side until the new one has been shown to be reliable.

Parallel Data Transmission: The method of transmission whereby each bit in a character (byte) flows through a separate line simultaneously.

Parallel Port: A type of port that allows lines to be connected so that bits can be transmitted simultaneously.

Parent Node: A node one level above the node being considered in a hierarchical database or network.

Parity Bit: An extra bit automatically added to a byte during keyboarding to test accuracy.

Pascal: A procedural programming language widely used on microcomputers. It is named after Blaise Pascal, a seventeenth-century mathematician.

Password: Secret word or numbers that limits access to information such as electronic mail.

Payroll: The activity concerned with calculating employee paychecks.

Periodic Report: Report produced at regular intervals such as weekly, monthly, or yearly.

Peripheral Device: Hardware that is outside of the system unit, such as disk drive or printer.

Personal Computer: *See* Microcomputer.

PERT (Program Evaluation Review Technique) Chart: Chart using lines and boxes that shows the time scale of a series of tasks for a project and the relationships among the tasks.

Phased Approach: The approach for systems implementation whereby the new system is implemented gradually over a period of time.

Physical Record: A block of records on magnetic tape.

Physical Security: Activity concerned with protecting hardware from possible human and natural disasters.

Picosecond: One-trillionth of a second.

Pilot Approach: The approach for systems implementation whereby the new system is tried out in only one part of the organization before it is implemented throughout the organization.

Piracy: *See* Software Piracy.

Pixel (Picture Element):   The smallest area on a screen that can be turned on and off or be made different shades of gray or different colors.

Plotter: Special-purpose output device for producing high-quality graphical images such as architectural drawings.

Plug-In Board: *See* Expansion Board.

Pocket PC: Hand-held or pocket-size portable computer, weighing 1–2 pounds.

Pointers: The additional connections in a network database between parent nodes and child nodes.

Pointing Device: Direct-entry device that uses pointing to input data.

Polling: The process whereby a host computer or file server asks each connecting device whether it has a message to send and then allows the message to be sent.

Port: A connecting socket on the outside of the system unit for devices such as video displays and printers.

Portable Computer: Microcomputer that can be carried around. *See also* Laptop, Notebook PC, Pocket PC, Transportable.

Portable Programming Language: Language that results in programs that can be run on more than one kind of computer.

POS (Point-of-Sale) Terminal: Terminal that consists of a keyboard, screen, and printer. It is used like a cash register.

Preliminary Investigation: The first phase of the systems life cycle. It involves defining the problem, suggesting alternative systems, and preparing a short report.

Presentation Graphics: Graphics used to communicate a message through the use of color, dimensionality, titles, and so on. Presentation graphics may make use of analytical graphics.

Primary Storage: The part of a microcomputer that temporarily holds data for processing, instructions for processing the data, and information (processed data) waiting to be output.

Printer: A device that produces printed paper output.

Privacy: Right to keep personal information from being used for purpose for which it was not intended.

Privacy Act (1974): Law restricting federal agencies in the way they share information about citizens. It prohibits federal information collected for one purpose from being used for a different purpose.

Problem-Oriented Languages: The fourth generation of programming languages. Designed to solve specific problems by allowing end users simply to describe what they want.

Procedural Languages: The third generation of programming languages, designed to express the logic that can solve general problems using English-like statements.

Procedures: The rules or guidelines to follow when using hardware, software, and data.

Processing Rights: The determination of which people have access to what kinds of data in databases.

Processor: *See* CPU.

Program: A set of step-by-step instructions that tell a computer how to accomplish a task.

Program Definition (Program Analysis): The first step in the programming process. During this phase, the program's objectives, desired output, input data required, and processing requirements are specified.

Program Design: The third step of the programming procedure. During this phase, custom software is designed, preferably using structured programming techniques.

Program Flowchart: Chart that graphically presents the detailed sequence of steps needed to solve a programming problem.

Program Maintenance: The process of updating and modifying a completed program that has been through the six-step programming process.

Programming: A six-step procedure for creating a program.

Programming Language: A set of rules that tell a computer what operations to perform. Usually written in a form resembling English for ease of use.

Program Module: A processing step of a program made up of logically related program statements.

Project: A one-time operation composed of several tasks that must be completed during a stated period of time.

Project Management Software: Program used to plan, schedule, and control the people, resources, and costs needed to complete a project on time.

PROM (Programmable Read-Only Memory): Chips that contain instructions that can be written but not changed.

Proprietary Database: Generally, an enormous database that an organization develops to cover certain particular subjects. Access to this type of database is usually offered for a fee.

Protocols: A set of rules for the exchange of information, such as those used for successful data transmission.

Prototyping: Building a model (prototype) that can be modified before the actual system is installed. Should be used along with careful system analysis and design procedures.

Pseudocode: A narrative form of the logic of a computer program.

Pull-Down Menu: List of software commands that "drops down" from a menu bar at the top of the screen.

Purchasing: The buying of raw materials and services.

Query Language: An easy-to-use language understandable to most users that is used to generate reports from databases.

RAM (Random-Access Memory): Temporary storage that holds the program and data that the CPU is processing.

Read: *See* Reading Data.

Reader/Sorter: A special-purpose machine that reads characters made of ink containing magnetized particles.

Reading Data: For floppy disks, the process of taking the magnetized spots from the disk, converting them to electronic signals, and transmitting them to primary storage inside the computer.

Read-Only Disk: Optical disk, such as CD-ROM, on which data is imprinted by the manufacturer and cannot be altered by the user.

Read-Write Head: Electronic head that can read data from and write data onto a disk.

Real-Time Processing: Processing performed at the same time that data is collected.

Recalculation: The process of recomputing values in electronic spreadsheets automatically.

Record: A collection of logically related fields.

Register: High-speed staging area that holds data and instructions temporarily during processing.

Relation: A table in a relational database that contains information on a specified subject.

Relational Database: The most flexible database organization, where data elements are stored in tables and there is no hierarchical structure imposed.

Rename: Give new filename to file on a disk.

Repetitive Strain Injury (RSI, Repetitive Motion Injury, Cumulative Trauma Disorders): Category of injuries resulting from fast, repetitive work that cause neck, wrist, hand, and arm pains. *See also* Carpal Tunnel Syndrome.

Replace: In word processing, command that enables user to search for a word and replace it with another one.

Return Key: *See* Enter Key.

RGB (Red-Green-Blue) Monitor: Monitor that allows the results of graphics software to be presented in a variety of different color designs.

Right to Financial Privacy Act (1979): Law setting strict procedures that federal agencies must follow when seeking to examine customer records in banks.

Ring Network: A network in which each device is connected to two other devices, forming a ring. There is no host computer, and messages are passed around the ring until they reach the correct destination.

RISC (Reduced Instruction Set Computer) Chip: Powerful microprocessor chip, such as the Motorola 88000, found in workstations.

Robot: Machine used in factories and elsewhere that can be preprogrammed to do more than one task.

Robotics: The field of study concerned with developing and using robots.

ROM (Read-Only Memory): Chips containing programs that are built into the system board at the factory. The instructions on these chips cannot be changed.

Rotational Delay Time: The time taken for the disk to rotate under the read-write head.

Row Headings: The labels down the left side of the worksheet area of a spreadsheet.

RPG (Report Program Generator): A procedural language that enables people to prepare business reports quickly and easily.

RS-232C Connector: *See* Serial Port.

Sales Order Processing: The activity that records the demands of customers for the company's product or service.

Satellite: A satellite is often placed in orbit so that it appears to remain in a fixed position with respect to the earth (that is, it is geostationary). Geostationary satellites are often used to relay microwave transmissions.

Scanning Device: Direct-entry device that converts images to digital data that can be processed by a computer or displayed on a screen.

Scheduled Report: *See* Periodic Report.

Screen: *See* Monitor.

Screen Resolution: A measure of the crispness of images and characters on a screen, usually specified in terms of the number of pixels in a row or column.

Scrolling: A feature that enables the user to move quickly through the text forward or backward.

Search: In word processing, command that enables user to find a particular term in a document.

Search Operation: Activity in which a disk drive rotates a floppy disk to proper position so that the read-write head can find the appropriate data on the disk.

Secondary Storage: Permanent storage used to preserve programs and data, including floppy disks, hard disks, and magnetic tape.

Sectors: Sections shaped like pie wedges that divide the tracks on disks.

Security: Activity of protecting information, hardware, and software from harm and from unauthorized use.

Seek Operation: Activity in which the access arm in a disk drive moves back and forth over the floppy disk to read data from or write data to the disk.

Seek Time: The time required for the access arm to get into position over a particular track.

Selection Structure: A logic structure that determines which of two paths will be followed when a decision must be made by a program.

Semiconductor: *See* Chip.

Sequence Structure: A logic structure in which one program statement follows another.

Sequential Access Storage: A method of storage where information is stored in sequence, and all information preceding the desired information must be read first.

Sequential Files: Files in which records are stored one after another in ascending or descending order.

Serial Data Transmission: The method of transmission in which bits flow in a series, one after another.

Serial Port: A port set up for serial data transmission.

Shared Database: *See* Company Database.

Shell: Special-purpose program that allows a person to custom-build a particular kind of expert system.

Silicon: Sandlike material used for making tiny circuit boards called chips.

Silicon Chip: *See* Chip.

Simplex Communications: A mode of communications in which data travels in one direction only.

Smart Terminal: A terminal that has some memory and allows users to perform some data editing or verification before the data is sent to the host computer.

Soft Copy: Images or characters output on a monitor screen.

Soft-Sectored Floppy Disk: Floppy disk that must be initialized (formatted) to place tracks and sectors on the surface.

Software: Another name for computer programs.

Software Copyright Act (1980): Law allowing owners of programs to make copies for backup purposes, and to modify them to make them useful, provided they are not resold or given away.

Software Piracy: Unauthorized copying of programs for personal gain.

Source Document: The original version of a document before any processing has been performed on it.

Special-Purpose Keys: Keys labeled *Ctrl, Del, Ins,* and so on, used to help enter and edit data and execute commands.

Speech-Recognition Device: *See* Voice-Input Device.

Spelling-Checker Program: A program used with a word processor to check the spelling of typed text against an electronic dictionary.

Spike: *See* Voltage Surge.

Spreadsheet: *See* Electronic Spreadsheet.

Spreadsheet Cursor: *See* Cell Pointer.

Star Network: A network of computers or peripheral devices linked to a central computer through which all communications pass. Control is maintained by polling.

Structured Programming Techniques: Techniques that consist of top-down program design, pseudocode, flowcharts, and logic structures.

Structured Walkthrough: A process in which several programmers, including the creator of the program, review the program, analyzing it for completeness, accuracy, and quality of design.

Supercomputer: Multimillion-dollar computers that are the fastest calculating devices made, processing over one billion program instructions per second. *See also* Massively Parallel Processing.

Supervisor: Lower-level manager responsible for managing and monitoring workers. Supervisors are concerned with operational matters—monitoring day-to-day events.

Supply Reel: The reel from which magnetic tape is being drawn into a tape drive.

Surge Protector: Device separating computer from power source of wall outlet, which protects computer system by activating circuit breaker when excess electricity appears.

Synchronous Transmission: The method whereby data is transmitted several bytes or a block at a time.

Syntax Error: Violation of the rules of whatever language a computer program is written in.

System: A collection of activities and elements designed to accomplish a goal.

System Board: A flat board that usually contains the CPU and some primary storage (main memory).

System Cabinet: The cabinet that houses the CPU.

System Clock: The clock that controls how fast the operations within a computer can take place.

System Flowchart: Chart that shows the kinds of equipment used to handle the data or information flow.

Systems Analysis: The second phase in the systems life cycle. During this phase, data is gathered and analyzed and a systems analysis report is produced.

Systems Analysis and Design: A six-phase problem-solving procedure for examining an organization's information system and improving it.

Systems Analyst: Computer professional who studies systems in an organization to determine what actions to take and how to use computer technology to assist in taking them.

Systems Audit: Part of maintenance phase of systems analysis and design in which systems analyst compares new system to the design specifications to see if new procedures are furthering productivity.

Systems Design: The third phase of the systems life cycle. It consists of designing alternative systems, selecting the best system, and writing a systems design report.

Systems Development: The fourth phase of the systems life cycle. It consists of developing software, acquiring hardware, and testing the new system.

Systems Implementation: The fifth phase of the systems life cycle. It is the process of changing (converting) from the old system to the new and training people to use it.

Systems Life Cycle: The six phases of systems analysis and design.

Systems Maintenance: The sixth (final) phase of the systems life cycle. It involves evaluating the new information system from time to time and modifying it if necessary.

Systems Software: "Background software" that includes programs that help the computer manage its own internal resources. The most important part of systems software is the operating system.

System Unit: The part of a microcomputer that contains the CPU.

Table Plotter: *See* Flatbed Plotter.

Take-Up Reel: The reel used to wind magnetic tape that has been drawn through a tape drive.

Tape Backup Unit: *See* Magnetic Tape Streamer.

Tape Library: Group of magnetic tapes stored by companies and other institutions.

Tape Streamer: *See* Magnetic Tape Streamer.

TB or T-byte (Terabyte):   A unit of capacity equal to 1,099,511,627,776 bytes (about one trillion bytes).

Terminal: A form of input (and output) device that consists of a keyboard, monitor, and communications link.

Thesaurus Program: A program used with word processing to find suitable alternatives for a typed word by presenting choices from an electronic thesaurus.

Time-Sharing System: A system that allows several users to share resources in the host computer.

Top-Down Analysis Methodology: The method used to identify the top-level component of a system and break this component down into smaller components for analysis.

Top-Down Program Design: The process of identifying the top element (module) for a program and then breaking the top element down into smaller pieces in a hierarchical fashion.

Top-Level Manager: Manager concerned with long-range (strategic) planning. Top-level managers supervise middle-level managers.

Touch Screen: A monitor screen that allows actions or commands to be entered by the touch of a finger.

Touch-Tone Device: A direct-entry device that sends data over telephone lines to a central computer.

Tracks: Closed, concentric rings on a disk on which data is recorded.

Tractor Feed: Printer mechanism with sprockets that advance printer paper, using holes on edges of continuous form paper.

Transaction File: A file containing recent changes to records that will be used to update the master file.

Transaction-Oriented Processing: *See* Real-Time Processing.

Transaction Processing Information System: Records day-to-day transactions.

Transactions: Events recorded in a database, such as employees hired or materials and products produced.

Transportable: Portable computer weighing 18–25 pounds.

Trojan Horse Program: Type of computer crime in which someone writes instructions that will destroy or modify someone else's software or data.

Twisted Pair: Copper-wire telephone line.

Typewriter Keys: The keys on a keyboard that resemble the regular letters, numbers, punctuation marks, and so on, on a typewriter.

Unix: An operating system originally developed by AT&T which has been adapted to run on a wide variety of computers, including microcomputers.

Unjustification (Unjustified Margins):   The process of having uneven or "ragged right" margins, such as the right margin in a typewritten letter.

Uploading: The process of transferring information from the computer you are operating to a remote computer.

Upper Memory: Located between 640K and 1MB of RAM. Although DOS uses this area to store information about the microcomputer's hardware, it is frequently underused.

Utility Program: Program that performs common repetitious tasks, such as keeping files orderly, merging, and sorting.

Value: The number contained in a cell of a spreadsheet.

VDT (Video Display Terminal):   An output display device that resembles a television screen.

VGA (Video Graphics Array):   Circuit board that may be inserted into microcomputer and offers up to 256 colors. It is superior in quality to CGA and EGA.

Video Privacy Protection Act (1988):   Law preventing retailers from selling or disclosing video-rental records without the customer's consent or a court order.

Virtual Environment: *See* Artificial Reality.

Virtual Fax Board: Expansion board that fits into microcomputer that enables user to write a document, which is then converted to a facsimile image and is sent electronically over telephone lines to a receiving fax machine, which recreates the image on paper.

Virtual Reality: *See* Artificial Reality.

Virus: *See* Computer Virus.

Voiceband: The bandwidth of a standard telephone line.

Voice-Input Device (Voice-Recognition System):   A direct-entry device that converts a person's speech into a numeric code that can be processed by a computer.

Voice-Messaging System: Computer system linked to telephones that convert human voice into digital bits and store telephoned messages in "voice mailboxes" for retrieval later.

Voice-Output Device: Device that makes sounds resembling human speech which are actually prerecorded vocalized sounds.

Volatile Storage: Temporary storage that destroys the current data when power is lost or new data is read.

Voltage Surge (Spike): Excess of electricity, which may destroy chips or other computer electronic components. *See also* Surge Protector.

Walkthrough: *See* Structured Walkthrough.

WAN (Wide Area Network): A countrywide network that uses microwave relays and satellites to reach users over long distances.

Wand Reader: A special-purpose hand-held device used to read OCR characters, such as that used in department stores to read price tags.

Window: An area defined on the screen for viewing data from a program.

Windowing Software: Software that allows a number of applications programs ("multiple tasks") to be used simultaneously.

Word: A unit that describes the number of bits (such as 8, 16, or 32) in a common unit of information.

Word Processing: The use of a computer to create, edit, save, and print documents comprised of text, such as letters, reports, and contracts.

Word Wrap: A feature of word processing that automatically moves the cursor from the end of one line to the beginning of the next.

Worksheet Area: The area of a spreadsheet consisting of rows and columns that intersect in cells.

Workstation: A more sophisticated microcomputer which can communicate with more powerful computers and sources of information.

Worm (Bacteria): Variant on computer virus, a destructive program that fills a computer system with self-replicating information, clogging the system so that its operations are slowed or stopped.

WORM (Write Once, Read Many) Drive: A form of optical disk that allows data to be written only once but read many times without deterioration.

Write: *See* Writing Data.

Write-Enable Ring: A ring that must be placed over the hub of a magnetic tape to allow data to be written to the tape.

Write-Once Disk: Optical disk on which data is recorded by lasers and cannot be erased by the user.

Write-Protect Notch: A notch on a floppy disk used to prevent the computer from destroying data or information on the disk.

Writing Data: For floppy disks, the process of taking the electronic information processed by the computer and recording it magnetically onto the disk.

WYSIWYG: Pronounced "wizzy-wig," stands for "What You See Is What You Get." That is, the image on the screen display resembles the image of the final document that will appear when printed out on paper.

XGA (Extended Graphics Array): Circuit board that can be inserted into a microcomputer and offers up to 256 colors under normal circumstances and 65,536 colors with special equipment.

The Student Buyer's Guide: How to Buy Your Own Microcomputer System

Some people make snap judgments about some of the biggest purchases in their lives: cars, college educations, houses. Merely on the basis of an ad, a brief conversation, or a one-time look, they may make an impulsive decision about something costing thousands of dollars. Who is to blame, then, if they are disappointed later? They simply didn't take time to check it out.

The same concerns apply in buying a microcomputer system. You can make your choice on the basis of a friend's enthusiasms or a salesperson's promises. Or you can proceed more deliberately, as you would, say, in looking for a job.

Four Steps in Buying a Microcomputer System

The following is not intended to make buying a microcomputer an exhausting experience. Rather, it is to help you clarify your thinking about what you want it to *do* for you, so you will get the best system for your needs with the money you want to spend.

The four steps in buying a microcomputer system involve answering the following two-part questions:

1. *My needs:* What do I need a computer system to do for me today? in another year or two?
2. *My budget:* How much am I prepared to spend on a system today? in another year or two?
3. *The software:* What kind of software will best serve my needs today? in another year or two?
4. *The hardware:* What kind of hardware will best serve my needs today? in another year or two?

We divided each question into two parts on the assumption that your needs may change, but so may the money you have to spend on a microcomputer. For instance, later in your college career or after college graduation, you may want a far more powerful computer system than you need now. At that point you may have more money to spend. Or you may not need to spend money at all, if your employer provides you with a computer.

Step 1: What Needs Do I Want a Computer to Serve?

The trick is to distinguish between your needs and your wants. Sure, you *want* a cutting-edge system powerful enough to hold every conceivable record you'll ever need and fast enough to process them all at the speed of light. But do you *need* this? Your main concern is to address the two-part question:

- What do I need a computer system to do for me today?
- To do for me in another year or two?

The questionnaire at the end of this guide will help you determine the answers to both questions.

Suggestions   The first thing to establish is whether you need a computer at all. Some colleges offer computer facilities at the library or in certain dormitories. Or perhaps you can borrow a roommate's. The problem, however, is that when you are up against a term-paper deadline, many others may be also, and the machine you want may not be available. To determine the availability of campus computers for your study needs, call the dean of students' office.

Another matter on which you might want advice is what type of computer is popular on campus. Some schools favor Apple Macintoshes, others favor IBMs or IBM-compatibles. If you are the owner of a system that's incompatible with most others on campus, you may find yourself stuck if your computer breaks down. Ask someone knowledgeable who is a year or two ahead of you if your school seems to favor one system over another.

Finally, look ahead and determine whether your major requires a computer. Business and engineering students may find one a necessity, physical education and drama majors less so. Your major may also determine the kind of computer that's best. A journalism major may want an IBM or IBM-compatible laptop that can be set up anywhere. An architecture major may want a powerful desktop Macintosh with a LaserWriter printer that can produce elaborate drawings. Ask your academic advisor for some recommendations.

Examples of Prices for New and Used Computers

Equipment	New	Used
Microcomputers		
Apple Macintosh Classic or si	$1500 – 2500	$1000 – 1800
IBM or IBM-compatible, including monitor and 40 MB hard disk	$1500 – 3000	$400 – 2000
Macintosh printers		
ImageWriter II	$500	$200 – 350
DeskWriter	$1000	Negotiable
LaserWriter	$2500	$1350 – 1500
IBM-compatible printers		
9-pin dot-matrix	$300 – 400	$100 – 150
24-pin dot-matrix	$400 – 600	$200 – 250
DeskJet Plus	$500 – 700	Negotiable
IBM laser	$1000 – 2000	$800

Example   Suppose you are a college student beginning your sophomore year, with no major declared. Looking ahead at the courses you will likely take this year, you decide you will probably need a computer mainly as a word processor. That is, you need a system that will help you write short (10- to 20-page) papers for a variety of general-education courses.

By this time next year, however, you may be an accounting major. Having talked to some juniors and seniors, you find that courses in this major, such as income tax preparation, will require you to do coursework necessitating elaborate spreadsheets. Or maybe you will be a fine arts or architectural major required to submit projects for which drawing and painting desktop publishing software would be helpful. Or perhaps you will be out in the job market and will be writing application letters and résumés that you want to have a professional appearance.

Step 2: How Much Money Do I Have to Spend on a Computer System?

When you buy your first computer, you are not necessarily buying your last. Thus, you can think about spending just the bare-bones amount for a system that will meet your needs while you're in college, with a view toward getting another system later on. After all, most college students who own cars (quite often used cars) don't think they will be the last cars they will ever have. Or, if you can afford it, you can buy an expensive system that will handle any kind of work required in your major and even after graduation.

You know what kind of money you have to spend. Your main concern is to answer this two-part question:

- How much am I prepared to spend on a computer system today?
- How much am I prepared to spend in another year or two?

The questionnaire at the end of this guide has a question on this.

Suggestions   You can probably buy a used computer of some sort for under $500 and a printer for under $200. On the other hand, you might spend $5000–8000 on a new state-of-the-art system that, when upgraded, might meet your needs for the next 5–10 years. (*See table, opposite, for examples of computer prices.*)

There is nothing wrong with getting a used system, if you have a way of checking it out. For a reasonable fee, a computer-repair shop can examine it prior to your purchase. Look at newspaper ads and notices on campus bulletin boards for good buys on used equipment. Quite often the sellers will include a great deal of software and other items (software file boxes, manuals) as part of the package. If you stay with recognized brands such as Apple Macintosh, IBM, Compaq, or AST, you probably won't have any difficulties. The exception may be with printers, which, since they are principally mechanical devices, may get a lot of wear and tear. This is all the more reason to tell the seller you want a repair shop to examine the equipment before you buy.

If you're buying new equipment, be sure to look for student discounts. Some college bookstores, for instance, offer special prices to students. Mail-order houses also steeply discount their products. These firms run ads in such periodicals as *Computer Shopper* (sold on newsstands) and other magazines. However, using mail and telephone for repairs and support can be a nuisance. Often you can use the prices advertised by a mail-order house to get a local retail computer store to lower its prices.

Example   Perhaps you have access to a microcomputer at the campus student computing center, the library, or the dormitory. Or you can borrow a friend's. However, this computer isn't always available when it's convenient for you. Moreover, you're not only going to college but also working, so both time and money are tight. Having your own computer would enable you to write papers when it's convenient for you. Spending more than $700 would cause real hardship, and so a new microcomputer system is out of the question. It looks like you'll need to shop the newspaper classified ads or the campus bulletin boards in hopes of picking up a used but workable computer system.

Or, maybe you can afford to spend more now—say, between $2000 and $3000—but probably only $1000 next year. By this time next year, however, you'll have a clear idea of your major and will know how your computer needs have changed. For example, because you'll be a finance major, you need to have a lot more computer memory (primary storage) to hold the massive amounts of data you'll be working with in your spreadsheets. Or because you'll be an architecture major or graduating and looking for a job, you'll need a laser printer to produce attractive-looking designs or application letters. Thus, whatever system you buy this year, you'll want to upgrade it next year.

Step 3: What Kind of Software Will Best Serve My Needs?

Most computer experts urge that you determine what software you need before you buy the hardware. The reasoning here is that some hardware simply won't run the software that is important to you. This is certainly true once you get into *sophisticated* software, such as specialized programs available for certain professions (e.g., certain agricultural or retail-management programs). However, if all you are interested in today are the basic tools of software—that is, *general* word processing, spreadsheet, and database management programs—these are available for all DOS-based and Macintosh-based hardware. The main caution to be aware of is that some more recent versions of applications software won't run on older hardware. Still, if someone offers you a computer for free, don't turn it down "because I have to figure out what kind of software I need first." You will no doubt find it sufficient for many general purposes, especially during the early years in college.

That said, you are better served if you follow step 3 after step 2—namely, finding the answers to the two-part question:

■   What kind of software will best serve my needs today?

■   Will best serve my needs in another year or two?

The questionnaire at the end of this guide may help you determine your answers.

Suggestions   No doubt some kinds of applications software are more popular on your campus—and in certain departments on your campus—than others. Are freshman and sophomore students mainly writing their term papers in WordPerfect on IBMs and compatible machines or in Microsoft Word on Macintoshes? Which spreadsheet is most often used by business students, Lotus 1-2-3 or Excel or Quattro Pro? Which desktop publishing program is most favored by graphic arts majors, Aldus PageMaker for Macintosh or Ventura Publisher for IBM? Do many students use their microcomputers to network with others, and, if so, which software is the favorite? Do engineering and architecture majors use their own machines for CAD/CAM applications? Start by asking other students and your academic advisor.

Whatever word processing software you buy, you'll probably find the addition of an electronic spelling checker and built-in thesaurus helpful also.

If you're looking to buy state-of-the-art software, you'll find plenty of advice in various computer magazines, several of which rate the quality of newly issued programs. Such periodicals include *InfoWorld*, *PC World*, *MacWorld*, and *PC/Computing*.

Example Suppose you determine today that all you need is essentially software that resembles a fancy typewriter on which you can write short papers. In that case, nearly any kind of word processing program would do. You could even get by with some older versions or off-brand kinds of word processing software. This might happen, for instance, if such software was included in the sale of a used microcomputer that you picked up at a bargain price.

But will this software be sufficient a year or two from now? Looking ahead, you guess that you will be majoring in theater arts, with a minor in screenwriting, which you may pursue as a possible career. At that point a simple word processing program won't do. You learn from juniors and seniors in that department that screenplays are written using special screenwriting programs, software that's not available for some computers. Or, as part of your major in advertising and marketing, you find you are expected to take promotional pieces composed with a word processing program and produce them as brochures with desktop publishing software. Or, as a physics major, you discover you will need to write reports on a word processor that can handle equations, which requires a machine with a great deal of memory. In short, you need to look at your software needs not just for today but also for the near future. You especially want to consider what programs will be useful to you in building your career.

Step 4: What Kind of Hardware Will Best Serve My Needs?

A bare-bones hardware system might include a five-year-old desktop or portable computer with two floppy-disk drives, a monochrome monitor, and a dot-matrix printer. With a newer system, the sky's the limit. However, as a student—unless you're involved in some very specialized activities—it's doubtful you'll need such things as scanners, voice-input devices, fax boards, and the like. Even so, the choices of equipment are many.

As with the other steps, the main task is to find the answers to the two-part question:

- What kind of hardware will best serve my needs today?
- What kind will best serve my needs in another year or two?

There are several questions on the questionnaire at the end of this guide to help you determine answers to these concerns.

Suggestions Clearly, you should let the software be your guide in determining your choice of hardware. If you've found that the most popular software in your department runs on a Macintosh rather than an IBM-compatible, then that would seem to determine your general brand of hardware.

Whether you buy IBM or Macintosh, a desktop or a portable, we suggest at a minimum you get two disk drives and at least 640K of memory. If you can afford a disk drive and a hard disk and even more memory, so much the better. Nowadays, most software requires a hard drive. And, of course, you need some sort of printer.

As with software, several computer magazines not only describe new hardware but also issue ratings. See *InfoWorld*, *PC World*, *MacWorld*, and *PC/Computing*, for example.

Example   Right now, let's say, you're mainly interested in using a computer to write papers, so almost anything would do. But you need to look ahead.

Suppose you find that WordPerfect seems to be the software of choice around your campus. It will run on either an IBM or compatible or on a Macintosh, but according to reviews in computer magazines the Macintosh version is not as good. You find that WordPerfect 5.0 will run on an IBM AT with 640K of memory and a 20-megabyte hard disk. A near-letter-quality dot-matrix printer will probably be acceptable for most papers. Although this equipment is now outdated, you find from looking at classified ads that there are many used machines of this nature around, and they cost very little—under $700 for a complete system.

If you're a history or philosophy major, maybe this is all the hardware and software you need. Indeed, this configuration may be just fine all the way through college. However, some majors, and the careers following them, may require more sophisticated equipment. Your choice then becomes: Should I buy an inexpensive system now that can't be upgraded, then sell it later and buy a better one? Or should I buy at least some of the components of a good system now and upgrade it over the next year or so?

As an advertising major, you see the value of learning desktop publishing, and that this will be a useful if not essential skill once you embark on a career. In exploring the software, you learn that WordPerfect 5.1 includes some desktop publishing capabilities. However, an old IBM AT and dot-matrix printer of the sort you previously considered simply aren't sufficient. Moreover, you learn from reading about software and talking to people in your major that other desktop publishing programs for the IBM are considered more versatile than WordPerfect—for instance, Ventura Publisher. Probably the best software arrangement, in fact, is to have WordPerfect for Windows as a word processing program and Ventura Publisher running under Windows for a desktop publishing program.

To be sure, the campus makes computers that will run this software available to students. If you can afford it, however, you're better off having your own. Now, however, we're talking about a major expense. A computer in the IBM PS/2 line, perhaps one running a '486 microprocessor, with plenty of primary storage and an 80-Mbyte hard disk, plus a color monitor and a laser printer, could run in excess of $6000.

Perhaps the tack to take is to buy now knowing how you would like your system to grow in the future. That is, you will buy an IBM PS/2 (or compatible) microcomputer, but at this point you will buy only a monochrome monitor and a dot-matrix printer. Next year or following, you can add to your system by selling off the less sophisticated peripheral devices and adding a color monitor and laser printer.

Developing a Philosophy About Computer Purchasing

It's important not to develop a case of "computer envy." Even if you were to buy the most expensive and up-to-date microcomputer system available, you would find in a matter of months that something better has come or is coming along. Computer technology is still in a very dynamic state, with more powerful, versatile, and compact systems constantly coming into the market place. So what if your friends have the hottest new piece of software or hardware. The main question is: Do you need it to solve the tasks required of you or to keep up in your field? Or can you get along with something simpler but equally serviceable?

Questionnaire: What I Want in a Microcomputer System

My Needs

1. What do I need a computer system to do for me today? in another year or two?

Check the following: I wish to use the computer for:	Today	In 1–2 years
Word processing—writing papers, letters, memos, or reports	_____	_____
Business or financial applications or exercises—balance sheets, sales projections, expense budgets, accounting problems, taxes	_____	_____
Record keeping and sorting—research bibliographies, scientific data, address lists	_____	_____
Graphic presentations—of business, scientific, or social science data	_____	_____
Online information retrieval—from campus network, electronic bulletin boards, CompuServe, Prodigy	_____	_____
Publications, design, or drawing—printed newsletters, architectural drawing, graphic arts	_____	_____
Playing video games	_____	_____
Other (specify):_____	_____	_____

My Budget

2. How much am I prepared to spend on a system today? in another year or two?

Check the following: I can spend:	Today	In 1–2 years
Under $500	_____	_____
Up to $1000	_____	_____
Up to $2000	_____	_____
Up to $4000	_____	_____
Over $4000 (specify):_____	_____	_____

Questionnaire: What I Want in a Microcomputer System

The Software I Want

3. **What kind of software will best serve my needs today? in another year or two?**

Check the following:

The *applications* software I need includes:

	Today	In 1–2 years
Word processing—WordPerfect, Word, MacWrite, other (specify):_____	_____	_____
Spreadsheet—Lotus 1-2-3, Quattro Pro, Excel, SuperCalc, other (specify): _____	_____	_____
Database manager—dBASE, Paradox, FoxPro, other (specify):_____	_____	_____
Presentation graphics—Harvard Graphics, Freelance Plus, Draw Applause, Graph Plus, other (specirfy): _____	_____	_____
Communications software—ProComm, Smartcom, Crosstalk, other (specify):_____	_____	_____
Integrated packages—Works, First Choice, Symphony Enable, Framework, SmartWare II, other (specify): _____	_____	_____
Desktop manager (appointment calendar, calculator, notepad personal telephone directory)—Sidekick, other (specify): _____	_____	_____
Hypertext—HyperCard, other (specify):_____	_____	_____
Video games or other entertainment (specify): _____	_____	
Project management software—Harvard Project Manager Microsoft Project for Windows, Project Scheduler 4, SuperProject, Time Line, other (specify): _____	_____	_____
Desktop publishing software—Ventura Publisher, PageMaker, First Publisher, Quark Xpress, other (specify): _____	_____	_____
CAD/CAM—VersaCAD, AutoCAD, other (specify): _____	_____	_____
Expert system (specify):_____	_____	_____
Other applications software (specify): _____	_____	_____
Programming languages—BASIC, Pascal, FORTRAN, COBOL, other (specify):_____	_____	_____

Note: The *specific* applications software packages you select will probably determine the kind of *systems software* you will need—which may well determine the kind of hardware you need to buy.

Questionnaire: What I Want in a Microcomputer System

The *systems software* I need includes:

	Today	In 1–2 years
DOS	_____	_____
DOS with Windows	_____	_____
OS/2	_____	_____
Macintosh OS	_____	_____
Unix	_____	_____
Other (specify):_____	_____	_____

The Hardware I Want

4. What kind of hardware will best serve my needs today? in another year or two?

Check the following:

The hardware I need includes:

	Today	In 1–2 years
16-bit processor	_____	_____
32-bit processor	_____	_____
Less than 640K memory	_____	_____
More than 640K memory	_____	_____
Expandable memory	_____	_____
Monochrome monitor	_____	_____
Color monitor—CGA, EGA, VGA, Super VGA, XGA (specify):_____	_____	_____
Keyboard with numeric keypad	_____	_____
Detachable keyboard	_____	_____
Single disk drive—5$\frac{1}{4}$" or 3$\frac{1}{2}$" (specify size of drive):_____	_____	_____
Dual disk drives (specify size of drives):_____	_____	_____
Hard-disk drive—20, 40, 60, 80, 100, or more megabytes (specify):_____	_____	_____
Expandable storage	_____	_____
Desktop microcomputer or workstation	_____	_____
Portable microcomputer—transportable, luggable, laptop, notebook (specify): _____	_____	_____
Dot-matrix printer	_____	_____
Daisy-wheel printer	_____	_____

Questionnaire: What I Want in a Microcomputer System

	Today	In 1–2 years
The hardware I need includes:		
Laser printer	_____	_____
Ink-jet printer	_____	_____
Color printer	_____	_____
Modem	_____	_____
Joystick	_____	_____
Sound	_____	_____
Manufacturer's reputation	_____	_____
Dealer's reputation	_____	_____
Method of financing	_____	_____
Local service and support	_____	_____
Maintenance contract	_____	_____
Clarity of documentation	_____	_____
Training	_____	_____
Other (specify):_____	_____	_____
_____	_____	_____
_____	_____	_____

Index

Illustration Credits

Figures 1-1; 1-3, 1-5, 3-1 (inset photos): West Stock, Zephyr Picture #991106.

Figures 1-6, 3-6, 3-4, 5-3, 12-2, and 12-3: Courtesy of Microsoft Corp.

Figures 1-4 (top), 1-10, 3-2 (left), 3-7, 4-2, 4-3, 4-5, 4-11, 4-24, 4-25, 5-1, 5-5, 5-13, 5-14, 5-19, 5-20, 6-5, 6-7, 6-17, 10-13, 11-15, 13-6: Courtesy of IBM.

Figures 1-4 (bottom), 4-8, 4-22 (John Greenleigh, photographer); 3-2 (right), 3-8 (Mosgrove Photo); 5-8 (John W. Lund, photographer): Courtesy of Apple Computer, Inc.

Figures 1-7, 4-1, and 6-4: Courtesy of Dell Computer Corporation.

Figures 1-8, 5-12, 13-2: Courtesy of NCR.

Figure 1-9: Courtesy of BASF.

Figures 1-12 and 14-9: Courtesy of Radius.

Figures 1-13, 4-9, 5-16, 5-17, 5-19: Courtesy of Hewlett-Packard.

Figures 1-14 and 7-6: Courtesy of Hayes Microcomputer Products, Inc.

Figure 2-4: Courtesy of WordPerfect Corp.

Figure 2-9: Courtesy of NEC.

Figure 2-10: Courtesy of Claris.

Figure 2-11: Based on a photo of Crosstalk Mk.420 screen, *PC World*, April 1991, p. 142.

Figures 2-12, 7-3, and 8-6: Courtesy of CompuServe.

Figure 3-9 (top): Courtesy of Open Software Foundation.

Figure 3-9 (bottom): Courtesy of Sun Microsystems.

Figure 4-6, 5-15, 6-15 (left): Courtesy of Toshiba.

Figure 4-10: Courtesy of Digital Equipment Corp.

Figure 4-12: Courtesy of Cray Research, Inc.

Figure 4-23: Courtesy of NeXT Computer.

Figure 4-27: Courtesy of Compaq.

Figure 5-6: Courtesy TSW, © Charles Gupton.

Figures 5-7, 11-16: Copyright © 1991 Matthew Borkoski/West Stock.

Figures 5-11, 7-2: Courtesy of Lanier Worldwide, Inc.

Figure 5-17: Courtesy of Tektronix and Dahlstrom Photography.

Figure 5-18: Courtesy of Okidata.

Figures 5-22 and 5-23: Courtesy of Calcomp.

Figures 6-11 and 10-3: Courtesy of Seagate.

Figure 6-12: Courtesy of Intel.

Figures 6-13, 13-3: Courtesy of BASF, © Carol Lee.

Figure 7-4: Courtesy of Lotus Development Corp.

Figure 7-8: Reprinted with permission of Arthur Andersen & Co. and adapted from *Trends in Information Technology.* © copyright 1987, Arthur Andersen & Co. All rights reserved.

Figure 8-8: Courtesy of Texas Instruments.

Figure 9-3: Courtesy of Bob Waldrop and Wilson Sporting Goods Company.

Figure 9-4: Copyright TSW, Chuck Keeler.

Figure 9-10: Copyright Canadian Airlines International.

Figure 9-12: Copyright TSW, Jon Riley.

Figures 10-2, 10-11: Copyright Darrell Peterson and West Stock.

Figure 10-10: Courtesy of Honeywell, Inc.

Figures 10-12, 11-2, and 11-15: Copyright © TSW, Tim Brown.

Figure 11-6: Courtesy of Patton & Patton.

Figure 11-15: West Stock/Michael Keller.

Figure 12-1: Based on a photo of Sidekick 2.0 screen, *PC World*, April 16, 1991, p. 38.

Figure 12-6: Adapted from illustration on pp. 6–7, *Syllabus,* published quarterly by Apple Computer, Inc. © Apple Computer, Inc. Permission courtesy of *Syllabus,* an Apple Higher Education Publication.

Figure 12-7: Adapted from illustration on p. 2 of October–November 1989 *Syllabus,* P.O. Box 2716, Sunnyvale, CA 94087.

Figures 12-9, 12-10: TSW, Andrew Sachs.

Figure 13-7: Copyright TSW, William S. Helsel.

Figure 14-1: Courtesy of Bank of America.

Figure 14-2: Courtesy of American Airlines.

Figure 14-3: Courtesy of Federal Express.

Figures 14-4, 14-5, 14-6, and 14-7: Copyright 1990 Bill Delzell.

Figure 14-8: Courtesy of The Interface Group, Inc.

Figure 14-11: Copyright TSW, Bruce Ayres.